LEGENDS OF THE

WILD WEST

James A. Crutchfield

Bill O'Neal

Dale L. Walker

Publications International, Ltd.

James A. Crutchfield has written 15 books, including *It Happened in Colorado, Tennesseans at War, The Natchez Trace: A Pictorial History,* and *Footprints Across the Pages of Tennessee History.* His articles have appeared in many magazines, including *Old West, True West, Early American Life,* and *Nashville.* He was a contributing writer to *Encyclopedia of the American West.* He is a member of the board of directors of the Tennessee Historical Society and is Secretary-Treasurer of the Western Writers of America, Inc.

Bill O'Neal's ten book credits include *Encyclopedia of Western Gunfighters, Henry Brown: The Outlaw Marshal, The Arizona Rangers,* and *Fighting Men of the Indian Wars.* He is a member of the Western Writers of America, Inc., a past president of the East Texas Historical Association, and a board member of the National Association for Outlaw and Lawman History. He has been a member of the history department of Panola Junior College since 1970.

Dale L. Walker is a freelance writer, historian, and editor. He has written 13 books, including *Mavericks: Ten Uncorralled Westerners, Will Henry's West,* and *Buckey O'Neill: The Story of a Rough Rider.* His contributing writer credits include *The Reader's Encyclopedia of the American West, Encyclopedia of the Old West, The West That Was,* and *Wild West Show!* His articles and reviews have appeared in many publications, including *Newsweek, The American West, Real West, Old West, Western American Literature,* and *Louis L'Amour Western Magazine.* He is a member of the Texas Institute of Letters and is a past president of the Western Writers of America, Inc.

Editorial Assistants: **M. David Key, Brett J. Olsen**
Photo Tinting Artist: **Cheryl Winser**
Illustrations: **Janet Hamlin**

Special thanks to Auggie Mastrioguiseppe and staff at the Western History Department of Denver Public Library for their help in locating prints of the Old West.

Photo Credits

The West produced many mythic figures, but none greater than Sitting Bull (seated, center) or Buffalo Bill Cody (standing, center).

Contents

Foreword

"**G**o West, young man, and grow up with the country!" advised Horace Greeley in an often-quoted editorial in the New York *Tribune*. And go west they did by the thousands.

During the 19th century, frontiersmen, home-steaders, cowboys, and other pioneers tamed the land west of the Mississippi in the swiftest mass settlement in the history of the world. Though settlers had been pushing westward since first landing on American soil, it was Thomas Jefferson's purchase of the Louisiana Territory in 1803 that sparked interest in expanding the nation from coast to coast. Once Lewis and Clark crossed the Mississippi, "the West" would forever be the land on the other side of the great river.

Yet all too quickly, the wilderness became a garden. By 1890, the Bureau of Census had surveyed the spread of towns and civilization and declared that the American frontier was closed. In 87 years—conceivably one person's lifetime—the frontier was gone.

The heyday of westward expansion—the "Wild West"—proved even more fleeting. The period that produced such legendary westerners as Hickok and Cody, Crazy Horse and Custer, and Butch and Sundance was but a brief 25 years between the end of the Civil War and the Battle of Wounded Knee.

However brief, the Wild West has been endlessly celebrated, interpreted, and exaggerated. From dime novels to classic pieces of literature, from television to fine films, the West casts a spell on America's collective imagination. Traits associated with cowboys, Native Americans, outlaws, and homesteaders have become standards that define America's national character. Davy Crockett's courage at the Alamo, Crazy Horse's boldness in battle, Jesse James's defiance against authority, Wyatt Earp's steely demeanor at the Gunfight at the O.K. Corral, and Calamity Jane's eccentricity all serve to describe America to itself and to the world.

Though the days of cowboys on the range, homesteaders in sod houses, and wagon trains on the trail have long since passed, we can still take Horace Greeley's advice. To "go West," simply turn the pages of this book and rediscover the Wild West through story and image. In vintage photographs and evocative text, *Legends of the Wild West* journeys to an era that is gone but not lost.

MOUNTAIN MEN

s early as 1783, when Thomas Jefferson was a 40-year-old congressman from Virginia, he entertained dreams of a government-sponsored exploration of the vast lands beyond the Mississippi River. As secretary of state in 1792, Jefferson again tried and failed to launch an overland expedition to the Pacific after the American sea captain, Robert Gray of Boston, had discovered the mouth of the Columbia River in the Pacific Northwest. Finally, as president, Jefferson realized his ambitions to move the nation westward. In 1803, President Jefferson directed the purchase from the French government of the Louisiana Territory, 1.5 billion acres of virtually unknown lands west of the Mississippi River. In so doing, he set the stage for the exploration and settlement of the American West, a period that lasted almost until the end of the 19th century. It was a time that witnessed the exploitation of the entire region—from the Mississippi River to the Pacific Ocean and from the Canadian border to the frontiers of Mexico—along with all of its native peoples. Jefferson's purchase of the Louisiana Territory spear-

Inspired by profit but driven by a taste for adventure, the legendary mountain men explored the untamed land west of the Mississippi.

headed the age of westward expansion. In 1845, newspaper editor John L. O'Sullivan coined a term that captured the zeal of the expansionists, whether they were politicians interested in national achievement or westward-moving pioneers caught up in the national state of mind. "Manifest Destiny," which held that the United States had a divine right to settle the land from coast to coast, became the catchphrase of the expansionists.

The journey of William Clark (above) and Meriwether Lewis (right) sparked America's imagination about the rich, wide-open West.

European trappers and traders—mostly Spanish, French, and English—had made frequent but limited excursions westward for many years before the first United States explorers arrived on the scene. The Lewis and Clark Expedition, the initial U.S. effort to probe the lands beyond the Mississippi, was President Jefferson's brainchild. In 1804, Captains Meriwether Lewis and William Clark, along with four dozen companions, one dog, and three boats, left the bounds of their known world to traverse an immense and uncertain landscape. For two years, they labored through the plains and across the mountain wilderness by land and by river, documenting the flora and fauna, establishing relations with the inhabitants, studying geologic characteristics, and charting the terrain. Late in 1805, they reached the Pacific shore at the mouth of the Columbia River, 14 years af-

The mountain men traversed practically every square mile of the West. Joseph Walker is best remembered for the trail he found through California's Sierra Nevada.

ter Captain Gray's discovery. Their return journey was completed in six months, and in the end they had traveled some 8,000 miles.

No doubt, President Jefferson is due credit for initiating the first official American excursion into the West, but it was the fashion industry in the East and in Europe that created the incentive for the extensive exploration and exploitation of the region. Felt, made from the fine inner hairs of beaver fur, had been used in the manufacture of hats for the preceding 300 years. The continuing demand for beaver fur had wiped out the species in Europe, and by 1800, most beaver habitats in the eastern United States were played out as well. When Lewis and Clark brought back news that huge beaver populations thrived in the mountains and river valleys of the West, the door was opened for the introduction of a unique breed of individual. He was the mountain man, and in the brief period of 40 years, he wandered over practically every square mile

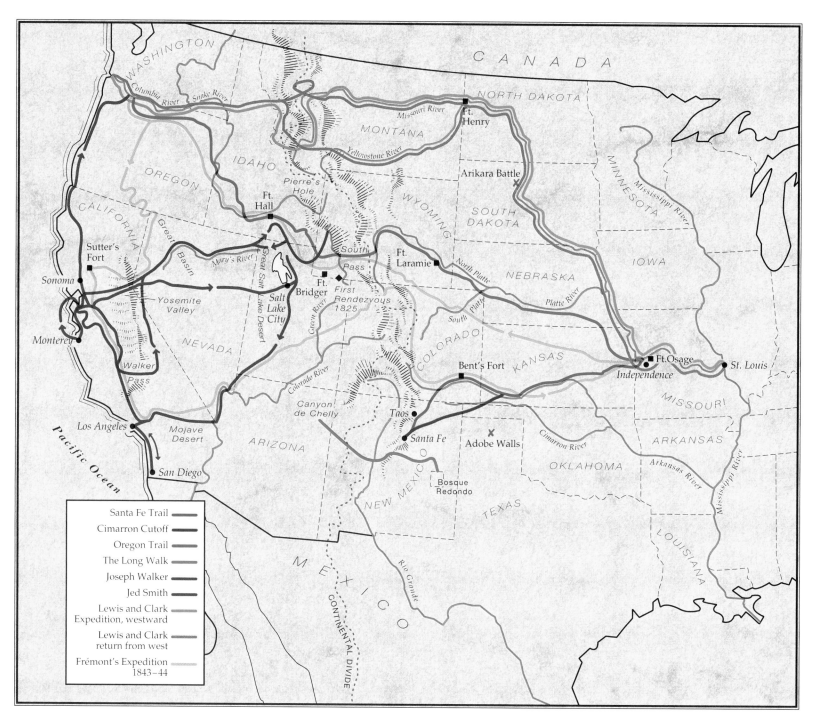

The passes and pathways founded by the trailblazers, trappers, and guides helped open
the West for commercial ventures and emigrant travel.

of the Great Plains, the Rocky Mountains, the Oregon Country, and the Great Basin and Plateau regions.

In 1806, when Lewis and Clark were on their way back to St. Louis from their premier journey to the Pacific Ocean, they encountered Joseph Dickson and Forrest Hancock, a pair of trappers making their way up the Missouri River in search of beaver. After hearing Lewis and Clark offer a description of the bountiful, untapped land to the west, Dickson and Hancock proposed that a member of the expedition join them and return to the wilderness as their guide and partner. John Colter volunteered his services, and as this small group set out in search of pelts, the Rocky Mountain fur trade began.

Trapper John Colter may have been the first Anglo-American to see the sites of what would later become Yellowstone National Park. Easterners were astonished by Colter's accounts of the fantastic sites of the Yellowstone region.

Colter spent a season trapping with Dickson and Hancock, after which he struck out on an odyssey that would easily qualify him as the prototype of the mountain man. Working sometimes as a guide, sometimes as a free trapper, sometimes as a fur company representative, he spent the next three years meandering across the Rocky Mountains. His goals were to navigate passage through the mountains, find untapped beaver ranges, initiate contacts with the Native Americans in the area, and simply stay alive; he achieved remarkable success on all counts. His journeys took him from a well-established base on the Yellowstone River across the northeastern range of the Rockies, over the Continental Divide to the Tetons on the western side of the mountains, and down the twisting Snake River.

During his time in the Rockies, Colter had regular encounters with native tribes, particularly the Blackfeet and the Crows. The Crows proved to be generally amiable and open to business overtures, and in later years they became strong allies of the trappers who followed Colter. The Blackfeet, on the other hand, were fiercely opposed to encroachment by outsiders, and Colter had several near-fatal clashes with them. Once after being captured by a group of several hundred Blackfeet, he was stripped naked, beaten, and told to run for his life through the rocky, bramble-covered passes near the Jefferson River. Colter somehow managed to kill one of his pursuers and stay ahead of the rest for some six miles, making it to the icy river where he took refuge for the night

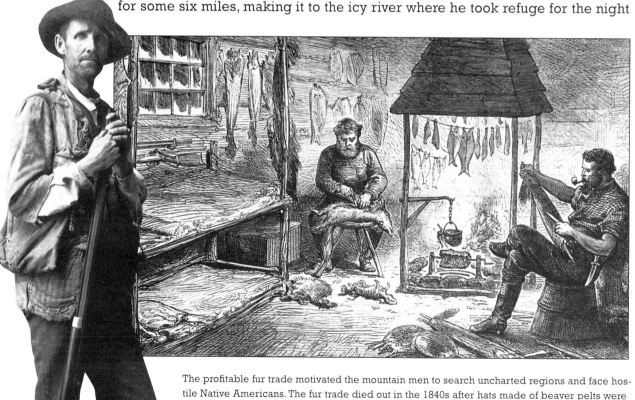

The profitable fur trade motivated the mountain men to search uncharted regions and face hostile Native Americans. The fur trade died out in the 1840s after hats made of beaver pelts were no longer fashionable.

under a float of driftwood. After the Blackfeet gave up the search, Colter stumbled 200 miles overland until—his feet and legs lacerated, his body dehydrated—he came upon his trading post on the Yellowstone River. After a few weeks of recuperation, he was back in the mountains trapping and blazing new trails again.

The mountain men who later swarmed into the newly explored lands of the Great Plains and the Rockies proved to be just as hardy as Colter. They came from all walks of life and from many different parts of the continent. Most of them had been born at a time when their own homes back East were situated on the fringes of the frontier, much like the wilderness they frequented as trappers in the West in search of beaver. Tennessee, Kentucky, Virginia, New York, and Pennsylvania all produced mountain men, as did several other states and a few foreign countries.

Sometimes called long hunters, mountain men managed to make a living by hunting deer and small animals after the beaver trade fell off.

Just as Daniel Boone, Simon Kenton, and James Robertson—the trailblazers of previous generations—braved the elements and wrestled land from the Native Americans east of the Mississippi, so did the mountain men of the West. The two groups differed in a major way, however. Boone, Robertson, and the other easterners were interested in opening new lands for settlement. They dreamed of towns, churches, and schools for their children and future generations. They cleared the forests for farmers to plant crops and raise livestock, and for businesses and communities to spring up. Mountain men, on the other hand, did not look ahead so far or so boldly. They braved the wilderness for themselves, looking for a fortune, for a living, or simply for solitude and escape from civilization. Although from time to time they would interact with other trappers, natives, and traders, this unique breed of men often lived in the remoteness of the wilderness, where they sometimes didn't see another human being for months on end. To survive in such isolation, they needed a knowledge of the land that was rivaled only by their neighbors, the Native Americans, with whom they would visit, trade, and fight.

Many mountain men were free trappers, making their own way up and down the beaver rivers and trading their pelts to the highest bidders they could find. Others worked for the large fur outfits that established forts and trading posts in the wilderness, such as Manuel Lisa's Missouri Fur Company or John Jacob Astor's American Fur Company. These two early companies were anchored in the northern plains east of the great mountain range, and they dominated the United States fur trade in the first quarter of the century. Later, the Rocky Mountain Fur Company provided the impetus to push the trade ever westward, into the heart of the mountains and beyond. There in the 1830s and 1840s, the fur trade reached its peak and began to wane. The near extinction of the beaver and the declining popularity of beaver hats made the mountain men obsolete before the middle of the century.

The American push westward was not dependent solely on the fur trade though. A strong coalition of politicians in the East was determined to take Manifest Destiny to its logical end and push the boundaries of the U.S. all the way to the Pacific. In 1838, a new branch of the military was formed—the Army Corps of Topographical Engineers. Following on the heels of the mountain men, this group paved the way for the next wave in the expansion to the West. A young, ambitious lieutenant, John Charles Frémont, led five separate army expeditions designed to identify and map passable routes and lands for settlement across and beyond the Rocky Mountains.

Frémont's abilities as a scientist and cartographer were impressive, but he wasn't much of a trailblazer or outdoorsman. He relied heavily on the skills and experience of others in his parties, most notably Kit Carson and Joseph Walker, to navigate the terrain. He had a reputation for sometimes ignoring both his guides and his superiors, and on several occasions good luck was the only thing that stood between his decisions and disaster. Still, Frémont's exploits were highly publicized and glorified, so that he became known to most Americans as the Pathfinder. His journeys made the wilderness seem less wild, producing detailed surveys of the South Pass over the Rockies, of the interior lands of the Pacific Northwest, of routes to California both from the north and from the east, and of the Great Basin that stretched out between the mountains and the ocean.

With this new view of the West, a new breed of pioneers was on the move. They were family men, like Boone and Robertson three or four generations earlier in Kentucky and Tennessee. These newcomers were intent on possessing the rich farm lands of Oregon and newly annexed California,

Currier and Ives chronicled 19th-century America in their popular prints. In "The Rocky Mountains: Emigrants Crossing the Plains," they immortalized the pioneers who followed the mountain men westward.

and they heralded a new age in westward expansion. Signs of this new era were apparent as early as 1843 when Jim Bridger, one of the most notable of the individualistic mountain men, built a post on Black's Fork of the Green River. The irony was that "Old Gabe" Bridger built his post not as a trading station to receive furs and pelts from his brother trappers but as a resting stop for the weary, westbound emigrants who were sure to be coming.

JIM
BRIDGER

1804—1881

Born two months before Meriwether Lewis and William Clark began their epic journey from the Mississippi to the Pacific, Jim Bridger was a legend by the age of 20. His exploits are recounted in any number of

Called Old Gabe by his friends, Jim Bridger was known as much for his tall tales as he was for his skills as a mountain man.

biographies and memoirs of those who lived west of the Mississippi before the Civil War.

The son of a surveyor and innkeeper, Bridger was born in Richmond, Virginia, on

March 17, 1804. He moved west with his family and in 1818 was apprenticed to a St. Louis blacksmith. Living along the Mississippi, he learned to handle boats, guns, and horses, making him an ideal recruit when he joined the Ashley-Henry fur-trading expedition to the Upper Missouri River in 1822.

With such comrades as Jedediah Smith, Tom Fitzpatrick, and James Clyman, Bridger learned the ways of the wilderness and the trapper's life as the band made its way by keelboat up the Missouri. At the mouth of the Yellowstone, he assisted in building the log outpost named Fort Henry and waded miles of icy streams to find beaver and lure them into his traps.

Unschooled and illiterate, Bridger had an instinct, perhaps the keenest of all the mountain men, for surviving in the wilderness. He knew he must understand the ways and languages of the Native Americans and learn the lay of the land. Within a few years, he had honed these rare skills to a phenomenal degree. General Grenville M. Dodge, who sought Bridger's advice while surveying a portion of the route of the Central Pacific Railroad, remarked about his trail-wise friend, "The whole West was mapped out in his mind."

Bridger, at the the ripe old age of 21, may have been the first white man to see the Great Salt Lake. At least, he liked to boast that he had discovered it. To settle a wager about the ultimate course of the Bear River, he traveled down river by boat until he came upon a large body of water. When he discovered that the water tasted salty, he assumed he had reached the Pacific Ocean. The following year, four other trappers made their way down the Bear River and established that it emptied into the famed saltwater lake.

In 1830, Bridger and four others bought out their employers to gain control of the Rocky Mountain Fur Company, coming into rivalry with the powerful American Fur operation owned by John Jacob Astor. With his partners, he continued to trap and engage in numerous skirmishes with Native Americans. Bridger was never much of a businessman and was relieved when the Rocky Mountain Fur Company sold out in 1834. That year he married Cora, daughter of the Flathead chief Insala, and visited St. Louis briefly before returning to the mountains.

Bridger attended the rendezvous at Green River in 1839, which turned out to be the last rendezvous, a sign that the beaver trade was playing out. Bridger decided he could make a living as a trader to the increasing emigrant traffic heading west along the Oregon Trail. For his post, he chose a grassy valley at Black's Fork on the Green River. In 1843, in partnership with veteran fur trader Louis Vasquez, he built cabins, corrals, and a blacksmith shop, and he bought supplies and stock from St. Louis. Fort Bridger became the only emigrant way station on the 620-mile stretch between Fort Laramie, at the junction of the Laramie and North Platte rivers, and Fort Hall on the Snake.

At his fort, Bridger settled down with his wife and three children. He sent his daughter Mary Ann to Marcus Whitman's mission school in Washington. Between 1846 and 1848, Bridger suffered three great personal tragedies: His wife Cora died, his daughter was killed by Cayuse Indians at the Whitman

Could this graffiti along the Oregon Trail be the work of the virtually illiterate Jim Bridger? Or did some would-be mountain man want to steal the mighty Bridger's considerable thunder?

mission school in Walla Walla, and his second wife, a Ute woman, died in childbirth. After each personal calamity, he escaped to the mountains to trap and hunt.

In June 1847, Bridger met Mormon leader Brigham Young on the trail to Fort Laramie. Young was leading his party of Mormon emigrants in search of a place to build a settlement. Bridger, in his customary forthright fashion, warned Young and his followers not to travel to the barren Utah country on faith alone. The old mountain man was skeptical

THE RENDEZVOUS

William Ashley, loaded down with supplies, left Fort Atkinson on a cold day in November 1824 for Henry's Fork on the Green River in the distant Rocky Mountains, a journey of some six months. His intention was to make a profit, not to begin one of the most colorful and raucous traditions associated with the early West. He did both, grossing $50,000 and having arranged the first of the annual gatherings known as the rendezvous.

The purpose of the rendezvous was to provide traps, weapons, liquor, trade goods, and supplies to the mountain men and Native Americans in exchange for the rich furs they had trapped during the previous fall and spring. The benefits of such a system were meant to be mutual. Operating a rendezvous allowed Ashley to obtain the best pelts at the point of origin, rather than forcing him to compete with other fur companies in the busy markets of St. Louis. It also allowed the trappers to acquire badly needed supplies and equipment in their home territory, thus saving them hundreds of miles of travel to and from St. Louis. From a social standpoint, the rendezvous was an opportunity for trappers to leave their lonely vigil in the remote Rocky Mountains to relax, drink, gamble, and womanize for several weeks in high summer.

At the rendezvous, the poor mountain men were often at the mercy of greedy suppliers: Whiskey selling at 30 cents a gallon in St. Louis was sold for three dollars a pint to the trappers.

Often the pricing structure at the rendezvous was weighted heavily in Ashley's favor. He paid the trappers as little as half the going rate in St. Louis for their pelts and marked up his goods tenfold or more.

The rendezvous became a fixture of the fur-trading industry during its peak years. Trappers, traders, and Indians met for the event each year between 1825 and 1840, except for 1831 when there was no gathering. The majority of the 15 rendezvous took place at various sites in the western part of present-day Wyoming, although two of them occurred in eastern Idaho and four were held in northern Utah.

that the Salt Lake region could support any farming enterprise no matter how assiduously pursued. The encounter apparently offended Young and his followers and began a period of enmity between Bridger and the Mormon church. In the decade that followed, the Mormons moved into the Green River Valley, opened rival trading posts, and accused Bridger of selling arms to Native Americans and inciting them to war. The church headquarters in Salt Lake City also resisted the attempt to convert Fort Bridger into an army post, claiming that the fort and the entire Green River Valley belonged to the Mormon-controlled Utah Territory.

In the meantime, Bridger had left his fort in the care of others and had returned to the wilderness. He lived for a time with the Shoshonis and courted Little Fawn, daughter of Shoshoni chief Washakie. Bridger and Little Fawn were married in 1850 at a Christian ceremony performed by his friend, the Jesuit missionary Father Pierre De Smet.

Bridger spent his summers at the fort and his winters with Little Fawn's people, but this tranquil period was marred when the Bridger-Mormon rivalry flared anew in 1853. A band of Mormons tried to arrest Bridger as an outlaw. He escaped with his wife and children into the mountains. When he returned to his fort, he found it burned and gutted, his trade goods and livestock stolen. His response to the depredation was to have a professional survey made of his 3,900-acre tract of land and to file

the paper with the General Land Office in Washington to establish his ownership. In the meantime, he bought a farm south of Westport, Missouri, where he took Little Fawn, now called Mary, and his children.

In the fall of 1854, Bridger met Sir George Gore, who was an Irish nobleman with a huge inherited fortune, and hired on as Gore's hunting guide in the Yellowstone and Powder River country. The hunting trek took two years, during which time Sir George read to Bridger and taught his rough-edged guide to love Shakespeare. By the time the long odyssey ended, the illiterate mountain man was able to recite long passages from the Bard's works.

After being paid by Gore, Bridger took a boat down the Missouri to visit his wife and

Old Gabe established Fort Bridger as a trading post and way station along the Oregon Trail in southwest Wyoming.

family and began thinking of his rebuilt fort on the Green River. He traveled to Washington to plead his case for ownership of the Fort Bridger lands at a time when anti-Mormon sentiment was being heard in the halls of Congress. He found sympathy for his case, and the Buchanan administration declared Utah Territory to be in a state of insurrection. The government ordered an infantry regiment under Colonel Albert Sidney Johnston to march from Fort Laramie into the Green River country. Bridger was selected as the guide.

In the ensuing Utah War of 1857–58, in which the Mormons under Young's leadership waged war against federal troops, Bridger leased his fort as a supply base. He led the infantrymen through winter blizzards with such skill that Johnston appointed him to his personal staff with the rank of major. When the war ended with a peaceful settlement, Bridger led Johnston's force in a parade through the streets of Salt Lake City. While he could take some satisfaction in having evened the score with the Saints, Bridger found little peace on returning home to Westport. During his absence or soon after his return, Mary Washakie Bridger died. He placed his children in the care of a tenant farmer and returned to the West.

So great was Bridger's fame that his name is attached to a city, a lake, a fort, a pass, a mountain, and a national forest.

After he sold Fort Bridger in 1858, he served as a guide along the Yellowstone and the Missouri throughout the Civil War years. He was employed as an army scout in the early Indian campaigns of 1865–66, including the Powder River Expedition against Cheyenne, Sioux, and Arapaho raiders, and he witnessed the establishment of Fort Phil Kearny on the Bozeman Trail. But, with failing eyesight and rheumatism, he was discharged from further duties in 1868.

He retired in Westport to a life of cultivating apple trees and telling tales of his adventures, true and tall, to his grandchildren. His mastery of the tall tale was recorded by many who knew him. One of his most oft-repeated stories involved his favorite camping spot, opposite a bald mountain so far distant that any sound made in his camp would take six hours to echo back. He said that just before he retired for the night he would shout, "Time to get up!" and the call would echo back to his camp at the precise hour he needed to awaken the next morning. "They said I was the damndest liar ever lived," he liked to say. "That's what a man gets for tellin' the truth."

Jim Bridger died on his farm near Westport on July 17, 1881.

TRADING
POSTS

Trading posts played an extremely important role in the North American fur trade. From the earliest days of fur exploitation in the Great Lakes region, the British and French built trading posts for dual reasons. First, the posts served as secure and tenable bases of operation for the traders. They also acted as storehouses for furs brought in by American Indians and for the numerous trade goods that were to be swapped with the natives for their furs. In later years, such posts became equally important in the Rocky Mountain fur industry. They were synonymous

Trading posts, such as the Hubbell Trading Post in Arizona, fulfilled many functions in the West, from serving as bases of operation for commercial enterprises to providing havens for weary travelers.

with forts until the American military arrived, and they were frequently a haven for the trappers during the most brutal months of the Rocky Mountain winters.

Fort Laramie, located in present-day eastern Wyoming, was a trading post built in 1834 on the bank of the Laramie River near its confluence with the North Platte. Its builder was William Sublette, a well-known and experi-

enced mountain man. The Fort went on to become one of the anchor points of the famous Oregon Trail traveled by countless emigrants to the West. Sublette became one of the primary partners in the Rocky Mountain Fur Company and a wealthy man.

Another notable trading post of the period was Bent's Fort, located on the Arkansas River in present-day southeastern Col-

orado. Completed in 1833 by Charles and William Bent and their partner Ceran St. Vrain, the fort was built of adobe, making it the only such structure in that part of the country. The building style may have been the contribution of St. Vrain, a naturalized Mexican citizen of French ancestry who had spent considerable time in the Southwest. With its two circular towers guarding opposite corners, Bent's Fort rose above the prairie grass like a castle in the wilderness and ruled the southern Great Plains for many years as the center of a far-reaching fur empire run by the Bents and St. Vrain.

JEDEDIAH
SMITH

1799–1831

Tall, lean, tireless, and intrepid, Jedediah Strong Smith has been called the perfect model of the mountain man. His restless eyes were forever turned westward, with his Bible always at hand and his Hawken rifle cradled and ready.

He was born on January 6, 1799, in Bainbridge, New York, and grew up in Erie County, Pennsylvania, and the Western Reserve of Ohio. He received only a rudimentary frontier education and was raised in a staunchly Methodist family. While a teenager and working as a clerk on a Lake Erie freighter, Smith supposedly read the journals of the Lewis and Clark Expedition. He soon made his way west, lured by the adventurous life of the trailblazer. By 1822, he reached St. Louis, where he answered an advertisement in the *Missouri Gazette* in which "enterprizing young men" were sought to ascend the Missouri River to locate fur-trapping grounds. The notice had been placed by Missouri Lieutenant Governor William H. Ashley and fur trader Andrew Henry of the Rocky Mountain Fur Company. From the time he threw in with Ashley and Henry until he died, Smith's life was one of relentless exploration through the trackless wilderness of the Northwest.

In the fall of 1823, he crossed the plains south of the Yellowstone River in search of new beaver grounds with a party that included Jim Clyman and Tom Fitzpatrick. He was mauled so badly by a grizzly bear that his scalp and ear were torn loose from his head. Clyman gingerly sewed them back on, and Smith survived to experience other adventures.

Smith's greatest venture began in August 1826 when he led a party of trappers on an overland journey from Utah to the Colorado River, then across the Mojave Desert, and into Southern California. Despite being ordered by Spanish authorities to leave the territory of California, Smith wintered in the San Joaquin Valley. He trapped along the Stanislaus River, and then with only a few of his men, he began the journey back, leading the first Anglo-American party to cross the Sierra Nevada and the Great Salt Lake Desert. The latter was an arduous trip as described by Smith. "We frequently travelled without water sometimes for two days across sandy deserts, where there was no sign of vegetation. . . . When we arrived at the Salt Lake, we had but one horse and one mule remaining, which were so feeble and poor that they could scarce carry the little camp equipment which I had along; the balance of my horses I was compelled to eat as they gave out."

Retracing his trail to California, Smith set out the following year with 18 men to relieve his hunting party and to explore the Oregon coast. At a Mojave Indian village at the Colorado River crossing, half of his group

Jed Smith lived a brief but furiously active life. He left his mark from the Great Salt Lake to the Pacific Coast, from the Columbia River to the Mojave Desert.

were massacred in a surprise attack. Smith led the remnant of his band into California. After being jailed briefly at the San Jose Mission, he journeyed on northward along the California coast. When he reached the Klamath River in Oregon, his party faced another attack by Indians, this time the Kalawatsets near the Umpqua River. Finally, in July 1828, Smith and the three surviving men reached Fort Vancouver.

Two years later, he sold out his interest in his beaver trapping enterprise to the Rocky Mountain Fur Company. He traveled down to St. Louis, moderately wealthy and semiretired. More devout and viceless than most of the hard-living mountain men, he had, in his own words, "missed the care of the Christian church."

Smith grew restless, however, because as one anonymous writer described, "His altar was the mountaintop . . . his sacraments were mountain skills." In 1831, he organized a trading caravan of 74 men, including his old friend Tom Fitzpatrick, and 22 wagons. They left St. Louis, bound for Santa Fe, New Mexico, in April. After several days of searching for water in the arid country between the Arkansas and Cimarron Rivers, Smith and Fitzpatrick rode ahead to find a stream bed to dig for water. The two men split up, and Smith soon found a small water pocket in a buffalo wallow in the Cimarron. Unfortu-

nately, he also found a Comanche war party. He managed to get one shot off with his Hawken rifle, which supposedly killed the leader of the Comanche band, before dying at their hands. The body of the legendary mountain man was never found.

Bible-toting Jedediah Strong Smith led the first group of Anglo-Americans across the daunting Sierra Nevada.

Jedediah Smith's achievements as a post-Lewis and Clark explorer are unparalleled. He was the first Anglo-American to discover and travel the length and breadth of the Great Basin. He pioneered the overland trail to California and was the first Anglo-American man to cross the Sierra Nevada and the Great Salt Lake Desert. He was the first to travel overland from California to the Columbia River in Oregon. Many of his trails were later followed by California-bound pioneers, making him one of the West's first and great pathfinders.

JAMES P.
BECKWOURTH

1798–1866

James P. Beckwourth's familiarity with several Native American nations lured him away from Anglo-American society.

Jim Beckwourth was what mountain men called a yarner, an adventurer who was never satisfied with the plain truth of his travels and exploits. Unlike Jim Bridger, another celebrated teller of tall tales, Beckwourth's yarns never had Bridger's elbow-in-the-ribs quality of obvious fun and ruse. Because he came to believe his own mythmaking, the real story of Jim Beckwourth—an eventful and tempestuous tale that required no embroidery—is cloudy and confused.

He was born James Pierson Beckwith in Fredericksburg, Virginia, on April 26, 1798, the son of plantation overseer Sir Jennings Beckwith (the title apparently inherited from a British baronet ancestor) and a black woman, probably a slave.

In 1810, Beckwith and his family moved to St. Charles, Missouri, then a part of the Louisiana Territory. At age 14, Jim, like his contemporary Jim Bridger, was apprenticed to a blacksmith in St. Louis. He may have also worked as a lead miner and hunter throughout his teens and early youth.

In 1824, Beckwourth (who changed the spelling of his surname for unknown reasons) became one of 25 men—including the redoubtable fur traders Tom Fitzpatrick and Jim Clyman—to join William H. Ashley's third trapping expedition to the Rocky Moun-

tains. The venture proved to be a dangerous and eventful debut to the life of a mountain man: The party trudged through snowdrifts in subzero temperatures; survived near-starvation in the Platte River Valley; tramped across northern Colorado and southern Wyoming in search of new beaver streams; lost several horses to a band of Crow raiders; and survived an Indian attack, which resulted in the death of one of Ashley's party.

Over the next few years, Beckwourth operated as a free trapper, meaning he was not associated with any fur-trade company. He trapped along the Upper Missouri, Platte, Snake, Green, Bear, and Yellowstone rivers, and he traded with Blackfeet, Snakes (Shoshonis), Cheyenne, and Crows.

Some time between 1826 and 1828, after trapping along the Powder River in Wyoming, Beckwourth abandoned his native society to live with the Crows. The Crows were generally friendly to the trappers, and he was welcomed among them. In his dictated memoirs, titled *Life and Adventures of James P. Beckwourth*, he stated that, with the Crows, he knew he could trap in their streams unmolested. He felt better protected with the Crows than with his fellow trappers. "I therefore resolved," he told his scribe, "to abide with them, to do my best in their company, and in assisting them to subdue their enemies."

Beckwourth claimed, and it may be true, that he became a chief among the Crows within a year. He learned their language, customs, and daily living habits, and he married at least two Crow women and fathered several children. He called one of his spouses Little Wife and the other Pine Leaf.

By his own account, he raided with and fought alongside Crow war parties, though it is not clear how often he participated. He supposedly learned how to steal horses while living with his adopted people.

He took advantage of his Crow connection to serve as a fur trader and agent among the tribe for the American Fur Company, John Jacob Astor's powerful enterprise. The American Fur Company had established the trading post of Fort Union on the Yellowstone River in 1828.

In the summer of 1835, Beckwourth made the first of several ventures to southern California to trade furs for cash and horses. Accompanying him on the expedition were trapper Thomas "Pegleg" Smith, a renegade

This likeness of Pine Leaf, one of Beckwourth's Native American brides, accompanied the mountain man's memoirs in *Harper's New Monthly Magazine*.

Ute chief and slave dealer named Walkara, and about 60 of Walkara's band. In the vicinity of Los Angeles, Walkara and his Utes stole 600 horses from a rancher and drove them off into the desert while Beckwourth and Smith were dickering with Spanish officials. Beckwourth and Smith followed after their companions, becoming horse thieves in the process. Neither man seems to have been guilt-ridden over the escapade since they sold their share of the stolen animals at Bent's Fort for a tidy profit.

Beckwourth grew weary of life with the Crows and joined the Missouri Volunteers as an army scout. He traveled to Florida and

THE ASHLEY-HENRY EXPEDITION

Americans had been trapping beaver on the Missouri River for more than a decade when General William H. Ashley and his partner, Major Andrew Henry, decided to give it a try. Henry had already been to the headwaters of the Missouri River in 1809, when he built a fur post at the Three Forks. Ashley, the lieutenant governor of Missouri, was new to the business. Following in the steps of Manuel Lisa and John Jacob Astor, they intended to establish a trading base in the wilderness so that they could offer freelance trappers transportation and supplies and get a share of the profits from shipping the pelts back to St. Louis.

In April 1822, Henry led a party up the Missouri from St. Louis and established a fort for winter quarters at the mouth of the Yellowstone River. The following spring, Ashley and some 70 adventurers started back upriver to begin trapping. They happened upon an encampment of Arikara Indians along the west bank of the Missouri River in present-day South Dakota. The timing was bad; the Arikara had never been sympathetic to encroaching easterners, and in a recent skirmish between the Arikara and their longtime enemies the Sioux, a group of white trappers had intervened on the side of the Sioux. The Arikara forced Ashley and his vastly outnumbered party back downriver. Ashley returned shortly with the U.S. 6th Infantry in tow, under the command of Colonel Henry Leavenworth. Leaven-worth's forces were far greater, but the Arikara had little trouble fending them off long enough to escape relatively unscathed.

This first battle west of the Mississippi between Native Americans and U.S. forces had significant ramifications. The natives of the area were left unimpressed by the performance of the army and so adopted a bolder attitude, making Ashley and Henry's plans for the area no longer tenable. As a result, the entrepreneurs took their Rocky Mountain Fur Company in a new direction—west. In later expeditions, they pushed overland into the very heart of the Rockies, opening up the secluded valleys and snakelike river systems that would, over the next two decades, produce the legendary mountain men.

Fur trade luminary William H. Ashley established a fort along the Yellowstone River in 1822 with the help of a party of trappers.

took part in the Seminole War, serving as a dispatch rider under General Zachary Taylor at the Battle of Lake Okeechobee in December 1837. Beckwourth's life seems a mixture of brave deeds and unscrupulous acts: After serving with Taylor, he returned to horse stealing. In 1840, he went back to California with Smith and Walkara for an unabashed horse rustling raid in the Santa Ana Valley.

After the beaver trade declined, Beckwourth—like most of the mountain men—worked a number of jobs. He settled in Taos, New Mexico Territory, married a girl from Santa Fe, assisted in erecting a fort on the Arkansas River in Colorado called Pueblo, and entered a partnership in a hotel and saloon in Santa Fe. During the Mexican War of 1846–1848, he served as a dispatch rider for General Stephen Watts Kearny during the New Mexico campaign and for Colonel Sterling Price in the Taos area.

After the hostilities ended, Beckwourth made his final journey to California, selling trade goods to '49ers in the Sonoma area. He discovered a pass through the Sierra Nevada that became part of a major pathway for settlers en route to California. He searched for gold in the Sierra Nevada, guided wagon trains over the passes to the supply base north of Sacramento, and operated a hotel and store in the vicinity.

Beckwourth settled near Denver in the early 1860s, married again, managed a store, and took occasional trips into the mountains

Beckwourth hunted along the Green River while operating as a free trapper. As "beaver waters" go, the Green proved to be lucrative.

to mine, hunt, and trap. He also found work as a guide for military parties. In this latter employment, he had a role, perhaps unwittingly, in one of the most reprehensible acts in the history of the American West. Beckwourth was a guide for the 3rd Colorado Volunteer Cavalry, under Colonel J. M. Chivington, in the massacre at Sand Creek on November 29, 1864, in which a camp of 500 Cheyenne and Arapaho were slaughtered.

After the Sand Creek atrocity, Beckwourth settled near Fort Laramie, where he worked occasionally as a scout, guide, and messenger. Not long after, he turned his back on Anglo-American society once again and returned to his Crow people.

Beckwourth died in 1866, though the precise date and circumstances are unknown. He probably died in a Crow village near Fort C. F. Smith on the Bozeman Trail near the Bighorn River in Montana Territory. He was laid to rest in Crow fashion on a tree platform.

JOSEPH REDDEFORD
WALKER

1798–1876

Joseph Reddeford Walker's encyclopedic knowledge of the lay of the land and his amazing memory for geography produced endless stories—documented ones—of his trail genius. When Walker was 63 years old, for example, he led a party of prospectors into New Mexico Territory. Around the present-day city of Deming, the men ran low on water and began to worry. After all, they were in the desert, in Apache country, and in the furnace-like heat of summer. Walker took it all calmly, remembering a trip he had made through the area many years before. He told his partners of a good spring several miles to the southwest and said the spring lay in a low, bald mountain and faced a large flat stone. Three days later, Walker led the miners to the mountain, the stone, and the spring—precisely as he remembered it.

Born on December 13, 1798, in either Roan County, Tennessee, or Goochland County, Virginia, Walker followed his older brothers to the Missouri Territory when he was about 20 years old. His transformation into a trapper and hunter occurred in 1821, when he joined a clandestine expedition to the southern Rockies and ended up imprisoned briefly in Santa Fe, capital of the province of New Mexico. He made the best of the situation by helping Mexican authorities wage war

In 1832, Walker began a trapping expedition with Captain Benjamin Bonneville that may have been a military reconnaissance mission. The party wintered along the Salmon River before journeying west to California.

against Pawnee raiders in the area, winning certain rare trade concessions in the bargain.

Walker could not have entered Santa Fe at a more auspicious moment. That same year marked the opening of the Santa Fe Trail, the famous trade route to the Southwest. The trail was so well used and profitable that the federal government decided it must be properly surveyed and mapped. Walker and his brothers, Joel and John, were hired to hunt game and to help the surveyors on the Santa Fe Trail. When treaties were presented to the

Pathfinder Joseph Walker discovered Yosemite Valley and founded the northernmost snow-free pass across the Sierra Nevada.

Osage and Kansas tribes along the route, Walker assisted in the signings.

By 1827, the Walker family home was established at Fort Osage, Missouri, and Walker busied himself in the development of newly created Jackson County. He may have actually picked the site of the county seat and selected the name Independence. He most certainly served as Jackson County's first sheriff, elected to two terms but refusing a third. When he left office in 1831, Independence had taken over as the chief outfitting post and point of departure for the Santa Fe Trail.

Walker returned to trading, though the fur-trade business was in decline. While trading in Cherokee lands in 1832, he met Captain Benjamin Bonneville at Fort Gibson, on the Arkansas River. Bonneville, an army officer on extended leave, was searching for men to accompany him on a trapping-trading expedition into the Rocky Mountains, though he may have also been on a secret government mission to determine the strength of British forces in the Northwest and of the Mexicans in California. Whatever Bonneville's mission, Walker signed on and soon became the captain's aide, embarking on an adventure of discovery that placed his name permanently in the pantheon of western trailblazers.

The Bonneville party left Fort Osage, Missouri, on May 1, 1832, with a party of 110 men consisting of American and French-Canadian trappers and a band of Delaware Indians. The group made its way up the Platte and Sweetwater rivers, crossed the South Pass of the Rockies to the Green River, and set up winter quarters along the Salmon River.

The expedition did not fare well that winter and spring. The spring trapping bare-

THE SANTA FE TRAIL

In 1821, an event occurred in the Southwest that was to dramatically change the economic climate of the region for decades. After years of futile attempts, Mexico finally won its independence from Spain and immediately opened its doors for business with the United States. A group of Missouri traders headed by William Becknell were bartering in Comanche settlements near the border when the news broke. They hastily loaded their few wares onto mules and picked their way across the rugged terrain, following the Arkansas River and crossing the Raton Pass to Santa Fe, where their goods were hungrily snapped up. Becknell's commercial success in the summer of 1821 marked the real beginnings of the Santa Fe Trail.

Becknell made the trip again the following year, bringing even more goods and realizing even greater profit. On this journey, he blazed a new portion of the Trail, called the Cimarron Cutoff. The Trail remained one of the Southwest's main economic routes until 1880, when the railroad finally reached Santa Fe.

Between 1826 and 1835, about 1,500 men accompanied 775 wagons carrying nearly $1.5 million of merchandise over the Santa Fe Trail.

ALFRED JACOB MILLER

While many artists traveled west in the early days of the 19th century, only Alfred Jacob Miller experienced and captured the spirit of the 1830s fur trade. The sweeping works of this young American painter provide a rare look at trappers, traders, and Native Americans in the pristine wilderness of the Rocky Mountains.

Captain William Drummond Stewart, a Scottish adventurer, brought Miller on a trek through the West that culminated with the 1837 rendezvous on the Green River in present-day Wyoming. Also at the rendezvous were some 3,000 Shoshoni, Crow, Nez Percé, Bannock, and Flathead Indians, along with several hundred trappers and traders. The 27-year-old Miller spent the next few years living in Stewart's castle in Scotland. There, he produced a collection of paintings based on sketches he had created in the Rockies, a collection that would offer one of the only visual records of the unique day-to-day life of the mountain man.

Miller's "Buffalo Hunt" was painted around 1850.

ly produced wages for Bonneville's men, and skirmishes with the Blackfeet became commonplace. When the party came to the summer rendezvous on the Green River in 1833, Walker, probably acting under orders from Bonneville, took the opportunity to put together a daring plan to journey west into California, perhaps all the way to the ocean.

The overland journey to the Mexican province of Alta California had been accomplished only twice before: Jedediah Smith had led a party of trappers across the Mojave Desert into southern California in 1826, and Hudson's Bay Company trapper Peter Skene Ogden had journeyed from the Rockies to California along the Mary's River (later named the Humboldt) three years later. Walker had no intention of following either Smith's or Ogden's routes. With 40 mounted men and 120 pack horses with provisions, Walker departed the Green River on August 20, 1833. His carefully planned route included traveling to the Bear River, along the north shore of the Great Salt Lake, and then southwest to the Mary's River, following it through northern Nevada to its terminus at Humboldt Sink.

The crossing of the Sierra Nevada took three weeks, and despite Walker's skilled leadership and careful planning, the party suffered from near-starvation in the punishing Sierra passes. They killed and ate many of their horses before making their way over to the divide between the Merced and Tuolumne Rivers.

After crossing the divide, Walker and his men had the privilege of gazing on a fabulous sight never before seen by white men—the Yosemite Valley. As they picked their way down the craggy slopes to the valley floor, gazing in wonderment at the ancient behemoth redwoods, the great waterfalls, and the lush virgin greenery, each man knew, and later stated, that November 13, 1833, was the greatest day of his life.

That winter, Walker and his men traveled westward to skirt the shore of San Francisco Bay, crossed the Santa Cruz mountains, and arrived in the Mexican capital of Monterey. The authorities and residents received the group hospitably and permitted them to trade their supply of furs for goods and horses. With a fresh supply of horses—almost triple the amount he began with—and cattle, Walker led his men east from the coast and then south along the Sierra. Close to the headwaters of the Kern River, he discovered a snow-free pass across the mountains that made a relatively easy return journey to the Mary's River. Subsequently named Walker Pass, the pathway became a principal route for California-bound emigrants.

The Walker expedition returned to the Bear River on July 12, 1834, in time for the trappers' rendezvous, having been gone 11 months. He had not lost a single man to the elements, Indians, or starvation, and the information he brought back to Bonneville produced the first dependable maps of the country west of the Rockies.

In the decade that followed his California expedition, Walker continued to lead the life of the trailblazing mountain man. He explored the Yellowstone River and the headwaters of the Missouri; traded with the Indians; trapped in Wyoming and Montana; worked with Kit Carson, Joe Meek, and others; and went into business with Jim Bridger and Louis Vasquez. In 1843, he guided emigrants to California across Walker Pass, led emigrant trains from Fort Laramie to Fort Bridger, and escorted others across the Oregon Trail.

As the fur trade declined, his career as a guide picked up steam. In 1845, he joined John C. Frémont's third expedition as it explored the Great Salt Lake and then crossed Nevada into California.

Mirror Lake in Yosemite Valley lives up to its name. Walker was the leader of the first group of Anglo-Americans to see the splendor of Yosemite Valley when they walked down to the valley floor in November 1833.

Well into the 1860s, Walker continued to work as a scout and horse trader. He even hunted for gold in the New Mexico and Arizona Territories. In 1867, nearly blind, he returned to California and lived with his nephew on a ranch in Contra Costa County, where he died of natural causes in 1876.

Of all of his expeditions and achievements, Joseph Walker ranked one as a supreme accomplishment. On his tombstone, he requested the epitaph read "Camped at Yosemite, Nov. 13, 1833."

JOE
MEEK

1810—1875

Many notables of the West achieved legendary status because their adventures were inflated by classic frontier exaggeration. No frontiersman was a more artful practitioner of the tall tale than Joe Meek, a tall, burly mountain man with a rollicking sense of humor whose range of exploits solidly substantiated his towering reputation. Joseph Lafayette Meek was born on February 7, 1810, in Washing-

ton County, Virginia. Though full of high spirits, he was lazy and avoided both work and school. At 16, he was still basically illiterate. He eventually learned to read and write, but his spelling was always an exercise in originality. A strong sense of adventure and a disagreeable stepmother sent him to Lexington, Missouri, where he joined the two brothers who had preceded him.

Early in 1829, Joe signed on with William Sublette's party of fur trappers, a venture that signaled the start of his life as a mountain man. Meek spent more than a decade as a mountain man, traversing almost every area of the West. He worked for the Rocky Mountain Fur Company for a couple of years before becoming a free trapper. Meek also accompanied Joseph Walker on his epic California expedition of 1833–1834.

Reveling in the adventurous life of a mountain man, no one found greater enjoyment in the annual trappers' rendezvous than Joe Meek. At the rendezvous, the mountain men drank, gambled, raced horses, swapped yarns, and enjoyed the company of Native American women. Over the years, Meek married three Native American women, including a Nez Percé princess.

Women and men alike found Joe a jolly companion. The full-bearded, six-foot-two mountain man cut a striking figure, and he radiated good humor. Joe could not resist a practical joke, and in a melodious voice and

Hardy Joe Meek gained fame as a killer of grizzly bears and as a teller of tall tales.

backwoods drawl he could reel off an inexhaustible string of tall tales.

Mountain men inevitably encountered grizzly bears, and Meek became renowned as a grizzly hunter. Joe happily embellished his struggles with bears, recounting, for example, the grizzly he tapped with a coup stick, which was a long stick used by some Native American nations to strike or touch a live enemy. Only Joe Meek would count *coup* before shooting a grizzly! He relished describing in rich detail his hand-to-paw battle with a grizzly that cuffed him severely before he sank a tomahawk into her brain, a bloody struggle that convinced Joe he "was satisfied with bar fighting."

He also fought warriors who resented the presence of mountain men in their homeland. In the spring of 1837, a division of trappers led by Meek clashed frequently with the Blackfeet, and during one battle he was nearly killed by a warrior who drew his bow while Meek was reloading his Hawken rifle. The Blackfoot's bow was strung too tight, causing his arrow to drop to the ground, which gave Meek time to fire a fatal shot.

By 1840, Meek was convinced that the trapping era was ending. Joe, his third wife, and fellow mountain man Doc Newell joined the trek to Oregon. Meek and Newell guided a wagon train, becoming among the first to use wagons on the Oregon Trail. The Meeks and Newell settled as farmers in the Willamette Valley, and Joe actively encouraged the Americanization movement. When a provisional government was organized in 1843, Meek was appointed territorial sheriff, and he was elected to the legislature in 1846 and 1847.

Converted to Methodism in 1847, the roistering mountain man became an advocate

THE OREGON TRAIL

Whereas the older Santa Fe Trail was primarily an avenue of commerce between Missouri and the New Mexican settlements, the Oregon Trail was a path of emigration that carried tens of thousands of restless settlers from their homes in the East to the promised land of Oregon. From Independence, Missouri, the Trail stretched westward all the way to Oregon City, just a few miles from the Pacific coast, a distance of some 2,000 miles.

In 1842, John Charles Frémont, an army topographical engineer, explored much of the route of the Oregon Trail, especially that part in the environs of the South Pass over the Continental Divide. By then, however, at least two settler parties had already successfully followed the trail to the West Coast.

The Oregon Trail was traveled by land-hungry settlers from its first use in 1841 until the mid-1880s, when the Union Pacific Railroad made it obsolete. Current estimates hold that during those four decades as many as 350,000 people crossed the Great Plains and the Rockies to the Pacific Ocean along the Oregon Trail and its split-off, the California Trail.

Pioneer Ezra Meeker sits alongside the rut created by prairie schooners heading west on the Oregon Trail.

THE
WAGON TRAIN

The prairie schooner, the ultimate symbol of America's westward expansion during the mid-1800s, actually evolved from the Conestoga wagon, a type of vehicle used in the French and Indian War in the valleys of Pennsylvania. Beginning in 1842 and continuing until late in the 19th century, a constant stream of land-hungry settlers from the East drove these prairie schooners and other types of wagons in an epic journey across the Great Plains to Oregon, California, and Utah.

By the 1840s, both the Santa Fe and Oregon Trails had their origins well established at Independence, Missouri. In any given week during warm weather, the town would see hundreds of settlers gathering for the journey to Oregon, as well as scores of traders bound for Santa Fe. The trading trains were usually well-planned business missions by seasoned travelers seeking profits in distant New Mexico. Settlement parties, on the other hand, sometimes formed at the drop of a hat, and a family never knew from one day to the next who their traveling companions might be. To maintain order, the emigrant wagon trains were organized somewhat like a military unit. The travelers would elect a captain who would exercise firm control over the wagons' movements. He selected the camp sites, appointed work details, settled disputes, and served as a military leader if the need arose.

Like the sailing ships that brought the pilgrims to America, these "Ships of the Plains," as painted by Samuel Colman, brought settlers West.

A typical wagon train with settlers bound for Oregon might consist of 100 wagons carrying 200 to 300 people with about as many cattle in tow. The prairie schooners could be pulled by either horses, mules, or oxen. Horses and mules usually covered 15 miles per day. Oxen could make about 10 miles daily, but they were hardier and easier to graze in the bare scrublands of some parts of the country. Everything an emigrant family owned was piled inside their wagon, and when an emergency made it necessary to lighten the load, pieces of furniture and other household goods were often tossed and left behind on the trail.

of temperance. Meek was a friend of noted frontier missionaries Marcus and Narcissa Whitman, whose mission had become a way station for Oregon settlers. When a measles epidemic broke out among the nearby Cayuse Indians, the natives went on a rampage, killing the Whitmans and a dozen others on November 29, 1847. Joe Meek led a delegation across the continent to Washington, D.C., to ask for protection and territorial status for Oregon. With good-natured braggadocio he announced en route that he was the "envoy extraordinary and minister plenipotentiary from the Republic of Oregon to the Court of the United States."

Although Meek arrived in Washington "ragged, dirty and lousy," he enthusiastically embraced the attention he received from the public. No doubt caught up in the spirit of the moment, Meek proclaimed that President Polk's wife was his cousin. He was spontaneously dubbed Colonel during this foray into Washington, and he proudly clung to the title for the rest of his life. On August 14, 1848—the last day of the session—Congress passed a bill making Oregon a territory. President Polk appointed Mexican War hero Joseph Lane territorial governor, and Colonel Joseph Meek a United States marshal. On his way back to Oregon, Marshal Meek picked up Governor Lane in Indiana and accompanied him west to the territorial capital of Oregon City.

Perhaps Meek's most notable duty as marshal was the execution by hanging of the five Native American chiefs convicted of the Whitman massacre. When Franklin Pierce became president in 1853, Meek lost his marshal's office.

From September 1855 through November 1856, the Yakima War plagued Oregon. The Yakima Indians were unhappy with reservation arrangements thrust upon them by a recent treaty, and in the fall of 1855, a few prospectors and Indian agent A. J. Bolen were slain by restless young warriors. A military column was met with determined resistance, and sporadic skirmishing occurred for more than a year. A veteran of combat with Native Americans, Meek was instrumental in organizing the Oregon Volunteers. "Colonel" Meek became a major of the volunteers, and participated in all activities until the Yakimas were pacified late in 1856.

During the troubled years preceding the Civil War, Meek was emphatically pro-Union, and he helped organize the Republican Party in Oregon. His final years were spent on his Oregon farm, and he died at age 65 on June 20, 1875. Despite his leadership role in Oregon affairs, Meek's half-blood children were ostracized by the anti-Indian sentiment of the times.

Joe Meek was the embodiment of the courageous, irrepressible frontiersman. Drawn to the West, he spent his life boldly enjoying the adventurous possibilities of America's harsh but magnificent frontier.

In his later years, Meek saw his beloved Oregon evolve from a wilderness to a U.S. territory in 1848 to the 33rd state in 1859.

KIT
CARSON

1809–1868

Christopher Houston Carson was born in Richmond, Madison County, Kentucky, on Christmas Eve, 1809, the sixth of ten children of Lindsey and Rebecca Carson. Kit's father served in the Revolutionary War before settling along the Kentucky River to farm. According to Carson's autobiography, Lindsey Carson pushed westward with his family about a year later, settling in Howard County, Missouri.

For a future frontiersman, Kit Carson seemed to have landed in a perfect spot: In 1821, the Virginian William Becknell and his partners left the settlement of Franklin, Missouri, to take their first pack train of trade goods to the town of Santa Fe in the Mexican province of New Mexico. That venture marked the opening of one of the most significant roads in western history—the Santa Fe Trail. But, at first, young Christopher—called Kit since childhood—was not in a position to blaze

Kit Carson's feats as a guide, scout, and Indian fighter are comparable to those of earlier mountain man Daniel Boone.

trails, forge pathways, or open territories, because in 1823, he became apprenticed to a saddle maker in Franklin.

After three years of watching from his saddle-shop window as the wagons wound westward to New Mexico, the teenaged Kit ran away from home and work. He joined a trade caravan heading first to Kansas, Colorado, and the Raton Pass, and then southward to the Sangre de Cristo Mountains of New Mexico and the fabled town of Santa Fe.

Over the next five years, while based in Taos, New Mexico, Carson learned the trades, crafts, and ways of the Southwestern mountain man. He worked as a teamster for a dollar a day on trade wagons. He rode with merchants into Chihuahua, Mexico, where he quickly learned Spanish, enabling him to serve as an interpreter. And he undertook his first California expedition, traveling with a brigade of 40 men led by veteran trapper Ewing Young. Though illiterate, Carson gained skills and experiences during this period that would save his life and those of his companions many times over.

Around 1831, Kit met the celebrated Irish mountain man Thomas Fitzpatrick in Santa Fe. Fitzpatrick was called Broken Hand by Native Americans because his hand had been mangled when his musket exploded. He offered Kit a billet among the free trappers he was leading north to the Rockies. Kit readily signed on for the adventure.

He also gained his experience as an Indian fighter. In January 1833, while Carson was trapping with 50 men on the Arkansas River in Colorado, nine of his party's horses were stolen by a band of Crows. Kit led a dozen men, including two Cheyenne Indians, 40 miles through the snow in pursuit of the thieves. He found the Crow camp, retrieved the horses, and attacked the band of Crows.

The Green River rendezvous in the summer of 1835 turned out to be an auspicious occasion for Kit Carson. There he fought his storied duel with a French-Canadian trapper named Shunar (probably Chouinard). Shunar took delight in insulting and bullying the Americans, aiming his sharpest insults at Carson. Kit quickly grew weary of it. "I did not like such talk from any man," he stated in his memoirs, "so I told him I was the worst American in camp. . . . and that if he made use of any more such expressions, I would rip his guts." The rivalry culminated dramatically, with the two men riding toward each other on horseback with pistols drawn. Kit not only won the fight but also a young Arapaho woman named Waanibe—who may have been the cause of the rivalry with Shunar. Waanibe became Kit's wife and bore him a child named Adaline. Carson does not mention Waanibe in his memoirs. All that is known of her is that she died of some unexplained illness around 1841.

With the fur trade in decline, Carson returned to Missouri in the

Carson led a life of such adventure that his exploits became the stuff of romance. Painter Charles Russell idealized Carson as a western legend in "Carson's Men" (left), while a print from a popular magazine sensationalized his celebrated fight with Shunar (above).

PORTRAIT OF A
MOUNTAIN MAN

The men who roamed the uncharted wilderness of the Rocky Mountains in the 1830s and 1840s made a remarkably diverse group—black and white, old and young, Irish, French, Scottish, and German, businessmen and backwoodsmen. Deeper than all that, though, they shared a characteristic resilience, self-reliance, and fierce individualism that served them well in their rugged environment. On the surface, the demands and rigors of their lifestyle also gave them a characteristic and unmistakable appearance, as described here by veteran trapper Rufus Sage.

"His skin, from constant exposure, assumes a hue almost as dark as that of the Aborigine, and his fea-tures and physical struc-ture attain a rough and hardy cast. His hair, through inattention, becomes long, coarse, and bushy, and loosely dangles upon his shoulders. His head is sur-mounted by a low crowned

The mountain men outfitted themselves for survival, not for appearances. In a harsh, demanding wilderness, their lives and their livelihoods depended on what they carried on their backs.

wool-hat, or a rude substi-tute of his own manufac-ture. His clothes are of buckskin, gaily fringed at the seams with strings of the same material, cut and made in a fashion peculiar to himself and associates.

The deer and buffalo fur-nish him the required cov-ering for his feet which he fabricates at the impulse of want. His waist is encircled with a belt of leather, hold-ing encased his butcher-knife and pistols—while from his neck is suspended a bullet-pouch securely fastened to the belt in front, and beneath the right arm hangs a powder-horn tra-versely from his shoulder, behind which, upon the strap attached to it, are af-fixed his bullet-mould, ball-screw, wiper, awl, &c. With a gun-stick made of some hard wood and a good rifle placed in his hands, carrying from thir-ty-five balls to the pound, the reader will have before him a correct likeness of a genuine mountaineer when fully equipped."

spring of 1842 to visit friends and relatives and to put his daughter Adaline in school. On a steamer on the Missouri, he met John C. Frémont of the U.S. Army's Corps of Topographical Engineers, who was beginning a series of expeditions into the Rocky Mountains and the areas beyond for the government. Frémont hired Carson, at $100 a month, to serve as a guide for the expedition.

In Carson, Frémont found the perfect guide for his expeditions, and together, the pair helped fulfill the goals of the western expansionists, who believed it was America's destiny to conquer and settle the West. In the three-month 1842 expedition, in which Frémont was to map the Oregon Trail, Kit led the group through the South Pass (in today's Frémont County, Wyoming) and into the Wind River Range.

Between the end of his first expedition with Frémont and the start of the second, Carson spent some time at Fort Laramie and at Bent's Fort, then returned to Taos. There, in February 1843, he married Josepha Jaramillo, the 15-year-old sister-in-law of his friend, the trader Charles Bent. Josepha proved to be the love of his life as well as his partner in a 25-year marriage that produced seven children.

In the spring of 1843, Carson rejoined Frémont. The second expedition explored the Great Salt Lake, made a dangerous winter crossing of the Sierra Nevada, and followed the Oregon Trail to Fort Vancouver. The party arrived at Sutter's Fort in March of the following year. Carson then led Frémont and his party south to the Mojave Desert, where the celebrated mountain man Joseph Reddeford Walker joined them for the return trip to the Rockies in Colorado. Frémont's reports of these first two expeditions made both Carson and Frémont famous and earned the ambitious surveyor his nickname, the Pathfinder.

Carson took time to build a cabin for Josepha on the Little Cimarron River near Taos and start up a small farming operation before he rejoined Frémont at Bent's Fort in the summer of 1845 for a new expedition to California. By the time the 62-man party reached Sutter's Fort, California, that November, the United States was poised for a war with Mexico. On May 13, 1846, war was declared, and Frémont's men were ordered to combat duty. Carson served daringly and

Carson fends off a couple of grizzly bears, as depicted in one of the many fictionalized accounts of his life.

Josepha Jaramillo Carson was 18 years old when this photo was taken— three years after she married Kit.

THE LONG WALK

In 1864, thousands of Navajo men, women, and children left their last refuge in Canyon de Chelly and marched under duress 300 miles to the Bosque Redondo reservation along the Pecos River in New Mexico. The Navajo were allowed to bring with them 3,000 sheep, a few hundred horses, and a mere 30 army wagons loaded with personal belongings. The leader of this final effort to subjugate the Navajo Nation was Colonel Christopher "Kit" Carson.

The barren Bosque Redondo was already a forced home to the Mescalero Apache, who could barely scratch out a miserable existence from the arid countryside. With the Navajo presence, life on the reservation became nearly impossible. An 1868 treaty granted the Navajo a reprieve, returning 3.5 million acres of their homeland near the New Mexico-Arizona border in exchange for their vow never to go to war with the United States.

The Navajo made their last stand against Carson's men around the rim of the red sandstone walls of the Canyon de Chelly. Their efforts failed, and they were forced to move from the Canyon to the Bosque Redondo.

earned a personal appointment from President James K. Polk as Lieutenant of Rifles.

Between the Mexican War and the outbreak of the Civil War, Carson and his friend Lucien Maxwell, who had served with Kit in the Mexican War, began a ranching and farming operation on Maxwell's enormous land grant at Rayado, New Mexico. Kit was never quite satisfied with the life of a gentleman rancher, however, and periodically took other, less mundane work. Late in 1849, he joined in the pursuit of a band of Jicarilla Apache who had kidnapped Mrs. J. M. White and her child after attacking the White caravan along the Cimarron River. Carson and a company of Taos dragoons found the Apache camp and routed it, but they proved too late to save the captives. Mrs. White's body was located, still warm, with an arrow in her heart. Her baby was never found. Though Kit v̄as a seasoned mountain man who had participated in skirmishes with Native Americans from the Canadian border to the Rio Grande, he never forgot this incident. In the rubble of the Jicarilla camp, he found a dime novel recounting the hair-raising adventures of Kit Carson. He wondered if Mrs. White, in her last hours, was waiting for the daring Kit Carson of the dime novel to rescue her.

In 1854, he was appointed Indian Agent at Taos with responsibilities among the Ute, Jicarilla Apache, and Pueblo nations. He served credibly in that capacity despite his near-illiteracy. During his tenure as agent, he dictated his memoirs to his secretary, John Mostin.

During the Civil War, Carson was named colonel of the 1st New Mexico Volunteer Infantry Regiment. He fought his single engagement against the Confederates at the

Battle of Valverde, on the Rio Grande above Fort Craig, on February 22, 1862.

More significant than his Civil War service was his return to fighting Indians, this time under the auspices of the U.S. military. In the winter of 1862, under the direction of Brigadier General James H. Carleton, commander of the Department of New Mexico, Carson began the long campaign against the Navajo, who had been rustling cattle from the New Mexican settlers. Carson and 400 men starved the Indians into submission by burning their crops and stores and killing their livestock.

Carson's last battle with Native Americans occurred late in 1864 when Carleton decided to put an end to depredations by the Kiowa and Comanche along the Santa Fe Trail. On Carleton's orders, Carson assembled a force at a fort along the Canadian River in the Texas Panhandle and marched against the Kiowa in their winter camps on the river. He led over 300 officers and troops, supply wagons, mountain howitzers, and an ambulance wagon across the Canadian in November to a large Kiowa village near an abandoned trading post called Adobe Walls. The Kiowa and Comanche, reinforced by other camps, made their stand there. They outnumbered Carson's force, but the odds were evened out by the military's deadly cannon fire. The Kiowa and Comanche bands, who suffered a combined loss of 60 men, retreated to their camps. Carson returned with only two men dead and 21 wounded.

After a brief command at Fort Garland in the Colorado Territory, Kit was mustered out of the army in November 1867. He settled with Josepha and his family at Boggsville, Colorado, where he was appointed Superintendent of Indian Affairs for the Colorado Territory. Unfortunately, by now he was growing increasingly ill.

His failing health notwithstanding, he made a final trip to Washington in February 1868, accompanying a delegation of the Ute to negotiate a treaty concerning their tribal lands. He returned to Boggsville in April, just in time to see Josepha give birth to their seventh child, a daughter. Ten days later, Josepha Jaramillo Carson died. Kit survived his wife by only a month.

Whether he was the simple, noble mountain man of Frémont's memoirs or the daredevil Indian fighter of the cheap dime novels, Kit Carson was painted in heroic tones with the broad strokes of hyperbole. His adventures and exploits helped construct the popular image of the self-reliant trailblazer who conquered the forces of nature for the good of the country. Yet, even without the exaggeration, his accomplishments—from leading Frémont's surveying expeditions to participating in the Mexican and Indian wars—helped settle the West for future generations.

KIT CARSON

Truly a legend in his own time, Carson lived long enough to see his life story interpreted and reinvented in the sensationalized dime novels.

GUNS

Few things connote the Wild West more clearly and strongly than the distinctive firearms that were so often used by the trappers, Native Americans, soldiers, gunfighters, and lawmen of the era. At a time when weapons were often the one and only means of acquiring food, safety, justice, or satisfaction, pistols and rifles were an indispensable technology, and their evolution came to play a key role in the history of the West.

The earliest explorers west of the Mississippi River—whether they were Spanish, French, or English—relied on somewhat primitive muzzle-loaded weapons that required the user to pour powder and ball down the barrel and then ram them into the breech for each shot. Not only did they take time to load, but their flintlock or wheel-lock ignitions, in which the powder is ignited by a spark from a flint, were not always reliable. In the early 1800s, this technology was still in use in the popular Kentucky rifle and the Harper's Ferry rifle, a special design brought along on the Lewis and Clark Expedition.

As the frontier moved westward, however, the sophistication of firearms improved. The Hawken brothers of St. Louis manufactured a rifle in the 1820s that quickly became the favorite of mountain men and their Native American neighbors. Early Hawken rifles employed the flint-lock mechanism, but later models took advantage of the more reliable percussion system, whereby the hammer struck a cap that would shoot fire through a flash hole to ignite the

Top: This Henry lever-action repeating rifle, serial number 1705, was a favorite of Native Americans. **Bottom:** Large caliber Sharps rifles were known for accuracy and stopping power. This Sharps buffalo rifle is .45 caliber.

powder. An average Hawken rifle measured .53 caliber, weighed about 12 pounds, and cost less than $25. Such rifles were clearly the preferred instrument due to their range and accuracy, but many trappers would also carry a single-shot, muzzle-loaded pistol for added protection.

In the 1830s, pistols became much more viable weapons when Samuel Colt patented a new design for the revolver, a gun that featured rotating chambers that allowed several bullets to be fired in rapid succession. The most popular versions were the .44-caliber Army and .36-caliber Navy Colts. While these

multishot breech-loaders were a substantial improvement over earlier pistols, they used paper cartridges that had to be hand-packed with a ball, powder, and percussion cap. Preparing the cartridges was a laborious task, and faulty packing could easily cause the round to misfire and even set off the cartridges in other chambers.

The breech-loading feature of the Sharps rifles of the late 1840s and 1850s allowed these single-shot guns to be re-

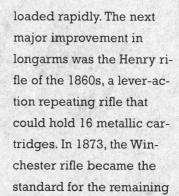

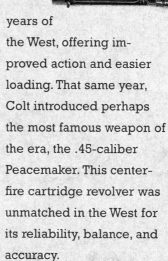

loaded rapidly. The next major improvement in longarms was the Henry rifle of the 1860s, a lever-action repeating rifle that could hold 16 metallic cartridges. In 1873, the Winchester rifle became the standard for the remaining

years of the West, offering improved action and easier loading. That same year, Colt introduced perhaps the most famous weapon of the era, the .45-caliber Peacemaker. This center-fire cartridge revolver was unmatched in the West for its reliability, balance, and accuracy.

Many gunfighters also relied on the crude but effective blast of a shotgun for settling disputes. Although the range and precision of such a weapon was severly limited, its

great firepower and wide spread proved overwhelming when working in close. With a loaded shotgun in his hands, even the most unskilled novice could become a deadly force to be reckoned with.

Left: This patterned powder flask features a military insignia.
Above: The Colt single-action Army revolver has long been identified with the Wild West. This Colt pistol was manufactured in 1872.

LAWMEN AND SHOOTISTS

The Law of the Gun. This description of law and order in the West was made popular in lore and literature, but it is not simply a colorful cliché. A double-edged phrase, it accurately conveys the absolute force needed to maintain order on the frontier and the power available to any man with the skill and nerve to wield a weapon.

Myth and legend have undoubtedly exaggerated the role of the lawmen in the taming of the Wild West. It was the continual mass migration and the coming of institutions such as the railroads that ultimately conquered the wilderness. Still the exploits of such lawmen and shootists as Wyatt Earp, Ben Thompson, Commodore Perry Owens, Tom Smith, and Wild Bill Hickok paint a telling portrait of the type of men who wore a badge in an era when the forces of civilization were resisted.

The West became a magnet for mayhem for a number of reasons. The 20 or so years prior to the opening of the West did much to familiarize Americans with violence. Recent history had been dominated by the bloody, chaotic struggle that culminated in the Civil War. Out of this intense turmoil came a substantial part of the West's population—young males, some foot-

A deputy U.S. marshal and his staff reveal that they are armed and ready for duty as they pose in front of the jailhouse at Fort Smith, Arkansas.

loose, some embittered and betrayed, some disillusioned, and all in some way witnesses to the destruction and upheaval of the war.

The combination of a sparse population and the vast expanses of land also played a major role in keeping the West wild and woolly. There were not enough

ordinary citizens and far too few lawmen, lawyers, and judges to enforce the law across the unsettled western landscape. The nearest law official could easily be 50 miles away. That knowledge tended to make outlaws bolder, which in turn made many citizens feel that they had to take the law into their own hands.

The frontier also held immense economic promise. Vast fortunes were available in the West to be won and lost, to be stolen and protected. Cattle companies and mining interests carved hordes of wealth out from the land, and many of the power-

After weeks on the trail of a cattle drive, cowboys wanted to cut loose in the wide-open cow towns. Their antics—fueled by money, guns, and alcohol—raised the level of lawlessness in these boisterous burgs.

ful leaders of these industries were eager to use or misuse the law or the gun to protect their holdings. Also significant was the region's strong, if volatile, economy. Fueled by the endless opportunities of the West, the economic engine of the frontier made towns such as Abilene and Dodge City swell with prosperity as shipping points to the East. Violence and crime swelled too as large numbers of cowboys, bored and lonesome after weeks on the trail,

In "Cowboys Coming to Town for Christmas," artist Frederic Remington captures the Wild West custom of hurrahing, in which cowboys raced down the main streets of cow towns, shooting six-guns while whooping and hollering.

poured into these cow towns with their pockets full of money. Liquored up and full of vinegar, they wreaked havoc in the saloons and brothels that peppered the business districts. Only the makeshift camps and boomtowns that sprung up around gold and silver deposits rivaled the freewheeling cow towns in their lawlessness and instability.

The coming of law and order to the frontier was a slow and haphazard process. Some of the lawmen who participated in that process were dedicated peace officers who swore to uphold the law, but many were politically motivated, more interested in power and profit than law and order. Some became lawmen to fill in between jobs, while others were gunfighters who simply drifted into a town at the right time. A few drifters and gunslingers took to the badge to avoid a vagrancy charge.

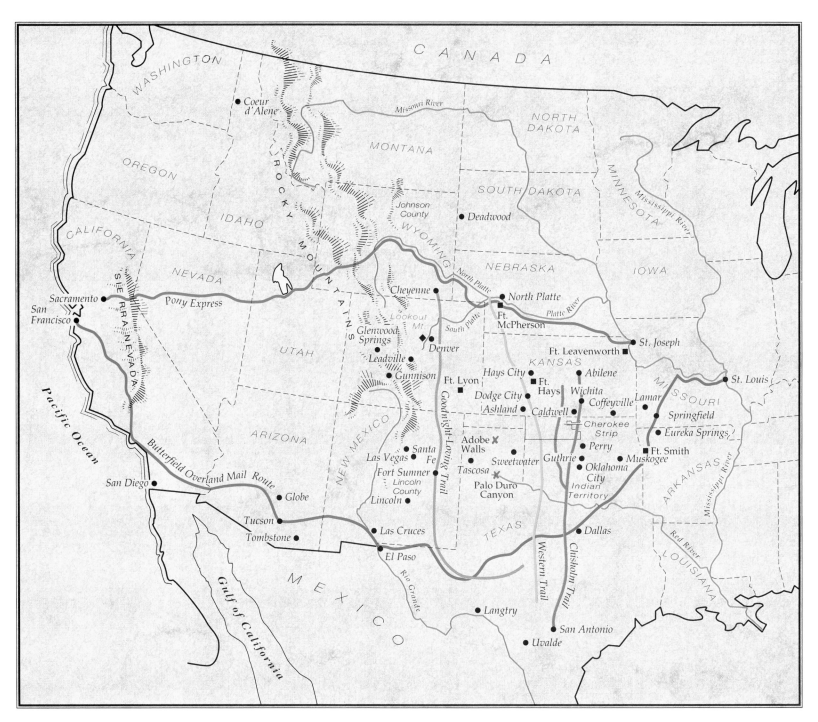

Such cow towns as Dodge City and Abilene were the end points of the famous cattle trails, but they weren't the only towns that needed law and order.

If the circumstances that led to the employment of these men seem to tarnish the image of the brave, righteous western lawman, then the tactics used by

most of them shatter the myth completely. The goal of any lawman was to stay alive by any means necessary. When up against an opponent, the lawman sought "to get the drop" on him, that is, to disable him in any manner. Getting the drop could include anything from clubbing the lawbreaker from behind to gouging him in the eyes to subduing him by grinding a well-placed boot heel in his face. Wyatt Earp preferred to pummel his opponents with his fists, a method that worked well on drunken cowboys. If a little more persuasion was needed, he was known to lay his gun butt to an opponent's head. Occasionally, the town fathers deemed the tactics of their peace officer to be too brutal, and the lawman was discharged or not re-elected, depending on the nature of the position.

In "The Magic of the Drop," Frederic Remington illustrates how shrewd lawmen were able to disarm and disable their opponents.

Law enforcement in the West consisted of a three-tiered structure that included federally appointed U.S. marshals, county sheriffs, and town marshals. The U.S. marshals and their deputies held the most authority and prestige. Appointed by the President, federal marshals had jurisdiction over entire states, districts, or territories. Their duties included apprehending mail thieves and army deserters. Federal officials could also hold additional positions as town marshals or county sheriffs.

The county sheriff's post was usually obtained through a hotly contested election, with the candidates having to engage in a great deal of politicking to win the post. In addition to protecting the town from unruly lawbreakers, the county sheriff collected taxes, from which he received a percentage of the take.

The sheriff also dispensed contracts for road building and other county services. This aspect of the job could easily lead to graft and bribery. John Behan, sheriff of Tombstone while Wyatt Earp was a deputy city marshal, reputedly collected close to $40,000 per year this way. The county sheriff's post could also include some less than glamorous chores. In a small Texas town, for example, the sheriff was responsible for getting rid of pesky prairie dogs.

A group of deputy U.S. marshals shows off their hardware at Fort Smith, Arkansas. In the West, U.S. marshals and their deputies held the most authority and prestige.

The town marshal was generally a hired position, with deputies appointed by the marshal himself. At this level, the number of odd jobs and unglamorous tasks proliferated. The town marshal might also serve as health inspector, fire inspector, and sanitation commissioner. He sometimes collected taxes as well as license fees for dogs, saloons, and houses of prostitution. He also served subpoenas, presided over the town jail, logged official records, and kept the courtroom or courthouse free of trash and garbage. While marshal of Abilene, Wild Bill Hickok not only kept the streets safe for ordinary citizens but also kept them clean of trash.

The lawmen who arrested the criminals could only do so much. The rest depended on a justice system that prosecuted the lawbreakers. When a territory was organized, the government appointed a handful of district judges, only gradually increasing the number as the territory became more populated. The vastness of their jurisdictions placed an enormous burden on these judges. A district judge could ride the circuit of his territory to try criminals in the various communities, or he might send out his U.S. marshals to bring the defendants to his district court for trial. Both were time-consuming approaches to bringing justice to the frontier.

District judges handled federal crimes such as train robberies, mail thefts, and the illegal sale of alcohol to Native Americans. They also handled major crimes that would later be tried in the state courts, including murder, rape, and armed robbery. About the only cases they did not handle were misdemeanors and violations of town ordinances, which were tried by locally elected or appointed justices of the peace or police court judges. The job of district judge was often made more difficult because of lawyers who were ignorant of the law. Few had any formal training, and the judges had to guide them through their cases.

Compared to district judges, local justices of the peace knew little of formal law. They handled only misdemeanors and violations of local ordinances, and they levied small fines as punishment. The formality of the federal courthouse was not found in the makeshift small-town courtrooms, where it would not be unheard of to find a judge clipping his toenails while holding court in a saloon.

In this illustration, a frontier justice of the peace is shown holding court in a saloon, a practice that was widespread in small, isolated western towns.

The law of the gun prevailed in its most brutal guise when this legal system proved weak, ineffectual, slow, or even nonexistent. In the absence of proper law enforcement authorities, ranchers and townspeople often employed professional shootists to protect their interests. The big cattle barons hired gunfighters, whom they called stock detectives or stock inspectors, to guard their herds from rustlers or small ranchers who sometimes picked up strays to build their own herds. The stock detectives were often little more than hired thugs that the cattlemen used to drive off the settlers and sheepherders who began to compete for the huge tracts of range land the cattlemen depended on for their business.

The gunfighter, shootist, or pistoleer hired by townspeople often straddled a thin line between lawman and outlaw. Playing both sides of the fence, the gunfighter might hire out as a town marshal one year and then find himself on the other side of the law the next. While deputy city marshal of Caldwell, Kansas, Henry Newton Brown attempted to rob the bank at Medicine Lodge with three accomplices, only to be caught and jailed. He was later shot by vigilantes. A lawman from Laramie, Wyoming, was hung after townspeople discovered that in his parallel career as a saloon owner, he was drugging and robbing his customers.

Some of the best peace officers had shady pasts. Only a public need or a change of circumstances was necessary to convert a man from an outlaw to a lawman. Once out of a job, his status could just as easily revert back. Perhaps it was hypocritical or contradictory to hire a gunslinger with a dubious past to be a representative of the law. Yet, in an era when there was no widespread respect for law and order—but a frank admiration for courage and skill with a gun—it was an approach that proved effective. Counting on their reputations to precede them, these gunfighters-turned-lawmen instilled fear and dread with their mere presence. Exaggerated stories and boldface lies circulated about their past exploits and gunfights, yet these men were rarely interested in setting the record straight because their notoriety gave them their edge.

The hyperbole that surrounded these lawmen and shootists during their lives was enhanced and circulated by dime novels. The exaggeration was such that even the lives of ordinary cowboys, such as Nat Love, became intertwined with the exploits of fictionalized heroes so that the line between fact and myth was blurred beyond recognition. The dime novels gave military scout William F. Cody an identity as a gunfighting western hero, an image embellished by Cody's own Wild West extravaganzas. Yet, neither Love nor Cody was a lawman, gunfighter, or shootist.

The violence that characterized the lives of the lawmen and shootists was romanticized in dime novels, Wild West shows, and later in film and television. In the popular mind, these men were fearless upholders of the law willing to shoot it out with badmen in a fair showdown on a dusty street; in reality, many were preoccupied enough with their personal safety to wait until their opponents were unarmed or too drunk to resist before attempting to bring them to justice. Still, those men who took to the badge often proved resourceful, tough, and daring. Their existence was often one of loneliness and danger, for which they received little pay. Collectively, they affected the course of frontier justice, and, in doing so, they left their mark on history.

Top: The fabled shoot-out in the street was more myth than history. **Bottom:** Sam Bass (center) was one of the many outlaws who had once been law-abiding.

WYATT EARP

1848–1929

Few western lawmen can surpass Wyatt Earp in legend and fame. Though dauntless, he was also cold and steely.

No more controversial shootist exists in western history than Wyatt Berry Stapp Earp. During his long life, Wyatt restlessly traveled throughout the West: He served as a peace officer in a succession of raw frontier communities; he worked as a buffalo hunter, saloon keeper, professional gambler, and prizefight referee; he joined in the rush to Alaska at the turn of the century; and he served as a technical adviser in Hollywood for such western movie stars as William S. Hart and Tom Mix. Wyatt was a principal in the most famous of all gunfights, then led a violent vendetta after the bloody ambushes of two of his brothers.

Born on March 19, 1848, in Monmouth, Illinois, Wyatt was named Wyatt Berry Stapp Earp after a captain under whom his father had served during the Mexican War. When he was two, the Earps moved to Pella, Iowa, where Wyatt spent most of his boyhood toiling on the family farm under the stern eye of his father, Nicholas.

During the war, Nick Earp was town marshal of Pella, and Wyatt watched his two-fisted father batter troublemakers into submission, thus preventing more lethal incidents. This is a lesson that Wyatt would repeatedly apply while wearing a badge in Kansas cow towns. The hard-bitten Nick once said, "I taught all my boys to fight and I'm damned proud of it!" The youngest Earp offspring, Adelia, later told her daughter, "All of your uncles—especially Wyatt—would rather fight than eat. They must have got it from Pa."

In 1864, Nick uprooted the family again, joining a wagon train for California. A couple of years later, Wyatt began chafing under his father's heavy hand at the Earp ranch in San Bernardino. One day, he lost his temper and hit Nick. Nick reacted with a kick to the groin, then wrestled Wyatt into a horse trough. Both understood that it was time for Wyatt to leave home, so he joined his brother Virgil in driving a freight wagon to Salt Lake City.

Wyatt and Virgil then worked as construction laborers on the westbound Union Pacific Railroad, before rejoining their father as he relocated the family to Lamar, Missouri. Wyatt became the town constable and in 1870 married Urilla Sutherland, with his father presiding as justice of the peace.

Less than a year after their marriage, Urilla Earp died in childbirth, along with her baby daughter. Despondent, Wyatt left Lamar and roamed the West. He was arrested in Indian Territory for horse stealing and then

THE EARP FAMILY

While Wyatt remains the most famous Earp, there were five other brothers and four sisters in the family. The patriarch of the family was Nicholas Porter Earp, born in North Carolina in 1813. Nick's first wife was Abigal Storm, who bore him a son and a daughter, but he later married Virginia Cooksey and sired eight more children. A veteran of the Black Hawk and Mexican wars, the hot-tempered and bellicose Nick spent time living in Kentucky, Illinois, Iowa, Missouri, and finally California, where he died in 1907.

Newton, Wyatt's half-brother, was the oldest of the Earp brothers. He was born in Kentucky in 1837 and died in California in 1928. Like most of the younger Earps, Newton followed a career in law enforcement, serving as town marshal of Garden City, Kansas, for a while. He was the only one of the six brothers to father children.

Left: Passive James Earp was never interested in being a lawman. **Middle:** Like Wyatt, Virgil was fearless and good with firearms. **Right:** Morgan, generally a pleasant man, became hot-tempered under duress.

James was born in Kentucky in 1841 and died in 1926 in Los Angeles. James preferred running a saloon to law enforcement duties, and although he may have been in Tombstone during the gunfight at the O.K. Corral, he did not actively participate in the fracas. James also differed in stature from most of his other brothers, standing only five feet eight inches tall, while the others stood around six feet.

Virgil was born in Kentucky in 1843. He worked as a stage driver and as a deputy marshal before joining his brothers in Tombstone as the city marshal. Later he would serve as the marshal of Colton, California. In 1905, Virgil died of pneumonia in Nevada.

Morgan, the only Earp brother not to live into the 20th century, was born in Iowa in 1851. He recovered from wounds he received at the O.K. Corral only to be murdered in 1882, most likely as retribution for his role in the famed shoot-out.

The youngest Earp brother, Warren, was born in Iowa in 1855. He was probably living in Tombstone in 1881 but did not join his brothers in the shoot-out. He died in Arizona in 1900 when he was shot in a run-in with John Boyett.

spent the next couple of years farming in Kansas, where he took on Cecila Ann "Mattie" Blaylock as a common-law wife. In 1873, he left farm work and joined his older brother James in Wichita, Kansas, the rowdy terminus of the Chisholm Trail. Wyatt again pinned on a badge, apparently as a member of a private force paid by subscription to keep law and order in the saloons and business houses. Later, he became a city policeman.

Wyatt frequently engaged in target practice with the Remington cap and ball revolver that he had used in Lamar. Unlike the famous Navy Colt, the Remington had a backstrap that reinforced the weapon as a club. Wyatt found it so

Wyatt's parents, Virginia and Nicholas Earp, moved their considerable brood around a great deal. Rugged Nick Earp—a cooper, bootlegger, and lawman—was married twice and sired ten children.

handy in knocking out drunks and other revelers that he later had it converted to cartridges. He also avoided shooting his opponents by using his fists. "There were few men in the West who could whip Earp in a rough-and-tumble fight 30 years ago," wrote his friend Bat Masterson in 1907. Wyatt was lean and tall and quick. "In his prime Wyatt was greased lightning," related James Earp. "I saw a couple of fights where guys swung at him and only hit thin air. And, he had a punch like a mule, with those long arms. Virge and I used to call him the Earp Ape."

On April 2, 1876, a candidate for city marshal named William Smith made remarks against opponent Mike Meagher, who was a friend of Wyatt's, and some of the Earp brothers. Angered by the remarks, Wyatt whipped Smith, causing Earp's dismissal from the force. "It is but justice to Erp [*sic*] to say he has made an excellent officer," observed the *Wichita Beacon*.

Wyatt promptly moved to Dodge City, an even wilder Kansas cow town. A man of his experience, rough skills, and courage was appreciated by the city fathers of Dodge, who appointed him to the police force. While Wyatt helped keep the peace in Dodge City, several other western legends lived there, including Doc Holliday and Bat, Jim, and Ed Masterson. During his four seasons as a Dodge lawman, Wyatt continued to buffalo troublemakers with his fists and gun barrel, resorting to gunfire only on July 26, 1878. At three o'clock in the morning, a small group of drunken cowboys began firing their guns into the air, bringing Wyatt and Jim Masterson on the run. The two parties traded shots, and as the cowhands tried to ride off, one young Texan, George Hoy, fell out of the saddle with a bullet in the arm. Infection set in and Hoy, who was under a $1,500 bond in Texas, died four weeks later.

Following the 1879 cattle season, Earp resigned as assistant marshal of Dodge and traveled to Las Vegas, New Mexico, where he joined other members of his family and Doc Holliday. Within a few months, Wyatt, Virgil, and James Earp moved to the Arizona boomtown of Tombstone and settled their families in three houses at the intersection of First and Fremont. Soon after, Morgan and Warren Earp, Doc Holliday, and Bat Masterson turned up in Tombstone.

Wyatt became a shotgun guard for Wells Fargo. He also gambled professionally and speculated in mining claims, and he acquired an interest in the flourishing Oriental Saloon. Twice Wyatt tried unsuccessfully to obtain an appointment as county sheriff. In July 1880, he did become deputy sheriff, stationed in Tombstone. His brother Virgil held a deputy U.S. marshal's commission.

Within a year, Virgil and Wyatt began tangling with rustlers Tom and Frank McLaury, who were involved in criminal activities with the Clanton clan. Earp detractors would later emphasize unsubstantiated rumors that the Earps had been involved with the Clanton-McLaury ring, and that the animosity between them was the result of a falling-out among thieves. They would also claim that James Earp's teenaged stepdaughter had been involved with a McLaury brother. When the McLaury brothers testified against Doc Holliday in connection with a March 1881 stagecoach robbery in which two men were killed, they earned the vengeful enmity of the Earps in general and Doc in particular.

The feud came to a head on October 26, 1881, erupting into a 30-second shoot-out that has generated more investigation than any other gunfight in frontier history. When the smoke cleared, Virgil had mortally wounded Billy Clanton; Doc Holliday had blasted to death Tom McLaury; and Wyatt and Morgan had shot and killed Frank McLaury, because according to Wyatt, "He had a reputation of being a good shot and a dangerous man." Meanwhile, Ike Clanton and Billy Claiborne had fled the scene. On the lawmen's side, Virgil had been shot through the calf, while Morgan had taken a bullet in the left shoulder. Doc had received a flesh wound. Only Wyatt remained unhurt.

The O.K. Corral incident climaxed but did not end the bitter, violent feud between the Earps and the Clantons. Two months after the shoot-out, on December 28, 1881, Virgil Earp left the Oriental Saloon half an hour before midnight. As he crossed the street, he was cut down by several shotgun blasts, throwing buckshot into his left side, back, and left arm. Virgil survived, but he lost the use of his arm. "Never mind," he comforted his wife, "I've still got one arm left to hug you with."

On March 18, 1882, Morgan was playing billiards as Wyatt and a number of other men watched. Suddenly two shots were fired into the room. The first slug entered the right side of Morgan's stomach, shattered his spinal column, and emerged to inflict a flesh wound on one of the onlookers. Morgan was carried into an adjacent card room and placed on a sofa, where he died surrounded by Wyatt, Virgil, James, Warren, and their wives. Friends of the Clantons were supposedly seen running away from the scene.

THE GUNFIGHT AT
THE O.K. CORRAL

John Behan, sheriff of Cochise County, Arizona Territory, was getting a shave in a barber shop in Tombstone on the afternoon of October 26, 1881, when someone bolted through the door with the news that there might be a shoot-out between the Clantons and the Earps.

Behan hastily wiped the lather from his face and hurried down Fremont Street to a vacant lot behind the O.K. Corral, where he found Ike and Billy Clanton, Tom and Frank McLaury, and Billy Claiborne. Only Frank McLaury and Billy Clanton were armed, and the group assured Behan that they were on their way out of town.

Behan looked up Fremont Street and saw Wyatt, Virgil, and Morgan Earp, along with Doc Holliday, rapidly approaching the corral. When the sheriff tried to tell the Earps that the Clantons and McLaurys were unarmed, they shoved him aside, effectively removing him from his precarious position between the two factions.

"You sons of bitches," snarled Wyatt to the group, "you're looking for a fight and now you can have it."

Virgil, standing only a few feet from 19-year-old Billy Clanton, whipped out his six-gun and triggered the first shot of the famous fight. Hit just below the left nipple, Billy was knocked onto his back, then a second bullet broke his right wrist. Gamely, he reached across and pulled his Smith and Wesson revolver, propped the gun on his knee, and fired until he was hit again in the stomach.

Doc shot and killed Tom McLaury with a double-barreled shotgun. Wyatt aimed for Frank McLaury, hitting him in the stomach. Clutching his abdomen with his left hand, Frank staggered into the street and managed to get his gun in play, while Ike Clanton and Billy Claiborne fled the scene. Virgil was shot through the calf, and Morgan took a bullet in the left shoulder. Morgan steadied himself and drilled Frank just under the right ear, killing him instantly. Billy Clanton, writhing in agony, was carried away to die. Doc had been grazed in the side, leaving Wyatt the only unscathed participant.

Three days later, murder charges were filed against all the Earps and Holliday. Within a month, they had been exonerated by Justice of the Peace Wells Spicer, who found that "the defendants were fully justified in committing these homicides."

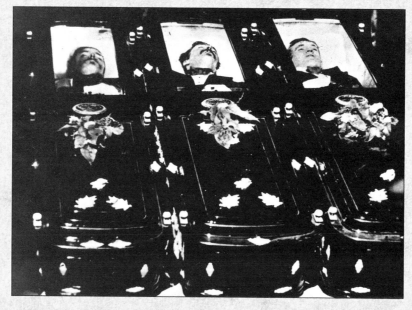

The bodies of Tom and Frank McLaury and Billy Clanton lay in state in the window of a hardware store.

Two nights later in Tucson, Wyatt, Warren, Doc Holliday, Sherman McMasters, and "Turkey Creek" Jack Johnson found Frank Stilwell, the chief suspect in Morgan's murder. Stilwell attempted to flee from the vengeful group, but he was headed off by Wyatt, wielding a shotgun. The entire party opened fire and riddled him with 30 slugs. Two days later, the vengeance-seekers located another prime suspect, Florentino Cruz, hiding at a wood camp near Tombstone and killed him with a volley of gunfire.

During that eventful year of 1881, Wyatt deserted Mattie for sultry Josephine Marcus. Wyatt married Josie the following year in San Francisco. Josie was Wyatt's companion until his death, and she lived until 1944.

Wyatt and Josie spent years wandering through the West. In 1883, he twice visited Dodge City, where he backed an old friend, gambler-gunfighter Luke Short, as a member of the celebrated Dodge City Peace Commission. He spent most of the next year in Idaho at the Coeur d'Alene gold rush, where he speculated with his brother James in mining claims and owned a couple of saloons. After jaunts to Wyoming and Texas, Wyatt returned to California, running a saloon in San Francisco until 1890, when he moved to San Diego to raise thoroughbreds.

In 1896, he refereed the Bob Fitzsimmons-Tom Sharkey prizefight and was widely accused of throwing the match to Sharkey. Attracted by the adventure and opportunities in Alaska at that time, he operated a saloon in Nome until 1901. For the next few years, Wyatt and Josie prospected in Nevada, visiting Virgil in the mining camp of Goldfield. Finally settling in Los Angeles, Wyatt tried to find someone to publicize his adventures, but he died in 1929 at the age of 80. Before he died, he worked as a technical consultant on Hollywood westerns, including those of cowboy movie star Tom Mix. A flamboyant, vain celebrity, Mix is said to have wept openly at Wyatt's funeral.

Two years after his death, Wyatt became the subject of more publicity than he could ever have imagined. Stuart N. Lake authored *Wyatt Earp: Frontier Marshal,* which presented him as an indefatigable gunfighter and a paragon of virtue. For

Earp (center) poses with Ed Englestadt and old friend John P. Clum in Nome, Alaska, around 1900.

many years afterward, books and films were laudatory about Wyatt Earp's life and career in the West, until revisionists tried to exploit every character flaw and rumor. Wyatt's most dedicated biographer, Glenn Boyer, collected documents, photos, and family testimonies for more than five decades. Boyer ridiculed Lake and other mythmakers, while systematically refuting detractors, leaving us with a human Wyatt Earp who marched combatively through an enormously adventurous life.

Throughout his career in the West, Wyatt Earp did prove himself to be tenaciously loyal and courageous—perhaps looming as a larger-than-life legend after all.

DOC
HOLLIDAY

1851–1887

Doc Holliday. The name is magical to western enthusiasts, conjuring up an image of a cadaverous but dapper gambler who fatalistically courted gunplay because a bullet was preferable to slow death by tuberculosis. The captivating persona of this quintessential gambler-gunfighter belonged to John Henry Holliday, who was born in 1851 in Griffin, Georgia.

Holliday's father was a Mexican War veteran who became a prosperous landholder in Griffin. He served as a Confederate major during the Civil War until he was forced to resign because of illness. Holliday's fortunes collapsed with the Confederate dollar, and the family moved to Valdosta, Georgia, where John Henry's mother died in 1870. At this time, John Henry became Doc when he began to study dentistry, probably as the apprentice to a practicing dentist. Doc practiced briefly in Valdosta, then moved his dental business to bustling Atlanta. Soon thereafter he was diagnosed with tuberculosis and advised to move west because the drier climate might prolong his life. By 1873, he had opened an office in Dallas, in partnership with another Georgian, Dr. John Seegar.

Only occasionally did Holliday practice dentistry, however. More frequently he engaged in gambling, usually as a house dealer. Doc gravitated to numerous frontier boomtowns during their heydays, including Dallas and Fort Griffin in Texas; Cheyenne in Wyoming; Dodge City in Kansas; Denver, Leadville, and Pueblo in Colorado; and Tucson and Tombstone in Arizona.

Holliday drank heavily, which accelerated the deterioration of his health as well as his opportunities for trouble. Over the years, Doc engaged in eight shootings, killing two men and wounding various adversaries and bystanders. He also assisted in the assassination of two other men. He first traded shots with a Dallas saloonkeeper named Austin, but neither man was hit. Holliday's next gunfight, in July 1879 in Las Vegas, New Mexico, was more lethal. Doc and a partner operated a Las Vegas saloon, and one of their saloon girls was the mistress of Mike Gordon, a former army scout. Gordon tried to persuade the woman to quit her job, but when she refused, he decided to shoot up the place. Gordon triggered two rounds at the building before Holliday coolly stepped outside and dropped him with one shot. Gordon died the next day.

It was said that Holliday was "drilled in the art of denistry, but for those who doubted his ability, he would drill 'em for free."

62

Holliday left town shortly thereafter. During his subsequent wanderings, he bullied a bartender named Charley White in Dodge City, causing White to leave town. White found employment in Las Vegas, and in June 1880, Doc drifted back into the New Mexico town and stopped off at the saloon to resurrect the old quarrel. Gunfire erupted and White was hit, collapsing behind the bar. Holliday departed, assuming White to be dead, but the wound proved to be superficial.

At this time, Holliday's female companion was a prostitute known as Big Nosed Kate. Frequently referred to as Kate Fisher, she was actually Katherine Elder from Davenport, Iowa. Born Mary Katherine Horony in Budapest, Hungary, in 1850, she migrated with her family to the United States during the 1860s. Kate lived until 1940, dying in the Arizona Pioneers' Home in Prescott.

Kate and Doc may have married in St. Louis in 1875, but their relationship ended in 1881 after Kate unkindly implicated him in the killing of Budd Philpot during a stagecoach robbery near Tombstone. Holliday was accused of the crime, but in one of several court appearances in the troubled year of 1881, he testified to his innocence. "Foresight is a virtue, they say," Holliday proclaimed at the time, giving insight into his constant readiness to do battle, "so I carried my .44 and a rifle in case some of my many admirers were unable to resist the desire to take a large chunk of my hair for a tender memento."

In Tombstone in April of that year, saloon owner Mike Joyce openly accused Holliday of participating in the stagecoach holdup. Doc angrily charged into the saloon with his revolver blazing, wounding Joyce in the hand and a bartender in the foot. In December,

Mike tried to shoot Doc, but he was arrested for carrying firearms within the city limits. A month later, on January 17, 1882, Holliday and John Ringo were arrested and fined 30 dollars on the same charge after bitterly quarreling on the streets of Tombstone. When Ringo, the West's most overrated gunfighter, was mysteriously shot dead and scalped on July 14, 1882, Doc was rumored to have killed him—but so were Buckskin Frank Leslie and Johnny-Behind-the-Deuce O'Rourke. A bizarre ruling of suicide officially cleared everyone.

A loyal friend to Wyatt Earp, Doc Holliday became deeply involved in the bitter feud between the Earp brothers and the faction led by the Clantons and McLaurys. Characteristically, Holliday helped push the trouble to a bloody end when, backed by Wyatt, Virgil, and Morgan Earp, he cursed an unarmed Ike Clanton in a Tombstone saloon. The next afternoon, October 26, 1881, Doc stood with Wyatt, Virgil, and Morgan against the Clantons and McLaurys outside the O.K. Corral.

As the firing commenced, Holliday pulled a shotgun from under his long overcoat and turned on Tom McLaury, who stood behind his horse unarmed except for a rifle in the saddle scabbard. Frank McLaury snapped off a shot that grazed Holliday in the side, but Doc blasted Tom McLaury with buckshot. He then drew his revolver and fired at unarmed Ike Clanton, who fled into a nearby doorway. Though only about 30 seconds had passed, the legendary gunfight was over, leaving

Tom McLaury was killed by a blast from Doc's shotgun during the Gunfight at the O.K. Corral.

COW TOWNS

In 1867, an Illinois-born entrepreneur named Joseph G. McCoy was looking for a place to gather and load cattle from Texas for rail shipment to the East. He settled on a small cluster of houses built

When cowboys drove 35,000 cattle up from Texas and through the streets the following summer, a new era began and a new kind of town was born. This was the first of the great cattle drives, and Abilene be-

For a time, Abilene held the distinction of being the wickedest city west of the Mississippi, but eventually the cattle drovers shifted the destination of their Texas herds to newer railhead towns in the West.

First came Baxter Springs and Coffeyville, then Newton, Wichita, and Great Bend. The most notorious of the Kansas cow towns was probably Dodge City. The town was established in the summer of 1872 as a center for the buffalo hide trade. The great cattle drives began to reach Dodge City in 1875, and the town quickly became the largest marketplace in the entire Southwest. Hand in hand with this rapid growth came its wild, lawless reputation. Said to attract men who were "as fearless as a Bayard, unsavory as a skunk," Dodge was home to at least 16 saloons, which sold only whiskey made on the premises.

Abilene became the first rip-roaring cow town when the Union Pacific established a railhead there for cattle drives. Abilene's heyday spanned the years 1867–1871.

around the railroad tracks in eastern Kansas. McCoy had stockyards, offices, a hotel, and holding pens erected near the railroad.

came the first of the Wild West towns known throughout the world for their hell-raising, gunfighting, whiskey drinking, and gambling.

Abilene settled down and other cow towns assumed the mantle of lawlessness and violence.

Even Dodge City's time passed however, and by 1885, when new depots for cattle shipment were being created by the railroad's ever westward progress, the wildest town of the West was tamed.

Morgan and Virgil Earp wounded and Billy Clanton and the McLaurys dead.

In the ensuing months, Virgil and Morgan were ambushed. Virgil was severely wounded in December 1881, and in the following March, Morgan was killed. Wyatt and Warren Earp, Doc Holliday, Sherman McMasters, and "Turkey Creek" Jack Johnson promptly set out in search of the killers. Within two days, they found Frank Stilwell in Tucson, exacting vengeance with some 30 shotgun and bullet wounds. Returning to Tombstone, the five avengers found another suspect, Florentino Cruz, in a nearby wood camp. He was executed with 10 or 12 shots.

After these killings, Holliday, along with Wyatt and Warren Earp, fled Arizona for Colorado, but Doc was arrested on old charges stemming from the stagecoach robbery and murder. Wyatt Earp appealed for assistance to his friend, Bat Masterson, who, despite his dislike for Holliday, helped foil efforts to extradite Doc to Arizona. As long as he remained in Colorado, Doc was safe from Arizona courts. He drank and gambled steadily and contracted pneumonia, becoming even more emaciated and gaunt in appearance.

Two years later, Holliday was down on his luck in Leadville, Colorado. He borrowed five dollars from a bartender named Billy Allen, who shortly after threatened to beat up the frail gambler. On August 19, 1884, Allen followed Doc into Hyman's saloon, but the 130-pound mankiller angrily whipped out his revolver and snapped off two shots. The second slug struck Allen in the arm and knocked him off his feet, but he scrambled outside while a barkeep grabbed Holliday's gunhand. As with other gunfights, Doc won a legal acquittal.

The encounter with Allen proved to be Doc Holliday's final duel. Weakened by tuberculosis and alcoholism, he took a stagecoach to the Colorado health resort at Glenwood Springs, where he died at the age of 35 on November 8, 1887. On his deathbed, he reflected on the irony of such a peaceful end, as he gasped out his last words, "This is funny."

Despite his efforts to go out in a blaze of gunfire, Doc died in a sanitarium in Glenwood Springs, Colorado (bottom).

BASS
REEVES

1840?—1910

In 1877, famed abolitionist Frederick Douglass became the first African American to receive appointment as a United States marshal. Two years earlier, however, another ex-slave, Bass Reeves, pinned on a badge for Judge Isaac Parker. In doing so, Reeves was probably the first African American to hold a deputy U.S. marshal's commission west of the Mississippi. For the next three and a half decades, Deputy Marshal Reeves battled badmen in lawless Oklahoma.

Bass was born around 1840, one of seven slaves on a farm near Paris, Texas. He grew into a big, powerful man, measuring six feet two inches and weighing 200 pounds. At some point during the Civil War, he left slavery behind him, apparently serving as a Union soldier in Indian Territory. By the end of the war, he had become an excellent shot, and he had learned to speak the Creek language as well as several other Native American dialects. When

Bass, or Baz, Reeves was one of several African-American lawmen who worked for Judge Isaac Parker, whose jurisdiction was the notorious Indian Territory.

the war ended, Reeves married and settled on a farm near Van Buren, Arkansas, where he and his wife eventually reared ten children.

In 1875, Isaac Parker became a federal judge operating out of Fort Smith, Arkansas. To quell the rampant outlawry in the Indian Territory, he appointed 200 deputy marshals—including Bass Reeves. A deputy U.S. marshal was unsalaried, receiving only mileage and fees, but like other deputies, Reeves counted on reward money as a primary source of livelihood.

The Oklahoma Native Americans disliked white men. Reeves, who could communicate in their own language, was able to readily uncover information that was unavailable to white officers. He was also clever at disguises and undercover work, and he often returned to Fort Smith with his prison wagon packed with prisoners.

Oklahoma homesteader Harve Lovelady remembered Reeves as "the most feared U.S.

marshal that was ever heard of in that country." Lovelady also mentioned that several times Reeves killed his prisoners. "He didn't want to spend so much time in chasing down the man who resisted arrest so he would shoot him down in his tracks."

Such an incident was related by Nancy E. Pruitt, a settler in the Creek Nation. "One time [Reeves] went after two mean Negroes and knew when he left that if he didn't kill them, they would kill him, for it would be impossible to bring them back alive." When Reeves located the fugitives, he lulled them with a ruse, then shot them dead before they could draw on him. "That looks like a cold blooded murder to us now, but it was really quick thinking and bravery," recalled Pruitt.

Reeves armed himself with a Winchester, a double-barreled shotgun, and a brace of revolvers, which he wore butts forward for a readier draw while mounted. His proudest accomplishment as an officer was halting the depredations of Bob Dozier, a farmer who had turned into a thief, rustler, and murderer. Reeves located Dozier in the Cherokee Nation, but the outlaw tried to shoot his way to freedom. After a sharp exchange of gunfire, Reeves collapsed into the mud, feigning a mortal wound while tightly gripping his cocked six-gun. Dozier emerged from his cover and walked toward Reeves, who suddenly sprang back to life and ordered the outlaw to surrender. Dozier tried to bring up his gun, but Reeves fired first, killing the fugitive with a bullet in the neck.

Dauntless in pursuit of criminals, Reeves proved cool and brave under fire. In 1884, while in pursuit of outlaw Jim Webb, Reeves rode into gunfire from the wanted man's Winchester rifle. The first shot clipped his saddle horn, the second tore a button off his coat, and the third round cut his bridle reins. Continuing to fire, Webb charged on foot, but Reeves unlimbered his own Winchester and pumped two bullets into the outlaw's chest.

Perhaps the most unusual entanglement in Reeves's career occurred a few months after he vanquished Webb. Reeves shot and killed his black cook, William Leach, after Leach threw hot grease onto Bass's dog. The lawman was eventually tried for murder, but he was acquitted.

Late in his career, Bass stated that he had killed 14 men. Not all of these executions can be substantiated, but without question, Reeves was an extremely competent and dangerous officer. His devotion to duty was tested when one of his sons, Benjamin, murdered his wife during a rage and then fled arrest. Reeves pursued and brought back Benjamin, who later earned a pardon and became a barber in Muskogee.

When Oklahoma became a state in 1907, federal jurisdiction gave way to local courts, and almost all of the deputy marshals relinquished their commissions. Reeves had served as a deputy marshal for more than 30 years. For two years after that, he walked a beat as a Muskogee policeman. Age forced him to use a cane, but he also carried a pistol on his hip and another in a shoulder holster. There was no crime on his beat.

At last failing health forced him to turn in his badge, and Bass Reeves died quietly on January 12, 1910. Hundreds of admirers and friends—black, white, and Native American—attended the funeral in tribute to a brave and dutiful man.

BILL
TILGHMAN

1854–1924

Bill Tilghman enjoyed the longest and most varied career of any peace officer in the West. Tilghman's Wild West adventures began almost as soon as he was born on July 4, 1854. Bill was but a few weeks old when his head was grazed by an arrow during a Sioux attack.

Raised on the Kansas farm of his parents, he became an excellent shot. Taking advantage of his skill, he left home when he was 16 to hunt buffalo, killing nearly 12,000 beasts during the next five years. He also poisoned coyotes, wolves, and bobcats for bounties on their pelts, usually selling his harvest in Dodge City. Tilghman married in 1878 and began ranching near Dodge, but his place was burned during the large-scale Cheyenne uprising led by Chief Dull Knife. Moving into town, Tilghman served an occasional stint as a deputy, worked on railroad construction jobs to support his growing family, dabbled at ranching once again, and operated two Dodge City saloons.

In 1884, Tilghman's law enforcement career began when he was appointed city marshal of Dodge. During the next two years, Marshal Tilghman served Dodge efficiently. He also held a concurrent commission as a Ford County deputy sheriff, utilizing his intimate knowledge of the countryside to hunt down a succession of lawbreakers.

A still youthful Bill Tilghman belied his 58 years when he served as Oklahoma City's police chief in 1912.

Tilghman's parents are shown on the porch of the family home in Dodge City, with his brother Frank standing to the left. The girls are Tilghman's nieces.

From 1887 through 1888, Kansas was plagued by the County Seat Wars, in which towns fought each other for the privilege of being the county seat. Riots, gunfights, and raids ensued as hired guns battled each other on behalf of town fathers. Tilghman became involved in two violent county seat wars. He briefly served as a deputy sheriff at Farmer City, a hamlet between Leoti and Coronado, two towns that were rivals for the county seat. An exceptionally violent shoot-out had recently occurred in the area, and hard feelings were rampant among citizens of all three communities.

Later, Tilghman accepted $1,000 and another deputy sheriff's commission to lead the faction representing Ingalls, Kansas, against Cimarron in the war over the Gray County seat. On January 14, 1889, Tilghman and several other gunmen piled into a wagon. A little before noon, they arrived in Cimarron with the intention of hijacking the county seal and archives. Tilghman led his men into the courthouse, but local citizens discovered the invaders and opened fire.

Badly outnumbered, the men from Ingalls fired back and scrambled to escape. Shooting on the run, Tilghman tumbled into an irrigation canal and sprained an ankle. He was helped into the wagon, and the vehicle rattled away toward Ingalls. Four Ingalls men were trapped inside the courthouse, and after a brief siege, they surrendered, to be released later. Two Ingalls men were hit during the shoot-out, and four Cimarron citizens were wounded, one mortally. The governor of Kansas eventually called out the state militia, and the presence of the soldiers prevented further conflict.

Attracted to the spectacular Cherokee Strip land rush in 1889, Tilghman built a home in Guthrie and opened a saloon. Two years later, he sold his Guthrie property to join another Oklahoma land run. He established a homestead near Chandler and named his little horse ranch the Bell Cow. Shortly thereafter, he accepted a post as deputy U.S. marshal, and in 1893, he was assigned to supervise Perry, Oklahoma, following the last great land rush. During this period, Tilghman began working closely with two other Oklahoma officers, Heck Thomas and Chris Madsen, and this formidable trio of lawmen became known as the Three Guardsmen.

The lawless element in Perry became so threatening that city fathers of the boom-

town hired Tilghman and Thomas as city marshal and assistant marshal, respectively. Marshal Tilghman, Deputy Thomas, and their police force engaged in a flurry of arrests, which rapidly tamed Perry. Early in 1894, U.S. Marshal E. V. Nix ordered the Three Guardsmen to concentrate on bringing in Bill Doolin and his gang.

Doolin's gang separated, but the lawmen arrested the gang's two teenage message carriers, Annie McDoulett and Jennie Metcalf— better known as Cattle Annie and Little Britches. On September 6, 1895, Tilghman cornered one of the Doolin gang, Little Dick Raidler, at a hideout. Raidler tried to flee, unlimbering his revolver and firing on the run, but Tilghman blasted him off his feet with a shotgun. Although riddled with six buckshot, Raidler survived to go to prison. Tilghman collected a $1,000 reward. With the money, Tilghman journeyed to Kentucky and bought two thoroughbreds, Chant, which won the Kentucky Derby in 1894, and Ceverton, victor in the Oakwood Classic. With these two splendid stallions, Tilghman operated a stud service.

Tilghman's most famous exploit as a law officer was his single-handed capture of Bill Doolin at an Arkansas hot springs resort.

Deputy U.S. Marshal Tilghman (left) poses with C. F. Colcord, a fellow deputy marshal, after being assigned to Perry, Oklahoma.

THE THREE GUARDSMEN

By the 1890s, the Old West had all but disappeared. Towns and cities were well established, range lands were largely fenced in, statehood was all the rage, and law and order had come to reign—except in the Oklahoma Territory. Formerly the Indian Territory, this area had only recently been opened for American settlers, and for the last decade of the 19th century, much of it remained as wild and wide open as the West had ever been.

A trio of U.S. marshals led the effort to bring order to this last frontier. Known as a crack shot with a rifle, Bill Tilghman had proven himself in the

Chris Madsen fought with Italian rebel Garibaldi.

streets of Dodge City, where he had served as marshal. Heck Thomas had been a courier in the Confederate Army as a boy, and he worked as a private detective before coming to Oklahoma in 1893. Chris Madsen, a Scandinavian, had seen military service under three different flags in earlier years, first in Italy, then as a member of the French Foreign Legion, and finally with the U.S. Cavalry. Working together to patrol the Oklahoma Territory, they came to be known as the Three Guardsmen.

While the Guardsmen would bring down a great many criminals in the 1890s, their most bitter and bloody quarry was the Doolin Gang. Led by Bill

Doolin, the gang included such dedicated criminals as Dan "Dynamite Dick" Clifton, "Arkansas Tom" Jones, George "Bitter Creek" Newcomb, "Tulsa Jack" Blake, and George "Red Buck" Weightman. Working from bases in the unsettled Oklahoma area,

Henry Andrew "Heck" Thomas was renown among outlaws as a man to avoid.

the outlaws targeted banks and trains throughout Kansas, Missouri, and Arkansas. The Guardsmen and other law officers hounded the Doolin Gang for years, following their trail of crimes, tracking them to various hideouts, and thinning their ranks in a number of bloody shoot-outs.

In the end, the Doolin Gang and most of the region's other badmen were brought to heel, and Oklahoma was brought into the Union. As the 19th century closed, the lawlessness that took its last refuge in the Oklahoma Territory was subdued, largely through the efforts of the West's last great law officers, the Three Guardsmen.

Troubled by chronic rheumatism and old wounds, Doolin sought relief at Eureka Springs, where Tilghman found him taking the waters and reading a newspaper on January 15, 1896. Tilghman got the drop on the outlaw and promptly took him by train to Guthrie. The capture of Doolin had a dime-novel ending. Tilghman's $5,000 reward vanished on July 5, 1896, when Doolin led an escape from the Guthrie jail. The following August 24, Heck Thomas located Doolin in Arkansas and killed him when he resisted arrest.

In 1897, Tilghman's wife, wracked by increasing physical and mental problems, filed for a divorce. Not long after the couple were divorced, she died. Bill served as the sheriff of Lincoln County in 1900, then moved his children to a two-story brick house in Chandler near the courthouse. Sheriff Tilghman won re-election in 1902, and the next year shortly after his 49th birthday, he married a 22-year-old schoolmarm, Zoe Agnes Stratton. The couple honeymooned in Kansas City, and Zoe learned that "Bill habitually slept with a loaded .45 under his pillow." Undaunted by his bedroom hardware, Zoe bore him three sons.

In 1908, Tilghman helped to make the film *The Great Bank Robbery*, persuading Heck Thomas, Chris Madsen, Chief Quanah Parker, and former outlaw Al Jennings to appear with him in the one-reeler. Two more one-reelers followed before the year ended.

Though Tilghman was elected to the State Senate in 1910, the next year he accepted appointment as police chief of Oklahoma City, now the state capital and a center of bootlegging, prostitution, and gambling. Selling his stud farm and resigning his Senate seat, Tilghman moved his family to Oklahoma City, then commenced a series of raids and other activities to curtail lawlessness. He resigned in 1913, and for years, he tried unsuccessfully to attain an appointment as U.S. marshal.

In 1924, at age 70, Tilghman answered another call to duty at Cromwell, an oil boomtown plagued by crime. Chris Madsen advised his old friend not to take the assignment. "Better to die in a gunfight than in bed someday like a woman," shrugged Bill, adding, "I should have things straightened out in a month or so."

Tilghman made impressive progress, but on the night of November 1, a drunken prohibition agent named Wiley Lynn fired a shot on the street. Despite his age, Tilghman slammed Lynn against a wall and jammed his gun into Wiley's ribs. Lynn surrendered his pistol, and Tilghman released him. Lynn suddenly pulled another weapon and pumped two bullets beneath Tilghman's heart. The last great western lawman collapsed and died within minutes.

Incredibly, a jury acquitted Lynn. Eight years later, the prohibition agent became involved in another scrap, shot three men, and was fatally wounded by four bullets. Zoe Tilghman observed, "No jury on earth can acquit him now."

When Tilghman brought outlaw Bill Doolin in to Guthrie, citizens cheered Doolin. Tilghman never understood the general public's admiration for outlaws.

PAT
GARRETT
1850–1908

When he triggered a bullet into the heart of Billy the Kid on the night of July 14, 1881, Pat Garrett won a permanent niche in the front rank of frontier lawmen. This spectacular success, however, was marred by unwanted but persistent criticism of the manner of the shooting, and Garrett's life went downhill after this legendary event in western history.

Born in 1850 in Alabama, Patrick Floyd Garrett was raised on a large Louisiana plantation. After the Civil War, his parents died, and the lanky teenager went west in 1869, spending the next several years as a Texas cowboy and buffalo hunter.

At a buffalo camp near Fort Griffin, Texas, in November 1876, Garrett made a remark that enraged a skinner named Joe Briscoe. Briscoe charged Pat with fists flying, but the six-foot-four Garrett quickly bested his smaller opponent. Furious at being beaten, Briscoe broke away and seized an ax, then charged Garrett again. Pat grabbed his Winchester and fired a slug into Briscoe's chest. Briscoe lasted less than half an hour, but just before dying, he reduced Garrett to tears by asking, "Won't you come over here and forgive me."

Garrett drifted to Fort Sumner, New Mexico, where he married in 1879. His teenaged bride died in premature childbirth, but Pat quickly remarried and began raising a large family.

By 1880, the Lincoln County War had been raging for two years. Garrett was elected county sheriff to restore order in general and to halt the crime spree of Billy the Kid in particular. The Kid was a daring killer and horse thief with many friends who helped him elude capture, but Sheriff Garrett launched a systematic, relentless manhunt.

After one series of arrests in December 1880, a belligerent hardcase named Mariano Leiva loudly proclaimed that " . . . even that damned Pat Garrett can't take me." Garrett slapped Leiva off a porch into the dusty street. Leiva palmed his revolver and snapped off a wild shot. Garrett pulled his .45 and fired twice, shattering Leiva's left shoulder blade.

A few days later, Garrett led a posse into Fort Sumner, launching an ambush when the Kid's gang rode in after dark. In the commotion that followed, Tom O'Folliard was mortally wounded, but the Kid and four other gang members galloped away into the darkness. Within four days, Garrett tracked the fugitives to a stone cabin at Stinking Springs. At dawn on December 23, 1880, Garrett and

With "journalist" Ashmun Upson, Pat Garrett penned *An Authentic Life of Billy the Kid.*

his men opened fire on Charlie Bowdre, who died on Pat's bedroll. The surviving outlaws surrendered that afternoon, and the Kid was quickly tried and sentenced to hang.

The Kid awaited execution in Lincoln. When Garrett was out of town on April 28, 1881, the Kid killed two guards and escaped. Garrett promptly resumed the manhunt, and on the night of July 14, he led two deputies into Fort Sumner. Leaving his men outside, Pat slipped into the bedroom of Pete Maxwell to ask the whereabouts of the Kid.

At that point, the Kid walked into the unlighted room. He had been with his Fort Sumner sweetheart and, deciding to eat a steak, had come to ask Maxwell for a key to the meat house. Hatless and in his stocking feet, the Kid was carrying a butcher knife but had a revolver stuck in his waistband. Passing the deputies, he pulled his gun and entered Maxwell's bedroom asking, *"Quien es? Quien es?"*

After Maxwell identified the Kid, Garrett whipped out his six-gun and pumped a bullet into his chest, killing him instantly. There was immediate criticism of the sheriff for shooting the Kid without warning and from the darkness. Garrett was forced to hire a lawyer to collect the reward money posted for the Kid. When election time rolled around, he was not even nominated for re-election to his post.

Garrett responded to his critics with a model statement of the deadly pragmatism of effective frontier peace officers. "I, at no time, contemplated taking any chances [with Billy the Kid] which I could avoid with caution or cunning. The only circumstances under which we could have met on equal terms, would have been accidental, and to which I would have been an unwilling party."

In the ensuing years, Garrett owned or managed several ranches, and he unsuccessfully tried to promote irrigation in the Pecos Valley. From 1884–1885, he headed a special group of Home Rangers against rustlers in the Texas Panhandle. In 1896, he returned to New Mexico as a territorial detective in charge of a search for the murderers of Judge Albert J. Fountain and his young son. Despite vigorous efforts and a wild shoot-out with suspects, the killers were never brought to justice.

Garrett (left) poses with John W. Poe (right) and James Brent (center). All served as sheriff of Lincoln County.

Finally moving his family to a ranch east of Las Cruces, Garrett was embroiled in a feud with a neighbor and was murdered on February 29, 1908.

TOM HORN

1860–1903

"Killing is my specialty. I look at it as a business proposition, and I think I have a corner on the market."

The lethal businessman who made this chilling statement was Tom Horn, one of the most mysterious and fascinating characters of the Old West. Horn possessed many of the most admirable traits of the traditional westerner. Repeatedly, he exhibited raw courage, tireless stamina, and unwavering loyalty. A man with a powerful physique, he was a superb horseman, a matchless roper, and a crack shot. But these attributes were offset by an inclination to drink, brag—and commit cold-blooded murder.

Born on November 21, 1860, in Memphis, Missouri, Tom was reared on the family farm. He often avoided farm work and school to roam the woods with a rifle and dog. Following a severe whipping by his father, the rebellious 14-year-old ran away from home to head to the West.

Working as a teamster, the strapping youngster made his way to Santa Fe, where

The life and times of shootist Tom Horn epitomize the image of the hired gun.

he learned to speak Spanish. He spent enough time on frontier ranches to master the cowboy skills, but by the early 1880s, he had signed on with the army as a packer in Arizona. His fluency in Spanish made him useful as an interpreter with the Apache who spoke Spanish, and he worked under the legendary scout Al Sieber.

In his famous but unreliable autobiography, Horn made exaggerated claims about his activities as an army scout during the Apache campaigns. His presence with the relentless General George Crook, however, testifies to his endurance and courage. In 1885, Captain Emmett Crawford selected Horn to lead the scouts in a pursuit of Geronimo. Horn was present at Geronimo's surrender in 1886 but was later discharged by the military during a sharp reduction of the scouting force.

In 1890, Horn joined the Pinkerton Detective Agency, working out of the Denver office. He left the Pinkertons four years later, declaring that he "never did like the work." That same year, he was hired by the Swan Land and Cattle Company as a range rider, or stock detective, to help eliminate rustling.

During this period, rustlers were often freed by sympathetic juries. This failure of the legal system irked the powerful cattle barons, who turned to hired guns to hunt down and kill cattle thieves. For the next several years, Horn worked for big Wyoming ranches, prowling the ranges to eradicate rustling. Working closely with such ranchers as John Coble, who ran the Iron Mountain Cattle Company northwest of Cheyenne, Tom Horn acquired a reputation for gunning down rustlers who refused to leave the country.

Horn's reputation was built on such episodes as the killings of William Lewis and Fred Powell. Lewis, who held a 160-acre homestead near the Iron Mountain ranch, bragged about stealing Iron Mountain cattle. He received a warning to pull out of the territory, but he did not heed it—at least not in time. In August 1895, his corpse was found riddled with three bullets fired from a range of 300 yards. Powell, a known confederate of Lewis, worked a homestead ten miles away. Defiantly, Powell invited cowboys from the nearby KYT Ranch to come to a supper consisting of their own beef. Shortly thereafter, a large rider shot Powell to death. Horn, who stood over six feet and weighed more than 200 pounds, was the obvious suspect in both killings, but everyone was wise enough not to accuse him publicly.

When not investigating stock thefts, Horn worked cattle on the ranches that employed him. He always carried a 40-foot lariat and liked to show off his roping skills. Horn usually packed a revolver along with a rifle, and he readily demonstrated his marksmanship.

A cowboy for the Swan Land and Cattle Company was sometimes asked to toss tin cans in the air for Horn, who would drill them twice with revolver bullets before the can would strike the ground. Horn's two primary enjoyments were participating in rodeos and drinking in a good saloon in Cheyenne, Laramie, or Denver. He drank heavily whenever in town, and when he was drunk he talked boastfully, often about his murders and gunfights. Much of this drunken boasting fell into the category of classic frontier exaggeration, but his murderous braggadocio doubtless added to his increasingly sinister reputation.

Horn roamed through much of Wyoming and Colorado, "working the pastures," as he called it. Though the range was mostly fenced, he would still be out for a week or two at a time, riding across the vast holdings of his employers. He also checked the smaller pastures belonging to the nesters who were likely to brand mavericks or rustle branded cattle.

Horn interrupted his career as a range rider during the Spanish-American War, serving in Cuba as a chief mule packer. When he returned to Wyoming, he was welcomed back by the big ranchers, who had become increasingly pressured by nesters and sheepmen. In 1900, he ventured into Brown's Park, a notorious haunt of outlaws. Yet, even in outlaw country, Horn proved to be a formidable figure, later bragging that "I stopped cow stealing there in one summer."

By 1901, Horn was once again working for John Coble at Coble's ranch north of Laramie. It seems Coble and the other large cattlemen were thoroughly disgusted with Kels Nickell. Nickell was a small cattle rancher who was suspected of having ob-

RANGE WARS

As soon as the open range was exhausted in the American West, the stage was set for range wars. When one rancher strung

During a range war in Custer County, Nebraska, circa 1885, a group of masked riders prepare to cut barbed wire on the Brighten Ranch.

wire that separated his neighbor's cattle from water, hostilities usually followed, often resulting in death and destruction on both sides.

Another type of range war occurred because of the intense hatred that cattlemen held for sheep and their owners. Sheep ruined the range, according to the cattle ranchers, and shouldn't be allowed anywhere near cows. Not so, replied the sheepherders, who maintained that their stock had as much right to graze the vast grasslands of the West as anybody.

The Pleasant Valley War of the 1880s became an example of the growing animosity between cattlemen and sheep owners. Although ill feelings had existed between the Tewksbury and Graham families for several years, it was the introduction of sheep to the Arizona range by the Tewksburys that resulted in several murders by both groups. On September 4, 1887, at Holbrook, Arizona, in one of the most famous gunfights in history, Sheriff Commodore Perry Owens single-handedly slew several Graham employees accused of killing John Tewksbury and a friend. In 1892, Tewksbury's brother was convicted of killing one of the Graham brothers.

Wyoming's Johnson County War had its beginnings in 1892. Frustrated members of the Wyoming Stock Growers' Association hired several "range detectives" to put a halt to rustling. Calling themselves the Regulators, the detectives invaded Johnson County and killed two suspected rustlers, Nate Champion and Nick Ray, in a dramatic 12-hour shoot-out. Concerned neighbors formed a 200-man posse and surrounded the Regulators at a ranch near the town of Buffalo. The U.S. Cavalry rescued the Regulators and escorted them to Cheyenne, where they stood trial. None of the Regulators were ever prosecuted for any crimes, and the dispute eventually subsided. In the long term, the Johnson County War hurt the local economy for several years and greatly affected the state's political makeup.

tained his herd through rustling. He then compounded the tension by switching to sheep. Another small rancher, James Miller, and his sons had been feuding with Nickell for years. On July 18, 14-year-old Willie Nickell, clad in his father's hat and coat as protection against a rainstorm, was murdered at a fence gate by a rifleman from a distance of 300 yards.

At first it was thought that Willie's murder was the result of the feud, and the Millers were subsequently questioned. Seventeen days later, Kels was wounded by a fusillade from concealed riflemen. Shortly thereafter, four riders killed about 75 sheep pastured by Nickell. The unfortunate rancher eventually sold his spread and moved away. Although blame might rest with the Millers, public suspicion began to center on the notorious Tom Horn.

Though attention surrounding the case had begun to fade away, detective Joe LeFors refused to give up the investigation. He laboriously deceived Horn into thinking his services as an assassin were needed by a Montana rancher. Pretending to be a middleman, LeFors lured Horn into an incriminating conversation, with a deputy sheriff and a court reporter listening from concealment. The resulting "confession" would not be admitted in a modern court, but the controversial transcript resulted in his arrest. Horn later insisted he was guilty only of drunken boasting.

Although the cattle barons provided Horn with an expensive legal team, Horn's lawyers were badly outdueled by the prosecution during the spectacular two-week trial in October 1902. Horn was declared guilty and sentenced to hang; all legal appeals were denied. On August 9, 1902, Horn escaped from jail, but he was quickly caught and beaten

into submission. To the end, the famed shootist denied that he had killed Willie Nickell.

In Cheyenne, on November 23, 1903, he ate a hearty breakfast, smoked a final cigar, and met his end impressively. Even if Horn had been innocent of the murder of Willie Nickell, there was a general certainty that he had gunned down four other men. There were also the rumors that he had slain countless others. Many people felt that Horn was a throwback to a more primitive and lawless era and that the West was well rid of an old-fashioned hired killer.

A jury deliberated only five hours before finding Tom Horn guilty of the murder of Willie Nickell.

BUFFALO
BILL CODY

1846–1917

More than any single historical figure, Buffalo Bill Cody has stood as the epitome of the Old American West. Eighty years after his death, his image remains indelible— a tall, handsome man dressed in fringed and beaded buckskins, gauntlets, and hip-high boots, with shoulder-length hair flowing from his wide-brimmed sombrero as he sat on a snow-white horse.

Between 1870 and the World War I era, an estimated 1,700 dime novels provided an eager public with lurid, totally fabricated tales of Buffalo Bill's exploits. These, together with Cody's spectacular record as an internationally beloved showman, overshadowed his genuine accomplishments as a frontiersman, Pony Express rider, scout, Indian fighter—and Indian friend. This triumph of myth over reality has resulted in a layer of varnish so thick that it must be scratched deeply to see what lies beneath it.

Born near Leclaire, Iowa, on February 26, 1846, William Frederick was the third of eight children of Isaac and Mary Ann Laycock Cody. Young Billy continued his country school education when the family moved to Kansas in

Bill Cody was quite conscious of the myth surrounding his life and readily embellished it through tall tales and grand posturing.

1854. Among the first families to settle in the newly opened territory, the Codys homesteaded in the Salt Creek Valley, a few miles east of Fort Leavenworth.

Within months of their settlement in Kansas, Isaac Cody was the victim of a violent incident that shaped the future of his oldest son. A religious man and an outspoken abolitionist in a pro-slavery district, Isaac was stabbed in the chest in a political argument. He survived the attack, but his health was broken. He died in 1857. Mary Ann took in boarders to make ends meet and took her son, then age 11, to Leavenworth to find him a job.

Billy landed work as a messenger for Russell, Majors and Waddell, the newly established but already important freight company. In his brief association with the outfit, young Cody had the first of a lifetime of adventures. He was among the horseback messengers who took instructions and orders from wagon to wagon when Russell, Majors and Waddell shipped supplies to the army in its expedition to Utah in 1857 to quell the Mormon rebellion. Brigham Young's troops attacked the caravan in Wyoming and captured many of its wagons.

In the three years that followed, Cody made several freighting trips to Forts Kearny and Laramie and learned the rudiments of mining and trapping. At age 15, he returned briefly to the Leavenworth freight company's employment for a stint as a Pony Express rider on the 116-mile run between Red

Buttes on the North Platte River and the Sweetwater in Nebraska.

In 1861, Cody joined a band of jayhawkers—Union guerrillas fighting Confederate sympathizers. The group stole horses from secessionists in Missouri and drove them back across the Kansas line. The next year, he worked as a scout for the 9th Kansas Volunteers on the Santa Fe Trail in Comanche-Kiowa country, and in 1863, he worked as a teamster. While en route to Denver, he received word of his mother's grave illness. He returned to Leavenworth in time to be at her bedside when she died that November. Thereafter, he credited Mary Ann Cody as guiding the course of his life.

Perhaps no other western figure was the subject of more dime novels than Cody.

While waiting to be mustered out of the army in St. Louis, he met Louisa Maude Frederici, three years his senior. After his discharge, Cody found work with Ben Holliday's Overland Stagecoach Line in Kansas, but he returned to St. Louis in the spring of 1866 and married Louisa. The marriage endured for 50 years, until Cody's death, despite being somewhat of a mismatch. The prim, temperamental, and jealous Lulu—as Cody called her— disliked the West, her husband's friends, his fame, and above all his inability to stay put long enough to have a stable family life. For his part, Will—as Louisa called him—remained a gregarious, free-spending, hard-drinking, philandering nomad, who was unwilling to conform to Louisa's homebody existence.

Cody made one half-hearted attempt at domesticity. He and Louisa returned to the Salt Creek Valley area soon after their wedding and opened a hotel, the Golden Rule House. Yet this mundane existence quickly debilitated Cody. "It proved too tame employment for me," he later wrote, "and again I sighed for the plains." Despite a promise made to his wife, who soon returned to St. Louis, the restless adventurer headed west.

Cody received his celebrated moniker, Buffalo Bill, around 1867–1868 when he began hunting buffalo for the eastern division of the Union Pacific Railroad, later the Kansas Pacific. A Hays City company, the Goddard Brothers, held the contract to feed the U.P.'s track gangs. Cody, who had a well-known skill with his .50 caliber Springfield breechloader, was hired at the handsome salary of $500 a month to supply the meat. He later estimated that he killed 4,280 buffalo in the 18 months at this job.

By July 1868, Buffalo Bill Cody was employed once again as a scout for the United States Army. In one daring exploit, he rode 65 miles from Fort Larned to Fort Hays to deliver to General Philip Sheridan news of the huge camp of Comanche and Kiowa that had sprung up near Larned. Sheridan then sent the scout on a 95-mile journey to Fort Dodge, carrying vital dispatches over a trail on which several other couriers had been killed. Cody made the trip unscathed, took a brief nap, and climbed back in the saddle. He rode into Larned, rested, and then returned to Hays—riding 350 miles through hostile country in under 60 hours. Sheridan, a man who was never easily impressed, called Cody's ride "an exhibition of endurance and courage" and appointed him chief of scouts for the 5th Cavalry at Fort Hays.

In the fall of 1868, the 5th fell to the command of Major General Eugene A. Carr and moved to Fort McPherson in central Kansas. There Cody had a fateful encounter with a 46-year-old New York writer named Edward Zane Carroll Judson. An author of dime novels and sensational magazine serials, Judson is best known by his penname, Ned Buntline.

Cody's real-life exploits as a young man became the basis for some of the acts in Buffalo Bill's Wild West show. Other acts were based on other famous western events.

and pointed to Cody, sleeping under a nearby wagon, saying, "There's the man you're looking for." Judson spent some time with Cody and returned home to write the first in a series of hair-raising adventures about his new-found hero, *Buffalo Bill, King of the Border Men*.

Between scouting assignments for the army, Cody served as a guide for various hunting expeditions, including a memorable one arranged for the Grand Duke Alexis, son of Czar Alexander II of Russia. This expedition also included General Sheridan, Lieutenant Colonel George A. Custer, and Spotted Tail, chief of the Brulé Sioux, who gathered 100 of his warriors to put on a war dance for the visiting nobleman.

On May 22, 1872, Cody was awarded the Congressional Medal of Honor for his gallantry as an army scout. The Medal was revoked in 1917, along with 910 others, in a purging of the award and retroactive tightening of the rules. Cody was declared to have been a civilian and therefore ineligible for the Medal. In 1989, 72 years after his death, the rules were rewritten once again, and the Medal was restored to him.

Buntline had come to Fort McPherson to meet the celebrated Major Frank North and to learn more about the work of North's Pawnee Scouts in the campaigns against the Sioux. Supposedly, North told Judson he was not interested in being heroized or novelized

Cody journeyed east during that eventful year of 1872 with fellow scout J. B. "Texas Jack" Omohundro after repeated appeals from Buntline. The prolific writer wanted them to appear in his melodrama, *The Scouts of the Prairies*. The play opened in Chicago's Nixon

NED BUNTLINE

Ned Buntline, the king of the dime novelists, was born Edward Zane Carroll Judson in New York in 1823. After serving at sea for a few years, Buntline participated in the Second Seminole War before choosing a literary career at age 21. A born prevaricator and ne'er-do-well, he had a knack for spinning entertaining yarns around just a handful of facts.

Buntline's first writing effort was *Ned Buntline's Magazine*, published for only two issues in New York City. Next, he founded the *Western Literary Journal and Monthly Review*. In order to save the magazine from failure, Buntline decided to set his sights toward the South for both contributions and subscriptions. He reorganized the magazine and renamed it *The South-Western Literary Journal and Monthly Review*. Unfortunately, it did little better than his earlier efforts.

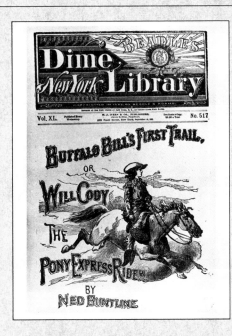

A prolific writer, Buntline is best-known for his wild yarns about Buffalo Bill Cody.

Buntline's life sometimes resembled the melodrama he was so good at fabricating. While promoting his fledgling magazine in Nashville, Buntline became involved with a married woman. The liaison caused quite a stir among Nashville society. After a preacher had observed the pair talking in a local cemetery, the woman's husband tracked Buntline down and shot at him several times. He missed, but Buntline did not. When a lynch mob attempted to capture the rakish novelist from authorities, he jumped out of the third story window of the City Hotel. He was recaptured and actually hanged on Nashville's Public Square, but friends were able to rescue him before the hangman's knot did its job. Finally, when a grand jury heard his plea of self-defense, he was freed. Buntline left Nashville immediately, never to return.

Untouched by his brush with death, Buntline returned east to continue his literary career. He gradually built his reputation and improved his income, which at $20,000 per year made him the highest-paid writer in the United States.

For many years, it was assumed that Ned commissioned the Colt's firearm factory to customize several 1873 Single Action Army revolvers to carry a 12-inch barrel and be fitted with a detachable walnut stock that converted the pistol into a rifle.

These mementos, called Buntline Specials, were supposedly given to several eminent lawmen, including Wyatt Earp, Bat Masterson, and Bill Tilghman. Recent research, however, has disproved parts of this story, yet the gun remains a major part of the lore and legend of Buntline.

Buntline was a prodigious writer, and before he died in New York in 1886, he wrote several hundred books, pamphlets, articles, and stories under both his own name and a variety of pseudonyms.

Amphitheater on December 17 to a packed house. The Chicago *Times* reported, "Such a combination of incongruous dialogue, execrable acting . . . scalping, blood and thunder, is not likely to be vouchsafed to a city for a second time—not even Chicago." But the participation of the *real* Buffalo Bill and Texas Jack gave the ludicrous play a semblance of authenticity, and audiences loved it. By the time the traveling melodrama's first season ended in New York, Cody had earned $6,000. He and Omohundro argued with Buntline over their earnings and soon parted company with the writer.

Looking out of place in a Venetian gondola, Buffalo Bill and a few of his cast members catch the sights while in Europe in 1890.

The cast of the retitled *The Scouts of the Plains* continued to perform the melodrama in the East and Midwest for several years, with a new manager. At the end of each season, Cody would rejoin Louisa and their growing family—daughters Arta and Orra and son Kit—in St. Louis and then report in at Fort McPherson for army duties. In the fall, he would gather with the rest of the cast to resume theatrics.

In the summer of 1876, Cody cut his theatrical season short and announced to his audiences that he was returning west to fight Indians once again. He rejoined the 5th Cavalry in Cheyenne, where he served under Major General Wesley Merritt.

In July, about 800 Cheyenne fled the Red Cloud Agency at Fort Robinson in northwest Nebraska. Merritt's command located the renegades about 30 miles from the agency on Hat Creek, strung out along a wide front. With Merritt's permission, Cody and eight troopers and scouts rode out to intersect one band of Cheyenne as they advanced on an army wagon train. In the skirmish that ensued, Cody fought with the Cheyenne chief Yellow Hair (often mistakenly called Yellow Hand). The experienced scout shot the chief's pony only to have his own horse stumble. Cody escaped a bullet that just missed him, returned the fire, and shot the Cheyenne through the head. He took Yellow Hair's scalp, and this grisly scene was depicted on countless garish posters, playbills, books, and magazines. It was even written into a five-act melodrama. The scalp and the Cheyenne chief's warbonnet became standard props in Cody's performances thereafter.

For the most part, the service with Merritt marked Cody's last official duty with the army. After two decades as a teamster, scout, buffalo hunter, and Indian fighter, he turned full-time to a career as showman, a calling he pursued the last 40 years of his life.

The open-air-extravaganza that became the internationally renowned Buffalo Bill's Wild West debuted at an Independence Day celebration in North Platte, Nebraska, on July 4, 1882. The show was officially launched in Omaha the following May, then moved eastward to Boston, growing in popularity with each performance.

Over its 25-year run, Buffalo Bill's Wild West underwent many script changes as the show traveled the United States and Europe, but certain features remained standard. The show almost always featured a Pony Express race, the Deadwood Stage attacked by bandits, Custer's last fight, the Battle of Summit Springs, Native American attacks on covered wagons, and a reenactment of the Yellow Hair duel. Also included were trick riding and roping, and appearances by frontier notables. The *pièce de résistance* was always Buffalo Bill himself. A grand figure, Cody would wave his wide-brimmed hat, bow to the audience, and race his snow-white horse around the ring.

Because of financial difficulty, Cody merged his Wild West show with a similar show owned by Gordon W. "Pawnee Bill" Lillie in 1908. The Buffalo Bill Wild West & Pawnee Bill Great Far East Show collapsed in Denver in 1913. Buffalo Bill became associated with the Sells-Floto circus and then with 101 Ranch Wild West Show, performing regularly up to two months before his death. Despite the many years of success and acclaim, Cody was not a wealthy man. He had gone through several fortunes, making bad investments, trusting too many people.

Near the end, he was also not a healthy man. Before each show, a member of the cast had to help the old man onto his horse. He would sit slumped in the saddle until the curtain parted. Then, as his assistant said, "Ready, Colonel," Cody would ride out into the arena, standing tall in the saddle with his back straight and chin held high. He would doff his white Stetson hat to the cheering audience and then gracefully bow just as he had done in the old days.

Yet Cody's lack of financial acumen, ill health, and hard times ultimately matter very little. As the champion purveyor of western lore and legend, he perpetuated the spirit of the Wild West just as his image captured the essence of the mythic frontier hero. For millions of people who never set foot west of the Mississippi, he provided the excitement and adventure of a time and place that had passed all too quickly. Buffalo Bill Cody died on January 10, 1917, and was buried on Lookout Mountain above Denver.

A crowd of 18,000 attended his funeral.

Though not a wealthy man when he died, Cody was beloved around the world as witnessed by the 18,000 mourners at his funeral.

ROY
BEAN

1827?–1903

In 1892, ten years after Roy Bean had set up his saloon-courtroom in Langtry, Texas, he received a letter from his putative boss, Governor James Hogg. Hogg was concerned that Judge Bean had not been turning over to the state a share of the fees and fines he collected. Bean's response to the Texas chief executive formed, in a dozen words, the sum of his entire professional philosophy: "Dear Governor: You run things up in Austin and I'll run them down here. Yours truly, Roy Bean."

For two decades, Bean did just that. From his headquarters at Langtry, a speck on the map a few miles west of where the Pecos River empties into the Rio Grande, he was the law in a vast and trackless territory that extended westward 350 miles to El Paso.

The Texas Rangers, the only other law in Bean's domain, loved him for the lightning justice he meted out. State officials were dubious of him because he was a mere justice of the peace, yet he was forever superceding his authority. And miscreants of every stripe— from simple drunks to killers—feared the bang of his six-shooter gavel that often dispensed unpredictable verdicts and capricious punishments.

One other feature of Bean's career is that he kept few records. He wrote no journal or memoir, scribbling only a handful of letters during his lifetime. Most of what we know of his early life derives from what Bean told others. Much of what we know of his Langtry career has been unearthed by folklorists who dote on him more for his peculiarly Texan sense of humor than for his outrageous administration of frontier law, though the two are perhaps inseparable.

Despite trying cases involving serious crimes, Roy Bean (foreground) was only a justice of the peace.

Born on the Ohio River in Macon County, Kentucky, in about 1827, Bean supposedly ran away from home at age 16. He visited New Orleans but seems to have gotten into some kind of trouble there. He claimed to have enlisted for the Mexican War and said that he drove ammunition wagons for General Zachary Taylor in northern Mexico.

With his brother Sam as partner, Bean gathered a wagonload of trade goods and journeyed from Westport, Missouri, to Santa Fe in 1848. He took the profits from this venture and continued south through the wild Trans-Pecos region of West Texas into Chihuahua. There, according to Bean, he killed a Mexican in an argument and had to flee the country, hiding in a wagonload of buffalo hides.

He made his way to San Antonio, where he ran a dairy for a time before abruptly leaving for California. One story about his sudden departure is too good not to be told but too good to be believed. Bean supposedly had been diluting his milk with water from the Rio Grande, a tactic that succeeded until a customer found a minnow in her milk.

He made his way to San Diego, where his brother Joshua operated a saloon. On February 24, 1852, Bean fought a duel on horseback with another man and wounded his opponent. The incident was written up in a local newspaper, representing a rare instance of being able to verify a story about Bean. He was jailed briefly but escaped and made his way to Los Angeles, where Joshua had just opened the Headquarters Saloon. Two years later, Joshua was murdered, probably over a woman, and Roy inherited the Headquarters.

According to Bean, he fell afoul of the father of a Spanish girl he was courting and came within a literal inch of being lynched for the indiscretion. The rope stretched, he claimed, and he had to stand on tiptoe to stay alive until his girlfriend cut him down. The story may be apocryphal, but, according to friends, Bean had a scar around his neck and could not turn his head independently of his body.

He turned up in Mesilla, New Mexico Territory, in 1858, where his brother Sam owned a hotel-saloon. During the Civil War, Roy claimed to have operated with Confederate irregulars serving with General Henry H. Sibley. He returned to San Antonio in 1863, and for 20 years, he worked as a bartender, saloonkeeper, and teamster. During this period, he married and fathered four children.

Bean was enamored with actress Lily Langtry. A world-famous beauty, she was once the mistress of King Edward VII.

Perhaps because of debts, unhappiness in his marriage, or simple wanderlust, Bean crossed the Pecos in 1882. With a wagonload of whiskey and canned goods, he opened a saloon along the Southern Pacific Railroad tracks at a place called Vinegaroon, which is the name of the ugly whip scorpion indigenous to the area. Soon after, he moved his establishment a few miles northwest to Eagle's Nest Springs. He supposedly renamed the village Langtry after an English actress named Lily Langtry. But once again, it is difficult to tell fact from folklore. The place may have been previously named Langtry, after a railroad contractor with that name. However, the possibility that Bean named it for his beloved actress makes better sense and most certainly a better story.

At Langtry, where he was named justice of the peace a few weeks after he moved there, Bean built his saloon. Made of roughly hewn boards, it was a boxlike building measuring 20 feet long by 14 feet wide, with a porch across the front. Inside there was a cast iron stove, two poker tables, a bar at the far end, and a rough courtroom table with two benches for defendants, lawyers, and witnesses. Bean rarely employed juries, but when he was forced to have one, he brought in a third bench.

He named his establishment the Jersey Lilly, a slight misspelling of the name of the woman whose visage he had seen in a magazine and doted on thereafter. He subscribed to theater magazines to follow Langtry's career, tacked up pictures of her over his bar, and stoutly defended her honor. When a visitor examined a picture of her over the bar and rudely likened Lily to a range heifer, Bean fined the man $20 for slander.

The signs over the Jersey Lilly proclaimed Judge Roy Bean a notary public, justice of the peace, and

the Law West of the Pecos. Another large sign read, "Ice Beer." From August 1882 to the end of his life, he dispensed whiskey, beer, and his personal brand of justice from the Jersey Lilly, tending bar and holding court, often simultaneously. He would trade his bar apron for an alpaca coat and use his six-shooter as a gavel. Frequently he could be found on the Lilly's porch, wearing a huge Mexican sombrero and playing cards with cronies.

Langtry never had a population above 150, but the the Jersey Lilly did a thriving business as a saloon and particularly as a courtroom. Judge Bean knew little about the law, and most of what he did know came from the single law book he owned, *Revised Statutes of Texas, 1878*. He took care of minor infractions such as drunkenness, assaults, and petty theft, but he also handled serious crimes, which were far outside his jurisdiction, including cattle rustling, horse theft, and murder. He never ordered a convicted person to prison because it would have involved state authorities, and this was a bother Bean avoided assiduously. His verdicts ranged from ordering a defendant to buy drinks for the house to ordering the accused to be hanged.

Bean holds court on the porch of the Jersey Lilly around the year 1900. He is supposedly trying a horse thief.

He kept no records of the transactions of his court, but some of his most memorable moments behind his makeshift bench were preserved by his Langtry friends, visitors, and lawyers. For example, Bean once held an inquest over the body of a railroad worker who had died in a fall from a bridge. In the victim's belongings were a pistol and $40 in cash. Judge Bean fined the corpse the $40 for carrying a concealed weapon, confiscated the weapon for use by the court, and gave the $40 to the railroader's friends to bury him.

In another inquest, in which the victim had been found with a bullet hole between his eyes, Bean declared the man had met his death "at the hands of a damned good pistol shot." He once threatened to fine a lawyer for using profanity in court when the attorney said he intended to obtain a writ of habeas corpus on behalf of his client. He performed weddings and granted divorces, the latter granted when he found that the marriages "didn't take." He once freed an Irishman accused of killing a Chinese railroad worker after consulting his law book and determining the statutes "did not say it was against the law to kill a Chinaman."

In February 1896, Bean put together one of the strangest events in sports history when he staged a heavyweight championship prizefight between Bob Fitzsimmons and challenger Peter Maher. Prizefighting was illegal in Texas, but Bean was undeterred. The 200 fight fans paid $12 per ticket, came to Langtry on a train from El Paso, and were led by the judge to the Jersey Lilly for prefight imbibing. He then directed them to a rickety pontoon bridge made of beer kegs and scrap lumber and guided them across the Rio Grande to a sandbar on the Mexican side of the border. The ring had been constructed on the sandbar, and spectator benches cut into the river bank. While Rangers stood on the American side to enforce Texas law, the fight began on schedule. Fitzsimmons knocked out Maher in 90 seconds, after which the crowd filed back across the river to Bean's now-famous saloon for libations and all-night postfight speculation.

The small burg of Langtry finally got on the map, or at least in the newspapers, in the 1890s when Bean wrote a letter to Miss Langtry to inform her that he had named the town for her. She wrote back, graciously thanking him for the honor and offering to finance the erection of a drinking fountain in the town square. Appreciative of her offer, the judge responded, saying he didn't think it would be necessary. "If there's anything these hombres of Langtry don't drink, it's water," he said.

Roy Bean died in his room at the Jersey Lilly on March 16, 1903, close to the age of 78 years. He had become such a national character by this time that newspapers across the country carried his obituary and recounted some of his expoits as the Law West of the Pecos. He was buried in nearby Del Rio.

Ten months after his death, Lily Langtry, on a tour of the United States, visited the town named for her. A celebration was held in her honor, and she was presented with a pistol that belonged to her long-time admirer. The Jersey Lily remembered Judge Bean when she published her memoirs, *The Days That I Knew*, in 1925. She regretted never meeting him and spoke of his "ready wit and audacity."

CHARLIE SIRINGO

1855–1928

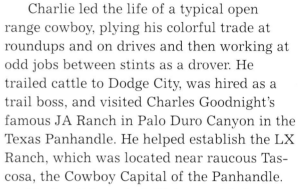

The year 1885 was the height of the "Beef Bonanza," in which wealthy easterners and Englishmen invested eagerly in western cattle ranches. During this time, the cowboy mystique permanently gripped the American imagination, and a 30-year-old drover released a colorful, atmospheric book that remains the best cowboy autobiography ever penned: *A Texas Cow Boy or, Fifteen Years on the Hurricane Deck of a Spanish Pony. Taken from Real Life By Chas. A. Siringo, An Old Stove Up "Cow Puncher," Who Has Spent Nearly Twenty Years on The Great Western Cattle Ranches.*

Charles Angelo Siringo was born on February 7, 1855, in Matagorda County, Texas, to an Italian father and Irish mother. In 1856, Charlie's father died, leaving his wife to care for their young daughter and infant son. Charlie learned to ride while still a boy, and when he was 12, he persuaded his mother to let him hire on with an area rancher "and learn to run cattle."

By the time Charlie was 16, he was employed on the Rancho Grande owned by legendary cattleman Shanghai Pierce. While still a teenager, Charlie registered his own brand, which he began to apply to mavericks on the ranges he worked. Like most cowboys, however, he was never able to build much of a herd.

Charles Siringo lived the life of the westerner to the hilt, then wrote about his exploits as a cowboy, Pinkerton agent, and lawman.

Charlie led the life of a typical open range cowboy, plying his colorful trade at roundups and on drives and then working at odd jobs between stints as a drover. He trailed cattle to Dodge City, was hired as a trail boss, and visited Charles Goodnight's famous JA Ranch in Palo Duro Canyon in the Texas Panhandle. He helped establish the LX Ranch, which was located near raucous Tascosa, the Cowboy Capital of the Panhandle.

During this period, Siringo got to know Billy the Kid, Tom O'Folliard, Henry Brown, and other fugitives from New Mexico's Lincoln County War. The Kid led a gang of rustlers who stole horses in New Mexico and then sold them in the Panhandle. He would then steal more horses in Texas to sell in New Mexico upon his return.

In 1882, Siringo drove an LX herd to Caldwell, Kansas, where the LX maintained a horse ranch. Caldwell was the terminus of the Chisholm Trail. "I immediately fell in love with the town," said Charlie about Caldwell, which was known as the Border Queen. He bought some lots and arranged to have a house built so that he could relocate his mother.

It was not only the town that the young drover became enchanted with. According to Charlie, "I fell head over heels in love with a pretty little 15-year-old, black-eyed miss, whom I accidentally met. It was a genuine case of love at first sight." Within a week,

Siringo was married, but three days later he led a large roundup crew back to Texas to drive a herd north to Caldwell. When he finally returned to his bride, he was ordered to take the crew to Texas once again for another drive to Caldwell. The potential for too many separations led Siringo to decide to stay in Caldwell with his family. He operated a tobacco and cigar store and then an ice cream and oyster parlor on the main street of the Border Queen.

When Siringo became a merchant in the fall of 1883, the city marshal of Caldwell was Henry Brown, a quiet but deadly gunfighter who was the first lawman to tame the rowdy Border Queen. Charlie had known Brown in the Texas Panhandle when Brown had been a fugitive from New Mexico with Billy the Kid. The Kid returned to New Mexico and was killed by Pat Garrett, but Brown pinned on a badge in Tascosa, then relocated to Caldwell. Like Siringo, Brown married a young girl from Caldwell. Siringo said nothing about the outlaw past of the two-gun marshal.

In April 1884, Marshal Brown led a gang in a bloody bank robbery at Medicine Lodge, and he and his confederates were chased down and killed by vigilantes. Siringo gave a lengthy interview to the Caldwell *Journal* about Brown's background, and soon afterward he contributed a "Sketch of Billy the Kid's Life" to the *Journal*. With his first published writing, he was encouraged to pen his reminiscences.

A Texas Cow Boy was released by a Chicago publisher in the fall of 1885 for one dollar per copy. It was the first authentic cowboy autobiography and only the second book of any significance about the cattle frontier. (The first, *Historic Sketches of the*

Cattle Trade of the West and Southwest, appeared in 1874 and was written by Joseph G. McCoy, a cattle buyer who developed Abilene, Kansas, and the Chisholm Trail). Although there was a flood of dime novels about the West, there was not another important book about the range country until 1902, when Owen Wister captivated the American public with *The Virginian*.

A Texas Cow Boy was reprinted in numerous editions, and Charlie moved with his

Siringo was one of the first to write authentically about the cowboy, whose everyday life on the range was not like that depicted in dime novels.

wife and daughter to Chicago. On May 4, 1886, shortly after the Siringos relocated, Chicago was wracked by the Haymarket Riot. In this violent confrontation, which took place in the city's Haymarket Square, policemen clashed with anarchists and laborers, resulting in the deaths of four workers and seven law officers.

The Siringos had taken up residence only a few blocks from the scene of the carnage, and Charlie, consumed by an impulse to track down the anarchists, applied for employment at the Chicago offices of Pinker-

THE PINKERTONS

Long before the Federal Bureau of Investigation and director J. Edgar Hoover hunted down such notorious gangsters as John Dillinger and Baby Face Nelson, such work was left to Pinkerton's National Detective Agency. The Pinkertons, as they came to be called, were founded before the Civil War by a young Scottish immigrant named Allan Pinkerton. Criminals referred to the agency as the Eye because of the company's wide-eyed logo and motto, "We never sleep." The symbol spawned the term private eye as a sobriquet for detectives.

Allan Pinkerton was the originator of the modern-day "rogue's gallery," in which critical information about major criminals is gathered, filed, and distributed. Personal data, physical traits, known acquaintances, and suspected hangouts for known law-breakers were gathered by Pinkerton agents and combined into the agency's rapidly growing information system. Supposedly, the Pinkertons never closed a suspect's file until he was declared dead.

Allan Pinkerton's company of detectives received a boost in recognition in 1861 when Allan uncovered a plot to assassinate President-elect Abraham Lincoln. After the incident, Pinkerton's agency became an intelligence organization for General George B. McClellan during the Civil War. Unfortunately for the Union, Pinkerton's numbers about Confederate troop strength were vastly overstated, and this misinformation contributed to the severe mismanagement of the Peninsula Campaign by McClellan. When McClellan was relieved of his command, Pinkerton's position went with him.

The Pinkerton Agency was more successful west of the Mississippi, where railroads and banks employed agents to pursue outlaws and gunfighters. In addition to their outlaw work, Pinkerton agents were involved in many labor disputes. Hired by mine and railroad owners, Pinkerton men would infiltrate the labor unions and then report the members' activities back to their employers. In many cases, only a thin line separated the violence committed by Pinkerton men and that perpetrated by the men they were watching.

Allan Pinkerton, who witnessed his detective empire grow so large that offices were opened in Denver, Seattle, and Kansas City, died in 1884, leaving the firm to his sons, who took over the Chicago and New York offices.

Allan Pinkerton sits atop his horse at Antietam, circa 1862. His work for the Union branded his agency a minion of business and the government.

ton's National Detective Agency. William Pinkerton interviewed Siringo in his Chicago office, and Charlie talked his way into a job. Although he received excellent training, Siringo quickly became disillusioned by brutal interrogation methods, perjured testimony, padded expense accounts, and other questionable methods. After a few months, the former cowboy was assigned to Pinkerton's newly opened Denver office, where he concentrated on rustling activities and outlaw gangs.

Pinkerton agents often were employed to head off labor movements through infiltration. Siringo detested such undercover work, but he was unable to avoid assignment to Idaho's troubled Coeur d'Alene mining district. There he experienced the violent riots of 1892. Charlie's testimony helped to convict 18 union leaders of murder and dynamiting mines.

Siringo spent four years around the turn of the century pursuing members of the notorious Wild Bunch. He journeyed 25,000 miles, mostly on horseback, through remote western regions. By the time he was taken off the case, Butch Cassidy and the Sundance Kid had fled to South America, and other Wild Bunch members had been killed or captured.

In 1907, Charlie left the Pinkerton Agency and moved to his Sunny Slope Ranch, a small spread on the outskirts of Santa Fe. He interspersed ranching activities with occasional detective work for the William J. Burns Agency. He also rode for two years for the New Mexico Mounted Police.

During this period, Charlie resumed writing, publishing, and peddling his books himself. *A Cowboy Detective, A True Story of Twenty Years with a World-Famous Detective Agency* first appeared in 1912. Three years later, Charlie released *Two Evil Isms: Pinker-*

tonism and Anarchism. By a Cowboy Detective Who Knows, as He Spent Twenty-Two Years in the Inner Circle of Pinkerton's National Detective Agency. Both books sold for 25 cents, and Charlie was harshly critical of the Pinkerton Agency. In 1919, Charlie published *A Lone Star Cowboy* and *A Song Companion of A Lone Star Cowboy.* The next year, he produced *History of "Billy the Kid."* In 1927, *Riata and Spurs* was published by Houghton Mifflin Company, but Pinkerton's launched legal action, and after the first printing, 148 pages of the book were suppressed.

By this time, Siringo had moved to California, living with his daughter in San Diego. His first wife had died in Denver in 1890, and by 1913, three subsequent marriages had ended in divorce. Siringo left San Diego to live in the Los Angeles area, where he became friends with William S. Hart, Will Rogers, and other celebrities.

Real-life cowboy and lawman Charles Siringo (right) meets movie cowboy William S. Hart (left) in Hollywood in 1926.

Siringo died at the age of 73 on October 18, 1928. He enjoyed decades of adventure in the West, encountering numerous frontier notables, and enjoying a variety of exploits. These activities, combined with a virtually unmatched autobiographical urge, allowed Charlie Siringo to become one of the most flavorful and important literary figures of the Old West.

He was born Bartholomiew Masterson in Canada in 1853. The American version of his name was Bartholomew, but later he changed his name to William Barclay Masterson. Still later, he became famous as Bat Masterson, a sobriquet that inspired as many yarns and tall tales as the events of his life. He may have acquired the nickname because it was short for Bartholomew, or maybe because he struck lawbreakers over the head with a cane, or perhaps because he was known to be a battler.

However it developed, few western names were better known in the late 19th century than Bat Masterson. The second of seven children of Thomas and Catherine Masterson, Bat lived with his family on a succession of farms in Canada and the northern United States. Finally, Thomas established a permanent home at a claim near Wichita, Kansas. Bat and his older brother, Ed, helped their father for a few months, then left home to seek adventure on the nearby frontier. Ed was 19 years old; Bat was a mere 17.

The Masterson brothers spent several months skinning hides for buffalo hunters. In the buffalo camps, Bat met Wyatt Earp, and he began to learn the art of gambling while drinking. In mid-1872, Bat and Ed undertook a grading contract for the Atchison, Topeka & Santa Fe Railroad. The job took them into a new town that was to be named Dodge City.

Their toil seemed to be for naught after contractor Raymond Ritter skipped town owing them $300. The Masterson brothers returned to hunting buffalo to restore their fortunes. When Ritter returned to Dodge on April, 15, 1873, he descended from the train to be met at gunpoint by Bat. The daring young man forced Ritter to hand over the $300, then treated a crowd of admiring onlookers to drinks. "He was a chunk of steel," observed noted scout and buffalo hunter Billy Dixon, "and anything that struck him in those days always drew fire."

By now a superb rifle shot, Bat resumed hunting buffalo, joining a party that ventured into the Texas Panhandle. On July 27, 1874, 20-year-old Bat was the youngest of 29 defenders at the famous Battle of Adobe Walls. There were two sod stores, a sod saloon, and a picket blacksmith shop at Adobe Walls to serve the buffalo hunters who swarmed through the Panhandle. The profusion of hunters and the resulting reduction of the buffalo herds inspired the Plains Indians to ally against the men who threatened to destroy their way of life. A combined force of several hundred Comanche, Kiowa, and Cheyenne warriors

In legend, Bat Masterson killed 27 men; in truth, he killed one.

planned to sweep through the Panhandle, beginning with a dawn attack on the congregation of white men (and one woman) at Adobe Walls.

When the big war party galloped toward the little cluster of buildings, the hunters scrambled for their Big Fifty Sharps buffalo guns. Forted up behind thick walls, the professional marksmen repulsed one charge after another. Masterson fought impressively.

The Battle of Adobe Walls opened the Red River War. When the army launched a major convergence on the Panhandle, Masterson signed on as a scout with the column of Colonel Nelson A. Miles. Later in the campaign, Bat worked as a teamster out of Camp Supply.

After the Native Americans were driven onto reservations, a new Panhandle community, Sweetwater (quickly renamed Mobeetie), was founded to service the hunters and soldiers stationed at nearby Fort Elliott. At the Lady Gay, a Sweetwater saloon and dance hall, Masterson notched his only fatality in a gunfight. Trouble erupted between Bat and Corporal Melvin A. King over a saloon girl named Molly Brennan. On the night of January 24, 1876, Corporal King apparently barged into the Lady Gay, found Bat and Molly together, and opened fire. As the story goes, Molly attempted to save Bat by throwing herself in front of him. Molly and Bat were hit, but as Masterson fell, he managed to shoot King, who had paused to cock his pistol. King died as a result of his wounds, and sadly, so did Molly. During his long recovery, Masterson used the cane that may have inspired his famous nickname.

Bat's brother, Ed Masterson, was gunned down in the line of duty.

Bat eventually returned to Dodge City, where he opened a saloon. On June 9, 1877, Masterson brawled with City Marshal Larry Deger. Deger had arrested a small man named Bobby Gill and was marching him to jail. Periodically, he kicked Gill in the backside to make him move faster. Masterson became angered at the display and grabbed the marshal around the neck, which helped Gill escape. With the help of a few bystanders, the 300-pound lawman pistol-whipped and arrested Masterson. Gill was rearrested the next day, and he was eventually fined $5.

Bat, who had made the mistake of resisting arrest, was fined $25. A short time later, Bat secured an appointment as undersheriff of Ford County—and subsequently relieved Marshal Deger of his concurrent commission as a deputy sheriff. In the fall, Masterson and Deger ran against each other for the office of county sheriff, with Bat edging his massive nemesis, 166–163.

Bat's jurisdiction as sheriff of Ford County ranged 100 miles from east to west and 75 miles from north to south. Just a couple of weeks after assuming office, Masterson led a posse in pursuit of a band of six train robbers. Outmaneuvering two other posses and the bandits themselves, he set a trap and captured two of them right away. Eventually, he found and captured three of the remaining four, which helped secure Masterson's reputation as an able lawman.

Ed Masterson had been appointed city marshal of Dodge in June 1877. Ed and Bat had differing approaches to maintaining law

Masterson's letter to the Dodge City *Times* appeared on November 15, 1879. This type of tough-sounding rhetoric maintained his reputation as an effective lawman.

and order. Bat had already developed a reputation as a gunfighter. Consequently, he rarely had to fire his guns during an encounter, because his opponents did not want to shoot it out with him. He constantly practiced his shooting skills, a habit that was made well known to the public. He filed the notch of the hammer off his gun so that the weapon would go off at the slightest touch.

Ed did not have the reputation that Bat did, and his easy-going manner and gentle ways contrasted Bat's tendency to be on the edge of trouble. Ed's policy was to keep his gun holstered as much as possible in order to talk out any difficulties with lawbreakers, a tactic that proved too tame for Dodge. As the raucous cow town grew, it attracted con men, rowdy soldiers, and petty thieves. Saloon brawls and midnight robberies increased, and Ed found his job more and more taxing. Bat tried to warn his older brother that he needed to instill fear amongst the rising tide of lawbreakers and desperados, but his warnings went unheeded. Ed was fatally wounded in a wild gunfight with two drunken cowboys outside a saloon on April 9, 1878. Dodge City mourned their marshal by closing down business the next day and

draping doorways with black crepe. His body lay in state in the parlor of the Dodge City Fire Company, because Ed had been a member. The firemen conducted the funeral, and 60 uniformed volunteers followed Bat to the military cemetery at Fort Dodge, where Ed was buried. Although griefstricken, Bat continued to lead posses and capture horse thieves, confidence men, jail escapees, and train robbers.

He garnered additional authority in January 1879 by accepting appointment as a deputy U.S. marshal. Two months later, Masterson temporarily left Dodge to hire his gun to the Atchison, Topeka & Santa Fe Railroad. He led a large posse of gunmen to back up the railroad in a dispute with the Denver & Rio Grande line over the right-of-way through Colorado's Raton Pass. This profitable diversion from his duties may have worked against him, because he was decisively defeated during his re-election bid for sheriff the following November.

After leaving office in January 1880, Masterson drifted into Colorado and then Nebraska. In Ogallala, Nebraska, he helped rescue gunman Billy Thompson, younger brother of gunfighter-lawman Ben Thompson. Local citizens were in a lynching mood over a gunfight involving Billy, who continually needed his brother's help in escaping trouble. Bat disliked Billy, who had been wounded in the altercation, but he loyally responded to the call for help from his friend Ben.

Early in 1881, Bat joined Wyatt Earp at the Oriental Saloon in Tombstone, Arizona Territory. While he was gambling in Arizona, his younger brother, Jim, became mired in dangerous difficulties in Dodge. In April, Jim exchanged gunfire with a business partner and an employee, A. J. Peacock and Al Updegraff. No one was hit, but Jim telegraphed Bat in Tombstone.

Bat's train arrived in Dodge at 11:50 A.M. on April 16, 1881. As he stepped off the train, Bat spotted Peacock and Updegraff walking together, and he aggressively made his way through a crowded street. "I have come over a thousand miles to settle this," shouted Masterson from a distance of twenty feet. "I know you are heeled—now fight!"

All three men drew guns. Bat dove behind the rail bed, while Peacock and Updegraff darted around the corner of the city jail. Bullets began to shatter windows and thud into the walls of surrounding buildings as two men from a nearby saloon (probably Jim Masterson and a friend) joined the gunplay. One slug kicked dirt into Bat's mouth before ricocheting and wounding a bystander. Updegraff was struck in the right lung, possibly by Bat or maybe by one of the men in the saloon.

When the antagonists paused to reload, the mayor and sheriff marched onto the scene brandishing shotguns. Updegraff was carried away to recover. Bat paid a small fine, then boarded the evening train out of town. At the age of 27, he had fought in his last shoot-out.

Masterson drifted around the West for several years, involving himself in minor altercations. In 1883, he returned to Dodge to answer a call for help from his friend Luke Short, but the widely publicized "Dodge City War," in which Short was pitted against reformers over his saloon and gambling operation, proved to be decidedly nonviolent. It seems Short had been arrested when shots were exchanged during a run-in with a local policeman. Forced to leave town, he headed

for Topeka, where he spoke to the press and spread the word that he was in trouble. The press speculated about what dire circumstances might occur if Short's friends, including Wyatt Earp, Bat Masterson, and Charlie Bassett, should appear on the streets of Dodge in defense of their associate. When Earp, Masterson, Bassett, W. F. Petilon, M. F. Mclain, and Neil Brown did arrive in Dodge, the town leaders quickly backed down, and Short returned to his business interests. In honor of the occasion, a photo was taken of Short and his friends titled "The Dodge City Peace Commission."

Later, Bat was present but uninvolved when Short killed Longhair Jim Courtwright in Fort Worth in 1887. In 1892, Masterson apparently served briefly as a peace officer in Creede, but he was never embroiled in bloodshed in the Colorado boomtown. In the course of drinking and gambling, Masterson sometimes became involved in altercations, but his early reputation tended to restrain adversaries from going for their guns.

During these years, Masterson became increasingly active as a sportsman, especially as an official and promoter of horse races and prizefights. Headquartering in Denver, he pursued those activities around the West. In 1896, he was part of the sporting crowd that accompanied heavyweight champion Peter Maher and challenger Bob Fitzsimmons as they tried to stage a championship bout. Frustrated repeatedly by reformers and do-gooders who attempted to ban boxing in many states, the crowd finally took a special train to Langtry, Texas, where Judge Roy Bean arranged to have the fight across the Rio Grande in Mexico.

A natty dresser, Masterson cut quite a figure with the ladies. On one occasion in 1886,

MASTERSON
ON HOLLIDAY

By the time Bat Masterson moved to New York City, he was making his career as a newspaper columnist. He became a sports writer for the New York *Morning Telegraph* just after the turn of the century. He also wrote about the gunfighters and Wild West characters he had known in the Old West in a series of articles for *Human Life* magazine in 1907. Bat wrote fondly of his old friend Wyatt Earp, but he clearly disliked Earp's friend, Doc Holliday.

"Holliday had a mean disposition and an ungovernable temper, and under the influence of liquor was a most dangerous man. . . . I have always believed that much of Holliday's trouble was caused by drink and for that reason held him to blame in many instances.

While I assisted him substantially on several occasions, it was not because I liked him any too well, but

In his later years, Masterson wrote about his Wild West acquaintances from days long past.

on account of my friendship with Wyatt Earp who did.

"Holliday had few real friends anywhere in the west [*sic*]. He was selfish and had a perverse nature—traits not calculated to make a man popular in the early days of the frontier.

"Physically, Doc Holliday was a weakling who could not have whipped a healthy 15-year-old boy in a go-as-you-please fist fight, and no one knew this better than himself, and the knowledge of this fact was perhaps why he was ready to resort to a weapon of some kind whenever he got himself into difficulty. He was hotheaded and impetuous and very much given to both drinking and quarreling and, among men who didn't fear him, was very much disliked. . . ."

Perhaps the most eloquent part of Masterson's reminiscences on Holliday involved Doc's devotion to Earp.

"His whole heart and soul were wrapped up in Wyatt Earp and he was always ready to stake his life in defense of any cause in which Wyatt was interested. . . . Damon did not more for Pythias than Holliday did for Wyatt Earp."

he drew his pistol and struck the husband of Nellie Spencer. Bat and Nellie ended up running off together, but the union did not last long. Soon thereafter, he began a permanent relationship with an actress named Emma Walters. The couple married in 1891, though they never had children.

Masterson had dabbled in newspaper writing since the 1880s. In the late 1890s, he became a sports editor for a Denver newspaper. Sadly, as time passed, Masterson turned to the bottle more and more. By the early 1900s, he was frequently drunk and disorderly and considered a troublesome frontier relic. He was asked to leave Denver.

A move to New York City in 1902 improved his lot considerably, because he became something of a celebrity in the big city. He cultivated friendships with heavyweight champions Jack Johnson, Jess Willard, and Jack Dempsey, as well as with writer Damon Runyan, newspaper columnist Louella Parsons, and owner of the New York Giants, Charles Stoneham. President Theodore Roosevelt hosted Masterson in the White House and offered him an appointment as U.S. marshal for Oklahoma. When Bat declined to return to western law enforcement, Roosevelt appointed him deputy U.S. marshal in New York at a handsome annual salary of $2,000.

When Masterson was named sports editor of the New York *Morning Telegraph*, he resigned his deputy's commission and happily immersed himself in sporting events and New York night life. On the morning of October 25, 1921, he arrived at his newspaper desk to catch up on his work. He wrote, "There are those who argue that everything breaks even in this old dump of a world of ours. I suppose these ginks who argue that way hold that because the rich man gets ice in the summer and the poor man gets it in the winter things are breaking even for both. Maybe so, but I'll swear that I can't see it that way. . . ." These became the last words that Masterson ever wrote. As he worked on his column, Bat Masterson slumped over his desk with pen in hand and died of a heart attack.

During the 1890s, Masterson worked as a sports editor in a rapidly expanding Denver. But, considered a drunken relic of the Old West, he was asked to leave around 1902.

JUDGE ISAAC
PARKER

1838–1896

"During the 20 years that I have engaged in administering the law here, the contest has been one between civilization and savagery, the savagery being represented by the intruding criminal class."

The criminal class intruded so rapidly into Indian Territory after the Civil War that lawlessness reigned unchallenged—until Isaac Parker was appointed federal judge with unlimited powers and no appeals, even to the Supreme Court. Parker tirelessly championed the cause of civilization against savagery, almost immediately becoming known as the "Hanging Judge." Undeterred by this unflattering appellation, Parker tried 13,490 cases in 21 years on the bench, securing 9,454 convictions and handing down 162 death sentences, of which 80 were carried out.

The Hanging Judge was born in Ohio on October 15, 1838. Reared on a farm, he was instilled with the stern moral principles of

Judge Isaac Charles Parker maintained a crushing schedule of cases throughout his career but still made time for civic activities.

the Methodist Church, and as an adult he readily battled evil in the cause of righteousness. As a young man he taught school, then studied for the bar, and in 1859 opened a law office in St. Joseph, Missouri. The next year, he was elected city attorney, and in 1861 he married Mary O'Toole, who would bear him two sons. After serving briefly as a Union corporal during the Civil War, Parker became prosecuting attorney for the Twelfth Judicial Circuit in 1864, then won election as judge of this court in 1868.

Two years later, he was elected to the first of two congressional terms as a Republican representative. In 1875, President Ulysses S. Grant appointed Parker chief justice of Utah Territory, but within two weeks, Parker decided he would be more useful as the ruling jurist of the lawless Indian Territory. Rustlers, murderers, thieves, and fugitives from other areas congregated in growing numbers in Indian Territory, rendering the region unsafe for honest settlers and travelers. Parker's judicial predecessor was corrupt, and it had become open season on law officers who dared penetrate the West's most lawless area.

At the age of 36, Parker was the youngest federal judge in the nation, but he arrived at judicial headquarters in Fort Smith, Arkansas, unintimidated. A tall, imposing, 200-pound man, he spent the rest of his life there ruling his court with a total commitment to crushing outlawry.

Because of the unprecedented degree of criminal activity in Indian Territory, Judge Parker was permitted to utilize the services of 200 deputy U.S. marshals, far more than in any other jurisdiction. So dangerous was Indian Territory that these officers often traveled in groups of four or five. Still, 65 of Parker's deputies were slain over the years. The deputies were unsalaried, collecting only mileage, fees, and rewards. And Parker would not pay arrest fees for dead fugitives unless there was a dead-or-alive reward. Despite the meager incentive, Parker's army of deputies fanned out into Indian Territory, hauling vast numbers of fugitives in prison wagons to Fort Smith.

The first session of Judge Parker's court lasted eight weeks, during which he tried 91 defendants. He sentenced eight murderers to hang simultaneously, although one, because of his youth, had his sentence commuted to life in prison, while another was killed trying to escape. On the morning of September 3, 1875, a crowd estimated at 5,000 jostled for a view of the massive gallows Parker had constructed. Big enough to accommodate a dozen felons, the gallows was 20 feet long and built of heavy timbers. In a ceremony that lasted over an hour, the sentences were read, hymns were sung, prayers were said, and farewell statements were made. Then, six black hoods were set in place, and six murderers plunged to their fate. A few months later, on April 21, 1876, five more killers were hung *en masse*.

Parker opened court at eight o'clock in the morning six days a week, and sessions often lasted into the night. Because of this staggering caseload, there were some years in which Parker's court was in recess no more than ten days. For 14 years, there was no appeal from his decisions, which dealt harshly with felons. Outside the region, however, there was criticism of the Hanging Judge, and in 1889 murderers he had sentenced to death were permitted to appeal to the U.S. Supreme Court. "I attribute the increase [in murder] to the reversals of the Supreme Court," complained an exasperated Parker in 1895. "These reversals have contributed to the number of murders in Indian Territory."

Parker dispensed law from this jail and courthouse at Fort Smith. Parker's jurisdiction included Indian Territory, where outlaws and killers escaped the restraints of white law.

As early as 1883, his jurisdiction began to be reduced in size, primarily to relieve his workload. Still, he maintained a crushing judicial schedule. Suffering from overwork and diabetes, Parker died at age 57 on November 17, 1896. The advance of civilization had made his swift, harsh style of justice obsolete, but the West had lost the most effective judge in frontier history.

NAT LOVE

1854–?

About one out of every three cowboys was of African-American or Mexican descent, a fact seldom reflected in western novels, films, or television series. Nat Love was born a slave in Tennessee in 1854, but after the Civil War, his imagination was fired by the colorfully dressed, free-spirited cowboys of the West.

In 1869, 15-year-old Nat left the South to become a cowboy, making his way on foot to Dodge City, where he was attracted to a Texas outfit with several black cowboys. Offered a job if he could ride a rank beast named Good Eye, Love, who had broken colts for a neighbor at ten cents apiece, was able to stay aboard. He began his career as a cowboy. Booted and spurred, sporting a bright bandanna and a broad-brimmed white hat, he worked as a cowhand, driving Texas longhorns to Kansas for several years.

After the Civil War, more than 8,000 black cowboys, including Nat Love, made their way west and worked the cattle drives. In 1876, Nat Love helped trail a herd from Arizona to the

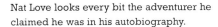
Nat Love looks every bit the adventurer he claimed he was in his autobiography.

In 1876, Nat Love arrived in the mining town of Deadwood, South Dakota, where he showed off his cowboy skills during their centennial celebrations.

Dakota gold-mining boomtown, Deadwood, where he entered the centennial Independence Day celebrations. Love related that he won a roping competition and a shooting contest. "Right there," he reminisced, "the assembled crowd named me 'Deadwood Dick' and proclaimed me champion of the Western cattle country."

Love thereby laid claim to having been the inspiration for the famous dime novel character, Deadwood Dick. The immensely popular dime novel was the creation of Erastus Beadle, a Buffalo, New York, publisher who envisioned that the development of the steam-powered, high-speed printing press made

AFRICAN-AMERICAN
COWBOYS

Although African-American cowboys were already at work west of the Mississippi River before the Civil War, thousands of emancipated slaves from the South turned their eyes westward when the great conflict ended in 1865. The age of the great cattle drives was about to begin, and hard-working men—regardless of color—could earn a fair if rough living wrangling the millions of Texas longhorns. Despite the ever-present threat of frontier violence, blacks were safer in the West than in the South, which averaged over 150 lynchings per year into the 1890s.

Although segregated bunkhouses were the norm on most ranches, African-American men found a readier acceptance on the frontier and far more integrated conditions in western towns than in southern communities. Cowboys judged each other by how well they could ride, shoot, tend cattle, and stand on their own. Family, breeding, nationality, and race mattered less amid the demands and dangers of a cattle drive. Although most African Americans worked as regular cowboys—watching after the herd, busting broncos, and the like—they also took on positions of authority, such as ranch foreman, trail boss, or ram-

A talented bronco-buster, Isom Dart was one of the many black cowboys.

rod. For the time, such a thing was remarkable; even in the most liberal parts of the North, it was all but impossible for a black man to find work supervising whites.

One of the most famous of all black cowboys was Bill Pickett. Born in Texas in 1860, Pickett is said to have been hired at age 13 at the famous 101 Ranch in Oklahoma. When he was about 20 years old, he created the sport of bulldogging, in which a rider leaps from his horse and wrestles a full-grown steer to the ground. As he perfected his bulldogging technique over the years, Pickett found that he could get a struggling steer to submit more quickly if he bit its upper lip. In the early 1900s, when the 101 Wild West Show was organized, Pickett accompanied such well-known cowboy stars as Will Rogers and Tom Mix on the wide-ranging show circuit. He performed in Madison Square Garden and in Europe before returning to Oklahoma and the 101 Ranch. In 1971, Pickett became the first African American ever inducted into the National Cowboy Hall of Fame in Oklahoma City.

NAT LOVE,
COWBOY

"In the spring of 1876 orders were received at the home ranch for 3,000 head of three-year-old steers to be delivered near Deadwood, South Dakota. This being one of the largest orders we had ever received at one time, every man around the ranch was placed on his mettle to execute the order in record time. . . .

"Our route lay through New Mexico, Colorado and Wyoming, and as we had heard rumors that the Indians were on the war path and were kicking up something of a rumpus in Wyoming, Indian Territory and Kansas, we expected trouble before we again had the pleasure of sitting around our fire at the home ranch. Quite a large party was selected for this trip owing to the size of the herd and the possibility of trouble on the trail from the Indians. We, as usual, were all well armed and had as mounts the best horses our ranch produced, and in taking the trail we were perfectly confident that we could take care of our herd and ourselves through anything we were liable to meet. We had not been on the trail long before we met other outfits, who told us that General Custer was out after the Indians and that a big fight was expected when the Seventh U.S. Cavalry, General Custer's command, met the . . . Indians . . . who had for a long time been terrorizing the settlers of that section and defying the Government. . . .

"We arrived in Deadwood in good condition without having had any trouble with the Indians on the way up. We turned our cattle over to their new owners at once, then proceeded to take in the town."

—from *The Life and Adventures of Nat Love*, 1907

it possible to reach mass audiences with inexpensive "steam literature."

Beadle's writers had little or no first-hand acquaintance with the West, but they still produced volumes on the subject. Formula writers such as Prentiss Ingraham, who churned out over 600 novels, described the fantastic exploits of imaginary heroes, as well as using the names of such real westerners as Wild Bill Hickok, George Armstrong Custer, Kit Carson, and Buffalo Bill Cody. In 1887, another of Beadle's prolific novelists, Edward L. Wheeler, introduced the genre's first outlaw hero: *Deadwood Dick, The Prince of the Road; or, The Black Rider of the Black Hills.*

This first book established the premise that Deadwood Dick had been victimized by powerful establishment figures, which vengefully pushed him into seeking justice. Wearing a black hat, a "jetty black" buckskin jacket, and a black mask "through the eyeholes of which there gleamed a pair of orbs of piercing intensity," Deadwood Dick took on a variety of powerful villains. A working-class readership that was oppressed by political bosses and robber-baron industrialists responded enthusiastically. Indeed, the popularity of Deadwood Dick spawned imitations, including characters based on Frank and Jesse James, who acquired a Robin Hood image as good badmen. The character of Deadwood Dick was instrumental in establishing the heroic outlaw as a staple of countless movies, novels, and television series.

There were 33 Deadwood Dick dime novels, as well as 97 Deadwood Dick, Jr., sagas. Titles ranged from *Deadwood Dick's Protegee; or, Baby Bess, the Girl Gold Miner* to

Deadwood Dick, Jr., in Chicago; or, The Anarchist's Daughter. Since there were so many dime novels with heroes who sported the names of actual frontiersmen, some Deadwood Dick fans assumed that he was a real westerner.

By this time in the real West, the trail drives were ending, the nature of ranching was changing dramatically, and large numbers of black cowboys were trying to find more stable work. During the era of open range ranching, most cowboys were employed only seasonally, during roundups and trail drives. By the 1880s, the cowboys of Nat Love's generation no longer were footloose teenagers in search of adventure and excitement; many men decided it was time to settle down and raise a family.

Nat Love gave up cowboying in 1890 and became a Pullman porter, the most reliable and renumerative job generally available to African Americans of that period. In 1907, he published the only book-length autobiographical account of a black cowboy: *The Life and Adventures of Nat Love, Better Known in the Cattle Country as 'Deadwood Dick.'* In addition to his claims about being the prototype for the famous fictional shootist, Love stated that he was a friend of Bat Masterson and that he had met Billy the Kid in 1877 and had various experiences with the

The first Deadwood Dick story described the title chracter as "an interesting specimen of young, healthy manhood."

Kid and Pat Garrett during the Lincoln County War. Love fearlessly endured two decades of harrowing escapades: "I gloried in the danger." He related a series of sensational adventures, from skirmishes with Native Americans (one nation supposedly adopted Love after capturing him), to cattle stampedes, to wild animal attacks, to gun battles. "I carry the marks of 14 bullet wounds on different parts of my body, most any of which would be sufficient to kill an ordinary man," he boasted, "but I am not even crippled." His book reads somewhat like a Deadwood Dick novel, and in *Sixguns and Saddle Leather,* the peerless western bibliophile Ramon Adams details "the author's many preposterous statements" and concludes that Love "either had a bad memory or a good imagination."

Perhaps Nat Love was not the inspiration behind the fictional Deadwood Dick. He spent most of his life as a cowboy rather than a daring shootist, but he was an adventurous man who went west to become a cowboy during the heyday of that captivating profession. And he was an African American who spearheaded the movement of his race into the last West, embellishing the deeds of his eventful life with the good-natured exaggeration that characterized entertaining frontier storytelling of every era.

1845–?

The nickname Mysterious Dave accurately describes the extent of knowledge about Mather's background and final years. Rumored to have been a descendant of the famed Puritan preacher Cotton Mather, Dave H. Mather was born in Connecticut in 1845. By the early 1870s, Mysterious Dave had begun a violent life on both sides of the law. He was involved with rustlers in Sharp County, Arkansas, in 1873, but a year later, he drifted west to hunt buffalo. After suffering a knife slash in the stomach during a fight in Dodge City, Mather left for New Mexico, where he consorted with horse thieves and stagecoach robbers. Mysterious Dave reputedly killed a man following a quarrel in Mobeetie, near Fort Elliott in the Texas Panhandle. In 1879, Mather and several other shady characters were arrested with the notorious outlaw leader Dutch Henry Born. Although Mather was released, he was arrested again a few months later for complicity in a train robbery near Las Vegas.

The band on Dave Mather's hat reads "Assistant Marshal," which dates this photo to 1883.

After winning acquittal, he secured an appointment as a constable in the very same town.

During a saloon fight on January 22, 1880, Las Vegas Marshal Joe Carson was slain, but Mather gunned down Tom Henry, James West, and William Dandall, wounding the latter two fatally. Three nights later, Constable Mather hurried to the scene of another drunken disturbance, where he was confronted by Joseph Castello. Castello leveled a revolver at Mather and threatened to shoot him if he took another step. Mather whipped out his own six-gun and shot Castello in the left side. The slug tore through Castello's lung and stomach, then ripped into his liver. Castello died at six o'clock the following morning.

After being accused of "promiscuous shooting," Dave resigned to travel with three prospectors to the gold fields of Gunnison, Colorado. By November, he was back in Las Vegas, where he helped some friends break out of the city jail.

Mather moved to Dodge City in 1883 and was appointed deputy marshal and deputy sheriff of Ford County. Complaints accused Deputy Mather of being a bully and being too cooperative with criminals, and he was defeated when he ran for city constable in February 1884.

A few months later, an old feud with Deputy Marshal Tom Nixon erupted into bloodshed. A former buffalo hunter, Nixon replaced Mather as assistant city marshal of Dodge. On the evening of July 18, Nixon and Mather quarreled outside the Opera House, where Mysterious Dave ran a saloon. Mather stood at the top of the stairs while his antagonist stood on the street. Suddenly Nixon pulled a revolver and fired a shot, which plowed into the woodwork and sprayed Mather with splinters. Sheriff Pat Sughrue appeared promptly and disarmed Nixon, who claimed that Mather had waved a weapon at him. Mysterious Dave swore that he was unarmed, and Nixon was forced to produce $800 bail.

Three nights later, Nixon was standing on the Opera House corner amidst numerous passersby. Mather came to the foot of the building's stairs and drew a Colt .45 revolver.

"Tom," whispered Dave, "Oh, Tom." His gun still holstered, Nixon turned to face Mather. Without further warning, Mysterious Dave fired.

"Oh," gasped Nixon, "I am killed."

Nixon died on the spot, and Mysterious Dave surrendered his gun to Sheriff Sughrue. Surprisingly, Mather was eventually acquitted.

On May 10, 1885, Mather became embroiled in another fatal shoot-out, this time in the Junction Saloon, where his brother Josiah was tending bar. As Sheriff Pat Sughrue looked on, a quarrel erupted over a card game. David Barnes produced a gun and fired a shot that creased Mather's skull. From behind the bar, Josiah Mather opened up with a six-gun, killing Barnes and wounding two bystanders. Sughrue arrested the Mathers. They posted a $3,000 bond and promptly jumped bail.

Mather later wore the city marshal's badge in New Kiowa, Kansas, and in 1887, he rode into Long Pine, Nebraska, where he had occasionally worked at the depot hotel. A year later, Dave permanently—and mysteriously—faded into anonymity.

Top: Dodge City looks deceptively peaceful in this photograph taken about the time Mather served as deputy marshal. **Bottom:** Dodge's notorious Long Branch Saloon was the scene of much violence.

WILD BILL
HICKOK

1837–1876

Frontier adventurer Wild Bill Hickok became the West's most famous gunfighter. A tall man with an athletic physique, he was a flamboyant dresser who affected shoulder-length hair and sweeping mustaches. "He always had a mistress," reminisced old friend Charlie Gross. Hickok was also acquainted with almost every noted westerner of his era. He pinned on a badge in several reckless frontier towns; he served as a daring scout during the Indian campaigns and the Civil War; at various times, he earned his living as a gambler, teamster, stagecoach driver, and Wild West show performer. And Wild Bill was the Prince of Pistoleers.

A fine shot with either hand, Hickok the dandy carried two revolvers tucked into a colorful sash with butts forward. In addition to Civil War combat, he engaged in at least eight

Wild Bill Hickok lives up to his name as he dons this dandified suit while working as a scout in Rolla, Missouri, circa 1864.

shoot-outs and killed seven or more adversaries during his short life.

"As to killing," he once reflected, "I never think much about it. I don't believe in ghosts, and I don't keep the lights burning all night to keep them away. That's because I'm not a murderer. It is the other man or me in a fight, and I don't stop to think—is it a sin to do this thing? And after it is over, what's the use of disturbing the mind."

This formidable character was born on May 27, 1837, in Homer (later Troy Grove), Illinois. James Butler Hickok was the fourth of six children of a Vermont couple who moved to Illinois the year before he was born. His father established a way station for the Underground Railroad, and young Jim often helped whisk away fugitive slaves.

By the time he was a teenager, Jim had become an excellent marksman. An older brother, Oliver, left home for the California gold fields, fueling the wanderlust that would come to characterize Hickok. His restlessness surfaced in 1852 after his father died. Upon leaving home, Jim adopted his father's name, Bill.

By 1855, 18-year-old Hickok had drifted into Kansas. "Bleeding Kansas" was torn by strife over slavery, and Hickok spent a year in the Free-State Militia of Jim Lane. A couple of years later, he began working his homestead claim. He often hired out as a laborer in Monticello Township, where he was elected constable in March 1858. This first brief tenure as a peace officer was perhaps too peaceful, and by 1859, Hickok was working for Russell, Majors and Waddell as a teamster on the Santa Fe Trail. He began acquaintanceships with other frontier notables: While in Santa Fe, he met Kit Carson, and he encountered 12-year-old Bill Cody at Leavenworth.

At Raton Pass, Hickok was mauled by a bear, although he managed to kill the beast with pistols and a knife. Russell, Majors and Waddell sent him to Kansas City for medical treatment, then assigned him to light duties at their Rock Creek Station in Nebraska, a Pony Express post along the Oregon Trail. Hickok worked as a stock tender under station manager Horace Wellman. Wellman's common-law wife was present, along with stable hand Doc Brink.

Across the creek, Dave McCanles lived with his family, and in a bold move, he installed his mistress, Sarah Shull, in a house nearby. McCanles began insulting Hickok by calling him Duck Bill, a slur upon his facial features, and hermaphrodite, a slur upon certain other features. Hickok retaliated by secretly seeing Miss Shull. McCanles also caused trouble with other employees, as well as with the company, and the festering situation came to a head on the afternoon of July 12, 1861.

McCanles told Sarah Shull that he was going to the station to take care of the people there. He appeared at the station backed up by his cousin, James Gordon; his 12-year-old son, Monroe; and an employee, James Woods. As Gordon and Woods headed toward the barn, McCanles exchanged angry words with the Wellmans. Spotting Hickok standing behind a curtain partition, McCanles threatened to drag Duck Bill outside.

"There will be one less son-of-a-bitch when you try that," challenged Hickok ominously. The 24-year-old frontiersman had never been involved in a shoot-out, but he boldly readied his weapon.

When McCanles stepped toward the curtain, Hickok pumped a slug into his chest. Staggering outside, McCanles died in the arms of his son as Gordon and Woods ran toward the sound of the gunshot. When Woods approached the kitchen door, Hickok shot him twice, then turned to wing Gordon, who had suddenly appeared at the front door. Woods and Gordon tried to flee, but Wellman and Brink, armed respectively with a hoe and a shotgun, gave chase. Brink killed Gordon with a blast from his shotgun, while Wellman easily caught Woods and hacked the life out of him.

Hickok had shot three men, at least one fatally. Tales about the gory fight spread rapidly, embellished with typical frontier exaggeration. In February 1867, the popular *Harper's New Monthly Magazine* published an article by Colonel George Ward Nichols entitled "Wild Bill." Wild indeed was

Nichols's account of the fight at Rock Creek Station, where Hickok, armed with a revolver, rifle, and bowie knife in the story, was attacked by Dave "M'Kandlas" and nine members of his "party of ruffians." Hickok supposedly told Nichols, "I was wild and I struck savage blows, following the devils from one side to the other of the room and into the corners striking and slashing until I knew that every one was dead."

J. W. Buel, who had been personally acquainted with Hickok while reporting for the Kansas City *Journal*, also wrote that Wild Bill killed ten outlaws, but in return he suffered four bullet wounds, a skull fracture, numerous knife gashes, and a slash to the head that left his scalp hanging across his eyes. In *Wild Bill, The Pistol Deadshot*, dime novelist Colonel Prentiss Ingraham stated that Hickok was shot 11 times while wiping out the McCanles gang.

Hickok lived for a decade and a half after first achieving notoriety, and during that time, he added immensely to the legend of Wild Bill. By the time of the Rock Creek fight, the Civil War had begun, and Hickok headed east to associate himself with the Federal army for the duration of the conflict. He experienced combat at Wilson's Creek, Missouri, and at Pea Ridge, Arkansas, and he served as a scout and spy under General Samuel P. Curtis. During the war he received his famous

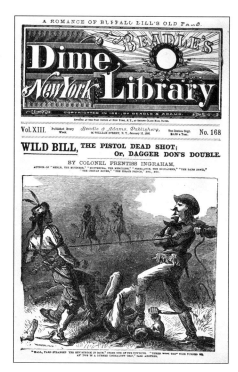

Colonel Prentiss Ingraham churned out many dime novels about Wild Bill, including this one in 1882.

nickname, and reputedly Wild Bill was involved in one dangerous scrape after another.

After the war, Hickok became a gambler in Springfield, Missouri, where he clashed with Dave Tutt over the affections of a girl named Susanna Moore. Hickok and Tutt, a former Union soldier, quarreled angrily over a card game at the Lyon House, then challenged each other to a duel the next day.

The dramatic showdown on a dusty main street that is a staple of western movies and novels almost never occurred in the real West. However, at six o'clock in the evening, as an excited crowd of onlookers jostled for a view, Hickok and Tutt confronted each other in the town square. At a distance of 75 yards, Hickok shouted "Don't come any closer, Dave!"

But Tutt defiantly drew a revolver and squeezed off a shot that went wild. Hickok steadied his own revolver in his left hand, then fired a ball squarely into Tutt's chest. Tutt pitched onto his face, dead in an instant. Wild Bill surrendered to the authorities, but he was tried and acquitted.

Following this cool display of courage under fire, Hickok ran unsuccessfully for the office of chief of police in Springfield, Missouri. On January 1, 1867, he began a six-month enlistment at $100 monthly to scout for Custer's 7th Cavalry. Though later in the

THE PONY EXPRESS

Many an adventurous boy longingly cast his eyes on an unusual advertisement that ran in the St. Joseph, Missouri, newspaper during the early days of 1860. Seeking young men with unique qualifications, the ad heralded the beginning of the short-lived Pony Express.

The successful firm of Russell, Majors and Waddell, a freighting company that operated across the Great Plains and the Rocky Mountains from Missouri to California, organized the Pony Express at the urging of Senator William M. Gwin of California. The primary goal was to speed up mail delivery between the East and California. The company's competition, the Overland Mail Company, advertised about a 20-day delivery, but when the Pony Express got underway, the Express's backers promised that mail from St. Joseph would be delivered

WANTED
YOUNG, SKINNY
Wiry fellows not over 18.

Must be expert riders, willing to risk death daily. Orphans preferred.

Wages $25.00 per week

Just 18 months after this ad ran, the Pony Express was made obsolete by the telegraph.

in Sacramento in ten days for the unheard of price of five dollars an ounce.

The Pony Express was inaugurated at 7:15 P.M. on April 3, 1860, when a young rider named Johnny Frey jumped on his horse at St. Joseph and set out for Sacramento, nearly 2,000 miles away. At about the same time, another rider started east from Sacra-

mento. Both men made their journeys within the allotted time.

After only 18 months in operation, the Pony Express went out of business, primarily because of the recent completion of the transcontinental telegraph. During the Express's brief life, 80 riders made 616 runs and covered more than 600,000 miles, delivering almost 35,000 pieces of mail. Unfortunately, the company

grossed less than $100,000—not enough to pay for the horses or the construction and maintenance of the 190 way stations along the route.

The Pony Express set the stage for a life of adventure for several frontier legends. Wild Bill Hickok worked for the system at a way station in Nebraska, while rider Buffalo Bill Cody once rode 300 miles nonstop when he discovered his relief man had been killed.

year Hickok was defeated in the sheriff's race in Ellsworth County, Kansas, he did obtain a commission as a deputy U.S. marshal, chasing army deserters and thieves of government livestock. On March 30, 1868, Wild Bill arrested 11 deserters who were operating as horse rustlers, and he engaged Buffalo Bill Cody to help him bring in the gang.

Hickok continued his haphazard career in law enforcement, despite his proclivity for hard drinking and rough living. In 1869, he was elected interim sheriff of Ellis County, Kansas. The county seat was Hays City, which, because of raucous buffalo hunters and reveling members of the 7th Cavalry stationed at Fort Hays, was as wild a town as any in the West.

From left: Hickok, Texas Jack Omohundro, and Buffalo Bill Cody all worked as scouts on the Great Plains.

On August 24, 1869, shortly after taking office as county sheriff, Hickok encountered an intoxicated ruffian named Bill Mulvey. Mulvey was accompanied by several equally drunken friends, and the gang was shooting up the town. Mulvey reacted belligerently when Wild Bill tried to arrest him. Sheriff Hickok shot Mulvey, who collapsed and died the next morning. About an hour past midnight on September 27, Sheriff Hickok and Deputy Peter Lanihan were called to John Bitter's Beer Saloon, where a local troublemaker named Samuel Strawhun and several drunken cronies were taking the place apart. When Strawhun turned on Hickok, the sheriff shot him in the head, killing him instantly and stopping the riot.

Instead of favorably impressing the electorate, Hickok's two killings in five weeks alarmed enough voters to give the November election to Deputy Lanihan, 144–89. On July 17, 1870, an inebriated ex-Sheriff Hickok became involved in a brawl at Drum's Saloon with five drunken troopers from the 7th Cavalry. The soldiers threw Hickok to the floor, and one trooper tried to shoot him, but the cap misfired. Wild Bill desperately pulled out his own guns and opened fire, wounding Private Jerry Lonergan in the knee and wrist and hitting Private John Kile in the torso. The other soldiers backed away, giving Hickok the opportunity to flee the town. The wounded soldiers were taken to the Fort Hays hospital, where Private Kile died the next day.

With commendable foresight but a lack of showbiz acumen, Hickok staged a Wild West show at Niagara Falls entitled The Daring Buffalo Chase of the Plains. When the show flopped financially, Wild Bill returned to the West and his career as a lawman. In April 1871, he was hired to be city marshal of Abilene at $150 per month plus a percentage of fines.

Abilene was just as raucous and raw as other cow towns of the period. Texas gamblers Phil Coe and Ben Thompson opened the Bull's Head Saloon and decorated it with a clearly depicted symbol of masculinity, which offended Abilene's respectable citizens. On instructions from the city council, Marshal Hickok ordered the alteration of the sign. Coe resented this interference, and trouble brewed between the two men.

On the night of October 5, 1871, Coe led about 50 Texas cowboys on a drunken spree through Abilene. Hickok was one of several citizens compelled to buy drinks, but the marshal warned the rowdies to control themselves, and he alerted Deputy Mike Williams. When a shot rang out at nine o'clock, Hickok ordered Williams to stay put and then hurried to investigate.

Hickok elbowed his way through the crowd and confronted Coe, who, along with several other Texans, brandished a revolver. When Hickok went for his guns, Coe, standing just eight feet away, snapped off a shot that cut through Wild Bill's coattails. Hickok's first slug tore through Coe's stomach and out his back. As Coe collapsed, he fired another wild round. Suddenly Mike Williams broke through the cowboys, intending to help Hickok. Glimpsing the movement amid a hostile crowd, Hickok whirled and fired, killing Williams with a bullet in the head.

An agonized Hickok scattered the crowd and shut down the town. One or two bystanders were treated for flesh wounds, while Phil Coe was carried away to die a lingering death three days later. Hickok paid Mike Williams's funeral expenses. After accidentally killing his deputy, Wild Bill Hickok was never seen firing a shot at another man.

During the next couple of years, Hickok traveled through the East with Buffalo Bill's troupe, somewhat ineptly performing in a production billed as *The Scouts of the Plains*. In 1872, he took time to join a royal Russian buffalo hunt in Kansas, and in 1874 he went back to the West, drifting from place to place as a gambler. His eyesight began to fail, perhaps as a result of gonorrhea, and on several occasions he was arrested for vagrancy.

By this time, he had renewed an old acquaintance with Agnes Lake, now a 50-year-old circus proprietor. The couple married on March 5, 1876, in Cheyenne, Wyoming. Shortly thereafter, Wild Bill left Mrs. Hickok for the Black Hills mining boomtown of Deadwood, where he was a regular at the gambling tables of the No. 10 Saloon.

On August 2, 1876, a young man named Jack McCall walked into the No. 10 Saloon and shot Hickok in the back of the head as he played cards at a table. As Hickok fell dead, McCall triggered the gun at the crowd, but every other cartridge was defective. McCall was quickly apprehended, and he was later tried and hung. Murdered at the age of 39, Wild Bill clutched a pair of black aces and a pair of eights, a poker combination immortalized as the Dead Man's Hand.

Hickok's gravesite in Deadwood, South Dakota, has long been a tourist attraction. Its appearance has been "improved" many times.

TEXAS
RANGERS

Although the Texas Rangers are known as a law enforcement agency, the group was actually formed to protect the frontiers of Texas from marauding Indians. Even before Texas declared its independence from Mexico on March 2, 1836, there were Texas Rangers.

Though Stephen Austin had formed Indian-fighting "ranging companies" about ten years prior, the Texas Rangers were offi-

Top: Company D poses during the early 1890s after capturing a bandit (seated far left). **Bottom:** Company D camps at Fort Inge around 1884. Several of these men were subsequently killed in action.

cially formed on November 24, 1835. Legislation called for three companies of 56 men each to be commanded by a captain, a first, and a second lieutenant. Privates received $1.25 per day for "pay, rations, clothing, and horse service." All Rangers were to provide them-

selves with 100 pounds of powder and ball, as well as a good horse, saddle, bridle, and blanket. Officers received pay comparable to officers in the United States Dragoons.

The Texas Rangers saw considerable service guarding the borders from Indians and Mexican

raiders from the days of the Republic to the beginning of the Mexican War. It was in the latter conflict that the organization first made a national name for itself. Several regiments of Rangers were activated into the U.S. Army and participated in most of the important battles of the war, ending with the occupation of Mexico City in September 1847. During the 22-month Mexican War, Rangers Samuel Walker, Rip Ford, John Coffee Hays, and Ben McCulloch gained fame as they claimed victory after victory.

Following the Mexican War, the Texas Rangers reverted to patrolling the borders and skirmishing with Indians and Mexicans. Although the organization took no official part in the Civil War, several of its veterans served the Confederacy in a regiment of volunteer cavalry called Terry's Texas Rangers. It was to this command that the famous rebel yell is accredited.

After the War and the advent of much lawlessness on the frontier, the Texas Rangers became an efficient and quick-acting law enforcement agency. Among the infamous outlaws that the force put out of business were Sam Bass, John Wesley Hardin, and King Fisher. For much of the Texas region's early history, the Rangers acted as the only organized regular force of military or legal authority, and at any given time there were usually less than 500 of them. While their numbers were always small, their deeds loomed huge, and they played a major role in shaping the destiny of Texas.

Left: As a Ranger, Ira Aten rounded up rustlers, caught smugglers, helped control range wars, and quieted political feuds. After a varied career, he died in 1953. **Bottom:** Captain D. W. Roberts's Rangers are shown taking mess in camp near Fort McKavett, Texas.

WOMEN
IN THE
WEST

In a faded photograph from a hundred years ago, a woman stands in front of a modest sod house with her children grouped around her. She wears the serious expression of the homesteader who not only survived the trek to the West with her family but also staked her claim on the sun-scorched Plains. In her homespun dress and sunbonnet, she is plain looking, yet her image portrays the strength and fortitude necessary to forge such a life.

Hundreds of photographs of pioneering women in front of their soddies have been left behind. These photos chronicle the contributions of women to this phase of western settlement and offer a testimony to the spirit of the pioneer. As much as these images honor the homesteading women, they convey only one of the many ways women participated in the settling of the West.

Women were drawn to the West for many reasons, and their contributions were as varied as those of men. While it is true that thousands of women accompanied their husbands, fathers, and brothers to settle

Fueled by an interest in Native American culture, Alice Fletcher expanded her horizons by taking a job directing the allotment of lands for Plains Indians.

on homesteads or small ranches, others came to take advantage of opportunities not available to them in the East or to build a new and better life. The more adventurous came "to see the elephant," which in the colorful vernacular of the Old West meant to visit the Mother Lode in search of personal fortune. By the end of the century, the phrase became more general, and it meant to experience any exciting aspect of life in the Old West. In this regard, many women who had left behind the comfort and familiarity of life in the East to make their mark in the West undoubtedly did see the elephant.

A pioneer woman sits with her family in front of their sod house on the Nebraska plains. On the prairie, a homesteading wife had to learn to make do: The pile of elk horns near her chair was probably used to dry clothes.

Despite the promise that the West offered and the desire by many women to claim that promise, the story of women in the West is not only one of adventure but also one of struggle. The majority of women who crossed the Mississippi made the journey alongside their husbands or families for the purposes of homesteading. Those looking for a new beginning in Oregon or California gathered at prearranged points along the Missouri River in the late spring of each year and then trekked westward in caravans of wagons. Most of the women walked alongside the wagons on the primitive trails, moving about 15 to 20 miles on a good day.

Some had been inspired by the journey of Narcissa Whitman and Eliza Spalding, two missionaries who were the first Anglo-American women to cross the Rocky Mountains. Longing to do missionary work among the Native Americans who lived in the Pacific Northwest, Narcissa Prentiss married Marcus Whitman and set out for the Oregon Territory in 1836. Their goal was to establish a mission post at Fort Walla Walla in present-day Washington. Reverend Henry and Eliza Spalding accompanied them for most of the journey, but the couples separated after they reached Oregon. Their successful trip spurred their missionary agency, the American Board of Commissioners for Foreign Missions, to dispatch a second party over the Oregon Trail and across the Rockies.

News of the missionaries' journeys may have encouraged other women to settle in the West, but few realized the hardships of the 2,000-mile, six-month trip. On the trail, women fulfilled a role similar to what they had been used to: They cooked, sewed, cleaned, doctored, raised children, and kept the family intact, often working longer hours than the men. On the trail, these familiar duties took on greater significance: They were essential to preserving the social order under the most primitive of conditions.

During harvest time, women often operated the food and water wagons for the hands in the fields.

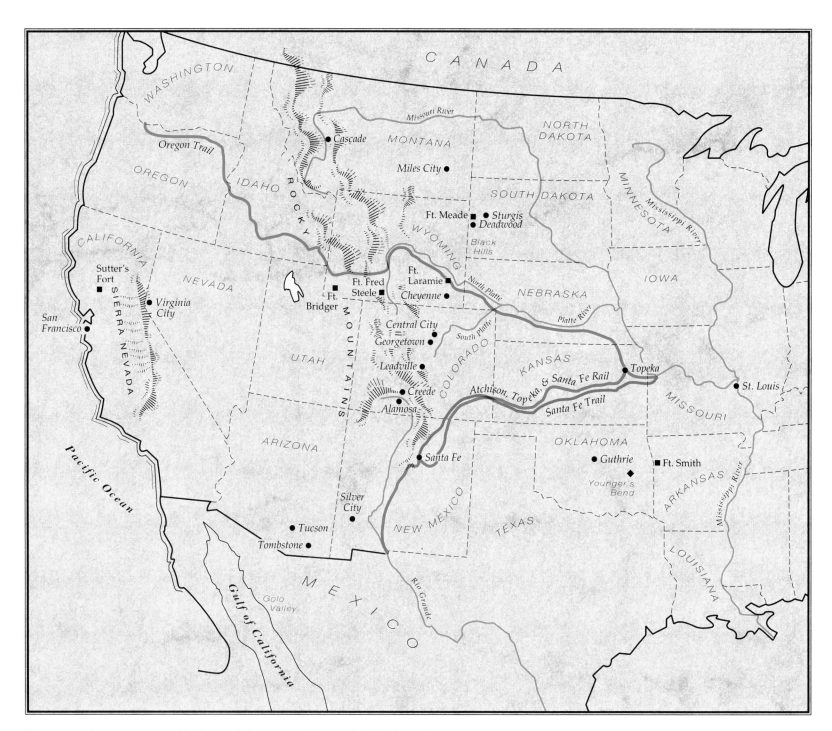

Whether running a restaurant in Tombstone, Arizona, or working as a bullwhacker in Deadwood, South Dakota, many women found opportunity in the West.

The trail proved to be a dangerous place for families, especially for children. Diseases such as the dreaded cholera wiped out entire families, while accidents such as drowning or snakebite claimed many a young victim. One in five women was pregnant on the trail, though having a baby was seldom cause enough to slow down the progress of the wagon train. Many newborn babies died on the road. Graves marked by makeshift wooden crosses or small piles of stones dotted the trails westward from the Missouri River all the way to the Oregon Territory.

Once settled on the homestead, whether in the Oregon Territory or on the Great Plains, women found the familiar terrain of marriage and motherhood to be a test of endurance. The isolation from other women, the grueling labor, the hardships of nature, and the lack of social institutions such as schools and churches thrust women into a difficult life.

The day-to-day life of the pioneer woman encouraged her ingenuity—that is, she learned the art of "making do." Slivers of dogwood bark served as sewing needles until the peddler could make his yearly visit, while such disasters as rattlesnake bites were alleviated by poultices of raw chicken meat or spoonfuls of ammonia diluted with water. Despite the hardships, some women chose this life for themselves. In parts of the West, a full 15 percent of settlers or homesteaders were single women, either unmarried or widowed.

Outside of homesteading, the history of the West brims with references to women who taught school, who ministered to the spiritually and physically ill, who entertained with performances from the latest eastern theater productions, who labored for years to get women the right to vote, and who toiled in jobs usually filled by men. Sometimes due to necessity, sometimes due to greater tolerance, frontier life afforded women opportunities unavailable to their eastern counterparts and freed them to some degree from the discrimination that was so entrenched in the East.

Settlers did bring with them much of the social structure of the East, and many of the standard social and economic divisions between men and women held sway over everyday life on the frontier. Still, the West was a land where notions of station and class proved less stringent, and women often encountered less resistance in the West when they stepped outside their traditional roles. Between 1840 and 1900, women earned a living as laundresses, teachers, shopkeepers, hotel and restaurant owners, entertainers, photographers, and even barbers. In the reckless mining camps and boomtowns of the Wild West, women found it easier to

In the Klondike region of Alaska, 60-year-old Nellie Cashman reflects on her life as a restaurateur, merchant, hotelier, and miner.

enter the professions, becoming doctors, dentists, lawyers, and journalists. Nellie Cashman was working as a bellhop in a Boston hotel when a chance conversation with General Ulysses S. Grant changed the direction of her life. Grant advised her to go west because the country needed people like her. Cashman became one of the most well-traveled entrepreneurs in the West: She followed the gold scent from Tombstone to the Klondike, establishing restaurants, boardinghouses, and mercantile stores along the way.

Former slaves journeyed west seeking a new and better way of life. Clara Brown, who purchased her freedom in the 1850s, started a laundry in Colorado and charged miners 50 cents per shirt. Laundry service was invaluable near the goldfields, and operating a laundry became one of the occupations most frequently pursued by women. Brown was so successful that she accumulated enough capital in a few years to help other former slaves settle in Colorado and to finance her search for her long-lost relatives.

A few women worked at jobs that were almost always held by men. There were a couple of women bullwhackers who drove huge teams of freight-pulling oxen along treacherous wilderness trails. A few, including Charley Parkhurst, drove stagecoaches, though Parkhurst did her driving disguised as a man.

Minnie Mossman-Hill had one of the most unusual jobs for a woman in the 19th century—she became the first licensed steamboat captain west of the Mississippi.

Considering the inroads women made into the male-dominated work force on the frontier, it is not surprising that women won the right to vote in the West before achieving suffrage in the rest of the country. In 1869, Wyoming Territory became the first territory or state to grant women the right to vote. They were followed by Utah Territory soon after, by Colorado in 1893, and by Idaho in 1896. In addition to gaining the right to vote, women could seek and hold office in some parts of the West, and western land-grant colleges were among the first to admit women.

Rugged Calamity Jane occasionally found work as a bullwhacker, cracking her whip over as many as ten oxen.

When frontier towns tamed down, prostitutes such as those from Bella Bernard's Parlor House in Denver (right) were no longer welcome.

Wherever women settled in the West, whether alone or as the wife of a settler or townsman, they tended to bring with them the comforts of civilization. As the supporters of culture, women saw to it that schools, churches, charitable societies, and libraries were not far behind them. Men in mining camps and boomtowns welcomed a stable female population as it generally signaled the beginning of a more civilized existence.

Not all women in the West stayed on the right side of the law, however. After domestic help, prostitutes may have been the second-largest

group of working women. Prostitutes and dance-hall girls followed the gold fever or cattle booms around the West. They frequently would drift from one settlement to the next when the gold strike played out; the cow trade moved on; or the town became larger, more civilized, and less tolerant of their presence.

In addition to prostitutes, other women led a bawdy existence outside of convention, if not the law. The West attracted free spirits and eccentrics of all kinds and allowed them room to follow their unusual lifestyles. Though the idea that the West offered women more freedom has been debated and women who thwarted convention often paid a price, the story of women in the West is made more colorful by the antics of such free-spirited legends as Calamity Jane, Belle Starr, and Pearl Hart.

The diminutive Hart pulled the last stagecoach robbery in the United States on May 30, 1899. On a treacherous road between Globe and Benson, Arizona, Hart and Joe Boot made off with $431 from the three stunned passengers onboard. Unfortunately, the thieves became lost in the surrounding mountains and were arrested three days later by a sheriff's posse. Hart was found guilty and sentenced to five years in the Yuma Territorial Prison. She served 18 months, was released in 1902, and then walked away into obscurity.

Another female outlaw, Eugenia Moore, served as an intelligence agent for the Dalton Brothers. Also known as Flo Quick, Mrs. Mundy, Mrs. Bryant, or Tom King, Moore was the sweetheart of Bob Dalton. Under the pretense of shipping valuables, she gathered information about the railroads so the Daltons knew which trains were best guarded. In 1892, just prior to the Daltons' infamous bank robbery attempt in Coffeyville, Kansas, Moore died of cancer.

Women, like the men of the time, performed many roles in the settlement and development of the West. They were teachers, missionaries, entertainers, homesteaders, and entrepreneurs, and they were outlaws, prostitutes, and dance-hall girls. In a measurable way, these women influenced the course of a young country as it expanded westward. The ingenuity, daring, and boldness of women in the West must have amazed and disturbed their counterparts in the East—who still thought that riding astride a horse in divided skirts was quite shocking!

After reading about the exploits of famous frontier outlaws, "good girl" Pearl Hart pulled the last stagecoach robbery in America.

CALAMITY JANE

1844–1903

Calamity Jane was born Martha Jane Cannary in 1844, according to the census of 1860. Other birth dates have been suggested, and with a vanity not typical of Calamity Jane, she reduced her age by claiming to have been born on May 1, 1852, in Princeton, Missouri.

Calamity Jane gained fame as a "character" but solidified her legend as a scout with General George Crook.

When Martha Jane was an adolescent, her family moved from Missouri, most probably to Calamus, Wisconsin. Her father, Robert Cannary, was a heavy drinker, and she left home after the Civil War to escape an intolerable home life. Martha Jane went west and supported herself as a prostitute in Wyoming. Shortly thereafter, she became known as Calamity Jane, although it is unclear how she acquired the famous sobriquet. Calamity Jane became a colorful frontier character of the first order. Although Calamity continued to work as a sporting lady from time to time, she decided that men had a better life. As her once-trim figure filled out to husky proportions, Calamity chopped off her hair and donned soiled buckskins and a slouch hat.

Calamity loved to belly up to the bar with the boys. She chewed tobacco and drank to excess. She cussed like a teamster and even worked as one on occasion. She enjoyed nothing better than spending a boisterous evening in a loud, smoky saloon, drinking and gambling, even though she was a poor gambler. In 1876, she was jailed in Cheyenne, and as the years went by, there were other arrests for rowdiness. During one raucous revelry, she reportedly bet everyone within earshot that she could enter a bordello, engage a prostitute, and, until a certain delicate moment, pass herself off as a man. Calamity swaggered into a red-light house

PROSTITUTION

It was inevitable that prostitution thrived in the West, where the ratio of men to women was ten to one. The cattle towns, the mining camps, and the military posts were all locales dominated by single males.

Many prostitutes were foreign-born, alone in a strange country with no other means of support: Chinese women on the West Coast, Mexican señoritas in New Mexico, and African-American ladies in the larger cities. These and other women added their individual personalities to a well-established business that boomed in the West when the first Texas cowboys arrived at Abilene soon after the end of the Civil War.

In one of the early cattle towns—Ellsworth, Kansas—the city fathers, rather than outlaw the profession, actually profited from it. A local newspaper of the times explained:

"The city realizes $300 per month from prostitution fines alone.... The city authorities consider that as long as mankind is depraved and Texas cattle herders exist, there will be a demand and necessity for prostitutes, and that as long as prostitutes are bound to dwell in Ellsworth it is better for the respectable portion of society to hold prostitutes under restraint of law."

Prostitutes were categorized into four groups. The streetwalker, the lowest rung on the ladder, solicited anyone from any social strata who could pay. Next came the saloon girl, who entertained the customers in the bars and saloons. The crib girl worked out of her crib, that is, a small room or residence. Crib girls catered to out-of-town visitors and guests. At the top of the scale were the women who worked in the large city parlors, often bestowing their talents on the town's leading citizens.

With such colorful names as Molly b'Damn, Contrary Mary, and Velvet Ass Rose, the prostitutes contributed much to the lore of the Wild West regardless of the moral stigma associated with them.

Prostitution thrived where there were lonely men and ample money. Some say Julia Bulette earned $1,000 a night at the Comstock Lode in Nevada.

and, with witnesses strategically positioned, proceeded to win the bawdy wager.

Calamity sometimes found employment as a bullwhacker, cracking a whip over teams of oxen. Posing as a male teamster, she accompanied the 1875 geological expedition of Professor Walter P. Jenney into the Black Hills. Supposedly, the next year she marched with George Crook's column into Montana, but when she went bathing with troopers and her gender was revealed, Calamity was ordered to return to civilization.

Civilization—of a sort—could be found in Deadwood, South Dakota, where she turned up not long before Wild Bill Hickok was murdered on August 2, 1876. Claiming a long and intimate association with the famous gunfighter, Calamity stated in her spurious autobiography that they had wed, then divorced so that Wild Bill would be free to marry Agnes Lake. She also claimed that she had borne Wild Bill a child.

She may have given birth to a son around 1882, although nothing further is known about this offspring. A daughter was born on October 28, 1887, but was deposited with St. Mary's Convent in Sturgis, South Dakota, eight years later. Thereafter, the little girl disappeared from history. The girl's father was El Paso cab driver Clinton Burke, who apparently married Calamity Jane in 1885. There were other husbands, perhaps of the common-law variety, in other places. Few documented details exist on Calamity Jane's attempts at romance, love, and family life.

Calamity drifted all over the West, gravitating to cavalry outposts, cattle towns such as Miles City in Montana, and boomtowns on the order of Deadwood. In Deadwood, she displayed a classic heart of gold by assuming the unlikely role of nurse. Working at times without pay, she cared for a stabbing victim, a smallpox patient, a dying girl, and a premature baby.

Her features coarsened, a reflection of her outdoor life and years of carousing. Calamity Jane eventually became an alcoholic and her habits were rough, but she was tough and resilient. She had to be to survive such a hard lifestyle.

With a ghost writer, she produced an autobiography, which put into print a boastful collection of falsehoods, including the claims that she had campaigned with Custer, married Wild Bill, and helped capture his killer. In 1896, Calamity made stage appearances as

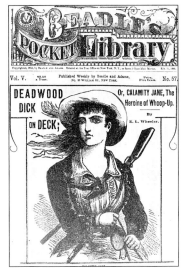

Calamity Jane's legend was enhanced by fallacious stories by *Beadle's* and other dime-novel accounts of the West. She did, however, live unconventionally for a woman of her time.

"the Famous Woman Scout," and at the 1901 Pan-American Exposition in Buffalo, New York, she appeared on the midway as a buckskin-clad cowgirl.

By this time, however, Calamity had sagged into alcoholic addiction. She was discovered sick and drunk in an African-American bordello in Horr, Montana, and she grumbled an uncharacteristic wish that people should "leave me alone and let me go to hell my own route." That route kept taking her back to Deadwood, where she fell ill at Terry, a nearby mining town. Delirious, she spoke lamentably of her daughter and then died on August 1, 1903.

Insisting that Calamity's dying wish was to be buried next to Wild Bill Hickok, her friends arranged to have her interred only 20 feet from his grave. They even changed the date of her demise to August 2, 1903, the 27th anniversary of Hickok's death.

Just 20 years later, a silent movie titled *Wild Bill Hickok* included the story of Wild Bill and Calamity Jane. Her character would continue to appear in the profusion of films about Hickok that followed. Calamity's tall tales and Hollywood had managed to insinuate a closeness between Martha

Jane Cannary and the Prince of Pistoleers that really never existed while Wild Bill was alive. This identification helped her become the most recognizable woman in frontier folklore.

Yet, Calamity Jane earned this fame and notoriety, if not for a supposed relationship with a legendary gunfighter, then for having the nerve to live as she pleased. The West was a man's world, and she entered that world not only by wearing the garb of a frontiersman but also by working at the occupations of a man and roistering in saloons, the western man's clubhouse. Calamity Jane was adventurous, rugged, courageous, strong-minded, and flamboyant, earning a place in the front rank of legendary western characters.

Calamity Jane visits the Deadwood, South Dakota, grave of Wild Bill Hickok around 1900. Her wish of being buried beside him was fulfilled after she died in 1903.

LIBBIE CUSTER

1842–1933

On February 9, 1864, a storybook wedding took place at the First Presbyterian Church in Monroe, Michigan. The bridegroom was 24-year-old George Armstrong Custer, the famous Boy General. Custer and his attendants, all fellow officers, were magnificently attired in blue and gold uniforms. The 21-year-old bride—Elizabeth Clift Bacon—was regarded as the prettiest girl in Monroe.

Libbie Custer received many long letters from George; he once wrote an 80-page epic to his wife.

Libbie Bacon, who was born on April 8, 1842, in Monroe, was the only daughter of Judge Daniel Stanton Bacon. Monroe's only judge, Bacon also served in the Territorial Legislature, as the director of a bank and a railroad, and as a lawyer and schoolteacher. Judge Bacon provided his lovely, personable daughter with a solid education, training in the arts, and a stylish wardrobe.

Libbie first encountered George Custer when he spent two years at an academy in Monroe. As Custer strolled past Judge Bacon's house, Libbie was swinging on the gate of the white picket fence. "Hello, you Custer boy!" she smiled, then ran into the house—and into 15-year-old George's heart.

A few years later, another chance encounter nearly derailed any future romance. From October 1861 until February 1862, Lieutenant Custer spent a sick leave in Monroe at the home of his half-sister. One day, he became drunk with some old schoolmates, and as he staggered to his sister's house, he passed the Bacon home. Libbie, a girl of strong religious convictions, observed the inebriated young officer with stern disapproval. Custer's sister apparently elicited a

In private moments at home, George insisted on having the constant presence of Libbie, even while he worked all evening at his desk.

pledge from him never again to indulge in liquor or tobacco, and he kept his word.

At age 18, Libbie was formally introduced to Custer while she was a student at Boyd's Seminary. Subsequently, Custer enthusiastically courted Libbie, besieging her with a barrage of letters.

Custer's spectacular successes during the Civil War resulted in swift promotion to general. In September 1863, he returned to Monroe and proposed to Libbie. Despite Judge Bacon's reservations, Libbie accepted.

Following the wedding and a brief honeymoon, Libbie accompanied her husband to brigade headquarters. It was not customary for respectable women to be at duty posts, but Libbie's presence noticeably improved behavior around headquarters, and other officers' wives began to join their husbands.

After the war, Custer, with Libbie alongside him, served with Reconstruction forces in Texas and saw duty with the frontier army. Libbie continued to live with Custer wherever he was stationed, and she often accompanied him on campaigns. When they were apart, he sent long letters to her. In 1867, Custer was court-martialed after leaving his regiment in the field to race 150 miles in 55 hours to see Libbie.

The 36-year-old Custer and more than 200 of his men were slain in 1876 at the Battle of the Little Bighorn. Libbie was only 34, but she remained a widow for the rest of her life. She promoted Custer's reputation through lectures and books, including *Boots and Saddles* (1885), *Tenting on the Plains* (1887), and *Following the Guidon* (1890). Libbie died in New York City on April 4, 1933. For nearly six decades, Libbie Custer had defended her husband as resolutely as he had ever defended the flag.

LIBBIE CUSTER ON FRONTIER LIFE

In *Following the Guidon* (1890), Libbie Custer wrote about what life was like for the wives of military officers stationed on frontier posts. In this passage, she offers a delicate description of those few flowers that existed in the western wilderness.

"We rarely had flowers to brighten our houses. Sometimes in the underbrush, where the sole trees we had—the cottonwoods—grew, we found clematis, and the joy of draping our pictures or mantles with this graceful vine, covered with its soft tufts of fluffy gray, was something to be remembered. For a brief time in the early summer the plains were aflame with wild flowers of the most brilliant dyes; but the hot summer scorched them, as well as the grass, out of existence. As ferns only grew in rather damp and shady places, it can be imagined that we never saw them. I had given [to] me some pressed ferns in the United States once, and pasted them on one of our windows when we reached the arid sun-baked plains. They seemed like a bit of fairy-land, and looking at them while they lasted transported us to cool nooks on a pretty brook overhung with thick foliage. Flowers are in such common use nowadays that few tables are without them. Perhaps only a cheap little basket of ferns and foliage plants, or a bowl of wild daisies, but that flowerless land seems like the desert of Sahara as I look back at it as it was after early summer was past."

CHARLEY PARKHURST

1812?–1879

Sometime between Christmas 1879 and New Year's Day 1880, the celebrated stagecoach driver Charley Parkhurst was buried in the Odd Fellows Cemetery near Wat-

Some speculate that Charley Parkhurst began her illusion as a male to succeed in her escape from an orphanage.

sonville, just east of Monterey Bay, California. It was entirely appropriate that Parkhurst, who had long been active in the local lodge of the International Order, be buried there: Charley was the oddest fellow in the graveyard. In fact, until Charley was embalmed, no one knew she was not a fellow at all.

Charley was born Charlotte Darkey Parkhurst (or Pankhurst, the record is not clear) in Lebanon, New Hampshire, in about 1812. In her teens, after abandonment by her parents, she ran away from an orphanage in Massachusetts and found work in a livery stable in Worcester owned by Ebenezer Balch.

There is no dependable historical record of Parkhurst's movements and work in the 20 years that followed her debut as a stagecoach whip under the tutelege of Balch, but there are some random facts and clues about these years. From her earliest days of learning to drive a coach-and-six, she called herself Charley and began wearing men's clothing. She worked in Providence, Rhode Island, for a time, then drifted to Georgia. There is no clue as to what she did or for how long in any of these ventures, but in 1849 she was back in Providence. There she learned about the gold rush north of Sutter's Fort on the American River in northern California.

One of Parkhurst's coach-driving colleagues in Providence, a man named James Birch, had quickly departed for California, intending to start up a coach line from the goldfields to Sacramento. He urged Parkhurst to follow, promising her employment.

She made the arduous six-month voyage to San Francisco via the Isthmus of Panama. In 1851, she made her way to the goldfields, where Birch hired her to drive coaches in the Mother Lode country around Georgetown,

Hangtown, and Coloma. By 1854, when Birch organized the California Stage Company, Parkhurst was one of his chief drivers. She was familiar with the entire Sierra Nevada foothill country, from as far north as Sacramento and Stockton to as far south as Monterey. Her regular runs were to San Francisco and Oakland.

Stories—some no doubt apocryphal—abound about her exploits during the period she worked as a stagecoach whip in California. The most notable instance involved a highwayman known as Sugarfoot, whose outsized feet wrapped in burlap sacks accounted for his unusual moniker. Sugarfoot stopped her coach, stuck a shotgun in her face, and ordered her to throw down the strongbox. Parkhurst did as she was told but warned the bandit, "Next time, I'll be ready for you."

She took to wearing six-shooters after this robbery. A year later, Sugarfoot and his gang held her up again. This time she began blazing away at them as they drew up to her coach. She whipped up her horses and flew down the trail. When a posse returned to the site, Sugarfoot was found dead, with two of his gang wounded.

Other dangers faced by Parkhurst as a stage driver involved the forces of nature as opposed to the follies of man. One of her stage routes crossed a dilapidated

bridge over the Tuolumne River. While on this run during a severe rainstorm, Charley grew apprehensive about crossing the bridge. Her fears proved founded when the stage drew up to the Tuolumne and she saw a raging, rain-swollen torrent beneath the swaying, creaking bridge. She gritted her teeth, laid the whip to her team, and bolted across the bridge at full speed. Just as the stage touched the other side, the bridge tore loose from its anchors and was washed down river by the swift floodwaters.

Despite taking a daring risk now and then, Parkhurst approached her job with great seriousness and professionalism. She did not drink while on the job and was highly critical of those who did. She maintained that stage accidents, particularly wrecks, were mainly the result of "whiskey or bad driving." She was openly affectionate with her horses, calling them her beauties and lavishing them with loving care. A good scrapper in a fight, she made short work of anyone who dared mistreat a horse or other animal in her presence.

Parkhurst retired from the rigors of the stage routes in the early 1860s, making her farewell run from San Jose to Santa Cruz. She was particularly proud of the fact that none of her passengers had suffered an injury, despite some hair-raising close calls.

The stagecoach was uncomfortable to ride in and just as arduous to drive. There were few private stops along a line, yet Charley Parkhurst was able to conceal her gender for years.

THE
STAGECOACH

By the middle of the 19th century, travel and transportation east of the Mississippi River had become a relatively simple affair. A proliferation of railroads and turnpikes had evolved over many years, while canals and regular coach service added to the convenience of personal travel and the transit of farm produce and manufactured goods.

No such conveniences existed west of the Mississippi River. Though the Santa Fe and Oregon Trails had led thousands across the Great Plains to the fabled markets of New Mexico and the promised land of Oregon, there were no organized services for travel like there were in the East.

Spearheaded by the migration of thousands of people to California, efforts were made in the early 1850s to alleviate the nightmare of travel and transportation between distant points in the West. The stage lines, such as those run by Wells, Fargo & Company and Overland Stages, solved the problem of consistent travel west of the Mississippi. By 1860, the stage had become the most popular means of carrying people, mail, and valuable freight across the West.

The Concord stagecoach, first manufactured in Concord, New Hampshire, in 1827, was the coach of choice for the stage companies. Costing about $1,050, a Concord coach could carry as many as 21 passengers and several hundred pounds of freight. The crew consisted of a driver and

This coach, on the Montrose-Ouray stage line, hits the end of the line at the Beaumont Hotel in Ouray, Colorado.

one or two guards who "rode shotgun," a slang term still used to describe front-seat passengers.

A full stage averaged about eight miles per hour. Horses were changed as often as every 12 to 15 miles, while passengers got a break at a comfortable stage stop about every 40 to 50 miles. The three-week journey from the Mississippi River to California cost about $200 per person.

Stage traffic tapered off after the railroad connected major towns, but in some remote areas of the West, it persisted into the 20th century.

In 1856, Parkhurst was living in the lumber town of Searsville when she was kicked in the face by a horse she was shoeing. She lost the sight in her left eye and wore a black patch, which added to her rough appearance. She acquired the nickname One-Eyed Charley as a result.

After her retirement, she purchased land in Rancho Soquel, near Monterey, raised some cattle, and grew vegetables. In 1867, she registered to vote in the local and state elections, listing herself on the voter rolls as: "Parkhurst, Charles D., age 55, Occupation farmer, Native of New Hampshire." The next year she voted in a federal election. About 43 years after Parkhurst voted in these elections, suffrage came to California!

In what proved to be her last venture, Parkhurst bought 25 acres of land in the Watsonville area in the 1870s. She took on a partner, Frank Woodward, and operated a small cattle ranch. Parkhurst became crippled by rheumatism and debilitated by cancer of the tongue. She died on her ranch on December 28, 1879. The physician who pronounced her dead and performed the autopsy was the first to discover Charley's secret.

Word of the decades-long masquerade quickly leaked out, with newspapers carrying the story all over the West. Reporters tended to embellish the story with outlandish speculation and exaggerated versions of her exploits. The doctor who examined her revealed that she had given birth to at least one child, but no record exists as to when or where this occured.

No one, not even her partner, seems to have ever questioned her gender, although she was only five feet seven inches tall, her face was suspiciously clean-shaven, and she spoke but a few words. She limited her speech to avoid suspicion, speaking in a voice described as a "whiskey tenor." She often wore pleated shirts over outsized trousers, and she was never seen without her leather gauntlet-like gloves in public. She tended to sleep in the stable with her horses while on the road and never bathed in a public bath house. Whenever an unsuspecting widow or single woman took a romantic interest in Charley, Parkhurst made sure her route was switched. To offset these peculiarities and ground her identity as a male, she swore like a longshoreman, smoked cigars, chewed tobacco, and was said to have known the inside of numerous saloons frequented by teamsters.

The question remains as to why Charlotte Darkey Parkhurst became One-eyed Charley. The challenge of keeping up the masquerade year after year seems daunting while the sacrifices involved were extreme. Friendships had to be kept to a minimum, while relationships with the opposite sex were not possible. Rumors that she was a cross-dresser and lesbian were spread at the time of her death, but the truth seems more complicated. In a male-dominated society, perhaps Charlotte became Charley to earn a decent wage and work at an occupation that offered excitement and challenge. Stage drivers were considered kings of the road, and many were celebrated for their daring as well as their skill.

In 1954, long after her original headstone had been stolen from the Odd Fellows Cemetery in Watsonville, her grave was rediscovered. A local historical society placed a new marker on the plot. The inscription reads: "Charley Darkey Parkhurst (1812–1879). One-Eyed Charley, the first woman to vote in the U.S., November 3, 1868."

POKER
ALICE

1851–1930

"At my age I suppose I should be knitting," reflected Poker Alice after several decades as the West's premier lady gambler. "I would rather play poker with five or six experts than to eat."

Alice Ivers was born on February 17, 1851, in Sudbury, England. As the only daughter of a schoolmaster, Alice was educated at a female seminary and instilled with strong middle-class values. Her father brought the family to Virginia when Ivers was in her late teens.

The family eventually moved to Colorado, where Alice married mining engineer Frank Duffield. Duffield's work took the couple to Lake City, Colorado, in 1875. When he spent evenings at a card table, she refused to stay at home, insisting on being permitted to stand behind him and watch. Alice began to sit in on games while Frank was at work, and she quickly demonstrated an affinity for poker. When Frank was killed in a dynamite explosion, she turned to the tables for a living, and soon the miners and other gamblers began calling her Poker Alice.

Alice Ivers received a fortune when she "bucked the tiger"—successfully predicting the winning cards at faro.

Alice Ivers's first husband, Frank Duffield, introduced the British native to poker.

Like other gamblers, Alice moved from one promising western community to another. Occasionally she engaged in high-stakes games aboard luxury passenger trains. In Colorado, she worked gambling rooms in Alamosa, Central City, Georgetown, and booming Leadville before heading south to Silver City, New Mexico. At Silver City, she bucked the tiger at a faro table and broke the bank, then left for New York City to enjoy her winnings. Alice spent $6,000 during one spectacular shopping spree before heading back west to replenish her bankroll.

Poker Alice gravitated to the 1889 land rush, spending two years at gambling tables in Guthrie, the new capital of Oklahoma Territory. Shortly thereafter, she was attracted by the rush to Creede, a new Colorado mining camp, where she managed a table for eight-hour shifts at Ford's Exchange. The owner of the Exchange was Bob Ford, infamous as "the dirty little coward" who had shot Jesse James in the back for reward money in 1882. Reputedly, Poker Alice was at her table on June 8, 1892, when Ford accused Ed O. Kelly of stealing his diamond ring, then tossed him out of the saloon. Moments later Kelly charged back into the Exchange and drove a collar button through Ford's throat with a blast from his shotgun.

By this time, Poker Alice was a well-known figure on the gambler's circuit. Blue-eyed and fair-haired, she dressed fashionably, but she acquired a taste for cigars from her patrons and constantly puffed on small black stogies. Because of her upbringing, she scrupulously refused to play on Sundays, an unprofitable quirk unfathomable to most professional gamblers. Much of the play centered in mining towns, and miners, who worked six-day weeks, crowded the tables on Sundays. But Alice steadfastly ignored potential profits and forsook the tables for church services.

Like most professional gamblers, Alice went heeled, packing a .38 on a .45 frame. She left Creede for Deadwood, South Dakota, where she took a job as a dealer in the saloon of a character named Bedrock Tom. The dealer at the next table was W. G. Tubbs, and one night a drunken miner pulled a knife on him. Alice deftly palmed her .38 and pumped a slug into the miner's arm, thereby triggering a romance between Tubbs and herself. Alice Ivers Duffield married Tubbs in 1907, and the couple abandoned the tables for a homestead north of Deadwood.

In 1910, Tubbs contracted pneumonia and died in Alice's arms during a blizzard. Alice drove his frozen corpse in a sled 48 miles to Sturgis, where she had to pawn her wedding ring to get the $25 to pay for her husband's burial. She promptly took a table in a gambling hall and resumed her old profession. With her first winnings, she reclaimed her ring.

While she gambled in Sturgis, she hired George Huckert to tend her sheep. He continually proposed to her, and when his back wages totaled $1,008, she married him. Alice noted, "It would be cheaper to marry him than pay him off."

During Prohibition, Alice opened a house near Fort Meade, west of Sturgis, offering liquor, gambling, and girls. Alice maintained her curious sense of morality by closing every Sunday. But after she shot and killed a

Poker Alice met up with the notorious Bob Ford on the streets of Creede, Colorado.

trouble-making trooper, her establishment was shut down, even though she was acquitted at a jury trial.

Alice spent her last years quietly in a Sturgis house that today is open to tourists. When she fell ill in 1930, doctors in Rapid City informed her that the odds of recovery were long. "I've faced big odds before," shrugged Alice. But on February 27, 1930, Poker Alice lost. She was buried in the Sturgis Cemetery. Female gamblers were not rare in the Old West, but the queen of them all was cigar-smoking, gun-totin' Poker Alice.

ANNIE OAKLEY

1860–1926

Though arguably America's greatest female sharpshooter, Annie Oakley was never an outlaw, a hellraiser, nor even a westerner.

Phoebe Anne Oakley Moses was born on August 13, 1860, in a log cabin in Patterson Township, Darke County, Ohio. She was the fifth of seven children of Jake and Susanne Moses.

From an early age, Little Annie seemed a natural at shooting a gun. "I was eight years old when I made my first shot," Annie related to an interviewer, "and I still consider it one of the best shots I ever made." Spotting a squirrel perched on a fence in front of her house, the child impulsively climbed onto a chair, dragged down a loaded rifle, then rested the gun on the porch rail. Remembering to shoot a squirrel in the head so as not to spoil the meat, Annie triggered "a wonderful shot, going right through the head from side to side." Annie's frightened mother refused to let her touch the gun again for eight months, but it wasn't long before the little girl was putting meat in the family pot.

Phoebe Anne Oakley Moses was dubbed "Annie" by her four older sisters.

Annie was offered a schooling opportunity if she assisted a housewife whose husband was superintendent of the county prison farm. It was while sewing for the inmates that Annie became fascinated by needlework. Eventually the quality of her embroidery would reach the level of art. When offered wages above the cost of schooling in return for babysitting duties, Annie moved to a farm 40 miles from her home. Unfortunately, she was underfed and sometimes beaten. Two years later, Annie broke away and made her way home.

By the time she was a teenager, Oakley was a dead shot. To help earn a living, she supplied game to a general store. The storekeeper began shipping her surplus to a Cincinnati hotel. The hotel keeper, Jack Frost, met Annie when she visited a married sister in Cincinnati. Frost set up a Thanksgiving Day shooting match between Annie and a traveling exhibition sharpshooter named Frank Butler. Butler always issued a challenge to local marksmen. Frost put up $50 on a 15-year-old girl wearing a sunbonnet and a pink gingham dress. Annie outshot Butler by one clay pigeon. The mighty marksman was so impressed that when he went on the road with his act, he began a correspondence. On June 22, 1876, Frank and Annie were married.

Butler, an Irish immigrant with a failed marriage in his past, was about ten years older than his young wife, but they became a devoted and inseparable couple. Butler and another crack shot named Billy Graham performed between acts of a traveling stock company, but when an ill Graham missed a performance, he was permanently replaced by markswoman "Annie Oakley."

Frank Butler and Annie Oakley toured the vaudeville circuits, then joined the Sells Brothers Circus. When Sells Brothers played New Orleans in 1884, Buffalo Bill's Wild West was also in town. Frank and Annie took in Cody's show, then asked the legendary westerner for a job. The Wild West had other shooting acts, but Butler offered to perform without pay as a tryout. Cody gave Frank and Annie a trial in Louisville early in 1885, and a crowd of 17,000 responded immediately to sweet-natured, beautiful Annie Oakley.

Oakley, a natural showman and crowd-pleaser, became one of the primary assets of Cody's Wild West. Annie traveled with Cody for 17 years but found it unnecessary to sign a contract with the old frontiersman, stating "His words were more than most contracts." Cody affectionately called her Little Missie, audiences regarded her as America's Sweetheart, and Chief Sitting Bull, who joined the Wild West shortly after Annie and Frank, gave her the name *Watanya Cicilia*—Little Sure Shot.

Annie lived up to Sitting Bull's nickname in performance after performance. She was a

shooting machine with a rifle or shotgun. The year before she joined Cody's Wild West, she shot 943 out of the 1,000 glass balls tossed in the air by Butler in a Tiffin, Ohio, exhibition. In Cincinnati in 1885, she fired a shotgun for over nine hours to register 4,772 hits out of 5,000 for 95.4 percent. In 1888 at Glouscester, New Jersey, $5,000 was wagered that Annie could not hit 40 of 50 clay pigeons, but Little

Annie Oakley was a star attraction in Buffalo Bill's Wild West for 17 years; she also was the star in other shows before and after her association with Cody.

Sure Shot hit 49. The next day she was challenged by the champion of New Jersey, Miles Johnson, whom she defeated by again hitting 49 of 50.

Oakley's act consisted of more than just shooting clay pigeons and glass balls. For a touch of showmanship, she liked to wait until two clay pigeons were released, then vault over a table, snatch up her gun, and shoot both targets. Other parts of their act featured Butler shooting an apple from the head of a trained dog. At 30 paces, Annie would shoot a dime from Butler's fingers or a lighted cigarette from his lips. She could also hit a dime tossed in the air or slice a playing card in half. Sometimes, Butler would toss a card with a picture of Oakley inside a heart-shaped bull's eye into the air, and Little Sure Shot would drill it six times.

Prominently advertised as The Peerless Wing and Rifle Shot, Oakley appeared second on Cody's bill of 19 acts. Following the grand entrance of riders, the diminutive Annie paraded in, bowing, and throwing kisses. In addition to her immense popularity, her early appearance was designed to accustom the audience to the constant explosion of firearms that accompanied the remainder of the show.

Annie Oakley was known the world over for her skill as a trick-shot artist.

Cody utilized several shooting acts, starting with himself. There were also Lillian Smith, a teenager who could break 495 out of 500 glass balls, and Johnny Baker, who consistently lost face-offs with Little Sure Shot. Audiences enjoyed the rivalry, and for those who thought that Baker always let the show's headliner win, he later admitted that he was never able to beat Oakley.

In 1887, Buffalo Bill's Wild West performed at Queen Victoria's Golden Jubilee in London, then launched a triumphal tour of Europe. In Berlin, Crown Prince William, later Kaiser Wilhelm II, horrified everyone except the confident Little Sure Shot by insisting that she shoot the ashes from a cigarette held in his lips. As always, she was successful. Cody's company numbered 640 performers and workers, as well as hundreds of animals and vehicles. The loading and unloading from trains and the feeding of the Wild West animals and crew had been perfected to a science, which impressed the military-minded Germans. "We never moved without at least 40 officers of the Prussian Guard standing all about with notebooks, taking down every detail . . . " wrote Oakley. Years later, when Kaiser Wilhelm was the detested villain of World War I, Annie stated that she should have missed the cigarette and shot the Kaiser.

Oakley, whose career was managed by Butler, broke away from Cody's Wild West to conduct a solo tour of European capitals, which immensely expanded her fame. Back in the United States, she appeared in a melodrama, *Deadwood Dick*, and in a variety act in New York City. Oakley and Butler joined Pawnee Bill's Wild West show, and Little Missie was reunited with Cody when Pawnee Bill and

Buffalo Bill merged their operations. Numerous competing Wild West shows capitalized on an enormous public appetite for the loud, colorful, exciting western extravaganzas, but aside from Cody himself, the most popular star during the long heyday of the Wild West shows was Annie Oakley.

On October 28, 1901, as Cody's show left Charlotte, North Carolina, for its final performance of the season in Danville, Virginia, their train collided head-on with a freight train, killing 110 horses. Oakley represented the most serious human casualty, suffering from severe internal injuries and partial paralysis. She underwent several operations, and her hair turned white. It looked as though Annie Oakley's career had ended.

After months of recovery, however, she resumed performing. She toured in 1902 and 1903 with the melodrama *The Western Girl*. Though her vigor was somewhat diminished, she demonstrated her old-time marksmanship in exhibitions. Annie Oakley never again appeared with Cody's Wild West, but in 1911 she began three seasons of touring with a show called Young Buffalo Wild West. In 1915, Annie and Frank joined the staff of the Carolina Hotel in Pinehurst, North Carolina, where they taught and

Later in her life, Annie Oakley taught rifle and shotgun shooting in Pinehurst, North Carolina, as well as in army camps during World War I.

demonstrated rifle and shotgun shooting. During World War I, they toured army camps, giving instruction as well as performances.

Offstage, Annie was quiet and prim, devoting herself to crafting her exquisite needlework and to reading the Bible. Although she sipped an occasional beer with the hard-drinking Cody, her favorite beverage was lemonade. Annie and Frank didn't have children, but she supported and educated 18 orphan girls.

In 1921, Oakley was crippled in an automobile accident. She and Butler moved to Greenville, Ohio, in her home county, where she died at age 66 on November 3, 1926. Butler passed away three weeks later, on November 23, and he was buried beside her in the Brock Cemetery near her birthplace.

Annie Oakley was not a westerner, and, except for her performance tours, she never experienced the Old West. However, through her countless exhibitions with Buffalo Bill's Wild West and other shows, and then later exposure in comic books, movies, television, and, most notably, Rodgers and Hammerstein's *Annie, Get Your Gun*, Annie Oakley became indelibly identified with the Wild West.

STAGECOACH MARY

1832–1914

The stagecoach driver stood six feet tall and weighed 200 pounds, smoked cigars, drank whiskey, never ducked a fight, and packed a .38 in addition to a double-barreled shotgun.

The stagecoach driver was named Mary Fields.

Mary Fields was born into slavery in 1832 in Tennessee. When the Civil War ended, the easiest way for ex-slaves to experience their new freedom was to move out of the South. Young African-American men headed west to become cowboys, and many African-American families moved to frontier homesteads. Fields left Tennessee, perhaps escaping before the end of the Civil War, and made her way north to Ohio, where she found work at a Catholic mission school.

Mary became close to an Ursuline nun named Mother Amadeus. When the Ohio school closed, Mother Amadeus was sent to Montana Territory in 1884 to help establish a mission school for Native American women, and she brought her big, loyal friend along to help. St. Peter's Mission School was built near Cascade, about 60 miles north of Helena. Mary was already past 50 years old when she arrived in Cascade, but for the next eight years she worked at hauling freight and performing heavy chores.

While ex-slaves moved west in considerable numbers, not many ventured as far north as Montana. When Mary Fields came to Montana in 1884, there were fewer than 350 African-Americans scattered across the vast territory, and she was called "Nigger Mary" and "Black Mary." Mary Fields quickly showed that she could meet any challenge of the raw Montana frontier.

Mary proved invaluable to Mother Amadeus as the mission slowly took shape. Mother Amadeus and Mary endured the extremely frigid winters in a log cabin. To protect herself against the cold, Mary togged out in a union suit, a pair of trousers, a long dress, a man's overcoat, and a fur cap. She regularly drove a wagon into Cascade, loading up supplies and lumber, then unloading these cargoes at the mission. At first, the sight of Fields driving her wagon with a cigar in her mouth and a jug of whiskey at her side intimidated and alienated some of the townsfolk. Mary tended to keep about her business and ignore the cold stares.

Although Mary Fields's first years in Cascade, Montana, were turbulent, she eventually became an honored citizen.

Like most men of the frontier, Mary went heavily armed. Once, while driving back to the mission after dark, she was attacked by a pack of wolves. Her team bolted, upending the wagon and dumping Mary and her supplies onto the prairie. She unlimbered her revolver and rifle and kept the wolves at bay throughout the night. While driving a load on another winter night, gusting winds suddenly brought a blizzard, and visibility through the swirling snow dropped to only a few feet. As snowdrifts piled around the wagon, Mary halted her team and got down. She stamped back and forth all night to keep from freezing to death.

Such a formidable character was not inclined to duck trouble. Although liked and appreciated by the nuns for her steadfast contributions to their work, Mary tended to clash with the workmen at the mission. Occasionally the strapping woman openly brawled with one of these men. Once, Mary and an antagonist went for their guns, shattering the peace of the mission with an exchange of gunfire. Although no one was wounded, the bishop in Helena directed Mother Amadeus to discharge her pugnacious friend.

Mother Amadeus helped Mary establish a restaurant in Cascade. Mary was a good cook but fed everyone regardless of their inclination to pay, and she went broke. Assisted again by Mother Amadeus, Mary reopened her business, only to shut down once more, although her generosity established a local reservoir of good will. By this time, the locals had been won over by Fields's determination, independence, and inherent kindness to those less fortunate.

"Black Mary" became "Stagecoach Mary" by riding shotgun and working as a driver on an area stagecoach line. When a mail route was established between Cascade and St. Peter's Mission, Mother Amadeus aided her 63-year-old friend in securing the position of carrier. Mary drove the route for eight years, becoming perhaps the second woman in history to deliver the U.S. mail.

When Mother Amadeus was transferred to a mission in Alaska, Mary felt she was too old to follow her longtime benefactor. Now in her 70s, she operated a laundry, babysat, and celebrated her birthdays by handing out candy to children. The New Cascade Hotel gave her free meals, and friends helped her build a house. When her home burned, townspeople helped her rebuild. Still fond of cigars and whiskey, she continued to pack a powerful punch. Legend has it that once, a customer in her laundry walked out without paying his bill. As he walked away, Fields tapped him on the shoulder. When he turned around, the 70-year-old woman punched him squarely on the jaw. Mary then announced that his bill had been paid in full.

By the end of her life, Mary Fields was revered as a local legend. Supposedly, Cascade's public schools were closed to honor her birthday. Sometimes they even closed twice a year, because Mary was unsure of her exact birth date. She also gained the distinction of being the first woman in Cascade to be allowed to drink in the town's saloons.

Mary died in 1914, and the grave of this redoubtable woman of the frontier may be visited at Cascade's Hillside Cemetery. Strong, industrious, loyal, generous, dependable, good with fists or guns, Mary Fields embodied many of the most admirable qualities of the men and women who settled America's last West.

NELLIE CASHMAN

1850?–1925

"Pretty as a Victorian cameo and, when necessary, tougher than two-penny nails," wrote Nellie Cashman's biographer, Suzann Ledbetter. Ledbetter describes in down-to-earth terms this remarkable frontier woman who was known during her lifetime by such heavenly appellations as Frontier Angel, Miner's Angel, Angel of the Cassiar, Angel of Tombstone, and Saint of the Sourdoughs.

Born in Queenstown, County Cork, Ireland, around 1850, her formal name may have been Ellen, but from childhood, she was called Nellie. It appears she and her sister Fannie emigrated to the United States in the 1860s and settled in Boston. Years later, in an interview with a writer, Nellie reminisced about those years. She recalled that she worked as a bellhop in a prominent Boston hotel, a job she acquired because of the shortage of available working men during the Civil War.

During this period, she not only had the honor of meeting General Ulysses S. Grant, but she actually had a chance to chat with the Civil War hero. Grant must have been impressed with her for he advised her to go west. "The West needs people like you," he supposedly told her.

Cashman took Grant's advice and used her hard-earned savings to travel with her sister to San Francisco in 1869. Within a year, Fannie married a man named Cunningham and began raising a family. Nellie hired out as a cook in various Nevada mining camps, including Virginia City and Pioche. With her savings from her months as a cook, she opened the Miner's Boarding House at Panaca Flat, Nevada, in 1872.

Forever footloose and willing to follow the gold scent, Cashman joined a party of 200 Nevada miners journeying north to the Cassiar gold strike around Dease Lake in northern British Columbia. Dressed in a colorful mackinaw, miner's trousers, boots, and fur hat, Cashman looked like a female Nimrod of the North among the prospectors who came to her boarding house near the diggings. Periodically, she came out of the wilderness to the city of Victoria, and during one of these visits, she learned that a scurvy epidemic had broken out among the miners at Dease Lake. She enlisted the help of six men, loaded pack animals with 1,500 pounds of supplies, including the antiscorbutics potatoes and lime juice, and began the long trip back to the Cassiar. The overland journey took 77 days.

Much of the time, the group had to sleep in the snow and subsist on short rations. One

The Angel of Tombstone, Nellie Cashman had a fine business sense but never let the pursuit of money overshadow her love of helping others.

Virginia City, Nevada, was home to Nellie Cashman when she was just starting her adventure in the West.

night, her tent was pitched on the side of a steep bank where the snow was ten feet deep. When someone tried to bring her coffee the next morning, Nellie was nowhere to be found. Nellie, her tent, and her belongings had disappeared. The men finally found her about a quarter of a mile down the hill. During the night, a small snowslide had carried her downhill and buried her under the snow.

United States officials at Fort Wrangel had tried to talk her out of making what she admitted was a "mad trip," but their advice failed to deter her. When reports leaked back to the fort that she and her party had perished on the trail, a detachment of men set out to find her. They did, relaxing with her partners beside a campfire on the Stikeen River. She politely offered her rescuers a cup of tea. Cashman's rescue party eventually reached the miners' camp in time for her to nurse 75 men back to health.

After the Cassiar strike, Cashman went to Tucson, Arizona, where she opened the Delmonico Restaurant in 1879, the first business in the town owned by a woman. The venture was a success despite her propensity for feeding down-and-out miners gratis. The next year, she moved to Tombstone, following the silver rush in the San Pedro Valley. She opened a boot and shoe store, sold it, and launched a restaurant. She sold the latter just before a fire gutted the entire Tombstone business district. Her last restaurant venture in Tombstone was the Russ House, which was named after the original in San Francisco. There, Nellie offered good meals for 50 cents. She advertised with the plain-spoken declaration that "there are no cockroaches in my kitchen and the flour is clean."

Cashman was a devout Catholic but also a pragmatist. While Nellie lived in Tombstone, a Reverend Endicott Peabody arrived in town. He had been educated in Cheltenham in England and graduated from Oxford University. Reverend Peabody did not have a church where he could hold his services, so Nellie prevailed upon the owners of the Crystal Palace saloon to lend him their premises. Nellie thought preaching in a den of iniquity was preferable to not holding services at all, so the barroom nudes were covered and faro games put away while Reverend Peabody attempted to turn sinners into saints.

The Crystal Palace saloon in Tombstone, Arizona, served whiskey and beer—and, on Sunday mornings, a measure of Christian services, thanks to Nellie Cashman.

During her years in Tombstone, Cashman became a prominent and revered local figure as she helped raise money to build the Sacred Heart Church and scrounged funds for the Salvation Army, Red Cross, Miner's Hospital, and for amateur theatricals. She also took up collections for individuals who had been injured or found themselves in trouble. In her missions of mercy, she often sought the

assistance of the inhabitants of Tombstone's red-light district, because she found them sympathetic and willing to lend a helping hand. One Tombstone resident recalled, "Nellie Cashman always called for help from Black Jack, known as the queen of the red-light district, and Nellie said her greatest help came from the back street which had no name on the map."

In an unusual use of her nurturing tendencies, she served as an impromptu officer of her church in hearing the confessions of two of the five men who were to be hanged for the Bisbee Massacre of December 1883, in which four Bisbee townspeople were killed during a store robbery.

Cashman didn't always take the side of the miners and the downtrodden; she took the side she believed to be the right one. When a group of miners wanted to hang mine owner E. B. Gage during a strike, Nellie rode into the middle of the foray in her buggy and rescued Gage from the lynching party. She escorted Gage from Tombstone to Benson, where he boarded a train for Tucson. Gage became one of Cashman's lifelong supporters.

Cashman joined a gold-seeking party on a futile expedition to the Golo Valley in the vicinity of Guyamas, Mexico, on the Gulf of California. The story goes that a dying Mexican arrived in Tombstone one day with his pockets stuffed with gold nuggets. He stumbled into the front of a hotel and then fell over, mumbling something about Mulege. Mulege was on the Baja Peninsula, so the gold would have been located in desert

BOOMTOWNS

Mining boomtowns sprang up throughout the West whenever gold and silver were discovered. Often miners' camps, which were usually ragtag collections of tents and thrown-together shelters, served as the basis of the boomtowns. The rate of development from camp to bursting boomtown frequently was just a matter of weeks—once word spread that the precious ore was just laying on the ground waiting for anyone to come along and pick it up! Eager entrepreneurs and merchants took advantage of the rapid growth to start much-needed businesses. Some were wholesome enterprises, some were not.

Tombstone, located in Arizona Territory, was typical of the western boomtowns. When silver was discovered in the vicinity in mid-1877 by Edward L. Schieffelin, Tombstone quickly grew as hundreds of the would-be wealthy arrived to try their hand at the mines. Christened with the fanciful names "Good Enough," "Tough Nut," "Westside," "Defense," and "Surveyor," five local mines produced enough silver for nearly half a million dollars worth of bars to be minted and stamped.

The Comstock Lode, a rich vein of silver discovered in western Nevada in 1859, made Virginia City one of the fastest-growing and most cosmopolitan of western towns. Within a span of a few weeks, its population soared to 15,000, peaking at 25,000 in 1875. Stores, hotels, saloons, and brothels were erected in rapid succession. Theatrical companies, tent shows, and minstrel shows played its many theaters. At one time, six Shakespearean companies played the Comstock at the same time.

Unlike many boomtowns throughout the West, Tombstone and Virginia City did not die out. They

Silver City, Idaho, was a typical boomtown. Sprawled across the valley, it was a prosperous, rough-and-tumble town before the lode played out.

maintained their position as viable, livable communities, surviving into the 20th century. Others, such as Goldroad, Arizona; Golden, New Mexico; Gold Point, Nevada; and Silver City, Idaho, died quickly as thriving mining towns, as soon as the precious metal that gave them their names was gone.

Today, vestiges of hundreds of former boomtowns, now called ghost towns, dot the landscape from Canada to Mexico and from the Rocky Mountains to California.

HARVEY GIRLS

Fred Harvey purchased a small lunch counter in the Topeka train depot in 1876. A few years after his purchase, Harvey persuaded officials of the Atchison, Topeka & Santa Fe Railway to allow him to open restaurants in depots along the main line.

Before the Harvey empire closed during the late 1950s, more than 100,000 women between the ages of 18 and 30 had been hired. The ladies became known as the Harvey Girls. Dressed in starched black and white uniforms, the Harvey Girls were regarded as symbols of hospitality throughout the Southwest.

Harvey Girls were never called waitresses. They were Harvey Girls, plain and simple. They lived by a strict code of conduct passed down by Fred Harvey himself. Even their personal lives were subject to scrutiny. As their historian, Lesley Poling-Kempes, has written, "They were expected to act like Harvey Girls 24 hours a day. They were told where to live, what time to go to bed, whom to date, even what to wear down to the last detail of makeup and jewelry."

The Harvey Girls were the mainstay of a restaurant chain that stretched from San Francisco to Chicago.

country. Unfortunately, the party underestimated the amount of water they needed to make the trip. When the group was perilously close to running out of water, Nellie volunteered to go for help alone. She came across a Catholic mission and organized a search party to find her companions. The gold-seekers were rescued and decided to abandon their quest.

Soon after Nellie's return, her widowed sister, who had been living in Tombstone in a cottage Nellie built for her, died of tuberculosis, leaving Nellie in charge of five children. She sold Russ House and took the children with her as she wandered mining camps in Wyoming and Montana and in the New Mexico and Arizona Territories. The youngsters, who never suffered for care and education, remembered their Aunt Nellie with great fondness. All grew up to lead successful lives, and one became a banker who managed his aunt's affairs.

In 1898, Cashman had her last adventure as an argonaut when she joined the gold rush to the Klondike in Canada's Yukon Territory. With a party of prospectors, she sailed to Skagway, port of entry to the goldfields far to the north. She made her way across Chilkoot Pass to the lakes leading to the Yukon River, then to Dawson, which was the center of the Klondike diggings. In Dawson, she engaged in several pursuits. She opened a short-order restaurant for a time and later a mercantile store. Always thinking of her beloved miners, she set aside an area in her store known as the "Prospector's Haven of Retreat," where the weary placer miners could write letters home, read, and smoke the free cigars she made available.

Many women might have been reluctant to reside in the rugged mining camps, which were dominated by rough and hardy men. But Cashman scoffed at the idea that she or her virtue were ever in any danger. Nellie told a reporter, "I never have had a word said to me out of the way. The 'boys' would sure see to it that anyone who ever offered to insult me could never be able to repeat the offense."

After years of helping miners and learning from their experiences, Cashman sometimes tried her hand at mining. While in Dawson, one of her claims along the Bonanza River panned out and garnered her more than $100,000. However, she spent most of that money either looking for or buying up other claims.

Cashman lived in Dawson from the most hectic period of the strike to its exhaustion. In those seven years, she became known as one of the greatest figures of the gold rush. Her champions included everyone from the richest of the Bonanza Kings to the lowliest of failed prospectors as well as such celebrated figures as Jack London, Joaquin Miller, Captain Jack Crawford, and Robert W. Service.

Around 1907 or 1908, Cashman's wanderlust took her farther north. She established herself at Fairbanks, Alaska, while running the Midnight Sun Mining Company in the wild Koyukuk region, only 60 miles from the Arctic Circle. She owned and operated 11 mines in the Koyukuk, but none of them paid particularly well. Still in excellent shape and full of life in old age, she once took a dog sled across 750 miles of rugged Alaskan wasteland.

In 1923, she retired to live in Victoria, British Columbia, where she died on January 25, 1925. Nellie Cashman never married, and if she had any lovers, she kept that information to herself. Once, during an interview with the *Arizona Star*, a reporter asked her about her lifelong status as a bachelor woman. She

This photo shows Nellie Cashman going down the Yukon River aboard the steamship *Casca* in 1921, a few years before she retired.

responded, "Why child, I haven't had time for marriage. Men are a nuisance anyhow, now aren't they? They're just boys grown up."

ADAH ISAACS
MENKEN

1835?–1868

"She is the most undressed actress now tolerated on the American stage," fumed an outraged reviewer. One of her starring vehicles, the racy melodrama *French Spy*, was branded a "leg show," and another critic stated that her stage assets were limited primarily to "*them limbs* and *that bust*." A wide-eyed reviewer, offended after viewing her in her most popular role—as a Tartar prince in *Mazeppa (or the Wild Horse of Tartary)*—once announced, "Prudery is obsolete now."

Who was this controversial performer who stirred up such extravagant reactions? She was a bold actress who became famous across the early mining frontier as Adah Isaacs Menken. Born around 1835 in the living quarters of her family's general store near New Orleans, she was christened Adah Bertha Theodore. According to one story, she was quite the well-rounded woman; Adah learned to ride and shoot in addition to experiencing a good education. Her schooling included instruction in the languages, poetry,

Beloved by mining audiences throughout the Southwest, Menken reclines seductively in costume as Prince Ivan Mazeppa.

dance, and voice. She made her stage debut as a child in a New Orleans ballet performance. Later, she said she danced in Texas and Cuba. Unfortunately, after her father died, Adah had to support her ailing mother with nontheatrical occupations.

In 1856, she wed Alexander Isaac Menken, the son of a wealthy Cincinnati manufacturer. Alexander Menken helped his wife join a small traveling troupe of performers, and she assumed the stage name Adah Isaacs Menken. She kept the name but not her husband, and she moved to New York City in pursuit of grander theatrical ambitions. In New York, she found another husband, a prize fighter, but not many roles. Adah divorced the pugilist, who was the second of four husbands, and found work as an assistant to the famed acrobat Blondin. She also managed to work up a vaudeville act of her own.

Producer James Murdoch learned of her riding ability and signed her to the role she would play for the rest of her life—Mazeppa. Ivan Mazeppa was a Tartar prince who fell in love with the betrothed daughter of a Polish nobleman. When Prince Ivan's overtures to his daughter were discovered, the nobleman had Mazeppa stripped naked and lashed "to a fiery, untamed steed." The steed galloped through the mountains to Tartary, where the king, outraged at his son's humiliation, organized a punitive expedition to march into

Poland. Prince Ivan rode—still unclad—to the rescue of his Polish princess.

In portraying Prince Ivan, Menken wore flesh-colored tights, but she was well-endowed, and her gender was obvious. However, it was not unusual for 19th-century actresses to play men's roles. The great Sarah Bernhardt, for example, appeared as Hamlet. Menken opened as Prince Ivan Mazeppa in 1861 in Albany, New York. *Mazeppa* proved to be a sensation, although a New York *Tribune* critic was unimpressed by Adah's acting ability, "Her talent is like gold in quartz veins—all in the rough."

Tom Maguire, a San Francisco theatrical impresario, knew that masculine audiences in gold mining country would be impressed by more than her thespian gifts. Western theaters in general provided enthusiastic receptions for melodramas and other performances. Adah Isaacs Menken was a spectacular hit in *Mazeppa,* and she toured throughout mining country. In Virginia City, Nevada, Samuel Clemens, beginning his writing career for the *Territorial Enterprise,* appreciated Adah as a "shape artist," penned a rave review, then spent a memorable evening with the star at her room in the International Hotel.

The dark-haired actress proved to be captivating company. Menken loved to gamble; she was one of the first women to smoke in public; and she was a delightful conversa-tionalist who enjoyed reading her own poetry and listening to the verse of others. She counted among her friends Walt Whitman, Charles Dickens, the elder Alexandre Dumas, hedonistic English poet Algernon Charles Swinburne, and French novelist George Sand. Sand, who smoked cigars and enjoyed wearing men's clothing, was another daring woman of her day.

Menken met these European literary figures when she starred in *Mazeppa* across the Atlantic. She toured Britain, then played in Paris. Sadly, she developed complications

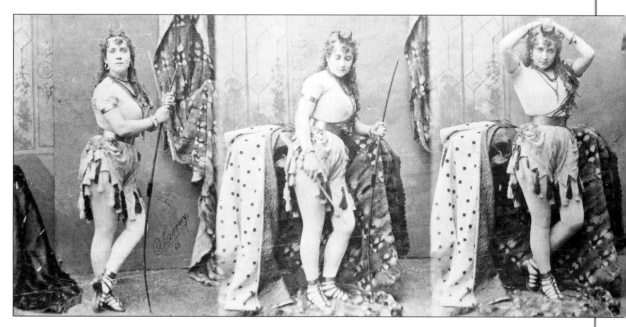

from an injury sustained while performing in the role that made her famous, and she died in Paris at the age of 33. A notable woman, Adah Isaacs Menken created a sensation when she toured the mining region of California and Nevada, where westerners recognized and relished a fine-looking woman—and a kindred spirit—when they saw one.

The well-rounded Menken wrote poetry and consorted with, among others, Samuel Clemens, Walt Whitman, and Charles Dickens.

BELLE STARR

1848–1888

"The ghost of Belle Starr still rides the Indian Territory." These words appeared in the *St. Louis Republican* in 1910, 21 years after Belle was shotgunned from ambush. They remain applicable today. Among the women of the Wild West, only Calamity Jane attained the degree of notoriety afforded Belle Starr, the Bandit Queen.

The "female Jesse James," as she would later be called, started life as Myra Maybelle Shirley on February 5, 1848, in Carthage, Missouri. Her father, John Shirley, prospered as a farmer and owner-operator of the Carthage Hotel. Called May by her family, she was educated at Carthage Female Academy, becoming quite well read. She was also a competent pianist. During the Civil War, her brother, Bud, rode as a Southern guerrilla until he was slain in 1864. Within a few months, John Shirley, sick over the loss of his son and the disruption of his business, sold his property and moved to Texas, where another son, Preston, had settled near Dallas. The Shirley family traveled to Texas in two Conestoga wagons, one driven by 16-year-old Myra Maybelle.

Belle Starr was accused of many transgressions in her life, such as robbery and rustling.

After the war, Myra fell in love with Jim Reed, a former family acquaintance from Missouri whose credentials included service as a guerrilla raider. Married in Collin County, north of Dallas, on November 1, 1866, Myra and Jim moved to the Reed home in Bates County, Missouri, a year later. In September 1868, Myra Reed gave birth to a daughter. Though the girl was christened Rosie Lee, she was always called Pearl.

Jim Reed exhibited more interest in horse racing and gambling than in farming, and he became involved with Tom Starr's gang of rustlers. Starr, a Cherokee, was a hulking desperado who trafficked in stolen livestock and illegal whiskey from a family stronghold. His favorite accessory was a rawhide necklace strung with the dried earlobes of men he had killed, and he was emulated by his admiring son, Sam. The family stronghold was located in the Cherokee Nation at a place Starr dubbed Youngers' Bend, because outlaw Cole Younger often sought refuge there. Younger visited Dallas about the time the Shirleys moved to Texas, and there were stories that he was Belle's first love and

Pearl's father, but he always denied any such connection.

With such wild companions, Jim Reed engaged in rustling, whiskey running, and a killing or two. When warrants were issued for his arrest, Jim fled to California, where he was joined by his wife and daughter. On February 22, 1871, the Reeds had a son, whom they named James Edwin after his father and his mother's slain brother. A month later, Jim was charged with passing counterfeit currency, and he bolted out of California. Lugging along her two babies, Myra followed Jim back to Texas.

The Reeds settled on a Bosque County farm set up for them by John Shirley, but Jim, a wanted man, could not stay out of trouble. In November 1873, Reed and two confederates ventured into Arkansas and brutally robbed Watt Grayson. During this period, Reed was unfaithful to Myra, and she and the children moved in with her parents near Scyene, Texas. The following April, Reed was part of another small gang that pulled a stagecoach holdup, and the reward money for Jim Reed quickly mounted. He shot his way out of an arrest attempt in Collin County and fled north to Indian Territory. He escaped from a posse and headed back to Texas, where he was finally killed near Paris on August 6, 1874. Myra testified that her husband "left me in a destitute condition."

The young widow rented her farm but realized no profit, although she found the means to send Pearl to school in Dallas. Myra's father died in 1876, and she drifted into Indian Territory, where she married Sam Starr, a handsome man who was four years younger than Belle, as she was now called. Because she was married to a Cherokee,

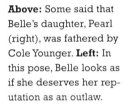

Above: Some said that Belle's daughter, Pearl (right), was fathered by Cole Younger. Left: In this pose, Belle looks as if she deserves her reputation as an outlaw.

Belle Starr was a citizen of the Cherokee Nation.

Sam built a log cabin on a timbered knoll at Youngers' Bend. The approach to the Starr

home followed a narrow defile that they called Belle Starr Creek. Jesse James later hid out at remote Youngers' Bend, causing Belle to complain that "My home became known as an outlaw ranch. . . ." She also complained, "I am the constant theme of slanderous tongues . . . " supposedly because of her refusal to let her neighbors hunt game on the Starr property.

Some of these slanderous tongues apparently belonged to ladies of a higher station, whom she avoided. "So long had I been estranged from the society of women (whom I thoroughly detest) that I thought I would find it irksome to live in their midst." Despite these protestations, Belle sometimes tended sick neighbors and occasionally shared favorite recipes with other women.

Uncovering the personality of Belle Starr from the facts and episodes of her life is not a simple task. Belle maintained her solitude, wandering off with a pillow and books for a day of reading, or after acquiring a piano, happily staying at the keyboard for hours. Belle's relationship with her children often seems contradictory. She doted on Pearl, but when her daughter later had an illegitimate baby, Belle arranged for the infant's adoption without Pearl's knowledge. Her son, Eddie, spent much of his boyhood with the Reed family. As an adolescent, he apparently stayed with Belle, and she often flogged him with a riding quirt.

Blue Duck and Belle Starr: This photo fueled rumors that they were lovers and that Starr hired the lawyer who helped get Blue Duck's sentence commuted.

In 1882 or 1883, Belle and Sam Starr were arrested for the theft of two horses and bound over to the Fort Smith court of the famous "Hanging Judge," Isaac Parker. Because of Belle's previous marriage to a criminal and the appearance of Jesse James at her home, sensationalized stories were printed that purported her to be the "queen" of a band of horse thieves. The courtroom was packed during the four-day trial, and Belle and Sam were declared guilty.

Because there had been no previous convictions, Judge Parker leniently sentenced Belle and Sam to one year in the House of Corrections in Detroit. Steadfastly refusing to permit Pearl to appear as a defense witness, Belle arranged for her daughter to stay with relatives. Belle wrote a long and reassuring letter to Pearl, promising "that never again will I be placed in such humiliating circumstances and that in the future your little tender heart shall never more ache. . . ."

Belle and Sam were released after nine months. Returning to Youngers' Bend, they resumed farm work. Belle became more solitary and withdrawn than ever. She brought Pearl and Eddie home. Belle hired a piano teacher for her children, but Eddie was indifferent. According to Belle, Pearl "tried hard, but had little talent."

By 1885, Sam returned to robbery and horse rustling. He hid out around Youngers' Bend where he was sheltered by relatives and friends. He also might have fled to New Mexico. As an ex-convict, Belle naturally was viewed with suspicion, and various charges were leveled against her in 1886.

That year, Belle consented to pose for a photograph in Fort Smith with a convicted murderer named Blue Duck. Belle was told that it would make Blue Duck feel better as he marched to the gallows, but his lawyer really hoped to call further attention to his client. The stratagem apparently worked, because Judge Parker later commuted the sentence to life imprisonment. A photograph of Myra Maybelle Reed that was taken when she was 22 years of age portrays a young woman with pretty features, but when Belle Starr posed with Blue Duck, she looked far older than her 38 years, revealing the toll exacted by a hard life.

In September 1886, while Belle was in Fort Smith winning acquittal from theft charges, Sam Starr was jumped by a posse as he rode his wife's mare, Venus, near Youngers' Bend. Venus was killed, and Sam was wounded. He escaped, but Belle persuaded him to surrender, and his trial was postponed until the next year. During this period, Sam's father, old Tom Starr, was sent to prison for whiskey running. Considering all of his bad luck, Sam was in a foul mood when he encountered a longtime enemy, Frank West, at Youngers' Bend. At a Christmas dance on December 17, 1886, Starr and West went for their guns. Both men inflicted fatal wounds, and Belle became a widow once more.

With Sam dead, Belle's claim to their Youngers' Bend property was in jeopardy under Cherokee law.

Belle Starr's body was returned to her daughter by a passerby. Pearl had Belle's tombstone engraved with an elegy, which ends, "The gem . . . sparkles yet."

Belle solved the problem by acquiring another Native American husband, Jim July. Tom Starr had taken July under his wing, even calling the young man Jim July Starr. July was 15 years younger than Belle, which did not please her children. Both children began to fall into trouble. Pearl turned to prostitution, and Eddie was arrested for horse stealing.

On Saturday, February 2, 1888, while riding on an errand, Belle was blasted out of her saddle in an ambush. As she tried to rise, the bushwhacker finished the job with the second barrel of his shotgun. The likeliest suspect was Edgar Watson, a neighbor who had clashed with Belle, but he was acquitted, and the killer was never officially determined.

Belle was buried near her cabin with no religious ceremony. She had spent her life in areas wracked by violence and lawlessness, and her taste in men linked her with thieves and killers. Her relationships with her children were troubled ones, and even though her reputation as a bandit queen was wildly exaggerated, she did serve time as a convicted felon. "It seems as if I have more trouble than any other person," she once lamented in a letter. Yet she brought on most of her trouble herself, which paints a picture of the West's most notorious female as more melancholy than nefarious.

HOMESTEADING
WOMEN

All through the history of the West, a steady flow of emigrant farmers poured into the vast grass-covered plains between the Mississippi and the Rockies. Thousands of women left their homes, families, and friends in the East to cross the Great Plains with their husbands in search of new lands and new opportunities. Most women who tramped the western trails ended up in isolated stretches of unsettled prairie or on remote farm lands in Oregon and California with little more than their land claim and a few household items. From the early 1840s, when the Oregon Trail opened for emigrant travel, until 1869, when it was replaced by the railroad, about 350,000 people journeyed west. Since the majority were families, a large percentage of these homesteaders were women.

Life was never easy for a homesteading woman. While her husband built their home, hunted for food, or broke ground for planting, she served as the housekeeper, cook, teacher for her children, doctor, and all-around handy-person. In most cases, she was miles from the nearest settlement, so she had to perform her duties with only the equipment and supplies that she had the foresight to bring with her. Sometimes, she had to undertake the grueling

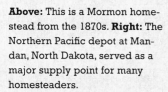

Above: This is a Mormon homestead from the 1870s. **Right:** The Northern Pacific depot at Mandan, North Dakota, served as a major supply point for many homesteaders.

chores traditionally reserved for men, including plowing, hauling, and planting.

Prairie homesteaders often made their homes from the very earth they owned because building materials on the plains were scarce. They hacked through the prairie to chop out bricks of sod to build the walls of their "soddies," using the bare ground for flooring. Roofs were also made of sod, unless a family was fortunate enough to find some willow branches or rushes to use instead. For the homesteading woman, keeping a soddie clean was nearly impossible. A rain shower could result in mud pouring down the walls, while dust storms or heavy winds left a layer of dust on every surface. If the lifestyle wasn't grueling enough, then nature often worked against the homesteading woman and her family. Insects, storms, hard winters, and extremes of temperature made farming or ranching a difficult way to make a living.

The isolation of this existence seemed particularly difficult for women. As the wife was sometimes the only adult woman on the homestead, women suffered from the absence of female companionship. The husband could hire a male laborer or hire himself out to a fellow homesteader, thereby expanding his social circle, but women were left with the occasional quilting bee, corn husking, or house raising to meet and greet other adult women.

A family of homesteaders sits out in front of their sod house on the Nebraska plains.

Regardless of the many trials and tribulations presented to the homesteading woman, she endured. The "winning of the West" was, in many ways, as much the result of the resolution and tenacity of the women as it was the drive and determination of the men.

Homesteading women did most (if not all) of the household chores and embodied the romantic western notion of self-reliance.

NATIVE AMERICANS

Many of the stories handed down through history about the conflict between the Native American and the white man in the West have been told from the perspective of the white victors. This commonly accepted perspective—tainted by greed, distorted by prejudice, and influenced by grandiose notions of Manifest Destiny—offers little insight into the identity or motivations of the vanquished Native Americans.

The white point of view established the erroneous idea, still present in some western lore and literature, that the Native Americans were a single force that offered a united front of opposition to the tide of emigrants flooding the West. This once popular view grouped Native American nations of the West under the blanket term *Indian* and depicted them as an obstacle to progress. In truth, they were diverse nations and tribes with different languages, modes of dress, spiritual beliefs, and political and social organizations. They viewed themselves in terms of individual tribal identity; they were Cheyenne or Sioux or Comanche—not "Indians."

Despite the diversity found among specific tribes, the western Indians shared some cultural attitudes that

Crow Indians such as these shared a similar economy with other Plains groups but saw themselves as culturally distinct from their neighboring Sioux and Blackfoot enemies.

The Comanche of the southern plains were among the first western nations to clash with white settlers over the use of land.

were very different from those of the white encroachers. Native Americans developed an intimate harmony with their environment in which they venerated the land and all things natural. No matter how widely they roamed, they kept a spiritual connection to their homeland, as it was a source of their identity. To Native Americans, the land was not something to be owned by individuals but was jointly occupied for use by the entire tribe or nation. Selling land was a foreign concept to Indians. To whites, the land was real estate—private property to be bought and sold to individuals for ranching, farming, mining, or other means of economic gain.

This differing concept of land was key to the conflict between whites and Native Americans in the West. When the U.S. government negotiated treaties with the western Native Americans, little if any consideration was given to the Indians' veneration for the land or their relationship to it. Prior to 1860, treaties persuaded Indians to grant hunting and fishing rights to their lands or to allow wagon trains the right of way—in other words, to share the land with white settlers. Later treaties, however, divorced them from their land, displacing them to reservations or cutting into the size of the homelands that were critical to their cultural identity. Between 1853 and 1874, 174 million acres of Indian land were transferred to white ownership. Staying within the confines of small reservations or relocating far away from their homelands proved to be jarring changes that destroyed or redefined the lifestyle of many tribes.

Though political systems for western Indian tribes varied widely, they had no governments in the white sense of the word. Leaders tended not to command or govern. Instead, social and spiritual sanctions guided individual behavior, or leaders guided by persuasion or example. When bands from one tribe came together, tribal councils made decisions, though large-scale unified actions were not customary. In some cases, such as with the Nez Percé, Indians maintained allegiance to their family first, then to their band, then to their tribe. This system tended to encourage factionalism within a tribe, even within a band. The focus was on individualism—whether in warfare, religion, or social interactions. A chief's agreement to a treaty, for example, might be binding only for his family. The rest of the tribe could refuse to comply. In warfare, leadership centered around personal influence rather than a command structure, and individual warriors could choose to obey a war chief or not.

Most western Indians exalted warfare, particularly the Plains Indians, and most pursued conflict as a way to exalt the individual brave. A war chief or leader fired up as many warriors as would follow him against an enemy, but the leader did not instruct the warriors once they were in battle. A warrior rode into battle for himself and did not often act in unison with other braves. Acts of bravery were used by an individual to garner prestige and position within his band or tribe. One of the bravest acts was to count *coup*, which referred to touching an

"The Last of His Race" by Frederic Remington captures the perseverance and strong individuality of a lone Native American brave.

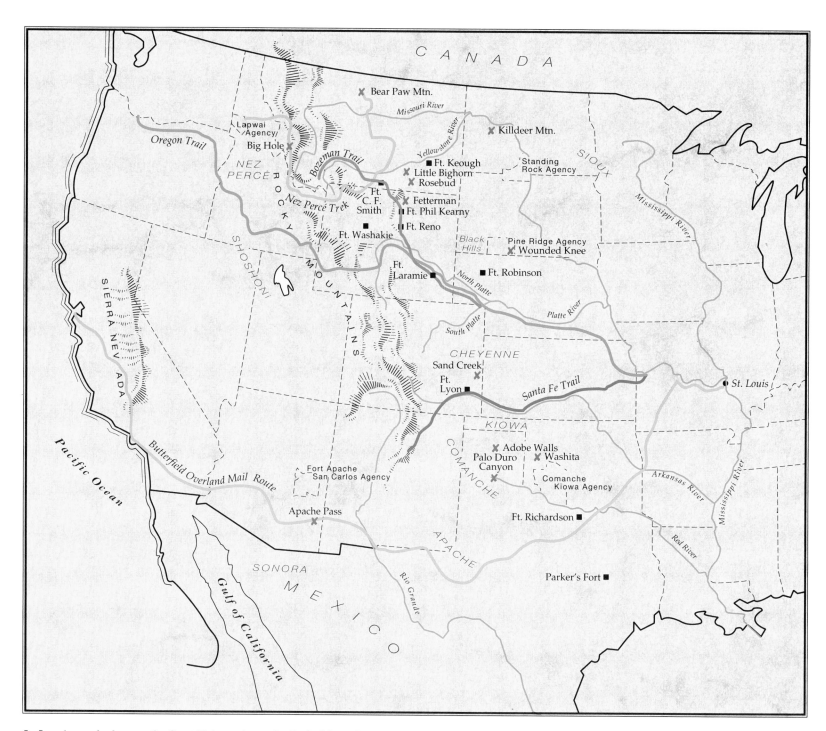

As America pushed across the Great Plains and over the Rocky Mountains, violent confrontations with the indigenous nations served as markers along the westward trails.

enemy while he was alive. This could be done with a gun, bow, lance, or *coup* stick, or even by hand. After touching an enemy, the warrior could then kill him, which garnered additional *coup*.

Intertribal warfare or skirmishing was frequent. Because each nation or tribe saw itself as distinct from others, differences between nations overshadowed any similarities and caused friction. Chronic fighting occurred, for example, in areas where hunting grounds overlapped. Warfare for the Plains and Southwestern Indians consisted of raids and counter raids, in which small groups of around 30 warriors might strike an enemy or plunder their camp for horses. This mode of warfare proved ineffectual against the U.S. Army in the long term,

because the army had the advantages of organization and long-range tactics.

Aside from warfare, the buffalo hunt was the most significant activity for many western tribes, specifically the Plains Indians. Buffalo hunts were communal and generally organized by civil chiefs, who determined when the hunts would occur. More than just a source of food, the buffalo pro-

The traditional hit-and-run tactics used by Comanche Quanah Parker (above left) and Apache Geronimo (left, center) were a viable short-term offense against army patrols but an inadequate defense against sustained U.S. campaigns.

Charles M. Russell's "The Buffalo Hunt No. 39" depicts Plains Indians in pursuit of their single most important resource.

vided all the basic elements of survival, including clothing and shelter. The hide was used to make lodge coverings, beds, or robes; rawhide was used to make moccasins, shields, bags, or pouches; hair was woven into ropes; horns became spoons, cups, and ladles; bones were turned into tools, knives, and game dice. Even the dung was used for fuel. Because of its importance, the buffalo was considered a sacred animal. Its strength was admired, and its spirit praised. Warriors were inspired to take names associated with the buffalo to serve them well in battle.

The mass slaughter of the buffalo by whites, which was sanctioned if not encouraged by the U.S. Army, contributed to the conflict between Native Americans and encroaching whites during the latter part of the 19th century. As they saw the buffalo disappear under the guns of white hunters, the Indians saw their very way of life threatened with extinction.

The conflict in the West was as much a clash of cultures as a physical confrontation, and the results for Native Americans were profound alterations to their way of life as well as political subjugation. Though the latter half of the 19th century brought the greatest changes to the Native American situation, the white man had been inflicting change on the Indians since first arriving on the continent. The introduction and spread of European diseases, for example, had devastating results. The Mandan and Arikara along the Missouri were decimated by smallpox, and other diseases such as tuberculosis, rubella, and syphilis ravaged tribes and nations across North America.

Contact with whites had other effects as well. The competition in the fur trade in the 18th and 19th centuries, for example, intensified hostilities among various Native American groups. Tribes raided other tribes for furs and hides to trade for alcohol and manufactured goods from the white man. White advancement also crowded Native American tribes into the homelands and hunting grounds of other tribes, resulting in warfare.

By the time of this photo in 1887, the cultures of virtually all western Indians had been redefined.

Of all the changes from contact with whites, the most profound for the western Indians were probably brought by the introduction of the horse and the gun. The Spanish brought horses to the Rio Grande area during the 1500s. Over the course of time, some escaped, some were stolen, while others were turned loose by the Spaniards. By the mid-18th century, many of the western Indians owned huge herds of horses and had become great horsemen. Called sky dogs, big dogs, god dogs, or medicine dogs by various tribes, horses replaced dogs as beasts of burden.

They also gave the Native American great mobility, which became the foundation for the buffalo-hunting culture of the Plains Indians.

With horses, the Plains nations turned away from being marginal farmers to become nomadic hunters, following the big herds of buffalo and embracing a whole new way of life. The mounted Plains Indians became mobile and fierce, reveling in the hunt for game and the charge against an enemy. With horses, tribes gathered surpluses of hides and game, they packed up and moved their

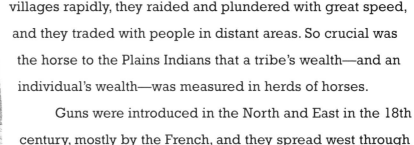

The horse allowed Plains Indians to develop a nomadic lifestyle based on expanded hunting, raiding, and trading.

villages rapidly, they raided and plundered with great speed, and they traded with people in distant areas. So crucial was the horse to the Plains Indians that a tribe's wealth—and an individual's wealth—was measured in herds of horses.

Guns were introduced in the North and East in the 18th century, mostly by the French, and they spread west through trade and warfare. The first whites to regularly appear in Native American villages were probably traders, who offered manufactured goods, including guns, as trade items. The adoption of guns by Native Americans made them dependent on whites in a way they had not been before because they needed powder and lead to make full use of these weapons. Indians grew dependent on trading for alcohol and other manufactured goods as well, which altered their material culture to some degree.

Thus, in the first half of the 19th century, when the western Indians began to encounter explorers, traders, and mountain men on a regular basis, they were not altogether unfriendly. And they were tolerant when the first emigrant wagon trains lumbered across their homelands. That tolerance soon faded.

By mid-century, several events occurred that prompted the sudden expansion of the United States. Texas was annexed in 1845, California and the Southwest were seized during the Mexican War, and the Pacific Northwest was added when a boundary dispute over the Oregon Territory was settled with

Great Britain. The floodgates were opened in 1848 when the gold rush lured thousands of fortune seekers over Native American homelands and hunting grounds to California. The suddenness of U.S. expansion set off a course of

confrontation and conflict between whites and western Indians that erupted into the Indian Wars during the latter half of the 19th century. The culmination of that course was the Battle of Wounded Knee in 1890, in which a band of Sioux men, women, and children were summarily shot by U.S. cavalrymen. After Wounded Knee, all Native American nations and tribes were subjugated to reservation life.

This 1885 drawing depicts the remnants of the Nez Percé being returned to their Northwest homeland after a forced relocation to the southern plains.

If many of the stories handed down about the conflict between Native Americans and the white man in the West have been told from a white point of view, then what of the Indian perspective? In 1877, as Crazy Horse lay on his deathbed, he spoke these words:

"We had buffalo for food, and their hides for clothing and our tepees. We preferred hunting to a life of idleness on the reservations, where we were driven against our will. At times we did not get enough to eat, and we were not allowed to leave the reservation to hunt.

"We preferred our own way of living. We were no expense to the government then. All we wanted was peace and to be left alone. Soldiers were sent out in the winter, who destroyed our villages. Then 'Long Hair' [Custer] came in the same way. They say we massacred him, but he would have done the same to us had we not defended ourselves and fought to the last. . . . I have spoken."

SITTING
BULL

1831?—1890

"**I** hate all white people. You are thieves and liars. You have taken away our land and made us outcasts." This hard-bitten view was expressed by an uncompromising Sioux war chief and medicine man called Tatanka Iyotake—Sitting Bull.

His father, a mystic and warrior named Returns-Again, had originally named the boy Slow because his habits were so deliberate. Born around 1831 near South Dakota's Grand River, the young Hunkpapa Sioux developed his own intimate association with the spirit world. He became devoutly religious, with the soul of a prophet, but he also possessed the ferocious instincts of a warrior and the leadership gifts of a general.

The Hunkpapa, a part of the Teton division of Sioux, were unsurpassed as fighting men. Slow grew up lusting for the prestige and honors of a warrior. When he was 14, he accompanied a war party who encountered a band of Crows. Slow raced ahead on his horse, rode over a Crow brave, and counted first *coup*, establishing himself as a warrior.

On the battlefield and at the negotiating table, Sitting Bull led the Hunkpapa Sioux in their fight to remain free.

His father, who had renamed himself Sitting Bull because of a dream, immediately gave the name to his only son.

Subsequent raids proved young Sitting Bull to be a daring warrior, and he was admitted to the elite military society, Strong Hearts. While his prowess as a warrior grew, he also developed a reputation as a visionary. His special ties to the spirit world were said to bring him guidance and insight into the future.

His exploits and engaging personality eventually brought him nine wives, several taken from other warriors, which was an accepted custom. It is notable that none of his wives were taken from Sitting Bull. He fathered at least nine children.

During an 1856 battle with Crows, Sitting Bull dueled with a chief who shot him in the left foot. Despite the injury, Sitting Bull felled the Crow leader with a ball from his muzzle loader and then limped forward to finish him with his knife. This impressive display of courage sent the other Crows galloping away from the battlefield.

Witnessed by 100 Hunkpapa warriors, the incident helped establish Sitting Bull as leader of the Strong Hearts, a position that included the responsibility of organizing buffalo hunts for his people. This responsibility proved to be a major one, as his tribe required as many as 30,000 buffalo each year. Sitting Bull's permanent limp from his encounter with the Crows was a constant reminder of his bravery in battle, and within a few years he became chief of the Hunkpapa.

Sitting Bull was a staunch opponent of the whites. He observed their unstoppable movement onto the lands of other tribes, and he sensed the danger of any contact between his people and whites. He began his lifelong struggle against the white man in 1863, skirmishing with soldiers of General H. H. Sibley who had attacked his hunting party.

Over the next two years, he frequently fought against American soldiers, and the fame of Sitting Bull as a war chief grew rapidly. He directed the Sioux in the Battle of Killdeer Mountain on July 28, 1864. With 2,000 men and eight artillery pieces, General Alfred Sully held the braves at bay.

Later that summer, during a brief clash with 600 of Sully's men, Sitting Bull was wounded at point-blank range by a soldier on foot. The pistol ball entered at his left hip and exited at the small of his back, but the chief stayed on his horse and galloped to safety. Sitting Bull scorned Sully's invitations to talk peace, and in September 1865, he and 400 warriors relentlessly badgered a 2,000-man column under Colonel Nelson Cole and Lieutenant Colonel Samuel Walker.

Feeling the pressure of the continued interference of the army, the Teton Sioux decided to coordinate their tribes under one chief.

Sitting Bull was the overwhelming choice for this unprecedented position. The chief began a campaign of harrassment against Fort Buford, a stockaded fort recently built in North Dakota. His warriors stole cattle and horses and picked off a few soldiers in skirmishes. When the sawmill at the fort was completed, Sitting Bull led a

When Sitting Bull surrendered at Fort Buford, the number of his followers had been reduced to less than 200, including these members of his family.

raiding party, stole the circular blade, and used it for a tom-tom.

The Hunkpapas were troubled by other Native American nations as well as by the encroaching whites. Late in 1869, 30 Crows killed a young Hunkpapa hunter, and Sitting Bull promptly led 100 warriors through the snow in pursuit. The Crows forted up at a rocky knoll now called Crow Rock, Montana, and conducted a fierce defense. The Hunkpapas overwhelmed the Crows and wiped them out in hand-to-hand fighting, but 13 Hunkpapa warriors died and 18 more were wounded. Sitting Bull counted three *coups*, adding to the total of 63 that he accumulated in his active years as a warrior.

Not long afterward, Sitting Bull directed an attack on a Flathead village on the Musselshell River. A small party of young braves drew 100 Flathead warriors in pursuit, whereupon 400 Hunkpapas launched an ambush that routed the surprised and outnumbered Flatheads. While leading a charge, Sitting Bull took either an arrow shaft or a bullet through his arm, adding to his honors.

Late in 1875, all the Sioux were ordered by the government to report to the reservation by the end of January 1876. Sitting Bull ignored the reservation directive. He was already angry that gold prospectors had been swarming into the sacred Black Hills, which had been promised permanently to the Sioux by treaty. A week after the deadline, the War Department was notified that Sitting Bull was hostile and should be dealt with by force.

Sitting Bull sent messengers to the Sioux, Arapaho, and Cheyenne, including bands living on reservations. He urged them to unite against the white threat. More than 10,000 Native Americans gathered, and with Sitting Bull's spiritual power and courage widely recognized, he was chosen war chief of all the camps combined. Three columns of soldiers converged on the northern plains. "We must stand together or they will kill us separately," counseled Sitting Bull. "These soldiers have come shooting; they want war. All right, we'll give it to them."

Sitting Bull did his best to arm his warriors, although at least half had no guns, and most of the firearms were obsolete. To provide numerous mounts for his unprecedented number of warriors, Sitting Bull sent small parties of young braves in search of horses to steal. "Listen, young men," he directed. "Spare nobody. If you meet anyone, kill him, and take his horse. Let no one live. Save *nothing!*"

Enormous organizational skills were required to keep more than 10,000 people and their animals fed and watered, and the huge camp had to be moved to new pasturage every few days. Sitting Bull presided over these demanding activities with his usual affable authority, though he radiated a fearful sense of purpose.

In preparation for the coming conflict, Sitting Bull underwent a ceremony. Each of his arms were sliced 50 times from wrist to shoulder. He then rose, blood dripping from his arms, and performed the sun-gazing dance, in which he stared all day into the sun as he chanted. The ceremony continued through the night and into the next day until Sitting Bull collapsed. During the ordeal, he received a vision of a great victory by his people over the whites.

On the evening of June 16, 1876, scouts rode into camp with reports that the nearby valley of the Rosebud River was filled with soldiers. General George Crook, at the head of 1,300 men, was on the march to make first contact with the rebellious Native Americans. A vanguard of warriors equaling Crook's numbers quickly assembled and rode through the darkness to the Rosebud. Having endured the bloodletting ritual three days earlier, Sitting Bull was too weak to take an active part in the fighting on June 17. Crazy Horse of the Oglala Sioux was the most prominent leader during the six-hour Battle of the Rosebud. When the Native Americans finally withdrew, perhaps hoping to lure the soldiers into an ambush, the fighting ended with nine dead troopers and 21 more wounded. Crook was so stunned by the unexpected size of the resistance that he went into camp for two months.

Sitting Bull's powerful dream had revealed great numbers of soldiers falling, but the limited casualties at the Rosebud did not seem to be the fulfillment of his vision. The big Native American camp was

Sitting Bull declined Buffalo Bill's offer to join a tour to England in 1887. Sitting Bull said that it was "bad for me to parade around" when there were negotiations to be settled regarding Sioux lands.

moved to promising hunting grounds along the Little Bighorn River. Sitting Bull was still expecting a major victory.

On June 25, Lieutenant Colonel George Armstrong Custer led his 7th Cavalry in search of the encampment. First, Major Marcus Reno and two companies crossed the Little Bighorn and attacked the southern end of the camp. Sitting Bull buckled on his cartridge belt, seized his .45 revolver and 1873 Winchester carbine, and mounted a black war pony.

Vast numbers of warriors also armed themselves and mounted war horses, and Reno's advance was checked, then thrown back into the river. As these desperately outnumbered soldiers were about to be overwhelmed, Custer approached the middle of the Indian encampment with five companies. While a few warriors stayed on the southern end of the camp to hold the ford, the mass of braves galloped to counter this new threat. As many as 3,000 armed braves battled Custer's 215 troopers, and within an hour, the so-called "last stand" ended with the death of all of Custer's soldiers. By this time, Reno's companies had been joined by others, and they dug in to present a determined defense.

Sitting Bull moved the Hunkpapa camp downriver, away from the bloating corpses of Reno's men and horses. He and his warriors then rode toward the defensive position, with the chief himself participating in some of the charges. After engaging in some sniping throughout the night, the warriors resumed fighting the next day. Yet Sitting Bull did not organize an all-out assault, feeling that enough of his braves had fallen. The victory was already enormous, with

more than 200 soldiers dead and many guns and horses captured. As another column of soldiers advanced from the north, the Native American camp was moved. A few days later, a new camp was set in the Bighorn Mountains, and a victory dance was held.

Eventually, the triumph over Custer proved hollow as hordes of soldiers descended upon the Native Americans, defeating almost all the nations by policy as well as by the gun. The murderous efforts of the buffalo hunters destroyed the Native Americans' major food source, a factor that aided the military in rapidly driving bands onto the reservations.

Sitting Bull fought to keep his Hunkpapas free. He engaged in unproductive conferences with Colonel Nelson A. Miles, and then fought the soldiers for two days before artillery fire sent the warriors into retreat. Miles pursued and forced the surrender of 2,000 Sioux, but Sitting Bull escaped with 400 Hunkpapas.

Top: Sitting Bull places a stone on a pedestal during ceremonies at the Standing Rock Reservation. **Bottom:** The Sioux police guard was sent to arrest Sitting Bull in December 1890.

In May 1877, Sitting Bull crossed the border into Canada. The Canadian government refused to assume responsibility for the Indians and urged the United States to persuade Sitting Bull to return. Sitting Bull refused to leave, though hunting was poor in Canada. When his band dwindled to less than 200 ragged followers, he reluctantly submitted to United States authority. Surrendering at Fort Buford on July 19, 1881, he was confined as a prisoner of war for two years, then released to the Standing Rock Indian Agency.

Lionized by the American populace as a legend of the Wild West, Sitting Bull made some public appearances and even traveled with Buffalo Bill Cody during the showman's 1885 tour. He wrestled unsatisfactorily with the government over the sale of traditional tribal territories. When a newspaperman asked him how Indians felt about giving up their lands, Sitting Bull growled contemptuously, "Indians! There are no Indians left but me!"

When the mystical Ghost Dance craze spread through the reservations, Sitting Bull refused to embrace the new religion. Despite his lack of interest, authorities ordered that he be taken into custody. They were concerned about the restlessness of the Native Americans under their charge and realized the influence a man of Sitting Bull's stature might have on them. Sioux policemen surrounded his cabin on December 14, 1890, but the chief's followers swarmed to his support. Fighting erupted, and there were a dozen casualities. Among them was Sitting Bull, shot through the torso and head by the Sioux police. He was buried in the military cemetery at Fort Yates, his coffin filled with quicklime. It was an end that the greatest of Sioux chieftains would have expected from his white enemies.

THE GHOST DANCE

As Native Americans faced cultural eradication, mystical religions that blended native beliefs and Christian-like concepts developed. Among those messianic movements was the Ghost Dance, a nonviolent cult inspired by a Paiute named Wavoka in the 1880s. Ghost Dance followers prayed, chanted, and danced to bring the return of the old world, in which dead relatives would come back, and the land would return to its original state—with the buffalo but without the white man.

Wovoka's message spread among several nations, including the Sioux, Arapaho, and Cheyenne. As it spread, the Ghost Dance took on added mysticism and its peaceful message was downplayed. White government agents near the Sioux reservations misinterpreted the religion and feared it might incite rebellion—a volatile situation that indirectly led to the Battle of Wounded Knee.

Wovoka prescribed nonviolence, ceremonial purification, and abstinance from alcohol for the followers of his religion, which whites called the Ghost Dance.

CRAZY HORSE

1841?–1877

Daring, aggressive, and courageous, Crazy Horse led devastating attacks against Sioux enemies and defended his lifestyle with fierce heroism.

Born most likely in the fall of 1841, Crazy Horse was first called Curly or Light-Haired

A work in progress, the Crazy Horse monument in South Dakota was designed by Korczak Ziolkowski. No known photos of Crazy Horse exist.

Boy. His mother was a sister of Spotted Tail, who became a magnificent warrior chief. His father was named Crazy Horse, a respected medicine man of the Hunkpatila band of the Oglala Sioux. Curly's hair and complexion were lighter than those of other Native Americans, although his eyes were black. He was a quiet boy, but he eagerly participated in the training activities that prepared young men for war.

Curly was out of camp on September 3, 1855, when a large column led by General William S. Harney launched an attack. Harney's assault on the Sioux encampment left 86 dead. Many of the casualties were women and children. Harney also marched off with 70 female captives. Stunned at the slaughter of his friends and relatives, Curly became a staunch foe of white men.

In 1858, Curly rode with a war party against an Arapaho village in central Wyoming. A small band of Arapaho warriors forted up behind some boulders on a hill and stood off the Sioux for a couple of hours. Suddenly, Curly's fighting qualities possessed him, and the youthful brave rode his pony at the Arapaho position. As their arrows whizzed by him, he counted *coup* on two Arapaho before pulling back. Twice more he charged the enemy, and when two warriors rode out to challenge him, he killed them both with arrows. When he dismounted to scalp the fallen braves, another Arapaho fired an arrow into his leg, but he managed to limp to safety.

At the victory dance celebrating his feat, Crazy Horse proudly gave Curly a new name—his own. Crazy Horse was a common name among the Sioux, but in more than two decades of valiant deeds, the fearless brave made it his own. The name came to symbolize the proud courage of the Native Americans of the last days of the Old West.

THE SIOUX

Fierce warriors and masters of their lands, the Sioux represent the prototype of the Plains Indians, and indeed of Native Americans in general.

The Sioux nation consists of three subgroups, the Eastern or Santee group, the Central or Yankton group, and the Western or Teton group. The word Sioux can be traced back to the Chippewa word for the tribe, *nadowe-is-iw*, which means adders, or enemies. This term was then corrupted by French *voyageurs* into *nadoues-sioux*. While Sioux remains the popular designation of this nation, the word Dakota, which is Siouan for allies, is a more correct term. In the Santee dialect, the tribe referred to itself as the Dakota. In the Teton dialect, it was the Lakota, while in the Yankton dialect, it was the Nakota. The name the Sioux nation used to refer to themselves was *Ocheti shakowin,* which means the seven council fires.

The aboriginal homelands of the once agricultural Sioux were the forests east of the Mississippi River. Conflict with other Native American nations, particularly the Chippewa, resulted in the migration of some of the Sioux sub-groups across the Mississippi. Once settled on the Plains, the Sioux turned away from agriculture. When they acquired horses, they became master buffalo hunters, gallant horsemen, and bold warriors.

Like other Plains Indians, the Sioux lived in tepees, or *tipis* (a Dakota word). Within Sioux tribes or divisions, a number of societies existed that performed various functions. Military societies performed policing duties and presided over the buffalo hunts; other societies were shamanistic. Men acquired prominence within their tribe by committing brave acts during warfare.

The most westward-dwelling and largest subgroup of the Sioux was the Teton. It consisted of several divisions: Brulé, Hunkpapa, Minniconjou, Oglala, Two Kettle, San Arcs, and Blackfoot (no relation to the Blackfoot nation). The wealth built up by the Teton in terms of fine horses as well as stores of food and hides to trade resulted in the Teton becoming the most powerful of the Sioux and thus the principal threat to whites. From the Teton came the Sioux's great leaders—Sitting Bull, Crazy Horse, and Red Cloud.

A Dakota couple stands outside their tepee. Covered in buffalo hide, it was waterproof, easily transportable, and well ventilated.

THE OTHER SIDE
OF THE STORY

Native Americans had their own stories to tell in regard to the Sioux campaign of 1876 and the Battle of the Little Bighorn. In drawings and in first-person accounts, warriors who participated in the fighting that summer offer different points of view. Skirmishes never reported in U.S. military accounts are detailed in Cheyenne drawings, for example, while some Sioux depictions of the Little Bighorn mention no last stand or offer any focus on Custer.

Flying Hawk was an Oglala Sioux warrior who participated in the Battle of the Little Bighorn when he was 24 years old. Sitting Bull was his uncle by marriage, and Crazy Horse was his cousin and best friend. Sometime during the 1920s, Flying Hawk dictated his version of Custer's last stand.

"When we got them [the soldiers] surrounded the fight was over in one hour. There was so much dust we could not see much, but the Indians rode around and yelled the war-whoop and shot into the soldiers so fast as they could until they were all dead. . . . We got off our horses and went and took the rings and money and watches from the soldiers. We took some clothes off too, and all the guns and pistols. Then we went back to the women and children and got them together that were not killed or hurt. . . . It was a big fight; the soldiers got just what they deserved this time. No good soldiers would shoot into the Indian's tepee where there were women and children. These soldiers did, and we fought them for our women and children. White men would do the same if they were men."

The introspective Crazy Horse joined a medicine society called the Thunder Cult, and he regularly sought visions. His mystical side fueled his warrior's instincts with confidence and dedication.

In 1865, Crazy Horse, who had counted a total of 240 *coups* by this point, was selected as one of four new chiefs by the Oglalas. Almost immediately, he assumed a prominent role under Sitting Bull in the harassing of a 2,000-man column of soldiers led by Colonel Nelson Cole and Lieutenant Colonel Samuel Walker. A year later, he played an even larger role in Red Cloud's War, which was a massive campaign against army possession of the Bozeman Trail.

During a fight near Fort Phil Kearny on December 6, 1866, Crazy Horse initiated an ambush by dismounting within sight of a detachment of soldiers, who eagerly charged the vulnerable warrior. Suddenly, other braves materialized to ambush the soldiers, killing two and wounding five others. This aggressive but impulsive reaction convinced Crazy Horse, Red Cloud, and other chiefs that a major force could be lured out of the fort and into a fatal trap.

On the frigid morning of December 21, 2,000 warriors concealed themselves on both sides of the road north of Fort Phil Kearny where the Bozeman Trail descended down a ridge to Peno Creek. A diversionary attack on a wood-cutting party drew a company of soldiers from the fort. Then, Crazy Horse and his party of ten decoys—two Cheyenne warriors, two Arapaho, and two each from the Oglala, Brulé, and Minniconjou Sioux—appeared within view of the post. An artillery round sent the decoys scrambling as though frightened, and Captain William J. Fetterman marched out with 80 cavalrymen and infantrymen.

Egotistical and scornful of Native Americans, Fetterman once snorted, "With 80 men I could ride through the Sioux nation." With fatal irony, he pursued the decoys with 80 men, defying orders by plunging out of sight of the fort. Concealed braves launched a barrage of 40,000 arrows and charged against a desperate defense. All 81 soldiers were slain and mutilated. Until the Battle of the Little Bighorn, the Fetterman Massacre was the army's worst defeat in the West.

On August 2, 1867, Crazy Horse led decoys against a group of woodcutters near Fort Phil Kearny. The soldiers were armed with new breechloaders and remained inside a barricade of wagon beds, successfully repelling an enormous war party during more than four hours of combat. Soon after this Wagon Box Fight, Crazy Horse was made war chief of the Oglalas.

Crazy Horse tried unsuccessfully to decoy George Armstrong Custer and his 7th Cavalry into traps during a Montana expedition in 1873. Custer's soldiers were too well disciplined to be ensnared, but during a skirmish, Custer's horse was shot out from under him.

In 1876, the army sent three large columns against unsubmissive Sioux and Cheyenne. The first clash occurred on June 17, 1876, at Montana's Rosebud River, where General George Crook's column of 1,300 men met an Indian force of approximately the same size masterfully led by Crazy Horse. Crazy Horse kept the soldiers off balance with a series of attacks and counterattacks, sending Crook back into camp for nearly two months. Eight days later, on June 25, Crazy Horse rode into combat against Custer's 7th, providing inspired leadership during the most famous battle of the Indian Wars.

These triumphs proved empty as the buffalo—the Plains Indians' major source of food—soon disappeared from the prairies. By 1877, Crazy Horse was forced to bring his starving people onto the reservation, after battling Nelson A. Miles, Ranald Mackenzie, and other noted soldiers. Assigned to the Nebraska reservation at Fort Robinson, Crazy Horse was constantly under watch as a potential escapee. On September 5, 1877, he

This illustration from *Leslie's Illustrated Newspaper* depicts Crazy Horse leading the Sioux to a reservation in 1877.

was arrested. When he realized he was to be confined in Fort Robinson's guardhouse, he went for a knife. Seized from behind, the valiant warrior was bayoneted through the kidney, and he died that night. His parents buried their 36-year-old son in a secret place.

For more than two decades, Crazy Horse had ridden as a Sioux warrior, counting hundreds of *coups*. He fought Crows, Shoshonis, and the white soldiers, leading his warriors with devastating skill in the West's largest conflict between the army and Native Americans.

BLACK
KETTLE

1803?–1868

"Although wrongs have been done me I live in hopes," reflected Cheyenne Chief Black Kettle with what proved to be tragically false optimism. No western chief lived in more consistent hope of maintaining peaceful relations with whites—and no chief suffered deeper wrongs. More than most of the stories of white encroachment, the tale of Black Kettle illustrates the tragic consequences of the white man's policies and prejudices.

Born around 1803 near the Black Hills, Chief Black Kettle (Moke-ta-ve-to) perceived the enormous power of the white man and was determined to avoid conflict for the good of his people. Whenever white soldiers or hunters arrived in large numbers near his camp in southeastern Colorado, Black Kettle moved his camp to avoid any possibility of hostilities. Government officials once presented Black Kettle with an enormous United States flag, and he proudly flew it from a pole above his tepee.

On May 16, 1864, about 100 Colorado Volunteers operating in Kansas initiated an unprovoked fight by gunning down Chief Lean Bear and two other Cheyenne. Warriors in the vicinity numbered at least 500. As large numbers arrived at the scene, the soldiers hastily withdrew toward Fort Larned.

Black Kettle, who sought early accommodation of the white man, is depicted in this drawing by John Metcalf.

Black Kettle rode among his warriors, restraining them from a general assault that might have destroyed the volunteers.

Black Kettle consulted with his old friend, William Bent, who had built Bent's Fort. Bent told Black Kettle that Colonel John M. Chivington of Denver had ordered his Colorado Volunteers to attack and kill the Cheyenne. "It is not my intention or wish to fight the whites," asserted Black Kettle.

Bent went to Fort Lyon, Colorado, to tell Chivington that the Cheyenne did not want to fight. Chivington, however, insisted that Black Kettle was "on the warpath" and that "the citizens would have to protect themselves." Called the Fighting Parson, Chivington had been a Methodist minister since 1844. When the Civil War erupted, he declined a chaplaincy in favor of a fighting commission, becoming something of a military hero. Back in Colorado, he organized nearly 1,000 volunteers who were eager to wage war against mostly peaceful Indians. He urged the killing and scalping of all Indians, even babies. "Nits make lice!" he crudely explained.

In 1864, Colorado's territorial governor, John Evans, officially announced that the war against hostiles would continue. A circular was printed ordering any Native Americans who wished to remain at peace to come to the reservation at Fort Lyon. The Cheyenne and Arapaho were spread across the plains engaging in their summer hunts. It was weeks before runners delivered the circulars to the scattered bands. The Indians' delay in responding to the circular made it appear they were defying the order. During this period, military campaigns against the Sioux in the north sent Sioux war parties on the rampage against whites. The Cheyenne and Arapaho were blamed for a number of Sioux raids, further inflaming sentiment against them.

In September 1864, the commander of Fort Lyon, Major Edmond W. Wynkoop, led a mounted column of 127 men toward Black Kettle's camp at the headwaters of the Smoky Hill River. Several hundred warriors galloped out to meet the badly outnumbered soldiers. Once again, Black Kettle and other chiefs managed to restrain the warriors from attacking.

Black Kettle established his camp on Sand Creek, about 40 miles northeast of Fort Lyon, while an Arapaho band moved their camp to the fort. Major Wynkoop was considered too friendly to the Indians and was removed from command of the fort. Meanwhile, support swelled in Colorado for Chivington's most recent order to the volunteers: "Kill all the Indians you come across."

Chivington prepared for a dawn attack at Sand Creek on November 29, 1864. Black Kettle's tepee was in the middle of the camp.

The warriors were away on a hunt, leaving about 600 women, children, and old men in the camp. When the soldiers were discovered, Black Kettle raised his big United States flag, then a white flag of surrender. Hundreds of his people gathered around Black Kettle, who assured them they were safe. Elderly Chief White Antelope walked toward the white men, holding up his hands and shouting in English, "Stop! Stop!" White Antelope was gunned down, and the volunteers, many of whom had been drinking heavily during their night march, opened a general fire. Ignoring Black Kettle's flags, the volunteers advanced, and the Indians fled. Black Kettle's wife was badly wounded, but the chief escaped up a ravine. Nine white men were killed and 38 were wounded, mostly by their own fire. Chivington reported that 400 to 500 warriors were slain, but in actuality 105 Cheyenne women and children were killed along with 28 men.

Left: This wanted poster calls for men to join the Colorado Volunteers a few months before the Sand Creek Massacre. **Below:** Robert Lindneux's 1936 painting depicts the *Sand Creek Battle*.

THE
CHEYENNE

Powerful and athletic, the Cheyenne were noted for their bravery as warriors. One of the major Plains nations, they called themselves *Dzitsi'stas*, meaning our people. The word Cheyenne comes from a Teton Sioux word, *Shahiyena*, meaning People of Alien Speech.

The Cheyenne originally lived in the dense evergreen forests of Minnesota. During their early years at the western end of the Great Lakes, they cultivated corn, beans, and other crops native to the area. Like other woodland nations in the region, the Cheyenne were eventually driven out of their traditional homelands by neighboring nations pushing westward. The Cheyenne were forced into what is now eastern North Dakota, then later settled along the Missouri River by the Mandan and Arikara

Before adopting their nomadic life on the Great Plains, the Cheyenne had lived in permanent villages of round earthen lodges.

nations. Additional pressure from the East, this time by the Sioux, eventually drove them farther west, into the Black Hills and along the headwaters of the Missouri River.

Once they settled on the Plains in the 18th century, the Cheyenne changed their lifestyle. They adopted a horse-mounted, buffalo-hunting economy, much like the rest of the northern Great Plains tribes. They became nomadic tepee-builders

who transported their furnishings and stores on horses as they searched for bison.

The Cheyenne nation was organized into ten major bands governed by 44 chiefs and seven military societies. There were also social, medicine, dance, and shamanistic societies. Of the military societies, the Dog Soldiers proved to be the most aggressive.

Some whites misconstrued this term and erroneously referred to all Cheyennes as dog soldiers, assuming the word Cheyenne to have come from the French word for dog, *chien*.

In the 1830s, the Cheyenne people split into two groups. Some remained in the northern plains while the others drifted south to the headwaters of the Arkansas River, where they became known as the Southern Cheyenne. Under the leadership of Black Kettle, members of this group were massacred at Sand Creek, Colorado, in November 1864.

The Northern Cheyenne—those who remained in Montana and Wyoming—became allies with their old enemies, the Sioux. They played a major role in harassing the United States Army along the Bozeman Trail and participated in Custer's defeat at the Little Bighorn.

cause of drunkenness, cowardice, and a lack of discipline, the volunteers let the majority escape. However, an orgy of mutilation ensued against the dead.

After dark, Black Kettle returned and found his wife. She was still alive, despite being shot nine times. The chief carried her out on his back.

The warriors lusted for revenge, and an alliance of Cheyenne, Arapaho, and Sioux began conducting raids on whites. This belligerent majority moved north to the more secure land of the Sioux, but Black Kettle refused to follow this war trail. A group of about 80 Cheyenne consisting mostly of women, old men, and wounded warriors moved with Black Kettle south of the Arkansas River. There they leagued with Southern Arapaho, Kiowa, and Comanche.

Chivington resigned his commission. A government investigation condemned his action, and he spent the rest of his life trying to evade the stigma of the Sand Creek Massacre. Government officials sought out Black Kettle and arranged a meeting at the mouth of the Little Arkansas in Kansas in October 1865. The commissioners expressed sorrow over the Sand Creek tragedy but stated that settlers now claimed Cheyenne lands in Colorado. A new treaty was proposed by which the Cheyenne and Arapaho would live south of the Arkansas in perpetual peace. "We have all lost our way," said Black Kettle sadly. Still, he determined on a course of peace.

The white man permitted Black Kettle to live only three more years. In 1867, Black Kettle was the first of 14 Cheyenne chiefs to sign the Medicine Lodge Treaty, in which the Cheyenne and Arapaho were granted a combined reservation in Indian Territory. He faithfully maintained his agreements while

other bands waged war. General Phil Sheridan launched a winter campaign to force all the Cheyenne and Arapaho onto a reservation around Fort Cobb in Indian Territory. Sheridan's favorite officer, Lieutenant Colonel George Armstrong Custer, led the 7th Cavalry toward a village that scouts had discovered on the Washita River. Custer orga-

No firm agreements were reached between U.S. Army representatives and Kiowa, Arapaho, and Cheyenne leaders when they convened in September 1864 at Camp Weld. Black Kettle is seated third from the left.

nized an attack from all sides for the frigid dawn of November 17, 1868.

The village was Black Kettle's. When the soldiers charged, Black Kettle immediately fired a warning shot, hoping to avoid another passive Sand Creek disaster. He leaped onto a horse, pulled his wife up behind him, then headed out of camp. Cavalrymen shot Black Kettle and his wife off their horse, and both were killed. In all, 103 Cheyennes were brutally slain—only 11 of them warriors—and 53 women and children were captured.

No chief west of the Mississippi was more committed to peace with the white man than Black Kettle, but he was victimized by two of the most murderous tragedies ever perpetrated upon Native Americans.

CHIEF
JOSEPH

1840–1904

"From where the sun now stands, I will fight no more forever." Chief Joseph pronounced these oft-quoted words in 1877, at the climax of an epic campaign in which his Nez Percé battled the U.S. Army with such skill and unity that they won the admiration of everyone familiar with the history of the West.

During the first half of the 19th century, the Nez Percé, whose homeland was the Pacific Northwest, had traded with fur trappers and had proven open to the Christian missionaries. An important convert was Tuekakas, later called Old Chief Joseph, a noted leader, warrior, and hunter of the southerly Wallowa band of the Nez Percé. Baptized shortly after a mission was founded at Lapwai in 1836, he was christened Joseph and in 1838 made a deacon. A disagreement with Lapwai Nez Percé leaders in 1846 triggered his move to the beautiful Wallowa Mountains.

The chief's son was born in 1840 and named Hin-mah-too-yah-lat-kekt, which means Thunder Rolling Down From the Mountains, but he was also called Joseph. He proved to be wise beyond his years, becoming a gifted orator and diplomat. His younger brother, Olikut, distinguished himself as a hunter and warrior.

In 1863, the government tried to impose on the Wallowa band a treaty signed by some of the Nez Percé leaders but not by Old Chief Joseph. Angered, the aging chief destroyed his United States flag and Bible, then tried to negotiate a just agreement that would not deny his small band their Wallowa home. The old chief's health began to fail, but Joseph the Younger ably represented the band. When Old Chief Joseph died in 1871, Joseph the Younger was elected chief even though he was only 31. Chief Joseph skillfully countered government efforts to move the southerly bands for the next six years.

Though the nontreaty Nez Percé were not legally bound to the 1863 agreement, the Indian agent wanted them at Lapwai Reservation under his supervision. In addition, the governor of Oregon coveted their lands for white settlers. In May 1877, General O. O. Howard, under instructions from the Commissioner of Indian Affairs and General William T. Sherman, gave the nontreaty bands 30 days to move onto reservation lands.

Several chiefs wanted to resist, but Chief Joseph persuaded the other leaders to comply rather than risk war. Gathering as much of their livestock as possible, the Wallowa band hastily moved to a campsite near the Lapwai Reservation. But a small party of hot-blooded young braves from other Nez

Chief Joseph remained resolute in his dealings with U.S. officials who wanted to enforce the treaty of 1863.

THE NEZ PERCÉ

The Nez Percé were the largest group of Sahaptian-speaking Indians. When this Native American nation was first encountered by the French, some of them were seen with shell ornamentation in their pierced noses (*nez percé*). Captain William Clark of the Lewis and Clark Expedition stumbled upon a Nez Percé village in 1805, becoming the first American to have contact with this group. "They call themselves Cho pun-nish or Pierced Noses," Clark wrote in his journal, despite the fact that nose piercing is not a custom of the tribe.

The Nez Percé lived in what is now western Idaho, northeastern Oregon, and southeastern Washington. Though related by language and culture to those Indian nations native to the Columbia Plateau, they lived just far enough east to be influenced by the Plains Indians. At first, the Nez Percé centered themselves around small villages made up of A-framed communal lodges. The villages were located on rivers or streams filled with salmon, which became their main source of food. There was no leadership above the village level, and each village operated independently.

The ways of the Nez Percé changed dramatically after they acquired horses during the 18th century. Unlike other mounted Native Americans, the Nez Percé became expert horse breeders, specializing in fine Appaloosa ponies. The horse allowed them to hunt buffalo, which became their main source of food, and to trade with nations beyond the Rockies. The organization needed for such activities led to the formation of larger bands and the evolution of a tribal government. Like the Plains Indians, they became tepee dwellers. They also adopted war practices, war dances, and horse tactics from their Plains neighbors.

When the Nez Percé acquired firearms, they became unusually adept marksmen. They sometimes battled war parties of other Indian nations in the traditional style of Plains Indians, but they enjoyed good relations with the white intruders who ventured into their magnificent homeland in the Pacific Northwest in the late 18th century.

The Nez Percé actually consisted of two groups, the Upper and Lower Nez Percé. Each occupied its own land, but they shared common hunting grounds. The U.S. government never fully realized the distinction between the two. When the Upper Nez Percé signed away the lands of both groups in an 1863 treaty, the stage was set for trouble between the whites and all the Nez Percé.

This photo of a Nez Percé tepee at the Yellowstone River was taken in 1871 by William Henry Jackson.

Percé bands went on a raid against offensive white settlers, putting the area into a panic.

General Howard sent for help from all outposts in the region. Captain David Perry led more than 100 troopers to protect settlers at Grangeville, only 15 miles from the camp of Chief Joseph. Adding several cowboy volunteers, Perry confidently rode toward the encampment on White Bird Creek. Perry deployed his men at dawn on June 17, 1877, but six Nez Percé rode out under a white flag. When this peace party was fired upon, Nez Percé marksmen opened fire on the soldiers. Both of the buglers fell, which rendered it impossible for Perry to readily communicate orders. The soldiers were routed, and the Nez Percé pressed their retreat for 18 miles. With 34 men killed and four wounded, Perry lost a third of his command.

Chief Joseph was not a warrior; he was responsible for the camp and stock herds during a battle or conflict. Since he had been the principal Nez Percé spokesman for years, however, General Howard assumed that Joseph was the primary leader. It was Olikut and

When Chief Joseph surrendered, he said, ". . . I am tired; my heart is sick and sad. From where the sun now stands, I will fight no more forever."

warriors from other bands who led the fighting in the ensuing Nez Percé War.

General Howard marched in pursuit of the Nez Percé with 500 men. The five non-treaty bands gathered for an exodus eastward through the mountains, hoping to find allies among the Crows. The Nez Percé mustered fewer than 200 warriors from 700 men, women, and children.

Although encumbered by infants and the elderly, the Nez Percé easily outmaneuvered Howard's column through rugged country. The warriors launched raids against the troopers. On July 11, 1877, Howard finally made contact with the Nez Percé camp at the South Fork of the Clearwater in Idaho Territory. Though the warriors were outnumbered three to one and faced artillery and Gatling guns, they outdueled the soldiers and then slipped away the next day.

After a difficult 11-day trek into Crow country, the Nez Percé found their way blocked by a timber barricade guarded by more than 200 soldiers and volunteers. Somehow, the Nez Percé clambered through where the whites claimed "a goat could not pass," and the barricade was derisively christened Fort Fizzle. The Crows wanted no part of a war against the army, so the Nez Percé found little help from them. Colonel John Gibbon intercepted the Nez Percé at Big Hole, Montana, on August 9. As soldiers charged into the camp, women and children were shot and clubbed. Joseph carried his infant daughter to safety. The warriors quickly counterattacked, enabling the noncombatants and wounded to retreat.

Continuing to outfox various pursuit columns, the tiring Nez Percé turned north toward Canada. Howard desperately sent orders to Colonel Nelson A. Miles at Fort Keough to try to block their path to the border; Miles mobilized eight companies within hours as Howard deliberately delayed his pursuit. Overestimating their safety, the Nez Percé camped at Bear Paw Mountain, a day's ride from the Canadian border. When Miles arrived, the Nez Percé women were taking down the camp. The soldiers hurtled into the camp, but they were repulsed by a counterattack.

The Nez Percé dug in and concentrated their fire on officers, taking a severe toll on army leaders. As a heavy snow fell on the second day, Miles called for a parley. When Chief Joseph came to negotiate, he was treacherously confined. The Nez Percé warriors countered by capturing an officer to exchange for Chief Joseph. When artillery was brought up, the Nez Percé pulled back to the cover of ravines.

By the time Howard arrived on the evening of October 4, Olikut and a majority of the warriors were dead. The next day Joseph surrendered. He delivered a bitter but moving oration that expressed the grief of his people, then turned over 431 Nez Percé, only 79 of whom were men.

Although Chief Joseph had not been a combat leader during the 1,600-mile campaign, abashed army officers and the press portrayed him as a military genius. As the starved and ragged Nez Percé were taken through Bismarck, admiring citizens turned out to cheer and hand out food. The captives were first taken to Kansas, then moved to Indian Territory in 1879. In the unfamiliar climate, large numbers of these mountain Indians sickened and died, including Chief Joseph's infant daughter. Joseph traveled to Washington, D.C., to make eloquent pleas with officials and the press on behalf of his people. Public sympathy finally resulted in the return of 268 surviving Nez Percé to the Northwest in 1885, although only 118 were permitted to rejoin their band on the Lapwai Reservation.

Chief Joseph and the others were placed on the Colville Reservation in Washington Territory, where he died suddenly on September 21, 1904. Prior to his death, he had traveled to Washington, D.C., to ask President Theodore Roosevelt to permit his return to the Wallowa Valley, but he was denied. Joseph reflected, "I have asked some of the great white chiefs where they get the authority to say to the Indian that he shall stay in one place. They cannot tell me."

This illustration from *Leslie's Illustrated Newspaper* depicts Colonel Nelson Miles's charge against the Nez Percé at Bear Paw Mountain.

WASHAKIE

1804?—1900

When Chief Washakie was at least 70, younger pretenders attempted to depose him as too old to lead his band of Eastern Shoshonis. Washakie left for two months, and when he returned from a solitary warpath, he produced six scalps as a testimony to his remaining ferocity. "Let him who would take my place count as many scalps," challenged the old chief belligerently. Little wonder that his enemies regarded him as the most dangerous of all war leaders.

Washakie's people camp in the Wind River Mountains in Wyoming. The Eastern Shoshoni adopted a typical Plains economy, hunting buffalo and living in tepees.

Washakie may have been a fierce warrior, but he made perhaps his greatest contributions to his people through his skills in diplomacy and historical foresight. It was he who decided that the Shoshonis would cooperate with rather than fight against the white man. In doing so, he secured for his people a rich and stable homeland at a time when most other nations were being corralled onto untenable reservation lands.

Washakie was not the first Shoshoni to help the white man. Sacajawea, who helped guide Lewis and Clark, was herself a Shoshoni.

Smells of Sugar—his boyhood name— was born around 1804 among his father's people, the Flatheads, in the Bitterroot Mountains of Montana. His father was killed by Blackfoot raiders while Smells of Sugar was still a child, and his mother, a Shoshoni, moved back to her people in Wyoming's Wind River Valley. As he grew to manhood, Smells of Sugar acquired a new name, Washakie. Raised to be a warrior, Washakie was big and powerfully built, and he possessed a fierce lust for combat. As a young man, the aggressive Washakie readily conducted war against all Shoshoni enemies, acquiring an arrow scar beneath his left eye and enormous prestige among his people.

By the early 1840s, numberless wagon trains were rolling across the plains and mountains along the Oregon Trail. Sioux, Cheyenne, Arapaho, and Crows looked upon the emigrants as disruptive invaders, and they sporadically killed, attacked, and robbed these intruders into their territory. At the same time, Washakie's strength of character and skill as a warrior had earned him leadership of the Eastern Shoshonis. As the new chief, Washakie pragmatically decreed that he would *assist* white travelers. Livestock that strayed from wagon trains would be rounded up and returned; wagons fording rivers would be helped; and Shoshoni warriors would drive off other war parties threatening wagon trains. In Washakie's farseeing eyes, the United States would be a valuable ally for the much-beleaguered Shoshonis in their traditional struggles against the powerful Sioux and Cheyenne.

When the Lander Road was laid out through Shoshoni territory in 1859, Washakie welcomed the situation, but with subtle threats of warfare against travelers on the new road, he coerced allotments of food, cloth, tools, guns, ammunition, and ornaments from the government. In 1868, after a decade of campaigning, he secured the rich Wind River Valley as a reservation. The government agreed to provide a school, hospital, mill, church, and military post to protect his people from enemy raiders.

Washakie also fought brilliantly alongside his U.S. allies, most notably at the Battle of the Rosebud. In the campaign against the Sioux and Cheyenne in the 1870s, about 250 Shoshoni and Crow warriors had been acting as scouts and an advance guard with General George Crook's 1,100 soldiers. Despite cautions from his scouts, Crook was taken unawares by some 1,500 warriors under the command of Crazy Horse near the headwaters of the Rosebud River. Fortu-

nately, Washakie and the Crow chiefs had positioned their few warriors in a strong defensive position and were able to hold off the first wave of Sioux long enough for Crook to ready his troops for battle. During the rest of the skirmish, Washakie constantly moved from the heated combat at the front line to the harried strategists at the rear, making valuable contributions in both areas. The Sioux were eventually turned away, and a potentially disastrous loss was averted.

Washakie, the skilled warrior, diplomat, and stern leader, remained vigorous well into

his 90s. He focused his last years on guiding his people as they adapted to life on the rich homeland he had so shrewdly acquired for them. When he died on February 20, 1900, he was still on the army payroll as a scout. He was buried two days later at the agency outpost—Fort Washakie.

Because of his cooperation, Washakie (seated, center) was able to garner land in the desirable Wind River Valley.

QUANAH
PARKER

1852?–1911

Kwahnah, meaning sweet odor, was the son of Comanche war chief Peta Nocona and Cynthia Ann Parker. He became famous on the Texas frontier as Quanah Parker, the most notable Comanche of his generation. Kwahnah established himself as a gifted young warrior, and his band of fierce Khwahada tribesmen were the last Comanche to surrender to reservation life. On the reservation, Quanah Parker proved himself a fine peacetime leader.

Nine-year-old Cynthia Ann was abducted during an 1836 Comanche raid on Parker's Fort in central Texas. Called Nadua by the Comanche, she married Peta, and their first child, Kwahnah, was born around 1852, according to the best calculations. The couple had two other children, a son named Pecos and a daughter called Topsannah.

Kwahnah rode with the Khwahadas, who snubbed a peace council in 1867 and were singled out for fierce retribution.

Kwahnah grew into a tall, strong man with bold features. His eyes were bluish grey, but aside from his large physique, little else about his appearance indicated that he was half white. He became a splendid rider and was taught to handle the traditional Comanche weapons.

Texas Ranger Sul Ross led a raid on Peta's camp on December 17, 1860. The chief, his young sons, and his warriors were on a hunt, although Ross mistakenly thought Peta was among the dead. Nadua, fleeing with Topsannah, was almost shot down by Charles Goodnight, but the young Ranger held his fire when he saw her light-colored eyes.

The raiders realized that Nadua was Cynthia Ann Parker, and she and her daughter were taken to the Parker family. There she pined for her husband and sons. When Topsannah died of a childhood disease, Cynthia Ann became grief-stricken and refused to eat. She died at her brother's home in 1864.

During this period, Peta Nocona also died. His half-white sons faced a harsh existence as orphans. Kwahnah established himself in the only way possible to a Comanche male, overcompensating for his biracialism by excelling as a hunter and warrior. By the time Kwahnah was 15, he had slain his first victim in a raid, and he soon displayed qualities of leadership.

Now a ready participant in raiding parties, Kwahnah proved himself as a war leader. He left his father's band of Nawkohnees to ride with the implacably warlike Khwahadas. While raiding with a war party in north Texas, Chief Bear's Ear was killed by soldiers, and Kwahnah skillfully assumed command. Thereafter, he led his own war parties, distinguishing himself during the 1870s when the Llano Estacado hunting grounds in Comanche territory were invaded by soldiers and buffalo hunters.

In the fall of 1871, Colonel Ranald Mackenzie led a column into the Llano Estacado in search of the Khwahadas. Taking the offensive, the Khwahadas under Kwahnah raided Mackenzie's horse herd. The cavalrymen had camped at the mouth of Blanco Canyon, and their mounts were staked out with iron picket pins. Screaming warriors galloped into the herd, waving blankets and ringing bells. The cavalry horses plunged against their pins as the troopers rolled out of their blankets to form skirmish lines and tried to control the frightened beasts.

While the U.S. Army could not thwart Kwahnah, the vast number of buffalo hunters who wiped out his food supply did.

The Comanche dashed out of the camp with a number of stolen animals, then scattered in several directions. At dawn, Mackenzie sent several detachments in pursuit. Captain E. M. Heyl overtook about a dozen warriors herding some of the cavalry mounts. The Comanche abandoned their stolen horses to outdistance the soldiers. After rounding up the horses, Heyl sent them back to camp with a detail, then led the balance of his men into broken country after the warriors.

Suddenly Kwahnah launched a counterattack, which quickly sent Heyl and his troopers in retreat. Mackenzie's adjutant, Lieutenant Robert Carter, fought a rearguard action so courageously that he earned a Medal of Honor. When Private Sander Gregg's horse gave out on him, Carter reported that Kwahnah galloped forward and killed the recruit with a revolver bullet in the head.

However much they outmaneuvered Mackenzie's men, the Comanche were running out of time. Their world was disintegrating as the

CYNTHIA ANN PARKER

On May 19, 1836, a Comanche raid resulted in the annihilation of almost everyone at Parker's Fort in east-central Texas. The Comanche spared nine-year-old Cynthia Ann and her 11-year-old brother but took them as prisoners.

Cynthia Ann grew up with the Comanche and became content with the Native American way of life. She was called Nadua, and she darkened her hair with buffalo dung to look more like her adopted people. Nadua became the wife of Peta Nocona, a Comanche leader. She gave birth to two sons, Kwahnah and Pecos, and a daughter, Topsannah.

On December 17, 1860, Cynthia Ann and her daughter were "rescued" by a group of Texas Rangers and returned to her American kin. Although she longed to be with Peta and her two sons, her relatives would not allow her to leave, putting her under guard when she tried to escape.

Within three years, Topsannah died of a childhood disease. Cynthia Ann horrified her relatives by mourning like a Comanche, howling and slashing her arms and breasts with a knife. Grief-stricken, she refused to eat and died at her brother's home at the age of 37.

Cynthia Ann Parker and her daughter Topsannah lived unhappily among whites.

buffalo disappeared under the onslaught of hordes of hide hunters. The Comanche responded to the messianic promises of Eeshatai, who brought large numbers of Native Americans together for a ritual dance that lasted three days and nights. Eeshatai pledged magical protection from hunters' bullets as excited warrior societies planned a war of extermination against the hide hunters in Comanche lands.

On June 26, 1874, Kwahnah was prominent among 700 Comanche, Kiowa, Arapaho, and Cheyenne warriors who assaulted a buffalo hunters' encampment at Adobe Walls in the Texas Panhandle. Kwahnah led a dawn attack to the walls, but the professional hunters, forted up behind adobe and armed with powerful Sharps buffalo rifles, broke the charge with deadly fire.

The outnumbered defenders—28 men and a woman—fought back with desperate courage. One sharpshooter knocked a brave off his horse from a distance of nearly a mile. Four white men were killed during the battle, including two brothers who had been sleeping in a wagon outside the buildings.

The warriors were punished by the professional marksmen. Kwahnah's mount was shot out from under him. As he scrambled for cover, a slug caught him in the shoulder. By the time he was rescued, the warriors had given up the attack and turned on Eeshatai.

The Battle of Adobe Walls triggered the Red River War of 1874–1875. Small groups of hide hunters were attacked across the Panhandle. The army launched a massive convergence against the so-called Wild Tribes. In September 1874, Ranald Mackenzie and his crack 4th Cavalry discovered and penetrated

Kwahnah led a disastrous attack on a buffalo hunters' camp at Adobe Walls in Texas. The hunters fended the Indians off using their Sharps rifles with telescopic sights, which could kill a full-grown buffalo at 600 yards.

Palo Duro Canyon, the great refuge of the Llano Estacado and the last remaining source of buffalo. Routed from Palo Duro Canyon during the winter, Comanche and Kiowa were hounded by army columns onto their reservations in the southeastern corner of Indian Territory. Kwahnah and 400 diehard Kwahadas held out, stubbornly roaming the plains until June 2, 1875, when this last band of Comanche drove 1,500 horses onto the Fort Sill Reservation.

Although only 30, the ambitious Kwahnah immediately sought the approval of white officials as a means of solidifying his leadership position. He became extremely reticent about his exploits against Texas frontiersmen, realizing that information about his warrior days might arouse resentment. From this point, he was called Quanah Parker by Texans.

Early in his reservation career, Quanah sold grazing rights to the 3,000,000-acre reservation ranges, extracting lease fees for his people from Charles Goodnight, Burk Burnett, and other cattle barons. These tough businessmen taught him much about negotiation and subsidized his frequent lobbying trips to Washington. Shrewd and pragmatic,

Above: Quanah Parker (with one of his eight wives) became a prominent citizen and a voice for Native American concerns in Washington. **Right:** Comanche women celebrate at the Parker Monument.

Quanah dressed in business suits and successfully invested his personal earnings. In 1892, after exhausting every conceivable delay, an unhappy Quanah attempted to pacify his people after their reservation land was apportioned into 160-acre plots, then the surplus land was opened to white settlement.

Burk Burnett helped Quanah erect the Comanche White House, a rambling 12-room residence near Fort Sill. Quanah served as chief judge of the Court of Indian Offenses, deputy sheriff of Lawton, and president of the local school board he helped to create. "No like Indian school for my people," he stated pragmatically. "Indian boy go to Indian school, stay like Indian; go white school, he like white men. Me want white school so my children get educated like whites."

Quanah's prominence reached celebrity status, and he was in great demand for parades, including President Theodore Roosevelt's 1905 inauguration. During all of his interaction with whites, Quanah proudly retained much of his Comanche identity. He remained polygamous, rejected Christianity, and used peyote and mescal. Quanah often shed his business suits in favor of buckskins and never cut his flowing hair.

When Quanah died of pneumonia on February 2, 1911, his demise was presided over by a Comanche medicine man. He was buried beside Cynthia Ann. Quanah first became known as a Comanche warrior who courageously defended his homeland until reluctantly submitting to reservation existence. For the last 36 years of his life, Quanah's fame grew steadily as a romantic relic of the old days who used diplomatic skill and tenacity to guide his people to their best advantage.

THE COMANCHE

Like their neighbors the Kiowa, the Comanche were members of the Shoshonean language family. Sometime in the 17th century, the Shoshoni split into two divisions—the Shoshonis and the Comanche. The Shoshonis occupied what is now Montana and Wyoming, while the Comanche migrated south and east until they reached the southern plains around the end of the 17th century. By 1700, the Comanche dominated vast areas of prairie in Texas and Oklahoma and had already made contact with the northern Spanish frontier in New Mexico. The name Comanche derives from the Spanish phrase *camino ancho*, which means wide trail.

Prior to migrating south, the Comanche had lived subdued lives and survived by gathering wild plants for food and by hunting small game. After their migration and the acquistion of horses, their way of life changed. The Comanche turned to buffalo hunting as a primary source of food. The buffalo also provided hides for robes, coverings for their tepees, and even sinews for thread.

One of the first nations to acquire horses from the Spanish, the Comanche became the premier horsemen and warriors of the southern plains. They were expert breeders and trainers and athletic riders. They initiated the equestrian-based nomadic lifestyle that was characteristic of the Plains Indians. The Comanche nation was organized into 12 or more bands that lacked the lineages, military societies, clans, and tribal government of later Plains Indians such as the Sioux.

Among the most warlike of nations, the Comanche represented a hazard to travelers and frequently mounted raids deep into Mexico for slaves and live-

The Comanche were fierce warriors and expert riders but were nomadic and did not develop a high level of tribal organization.

stock. After 1790, they were sometimes accompanied by their allies, the Kiowa. Although other nations took prisoners from time to time, the Comanche were masters at kidnapping, especially when it came to Mexicans and Texans. The Comanche raided against the encroaching whites from the time of the California gold rush to 1875, when the depletion of the buffalo led to their acceptance of reservation life.

SATANTA

1830?–1878

No Native American of the West provides a sadder example of the tragic effects of the clash of cultures than Satanta, or White Bear. A fierce but jovial Kiowa chief who exulted in the wild, free life of his people, Satanta was imprisoned by soldiers because of his frank admission of his warrior activities. When he was confined to the white man's penitentiary, the old war chief resorted to a crude form of suicide as the only means of regaining some measure of freedom.

Satanta was born around 1830 and bred to Plains Indian warfare. He grew into a tall, strong man who was a bold and fearless hunter and warrior. Excelling in combat against other Native Americans and Texans, he was elevated to the rank of chief while still in his 20s.

In 1867, Satanta told U.S. officials, "When we settle down, we grow pale and die."

Confident that he was one of the great men of his tribe, Satanta had a booming laugh, and he relished a fight or a feast. He was a gifted orator and diplomat. He signed the 1865 treaty of the Little Arkansas and the Medicine Lodge Treaty of 1867, which established a Kiowa reservation just above the great Comanche preserve in the southwest corner of Indian Territory.

The Kiowa were supposed to receive government provisions at Fort Cobb, but it had been agreed that they could hunt buffalo below the Arkansas River. For more than a year, the Kiowa continued their nomadic way of life, never venturing near Fort Cobb. Then, General Philip Sheridan ordered all Kiowa, Comanche, Cheyenne, and Arapaho to report to the fort or face military assault. In December 1868, Lieutenant Colonel George Armstrong Custer and his 7th Cavalry mauled the Cheyenne village of Chief Black Kettle on the Washita. Cheyenne, Arapaho, and some Comanche surrendered at the fort, but the Kiowa remained in their winter camp on Rainy Mountain Creek.

Custer led a column of soldiers toward the Kiowa camp. Chiefs Satanta and Lone Wolf, escorted by several warriors, rode out to parley. Custer directed his interpreters to order the Kiowa onto the reservation, then arrested the chiefs and their escort, informing them that they would be held at Fort Cobb until their people submitted to reservation authorities. Calmly pointing out that he needed to send a messenger into camp to give these orders, Satanta directed his son to tell the Kiowa to flee west. By the time the party reached Fort Cobb, even the escort warriors had slipped away, leaving the two chiefs still in custody.

THE
KIOWA

Compared to other Plains Indians, the Kiowa do not have a lengthy, complex history and involved system of subgroups, clans, and tribes. The name Kiowa comes from *kai-gwa*, meaning principal people.

According to tribal tradition, the homeland of the Kiowa may have originally been around the headwaters of the Missouri River. By the 18th century, they had migrated to the southern plains of present-day Oklahoma, Texas, New Mexico, Kansas, and Colorado. They acquired horses from the Spanish, and like other Plains Indians, they became nomadic buffalo hunters. They lived in tepees covered in buffalo skins.

The Kiowa were divided into seven bands, including the Kiowa-Apache, a small group who retained their own Athabascan language. The Kiowa had warrior societies, and members of these societies attained rank through heroic acts during war, including counting *coup*, or touching the body of an enemy during battle.

The Kiowa nation was known for the historical record they kept in the form of a pictographic calendar painted on buffalo skin. Between 1832 and 1839, two drawings were added to the record each year, one of an event from the summer and one of an event from the winter. The chronicler usually depicted subjects that had affected the whole nation, but sometimes a more personal story was selected.

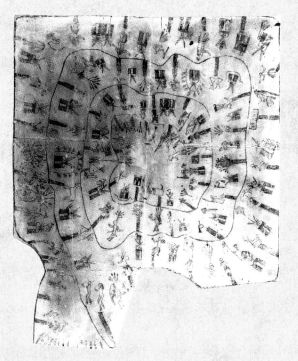

This pictograph is a chronicle of significant events from Kiowa history.

Originally, the Kiowa were enemies of the dominant Comanche nation, but by the 19th century, the two peoples had reconciled their differences and become allies. From that point on, Texans and New Mexicans referred to the Kiowa and Comanche as if they were one people, although the two nations spoke distinct languages.

The Kiowa were at first friendly with Americans, dating from an incident in 1834 when Colonel Henry Dodge returned a captive Kiowa girl to her people. But continued white pressure along the Santa Fe Trail and throughout the southern plains eventually drove the Kiowa to make war on all whites. Before their very eyes, the vast herds of bison disappeared under the guns of white hide hunters, and times became hard for all the buffalo-hunting nations. "Has the white man become a child, that he should recklessly kill and not eat?" asked the Kiowa chief Satanta.

Sheridan angrily announced that Satanta and Lone Wolf would be hanged unless their people turned themselves in at Fort Cobb. As the Kiowa began to appear, the captive chiefs were taken to the newly completed Fort Sill on the reservation. When Sheridan arrived at Fort Sill, he released Satanta and Lone Wolf. He admonished the chiefs and ordered them to follow the orders of Indian agent Lawrie Tatum. These orders included a directive to become farmers. Soon 2,000 Kiowa as well as 2,500 Comanche arrived at the new reservation. But Satanta was dissatisfied. He had no intention of digging in the dirt like women. He asked Tatum for guns and ammunition to hunt buffalo because he found neither stringy government beef nor reservation corn to his liking. "I don't like corn," he stated flatly. "It hurts my teeth."

When Tatum gave permission for the hunt, several Kiowa happily rode off to Texas in search of buffalo, with raids against white settlers as a satisfying bonus activity. During that summer of 1870, braves who remained on the reservation taunted Chief Kicking Bird because he had strongly urged his people to become farmers. Finally, Kicking Bird challenged the warriors to follow him on a Texas raid, and 100 men rode south toward Fort Richardson. During an eight-hour duel with soldiers, Kicking Bird outflanked his adversaries and conducted the action with consummate skill. Kicking Bird returned triumphantly to the reservation—then resumed his policy of cooperating with white men for the good of his people.

Satanta grew restless on the reservation, but Chief Big Tree was downright angry. He tried to persuade Kiowa warriors to set Fort Sill ablaze one night, then kill the soldiers as they ran out of the burning buildings. In the spring of 1871, a large Kiowa and Comanche war party, including Satanta, Big Tree, old Satank (Sitting Bear), and other noted chiefs, eluded army patrols along the Red River and rode toward Fort Richardson. On May 18, concealed near the Butterfield Trail, the warriors attacked ten freight wagons, killing seven teamsters. They looted the wagons while the remaining drivers escaped. The war party headed back to the reservation with scalps and stolen draft animals.

A few days later, General Sherman arrived at Fort Sill and directed Tatum to find out if any of his charges knew about the recent raid in Texas. When Satanta and other chiefs came to agency headquarters to receive their weekly provisions, Satanta announced that he had led the raid. "I have repeatedly asked for arms and ammunition,

Satanta, passing the pipe at a council, had an attitude of accommodation to a point: "The good Indian . . . gets nothing. The independent Indian is the only one rewarded."

which you have not furnished, and made many other requests, which have not been granted." Satanta stated that these grievances had been the motivation for the raid.

Tatum sent a note to post commander Colonel Benjamin Grierson, informing him of Satanta's arrogant confession. The message was passed on to General Sherman. Satanta marched alone to headquarters and demanded to see Great Warrior Sherman. Stepping onto the broad gallery, Sherman shook hands with Satanta and announced that all of the chiefs should assemble for a council.

Grierson and Sherman hastily arranged to meet the chiefs on the big gallery, where Sherman promptly arrested them. Satanta shouted in Kiowa that he would rather die than be taken prisoner, and he groped under his blanket for a revolver. Sherman snapped a command, and soldiers inside the building threw open the front shutters, momentarily quelling the chiefs by the unexpected sight of leveled carbines. Lone Wolf and a Kiowa brave instigated a scuffle, but they were wrestled to the gallery floor. The two warriors and others, including Satanta, were seized and hustled off to the guardhouse.

Handcuffed and placed in two wagons with a cavalry escort, Satanta, Big Tree, and Satank were taken toward Texas. Old Satank had hidden a butcher knife on his person, and he decided he would use it to die like a Kiowa warrior. Chanting what proved to be the death song of the Society of the Ten Bravest, Satank ducked his head beneath his blanket and gnawed off enough flesh to free his hands. He stabbed a guard and seized his carbine before being shot dead by another guard.

The other two chiefs proceeded on to Fort Richardson for trial in a civilian court in nearby Jacksboro. Satanta and Big Tree were convicted of first-degree murder and sentenced to hang. Texas governor E. J. Davis commuted the sentence to life imprisonment—a crueler fate than death for Plains warriors. Besieged with humanitarian requests, Governor Davis paroled the two chiefs to the reservation in 1873.

Angrily, General Sherman wrote to Governor Davis, "I now say to you that I believe White Bear and Big Tree will have their revenge and that if they are to have scalps, yours is the first that should be taken." Sherman's prediction was partially accurate. The two chiefs led small bands of warriors off the reservation in the summer of 1874. Numerous Kiowa, Comanche, and Cheyenne war parties made raids during that troubled summer, prompting Sherman to send five columns and a total of 3,000 men to scour the southern plains. By October 1874, Satanta and Big Tree had been run into the ground. The two chiefs finally surrendered themselves, along with 143 followers; only 35 were warriors.

Most of the Kiowa chiefs faced tragic ends. Lone Wolf was the last Kiowa chief to surrender, and he was exiled to Florida with some other militants. Kicking Bird was killed with a dose of strychnine by resentful Kiowa. Allowed to remain on the reservation, Big Tree became a Baptist deacon and Sunday school teacher. Over his bitter protests, Satanta was sent back to the Texas State Penitentiary in Huntsville. Depressed and wasting away in the prison hospital, Satanta committed suicide on October 11, 1878, leaping headfirst from a second-story window.

RED
CLOUD

Red Cloud spent the first half of his lengthy life span as a free Oglala Sioux, a gifted warrior and hunter who reveled in the exhilarating life of the Indians of the northern plains. As a noted leader in his 40s, however, he recognized the impossibility of resisting the inexorable white advance. Submitting to reservation life for more then four decades, he was subjected to maddening injustice from whites and to endless criticism from fellow discontented Sioux.

Born in 1822 at the fork of Nebraska's Platte River, Red Cloud (a name probably not given until he became a warrior) was orphaned while very young. The boy grew up in the band of his maternal uncle, Chief Smoke, leader of the fierce Bad Faces clan. Taking up the warpath as a youth, he rode on raids against Crows and Pawnee. When he was 16, he claimed his first scalp while riding against the Pawnee. During a raid against a Crow camp, he killed a boy guarding the Crow pony herd and rode off with the horses. When the Crows pursued, Red Cloud boldly turned and killed the enemy chief. He earned even greater glory on another raid by killing four Pawnee braves. Red Cloud confirmed a growing reputation for cruelty during a fight against the Ute, when he dragged a drowning enemy out of a stream in order to scalp him.

By 1841, a dispute had arisen between Chief Smoke's Bad Faces and the Koyas of the noted Chief Bull Bear. The ambitious and brutal Red Cloud shot and probably killed Bull Bear near Fort Laramie. Although his repu-

Red Cloud led such intense assaults on the traffic along the Bozeman Trail that the U.S. government was never able to establish firm control of the area.

tation as a deadly warrior was still further enhanced, Red Cloud would never be trusted as chief of all Oglalas. The breach between the Bad Faces and Koyas was not healed for half a century; the Bad Faces allied with the Northern Cheyenne while the Koyas affiliated with the Southern Cheyenne. Red Cloud's ability as a fighting man remained unquestioned, as he continued his bloody career against traditional enemies of his people. Soon after assassinating Bull Bear, he caught a Pawnee arrow in his leg, a wound that would never cease to trouble him.

Red Cloud's first significant action against U.S. soldiers occurred spontaneously on August 19, 1854, near Fort Laramie. A Sioux brave killed a cow belonging to an emigrant, but Chief Conquering Bear's offer of a fine horse in compensation was ignored. Instead, a young officer named John L. Grattan led 30 men to Conquering Bear's camp, then belligerently opened fire. The chief was killed, but all Sioux warriors present, including Red Cloud and a number of Bad Faces, immediately swarmed the soldiers, who fled and were chased down and killed individually.

Red Cloud came to be widely acknowledged as the best war leader of the Oglala, a position he would solidify during the next few years with a bloody and successful campaign called Red Cloud's War. In the early 1860s, the Bozeman Trail cut through some of the richest hunting grounds of the Sioux and Cheyenne. The natives of the area, including Red Cloud's people, constantly harassed the intrusive whites along this trail, and in 1865 the federal government decided to establish and protect this dangerous route.

General Patrick Connor commanded the Powder River Expedition, directing three columns that were to shatter hostile resistance. Connor's column built Fort Connor (later renamed Fort Reno) to anchor the trail, then moved on to attack Arapaho, who had been peaceful until this unprovoked assault. Meanwhile, the other two columns, commanded by Colonel Nelson Cole and Lieutenant Colonel Samuel Walker, linked together and marched into Wyoming from the Black Hills toward a rendezvous with Connor.

In mid-August, Red Cloud and Chief Dull Knife of the Cheyenne learned of a large wagon train proceeding through the region, and they led about 500 braves against the intruders. The train, consisting of 80 wagons loaded with supplies for Virginia City, 73 civilians, and an escort of two infantry companies, circled up and held off the big war party. After a parley, Red Cloud and Dull Knife agreed to accept a wagon of supplies in exchange for safe passage, and during negotiations they heard for the first time about Connor's fort and expedition.

Red Cloud and other leaders rode to inspect the fort. Red Cloud decided that the fort's stockade and cannons rendered a direct attack too costly, so a series of raids was launched against travelers and soldiers. The hard-pressed Cole-Walker column ran out of supplies and staggered, battered and half-starved, into Fort Connor. General Connor was abruptly removed from command and the Powder River Expedition was terminated.

But the army soon returned in force, ordering Colonel Henry Carrington and his

American Horse (left) participated in the skirmishes along the Bozeman Trail led by Red Cloud (right).

THE BOZEMAN TRAIL

The rush started in Idaho and moved steadily eastward. Gold had been discovered in 1860, and a stream of prospectors poured across the land. Eventually, a creek-riddled gulch in southwestern Montana had become the focus of their activity. Thousands of miners wrested some ten million dollars from the ground, and Virginia City became the latest boomtown.

The diggers required a constant influx of supplies, and current overland trails to the area were arduous. In 1864, John M. Bozeman left Fort Laramie intending to find a more direct path to the gold. As later mapped out, the Bozeman Trail stretched from Julesburg in northeastern Colorado through Nebraska and Wyoming to Virginia City in Montana. For several years, it remained one of the main supply routes to Virginia City.

Bozeman's route ran through the coveted hunting grounds of the Sioux and Cheyenne along the Powder River east of the Bighorn Mountains. Use of the trail led to bitter conflict with the Oglala Sioux.

Cattlemen used the Bozeman Trail to drive beef north to the Montana goldfields.

18th Infantry to fortify and secure the Bozeman Trail. Carrington requested the Sioux leaders to negotiate with him at Fort Fetterman, and when Red Cloud finally arrived, he sullenly disdained to be introduced to the officers. Unable to secure acceptable terms, Red Cloud stormed out of the meeting, making angry threats to wage war with the intruders.

Carrington soon marched his regiment up the trail to Fort Connor. Red Cloud promptly launched a raiding party that stole the horses and mules brought to the post and then struck a civilian wagon train for good measure. Carrington detached one company to strengthen Fort Reno, then pushed on up the Bozeman and began construction of Fort Phil Kearny in July 1866. Two companies were sent to erect Fort C. F. Smith farther north on the Bighorn River, and Fort Phil Kearny was completed within four months.

Throughout the summer and fall, Carrington's command was constantly engaged against Sioux warriors under Red Cloud, who directed a deadly guerrilla war at the army and at travelers along the trail. By the end of the year, Carrington's force had faced the enemy in more than 50 skirmishes. Red Cloud's warriors had killed and mutilated 5 officers, 91 troopers, and 58 civilians and had stolen 306 head of oxen and cattle, 304 mules, and 161 horses from the vicinity of Carrington's fort. The garrison was virtually in a state of siege behind the elaborate fortifications of Fort Phil Kearny. The climactic battle occurred on December 21, 1866, a few miles north of the fort. After careful planning, a young warrior chief named Crazy Horse and a group of decoys enticed a pursuit column into an ambush, and Captain William Fetterman and all 80 of his men were slain. It was the worst loss the U.S. Army had suffered in the West up to that time.

Carrington was removed from command, but the military presence was maintained along the Bozeman Trail and hostilities continued in 1867. On August 1, warriors struck a hay-cutting party near Fort C. F. Smith, and the next day Red Cloud directed an attack against woodcutters near Fort Phil Kearny. At each battle site, large war parties swooped down on small bands of civilian employees and infantry escorts. The beleaguered soldiers had recently received new .50 caliber breech-loading Springfield rifles, though, and they fought for their lives with impressive firepower and courage. Each battle lasted for several hours, but the Oglala warriors finally withdrew after suffering heavy casualties.

In the end, Red Cloud's campaign proved effective. His warriors skillfully continued to strike civilians and soldiers at every opportunity. The War Department at last relented, pulling the garrison out of Fort C. F. Smith on July 29, 1868. The next morning, Red Cloud and a jubilant band of warriors rode in and burned the fort. A month later, Fort Phil Kearny also was abandoned, then burned, and within a few days the army marched out of Fort Reno. The Bozeman Trail was closed. Red Cloud had engineered the only successful Native American campaign against the U.S. government.

Red Cloud rode triumphantly into Fort Laramie in November and signed a treaty pledging never to fight again, but his triumph was short lived. After the government began to ignore the Fort Laramie treaty in

1870, Red Cloud traveled on a train to Washington, D.C., and met with President Grant. This trip, and his six other visits to the capital, revealed to him the true extent of his enemy's size and power. Red Cloud eventually brought his people onto reservations, and he helped to persuade his old ally, Crazy Horse, to yield to reservation life in 1877. He clung to power within his tribe by fighting political battles with government officials skillfully but with little success. For 40 years, he precariously remained his peoples' leader, but both he and they saw the steady erosion of the Oglala Sioux culture. Red Cloud died on December 10, 1909, a great victor in war but an ineffective victim of peace.

Top: In this 1868 Mathew Brady photograph of a peace council, Red Cloud appears at the far left.
Above: Chief Red Cloud poses with his children in 1909. He became convinced of his enemy's power during several trips to Washington, D.C.

COCHISE

?–1874

Destined to become perhaps the greatest of all Apache chiefs, Cochise was born in the early 1800s in the Chiricahua Mountains, probably in southeastern Arizona but possibly in northern Sonora. His father and grandfather were chiefs of the Chokonen, or Central Chiricahua Apache, which made Cochise a hereditary candidate for leadership.

Like all Chiricahua boys, he was trained for war. Toughened to existence in a harsh land, Chiricahua warriors could cover 70 miles in a day through rugged terrain, keeping a pebble under their tongues in waterless desert. They became masters of concealment, with ambush a common tactic. Youthful captives might be absorbed into the band or ransomed, but most prisoners were cruelly tortured to death. Especially hated were the Mexicans, against whom Cochise's people waged ceaseless war. Of course, there was a bounty for Apache scalps in Mexico, which fueled the murderous animosity of the Chiricahuas. By the 1830s, Cochise was a constant participant in raids

Cochise at first sought compatibility with whites, but after he was falsely accused and arrested, he started to fight the invaders of his homeland.

against Mexico. An 1835 truce between Chiricahuas and Mexicans was rejected by Cochise and a chief thought to have been his father or grandfather.

Cochise married twice, fathering two daughters by his first wife. His second marriage, to Dos-teh-seh, had political consequence. Dos-teh-seh was the eldest daughter of the legendary Mangas Coloradas, chief of the Eastern Chiricahuas, who farsightedly tried to forge Apache alliances that might be powerful enough to resist the invasion of white men. An imposing powerhouse among his people, Mangas Coloradas married all three of his daughters to promising young leaders. Cochise and Dos-teh-seh produced two sons: Taza, who never married and sired no children; and Naiche, who was born in 1856 and died in 1921 as the last Chiricahua chief.

Cochise apparently became a member of the most warlike band of Central Chiricahuas, led by Miguel Narbona. In 1848, the band took five Mexican prisoners near Frontreras in Sonora, but while a ransom was being arranged fighting erupted. Cochise was captured and subsequently released in exchange for 11 captives—testimony to his rising prominence. When Miguel Narbona died in 1856, Cochise succeeded him as head of the band, and soon after he became chief of all Central Chiricahuas.

Cochise frequently aided Mangas Coloradas in raids into Mexico. When Cochise's father-in-law suffered the loss of two sons in Mexico, he launched a brutal assault into Sonora in May 1858. The following September, after drunken Apache were brutally murdered during a parley at Frontreras, Mangas Coloradas and Cochise launched a retaliatory attack on the local presidio.

The thrust of his activities as a warrior always had been aimed at Mexicans, and for the early part of his life, Cochise seems to have experienced little conflict with whites. At a conference with Major Enoch Steen of the 1st U.S. Dragoons in 1856, Cochise agreed to let white travelers pass through Chiricahua country as they followed the southern route to California. Three years later, Cochise met with Indian Agent Michael Steck at Apache Pass and consented to the construction of a Butterfield stagecoach station at a nearby spring.

Such generosity disappeared in January 1861. Asked to attend another conference at the Apache Pass station, an unsuspecting Cochise arrived with his brother, two nephews, his wife, and four-year-old Naiche (also known as Nachez). An army tent had been set up by Second Lieutenant George N. Bascom, who had marched to Apache Pass with 54 men of the 7th Infantry. Cochise and his family entered the tent, and Bascom accused him of recently stealing cattle and capturing a boy from the ranch of John Ward. The raid had been conducted by the Coyotero Apache, but Bascom believed that Cochise was the culprit. Astounded, Cochise stated that he knew nothing about the incident but would make inquiries. Bascom stubbornly ordered his men to arrest Cochise. But the chief whipped out a knife, slit the tent open, and dashed through soldiers, reaching safety despite a slight wound but leaving his family behind.

An enraged Cochise hastily collected a few of his warriors, including Geronimo, and attacked three Butterfield employees, killing one, wounding one, and capturing another. Next, Cochise assaulted a wagon train, taking two soldiers prisoner but lashing the eight Mexican teamsters to their wagon wheels and burning them along with the wagons.

Having established the seriousness of his intentions, Cochise took his captives to within shouting distance of Bascom and tried to exchange the white men for his family. Ignoring the pleas of the captives, Bascom refused to negotiate, whereupon Cochise dragged off his prisoners and tortured them

Cochise's son Naiche (left) rode with Geronimo (right) during the Apache Wars after his father's death.

to death. Bascom retaliated by hanging Cochise's brother and two nephews, along with three Coyotero captives.

Assaulting ranches, mines, stagecoaches and wagon trains, Cochise and his warriors killed 150 whites during the next two months. The start of the Civil War took many of the area's troops to the East, so Cochise waged his war with scant opposition. Five stage stations soon had been destroyed, and on April 28, 1861, Cochise and Mangas Coloradas killed five whites riding a stagecoach near Stein's Peak, New Mexico. A band of civilian volunteers soon found six other burned stagecoaches and numerous dead citizens. In July, Cochise and Mangas Coloradas jumped a stagecoach a mile west of Cooke's Spring, New Mexico. The driver, conductor, and five passengers forted up atop a nearby knoll and defended themselves for three days, inflicting about 40 casualties before being wiped out.

Cochise continued to lead forays into Mexico whenever possible. During yet another raid near Frontreras, he was shot in the leg, and within a few years he was wounded in the neck while fighting in northern Mexico. Years later, after he had established peace terms with the U.S., he raided at

Tom Jeffords, an Indian agent and a friend of Cochise, worked hard to improve reservation life for the Apache. He is shown here on his ranch.

will below the border, pointing out that he was never at peace with Mexicans.

Confederate troops had penetrated New Mexico and Arizona by 1862, and the Union countered with the California Column led by General James Carleton. Carleton sent Captain Thomas Roberts and 126 men into Arizona. When Cochise learned of the approaching soldiers, he collected 700 warriors along with Mangas Coloradas and Geronimo to create the largest Apache fighting force ever assembled. An ambush was launched at Apache Pass on July 15, 1862, but Thomas unlimbered two mountain howitzers and blasted his way to victory over the surprised warriors.

The next year Mangas Coloradas, who was in his late 60s, sought to negotiate peace under a white flag at Fort McLane, New Mexico. During talks he was abruptly arrested by U.S. forces and charged with attacks on wagon trains. While in custody the night of his arrest, the great chief was cruelly tortured by soldiers who held heated bayonets to his feet and legs. He was then shot, scalped, and decapitated. Despite the loss of his formidable father-in-law, Cochise continued to carry on the fight. In October 1869, Cochise and a war party jumped a stagecoach west of Dragoon Wells and killed everyone onboard, then killed a cowboy and stole a herd of 250 cattle. A determined pursuit by the cavalry brought about a clash in which Cochise's band suffered a dozen casualties.

The army built Fort Bowie in Apache Pass, and from 1869 through 1872, the commander of this key outpost was Captain Reuben Frank Bernard of the 1st Cavalry. Bernard was a veteran of numerous patrols in Arizona and New Mexico prior to the Civil War, and he hounded the Chiricahua warriors with resourceful tenacity. Bernard's most notable action against Cochise was fought when the wily chief ambushed the Captain and 61 men at Chiricahua Pass on October 20, 1869. Bernard steadied his men and, battling until sundown, tried to turn each flank. Two soldiers were killed and several wounded, but Cochise held the pass at a cost of 18 warriors.

Cochise forged an unusual friendship with Tom Jeffords, whose stagecoach line had lost 14 employees to Chiricahua attacks. In 1867, Jeffords courageously sought out Cochise to try to negotiate on behalf of his business. Impressed by his obvious bravery, Cochise became friends with Jeffords and called him *shik-isn* or brother, even though the white man occasionally served the army as a scout. Jeffords tried to influence Cochise toward a permanent peace and established contact between the chief and government officials, most notably with General O. O. Howard in 1872.

A Chiricahua reservation was organized with headquarters at Apache Pass, and at the insistence of Cochise, Jeffords served as Indian agent. Cochise remained at peace with the white man, but soon he began to suffer health problems (probably cancer), and he died on June 8, 1874. His warriors buried him in a secret place in his beloved Chiricahua Mountains.

Although the Apache were one of the most scattered, loosely organized nations, Cochise played a major role in galvanizing his people against the white forces. During a decade of war against the United States, his braves had slain more than 4,000 victims and constantly thwarted all efforts to subdue them. The great Apache chief proved himself to be one of the most effective guerrilla leaders in the history of American warfare.

INDIAN AGENTS

As Native Americans moved onto reservations, the role of the Indian agents changed dramatically. Whereas once they had been ambassadors and negotiators, they now became tribal administrators of a sort. They were responsible for distributing annuities, maintaining relations between Native Americans and whites in the region, executing federal policy, and helping the Indians to adapt to reservation life. This last task— the most difficult of all— came in a variety of forms: farming or some other stable economic industry, Christianity, or formal education, all of which were incompatible with the traditional cultures of the Plains and Southwestern Indians.

Few if any agents achieved long-term success in their efforts. Some were not qualified as administrators or had no understanding of the culture they were dealing with. Others were shamelessly corrupt, pocketing federal

Originally with the War Department, Indian agents moved under the Department of the Interior in 1849.

monies, selling goods meant to be used on the reservation, or parceling out Indian lands to the highest bidders. The qualified and dedicated agents could really achieve little with the resources given them. Reservation lands were typically poor, and supplies and equipment were often inappropriate, outdated, or in disrepair.

GERONIMO

1820s ?—1909

"We were reckless of our lives, because we felt that every man's hand was against us . . . so we gave no quarter to anyone and asked no favors." Geronimo's narra-

Even in a posed photograph, Geronimo presents a fierce and imposing countenance that identifies him as a formidable warrior.

tion of his final hostile activities aptly describes the warrior's philosophy that made his name synonymous with terror on the Southwestern frontier.

Despite the turbulence associated with his last days as a warrior, his early life was tranquil. He was born in the wild mountainous country near the headwaters of Arizona's Gila River in the mid-1820s. Known as Goyahkla (One Who Yawns), he was the grandson of a chief of the Nedni Apache. Goyahkla's father married a Bedonkohe Apache and joined her tribe, thereby forfeiting his hereditary right as leader and opening the way for the great Mangas Coloradas to become chief.

When Goyahkla was an adolescent, his father died. He took his mother to live with Nedni relatives among a band that was later led by his friend Juh, who proved to be a superb chief. Goyahkla performed four novice raids and completed other required activities to gain admittance to the council of warriors when he was 17. Soon afterward he married Alope, who bore him three children within a few years.

At Janos, Goyahkla's entire family, including his wife, three children, and mother, were slain during an 1850 massacre by Mexican soldiers while the Apache men were absent from their camp in Chihuahua. Stunned by his loss, the One Who Yawns lusted for vengeance. "My feelings toward the Mexicans did not change—I still hated them and longed for revenge. I never ceased to plan for their punishment."

At this point, Goyahkla, previously known as more of a medicine man than a fighter, gained prominence as a resourceful and merciless warrior. The following year, he was called Geronimo after he led a wild charge against Mexicans who screamed, *"Geronimo!"* They were appealing for help to their patron saint, Jerome, or Geronimo in Spanish. Goyahkla's fellow warriors took up the cry, and he became infamous as Geronimo.

Contrary to popular assumption, Geronimo was not a chief. He led war parties numbering as few as three braves into Mexico. He willingly followed the leadership of such great war chiefs as Juh, Mangas Coloradas, and Cochise, and for decades he looted and killed ceaselessly. His fierce countenance accurately reflected a murderous temperament, and although he stood just five feet eight inches, he was barrel-chested and possessed seemingly limitless stamina. He took several wives and sired several more children during his life, but he could never abandon the warrior's life for long.

Eventually, Geronimo's enemies included whites. Shortly after the Bascom incident of 1861, which resulted in the capture of part of Cochise's family, Geronimo joined the enraged Chiricahua chief as he sought vengeance against white soldiers and civilians. During the first two months of Cochise's retaliation, 150 whites were slain, and Geronimo participated in his share of raids on stagecoaches, ranches, and small settlements. Cochise and Mangas Coloradas brought together 700 warriors, the largest Apache fighting force ever assembled. Geronimo was part of this unprecedented war party, which set an ambush in Apache Pass on July 15, 1862. However, the 126-man army column, which became the target of the ambush, brought two mountain howitzers into play. The resulting defeat at the Battle of Apache Pass convinced Apache leaders that in the future they should rely on small raiding parties—a tactic that perfectly suited the wily Geronimo.

In the 1870s, Geronimo ostensibly settled on the Chiricahua Reservation in Arizona. Later he was placed on the Warm Springs Reservation, but he continued to slip away on raids. On January 9, 1877, Geronimo's band was struck by a patrol under Lieutenant J. A. Rucker in southwestern New Mexico. Geronimo lost ten warriors. He turned up at Warm Springs with livestock stolen during recent raids. Angered when he was not permitted to draw rations for the time period he had been absent on raids, Geronimo traveled

Taz-Ayz-Slath, one of Geronimo's wives, poses with their child sometime around 1885.

to New Mexico's Ojo Caliente Reservation to try to draw rations there. Agent John P. Clum regarded Geronimo as a renegade, and Clum had him arrested and shackled, along with seven of his braves.

Geronimo was moved to the San Carlos Reservation, then released a few months later by Clum's successor. Less than a year later, he broke away from San Carlos and headed for Mexico. During the Victorio War of the late 1870s, in which Victorio led an uprising of attrition against the whites, Geronimo operated with Juh in coordination with Victo-

Although Geronimo was not a chief, his personal magnetism drew many Apache warriors to follow him.

rio's Mimbres Apache. Late in 1879, Geronimo and Juh returned to San Carlos, but two years later they bolted the reservation once again to do battle in their own rebellion.

In the spring of 1882, Juh and Geronimo led 60 men back to San Carlos. At dawn on April 18, they audaciously broke Chief Loco and several hundred unarmed Mimbrenos off the reservation. Fighting their way back into Mexico, the renegades were attacked in camp by cavalrymen under a new agreement between the United States and Mexico. This so-called "hot pursuit" agreement permitted troops from either country to cross the border while chasing marauders. The Apache suffered numerous casualties, but they finally fought through to mountain hideaways in Mexico where they resumed their perpetual war against Mexicans.

During this period, Juh fell from his horse, either because of a heart attack or because he was drunk, and he drowned in a river. At six feet and 225 pounds, Juh was an imposing and cruel fighting man, but he was also a talented leader. His loss placed Geronimo in the forefront of the Chiricahuas who wanted to continue the life of mountain raiders.

The relentless effort of General George Crook was making that way of life increasingly more perilous. The Apache called the middle-aged general Gray Wolf because he operated like a cunning timber beast. Crook had been fighting Native Americans since the 1850s. He tried to think like a warrior so that he could understand their guerrilla warfare and methods of operation.

As Crook hounded the Apache in their Mexican lairs, one band after another headed north to the reservation. Geronimo agreed to parley with Gray Wolf in May 1881, but it was nearly a year before the vicious old warrior finally crossed the border, accompanied by nearly 100 diehard followers and 350 stolen cattle. San Carlos Reservation officials, however, confiscated his herd. "These were not white men's cattle," Geronimo resentfully complained, "for we had taken them from the Mexicans during our wars."

Geronimo located his reservation home on Turkey Creek, 17 miles southeast of Fort Apache. Although inclined toward stock-raising, the Apache were issued plows by the Indian Bureau and ordered to become farmers. While Geronimo's wives did the work on his farm, he remained peaceful for a year.

Geronimo and other leaders resented the bans on wife-beating, the drinking of *tizwin* (a weak beer brewed from corn), and other traditional practices. The wisdom of the prohibition against *tizwin* was verified in May 1885, when Geronimo and other Chiricahua leaders went on an all-night drinking spree. A few days later, Geronimo, perhaps fearful of repercussions and certainly restless for his old lifestyle, led four other chieftains, 38 braves, and 92 women and children in another outbreak. The renegades cut the telegraph wires, then headed for Mexico, pushing 120 miles before halting for their first camp.

The Apache scattered, with each of the five leaders taking a small band into a remote location. Crook coordinated the pursuit on the American side, while Mexican troops also rode to the chase. Thousands of soldiers tracked the fugitives relentlessly, yet Geronimo and a handful of followers remained elusive. Guided across the border by Apache scouts, one of Crook's detachments attacked Geronimo's camp on August 7, 1885, and captured one-third of the band's women and children. Six weeks later Geronimo slipped back into San Carlos, recovered a wife and child, then returned to northern Mexico with his family.

On January 10, 1886, Captain Emmett Crawford and a column of Apache scouts located Geronimo's *rancheria* near the Haros River in Sonora. Crawford routed the Apache with a dawn attack and seized most of their horses and camp gear. Geronimo sent a woman to arrange for a meeting with Crawford the next day, but dawn brought the approach of a Mexican column. The Mexicans apparently thought Crawford's scouts were hostile Chiricahuas and opened fire. Crawford was shot in the head, and four scouts were wounded, but the American party fired back, killing four and wounding five. Watching from concealment, Geronimo and his men enjoyed the unaccustomed role of spectators. Crawford never regained consciousness and died a week later.

Despite the efforts of two nations and thousands of troops, Geronimo remained at large until he chose to surrender.

When Mexican troops invaded his Sierra Madre sanctuary, Geronimo agreed to meet with Crook just below the border. Gray Wolf promised to try to persuade government officials to let the Apache return to their reservation after spending two years as prisoners in Florida. Crook hurried ahead to telegraph Washington about the surrender, only to receive the reply that Geronimo's terms were unacceptable.

Geronimo left the custody of Crook's scouts, however, and was on the loose in Mexico with a few followers. A bootlegger had provided the Apache with whiskey, and

APACHE

The most nomadic nation in the Southwest, the Apache became the last major Indian group to submit to American authority. The Apache called themselves the *Diné*, or the people. The word Apache derives from the Zuni word

This Apache camp in Arizona was quickly raised and could just as quickly be left behind.

for enemy, *apachu*. Along with their kinsmen, the Navajo, the Apache are members of the Athapaskan language family.

Some time in the distant past, while Europeans were still living in the Dark Ages, the Athapaskans migrated south from Canada to inhabit the parched lands of New Mexico, Arizona, and northern Mexico. In the vast lands of the Southwest, the Athapaskans drifted apart. One group became the Navajo, who based their way of life on sheepherding and farming; the other became the Apache, who adopted a nomadic life.

The Apache way of life reflected the significance of mobility. They lived in hastily constructed thatch *wickiups* and did not rely on craftmaking like their counterparts, the Navajo. During the 18th century, raiding became a major source of meat and supplies for the Apache, although some of the Apache depended on farming and hunting small game for subsistence. Of the little farming that occurred by the Apache, it was the women who tended the crops and fields.

A characteristic of the Apache was their lack of tribal solidarity, which was indicated by the many subtribes, bands, and families. The Apache group was divided into six distinct subgroups: the Lipan, now extinct; the Western Apache; the Chiricahua; the Mescalero; the Jicarilla; and the Kiowa-Apache. The Western Apache was further subdivided into 14 bands.

The Apache were fierce fighters, known for their guerrilla tactics. They fought with the Comanche to the north, the Navajo to the west, and the Spanish to the south. They were feared by the Pueblo Indian groups as well as by the Mexicans and Anglo-Americans. The U.S.'s post-Civil War policy of controlling all Native Americans included the Apache, who proved to be the most tenacious of the Indian guerrillas. Though most of the Apache were subdued during the 1880s, a few camps were never defeated, hunting and raiding in the mountains of Northern Sonora until 1930.

as Geronimo became drunk, his misgivings increased. "I feared treachery, and when we became suspicious, we turned back."

Crook was criticized by civilians, newspapers, and his superiors, which prompted the resignation of the army's finest strategist in the campaign against Native Americans. The capable and ambitious General Nelson Miles assumed command, throwing 5,000 troops into the field and establishing 30 heliograph stations to facilitate communications. Thousands of Mexican soldiers scoured Geronimo's old haunts, but the Apache somehow avoided contact. Only after Geronimo learned that the other Chiricahuas, including the families of those still at large, were about to be shipped to the East did he finally decide to surrender. Geronimo turned himself in to Miles in September 1886, and he shortly found himself aboard a train for Florida.

Geronimo was incarcerated at Fort Pickens, outside Pensacola, for the better part of two years. In May 1888, the Native Americans were moved to Mount Vernon Barracks, Alabama, an unhealthy site that decimated the Apache prisoners. Not until 1895 were they removed to a more favorable climate, Fort Sill in Oklahoma, where Geronimo spent the final 14 years of his life.

The old Indian warrior picked up a little English and learned to write his name. He became something of an entrepreneur, selling buttons from his coat for a quarter apiece, his hat for five dollars, and hawking bows and arrows that he made. For an extra 50 cents, the customer could purchase the old warrior's autograph. He proudly showed off his many battle wounds. He was a popular attraction at the Exposition in Omaha in 1898, the Pan-American Exposition in Buffalo in 1901, numerous Oklahoma celebrations, the St. Louis World's Fair in 1904, and Teddy Roosevelt's inaugural parade in 1905. Despite these extensive travels, he was never permitted to return to Arizona. As an old man, he remained a crack shot, and he enjoyed robust health into his 80s. He also continued to imbibe alcoholic beverages, and on a winter night in 1909, he drunkenly toppled from his horse and spent hours on the cold ground. Geronimo died of pneumonia on February 17, 1909, already a legend as the last renegade leader to surrender to the army.

Geronimo (front row, second from right) sits with other Apache captives on their way to Florida in 1886.

WEAPONS AND
FIGHTING TACTICS

With a life and economy indelibly tied to the wilderness and intertribal warring, Native Americans depended on their weapons as the primary tools of everyday life. The staple weapon of the Plains Indians was the bow and arrow. Introduced into North America around 1000 B.C. by new waves of Asian emigrants crossing the Bering Strait, the bow and arrow quickly became a standard tool for most nations. Made from tough wood and sometimes reinforced with bone, the average bow in the 18th and 19th centuries measured about three feet—long enough for distance shooting, but short enough for a horseman to use while on the move. Arrows tipped with points made from flint, obsidian, or—after the arrival of the whites—metal could be fired with extreme accuracy up to a distance of 150 yards. The bow and arrow also allowed a very rapid rate of fire. A bowman could easily let fly several arrows in the time it woud take a rifleman to prepare a muzzle-loader to fire a single shot. With the development first of

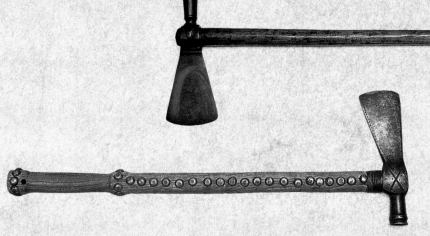

Top: This tomahawk from South Dakota likely belonged to a Sioux warrior. Bottom: Brass tacks were a common adornment on all types of 19th century Indian weapons.

breech-loading rifles and then of repeating rifles, the bow and arrow eventually lost its advantage.

The lance had been the weapon of choice for hunters and warriors before the bow and arrow. These spears tipped with flint or metal points remained a part of the Native American armory, but they were eventually limited to ceremonial use. Other offensive weapons for a warrior included a tomahawk, a knife, a stone war club, or perhaps a sling. Defensively, an Indian warrior might use a buffalo-hide shield, which in many cases could stop an arrow but not a bullet.

Of course, after white contact, many individuals obtained firearms from traders and from defeated enemies, and in time, the rifle became a prominent weapon among many tribes. Rifles were hard to come by for Native Americans, though. For the most part, they had access only to technologically outdated firearms, and it was often difficult for them to keep guns in good repair and find ready supplies of ammunition for them.

Native Americans had a very personal concept of battle. War with other tribes was generally not a protracted affair with specific military or political objectives. Sometimes groups would battle over hunting rights to a certain area, but most often skirmishes were opportunities to acquire horses or other property, to seek vengeance or restitution in personal matters, or to establish prowess as a warrior. In some instances, though, bitter tribal feuds lasted for generations, as with the Blackfeet and the Crows, who would typically engage each other on sight.

Sometimes large forces of warriors were amassed, particularly after whites became a primary adversary, but typical war parties might consist of as few as ten or twenty young warriors. Such a party would not necessarily be executing the will of their tribe. More often, they

were acting independently. Any brave who could command the respect of others and convince them to follow him had the right to assemble a group of warriors and lead them into battle, sometimes even over the objections of their tribal leaders.

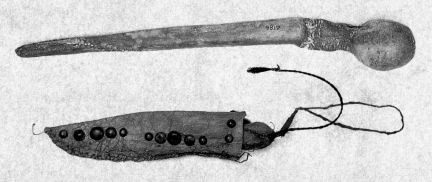

Left: The Native American owner of this musket cut the barrel down. **Below:** These were two Apache weapons: a simple but effective war club and a knife in a rawhide scabbard.

By a process known as counting *coup*, a brave could establish his prowess as a warrior. To count *coup*, one literally rode up to and touched an enemy, sometimes with a *coup* stick. To Indians, this was the ultimate demonstration of bravery. Each *coup* would earn a warrior the respect and admiration of his tribesmen. Such accolades could also be won for

other specific deeds, such as rescuing a fallen comrade, receiving a wound, or rushing into an enemy's camp. By demonstrating their skill and bravery, warriors could rise to prominence within their group.

SOLDIERS AND CAVALRY

A soldier in the isolated outposts and forts of the West spent his day drilling, doing hard physical labor, or pulling guard duty. At the end of the day, he could look forward to a meal of boiled or baked beans, range beef, and coffee. If he were lucky, he could retire to barracks that were well built and comfortable; if not, he shared crowded, leaky barracks with assorted vermin. The monotony of garrison life was interrupted by arduous field duty, which sometimes included skirmishes and battles with hostile Native Americans. For this thankless and often perilous job, he received $16 per month, reduced to $13 in 1871 after Congressional cutbacks. The soldier may have wondered why he chose such a rugged life and pondered the value of his service.

In the long term, the value of his service was immeasurable because the military proved to be a key to the settling of the West. The doctrine of Manifest Destiny maintained that it was the divine right and national destiny of the United States

Some of the key figures who developed and executed military policy in the West gather at Ft. Sanders in 1867.

to possess the whole continent in order to inspire liberty and encourage self-government. If the government sanctioned the expansionist goals of Manifest Destiny and the people aspired to fulfill those goals, then it was the military that acted to protect and serve them. This role was never an official directive for the military. However, in retrospect, the army aided the fulfillment of Manifest Destiny by surveying the land for potential commercial use, by escorting and protecting emigrant settlers in the West, by participating in military action that

helped acquire new territories, and by checking Native American resistance to white encroachment and settlement.

Military involvement in the West began in 1804, when Captains Meriwether Lewis and William Clark led a detachment of soldiers on their famous expedition. Later army exploration in the West was led by such notables as Lieutenant Zebulon Pike, Major Stephen Long, and Lieutenant John C. Frémont.

While in the field in South Dakota, General Nelson Miles and his staff (right) enjoyed somewhat better mess accommodations than did their enlisted men in the 1st Infantry (above).

"A Cavalryman's Breakfast on the Plains" by Frederic Remington depicts an army patrol in camp.

The Corps of Topographical Engineers was organized by the army in 1838. Their mission was to explore and survey U.S. possessions in the West, to collect natural and scientific specimens, and to document their findings. Although many of the places surveyed had been visited by mountain men years earlier, the engineers were the first to investigate locales for America's future use. They laid out roads, discovered landmarks, participated in boundary delineation, and were responsible for the transcontinental railroad surveys of the late 1850s. Their work helped pioneers and merchants navigate the lands west of the Mississippi—a major step in turning the wilderness into a garden.

Soldiers constructed the first military fort in the West, Fort Osage, near present-day Kansas City, in 1808. Built by part of the 1st U.S. Infantry, Fort Osage doubled as a government factory and depository for furs that had been garnered from nearby Native American tribes.

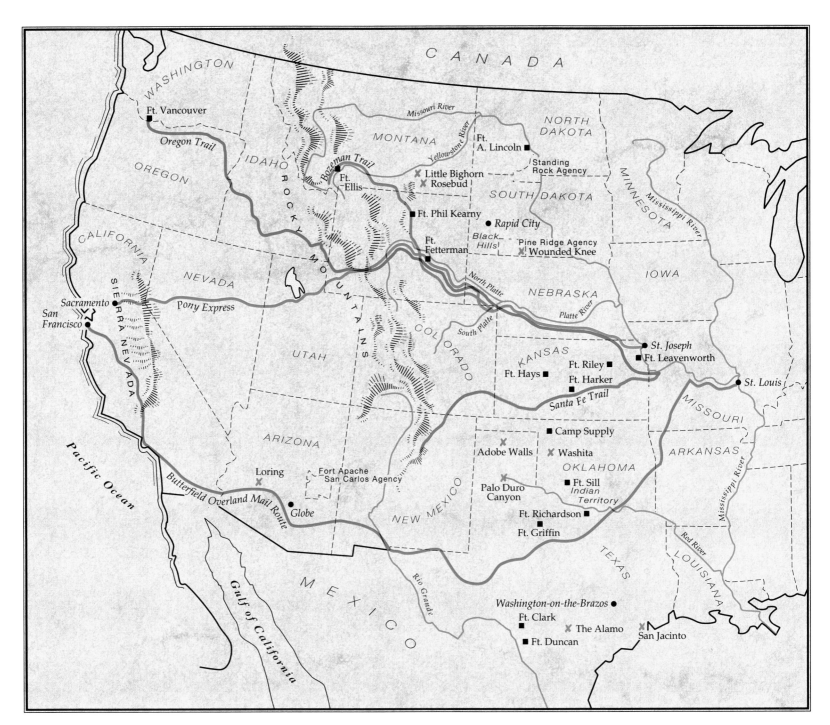

As America pushed westward to fulfill its Manifest Destiny, the army became embroiled in complex issues of economics, politics, transportation, foreign relations, and military confrontation.

Trade in fur and other goods involved the military in other ways as well. Missouri traders and merchants began to encounter Native Americans along the Santa Fe Trail during the 1820s. In 1829, Major Bennet Riley provided an army escort for traders on their way to New Mexico. Riley's escort became the first of several attempts by the army to offer protection for civilian traders. Army protection for traders and merchants was not extensive or universal, partly because there were few soldiers stationed at posts in the West. In 1820, there were only 6,000 soldiers in the U.S. Army, with very few of them west of the Mississippi.

During the mid-19th century, the United States expanded its territory west of the Mississippi quickly and significantly. Expansionist fever during this period elected James K. Polk as President and launched the phrase Manifest Destiny. The idea behind Manifest Destiny—that the moral superiority of freedom-loving Americans gave them the right of conquest—had influenced the rebellion of Texas against Mexico during the 1830s. When Sam Houston, who commanded the Texas forces, called for more volunteers in newspaper ads, scores of men from the East rushed to help release their fellow Americans from the yoke of Mexican (that is, foreign) rule. Texas declared itself an independent republic in 1835 and achieved statehood ten years later, the same year that newspaper editor John L. O'Sullivan defended America's expansion with the term Manifest Destiny.

Polk used the army in 1846 to force Mexico's hand and gain more territory for the United States. He sent ten regiments headed by General Zachary Taylor to the Rio Grande to encourage Mexico to sell California and the Southwest. Because the Rio Grande area was in dispute, Mexico regarded this as an act of invasion and declared war. A force of 50,000 volunteers was called up to reinforce Taylor's 2,000 U.S. Army regulars. The Mexican War ended in 1847 with a

Troop numbers varied over time in the West, but they were typically low. In 1860, 10,000 men patrolled 2½ million square miles of U.S. territory.

swift victory for the U.S. Army. The Mexican War, the Gadsden Purchase, and a border settlement with Great Britain added California, the Southwest, and the Oregon and Washington territories to the United States.

The most well-known role of the U.S. Army in the West was as an Indian-fighting force, but the army's interaction with Native Americans throughout the 19th century proved more multifarious than western legend allows. For example, the army was charged with the welfare of Native Americans and the implementation of all Indian policy until mid-century, when the Department of the Interior assumed those responsibilities. As huge numbers of emigrants began moving westward along the Oregon and California trails in the 1840s and 1850s, relations between the U.S. government and the various Indian nations of the West intensified. With this age of westward expansion, the military's role changed, becoming more complicated.

Treaties between the Plains Indians and the U.S. government during the early 1850s divided the Great Plains among the Plains nations. Each nation was to receive supplies from the government every year for 50 years. In return, emigrants were granted safe passage across tribal homelands, and the government was allowed to build roads and forts on Native American lands. Other treaties designated specific reservations for the various tribes and nations, again with the hollow promises of regular supplies. The government did not always live up to the treaties. Consequently, Native Americans continued to roam the plains to hunt, but the competition for the game supply was increased by the presence of whites. Tensions ran high, and violence erupted against the emigrants and settlers.

A string of forts and outposts was constructed along the frontier throughout the 1850s. On the central plains, army personnel from these forts protected emigrants on the Oregon and California trails; toward the south, the forts were constructed to block tribes on the southern plains from raiding into Texas. Settlers requested military protection and escorts across the plains, despite violating government treaties by settling or hunting on Indian lands. Civilians were just as likely to demand help on petty matters, such as missing livestock, as they were for protection against raiding warriors. Paradoxically, the army was also delegated the job of enforcing treaties to protect Native American ancestral lands from settlers and hunters—a job not likely to be carried out. Even if officers wanted to do this—and most did not—the army did not have sufficient manpower to seal off the reservations from settlers. No clear, all-encompassing policy existed for dealing with Native Americans, making the military's role in the West a difficult one.

This drawing depicts one of the army's many duties in the West, as soldiers arrest an illegal trader in Indian Territory.

When the Civil War began, large numbers of soldiers were evacuated to the East. As the military presence abated, Native American resistance grew stronger and attacks on settlers, miners, and ranchers became more frequent. By the end of the Civil War, the Native Americans were galloping toward a final phase of resistance—a series of mostly small engagements and skirmishes that crystallized the army's role in the West as Indian fighters.

After the Civil War, the government still had no set policy for the Native American "question." By 1868, most of the Plains Indians had been assigned to reservations, but significant numbers of them still roamed the Great Plains. The government vacillated between not wanting to face the issue at all and deciding it was not that serious, and so the United States had no official strategy for decisively dealing with the situation. Easterners were tired of war and military expenditures, so their representatives in Congress slashed the military budget and reduced the army's size to 54,000 in 1866 and to 27,000 in 1874. Only a fraction of that total was posted in the 100 forts scattered from the Mississippi River to the Pacific Ocean.

The government may not have had a concrete policy, but the attitude of some of the soldiers—from the generals to the enlisted men—determined a course of action. Both officers and enlisted men tended to believe in the idea

Off-duty soldiers relax in a canteen at Ft. Keogh in Montana.

behind Manifest Destiny. They believed in the expansion of whites across the West and the progress that came with it, and they determined that the Native Americans stood in the way. This attitude was reflected in the words of General William T. Sherman, who described Native Americans as "a class of savages displaced by the irresistible progress of our race." Sherman commanded the Division of the Missouri from 1866 to 1869, and he was appointed commanding general of the army in 1869. Essentially, he was in charge of the military during the Indian Wars, and he had the authority to put his opinions into action.

The small forces of men stationed at remote outposts, the harsh and unfamiliar terrain, and the hit-and-run guerrilla tactics of the Native Americans made subduing the Indians a formidable task. However, two major aspects of military strategy resulted in the eventual vanquishing of the Native Americans. First, the army was engaged in total warfare against recalcitrant Indians. Contrary to what some tribes or bands thought, the army was not going to pack up and leave after a poor showing in a couple of skirmishes. Manifest Destiny made the white dominance of the West inevitable, and the military fought to win the continent for their country. Their unity of action toward that goal was more than a match for the Native Americans' individualistic approach to warfare.

Secondly, an offensive strategy involving winter campaigns helped destroy the Plains Indians' structure of life, forcing them to surrender to reservation life. Traditionally, these Native Americans fought during the summer months when they roamed the plains, following the grass and game. In the winter, they set up semipermanent camps to wait out the harsh prairie winters. As devised by General Philip Sheridan in 1868, the winter campaigns involved going into the field to search for these winter villages. On finding them, the soldiers killed as many Native Americans as possible, burned the shelters and food supplies, killed the horses, and drove the survivors on to the plains to face death by star-

vation or exposure. Survivors had no choice but to head to the nearest fort and surrender. The military's approach to subduing the Native Americans was subjugation or annihilation, and their tactics were brutally effective.

For all its long-range optimism and ambition, Manifest Destiny had a dark underside of racism that culminated in the vanquishing of most native peoples,

The military's sustained campaign of total war eventually overwhelmed the western Indian nations that fought to keep their homelands.

and the military became the vehicle of that devastation. The common soldier would not have seen it that way. His image of himself was as an Indian fighter who was often outnumbered and surrounded by a capable foe. Underpaid, underfed, and pushed to his limits, he nonetheless proved himself steadfast under fire and a worthy opponent in battle.

SAM
HOUSTON

1793–1863

Sam Houston endures as the human embodiment of the phoenix. He rose from the ashes of several ruined careers and a reputation as a drunk to become, in the words of Andrew

In 1835, Sam Houston went to New Orleans for money and volunteers; he returned to Texas with a company of fighters and more than $10,000.

Jackson, "enrolled as amongst the greatest chieftains." Samuel Houston was born in 1793 near Lexington, Virginia, the fifth of nine children of Major Samuel Houston, a career army officer and veteran of the Revolutionary War, and his wife, Elizabeth. After Houston's father died in 1806, his mother moved across the Alleghenies to a farm near Knoxville, Tennessee. Sam left home at age 16. He was curious about the Cherokee living along the Tennessee River and went to live with them, learning their language and customs. He was given the first of his two Cherokee names, Co-loh-neh, or the Raven.

After his sojourn among the Cherokee, Houston returned home. When army troops passed through Knoxville offering silver dollars for enlistees in 1813, the young adventurer joined the 7th U.S. Infantry and accompanied General Andrew Jackson's force to Alabama to wage war against the Creek nation.

At the Battle of Horseshoe Bend on the Tallapoosa River on March 27, 1814, Houston was among the first to scale a high stockade and fight hand-to-hand with the Red Stick band of the Creeks. He suffered wounds from arrows and gunshots in his leg, arm, and shoulder. The boldness of this young ensign came to the attention of General Jackson.

After the campaign, Houston completed a law course in Nashville and set up practice in nearby Lebanon. He was a frequent guest at the Hermitage, Jackson's estate in Nashville, and became a friend, ally, and protégé of the great soldier. With Jackson's endorsement, Houston was elected district attorney for the Nashville district and in 1823, at age 30, was elected to Congress. He served two terms as a Jacksonian Democrat, and after leaving office, he helped elect Old Hickory president. Jackson, in turn, showed his appreciation by putting Houston's name forward as governor of Tennessee.

Houston married 20-year-old Eliza Allen in 1829. Unfortunately, the marriage dissolved in three months for reasons unknown. Despondent, Houston resigned the governorship and drifted to Arkansas to live among his beloved Cherokee. On the Verdigris River near Fort Gibson, Arkansas, Houston set up a trading post called Wigwam Neosho. And he drank. So deep ran his whiskey addiction that the Cherokee called him Oo-tse-tee Ar-dee-tah-skee, or Big Drunk.

He still was respected enough by the Cherokee to become their counselor and public spokesman. He bid for a contract to supply food and trade goods to the Cherokee after learning that corrupt agents had been supplying them with inferior goods and pocketing enormous profits.

Through the influence of Jackson's secretary of war, John Eaton, and perhaps the President himself, Houston was awarded the contract. Ohio congressman William Stanbery questioned the arrangement, and on the floor of the House of Representatives, he accused Houston, Eaton, and Jackson of fraud. After Stanbery repeated his accusation, Houston met the

Sam Houston, here in Cherokee garb, wisely retreated from Santa Anna's army in 1836 until he could organize a tangible fighting force.

congressman on a Washington street and used his hickory cane to beat him senseless. Houston stood trial for contempt of Congress and was given a light reprimand.

Houston ventured to Texas for the first time in 1832. He had not been in the Mexican territory long before he began hinting at the acquisition of the province by the United States. Houston settled in Nacogdoches and quickly involved himself in the Texas independence movement.

By the end of 1835, the province was on the verge of war with Mexico. Houston was named Commander-in-Chief of the Texas army, and he appealed for volunteers in the newspapers. Land was offered to those who helped defeat the "usurper," President Antonio López de Santa Anna.

In a crude frame building in the village of Washington-on-the-Brazos, 59 Texas leaders declared Texas's independence and adopted a constitution on March 2, 1836. Houston began to plan his strategy to fight Santa Anna's 4,000-man army, which had surrounded the Alamo in San Antonio de Bexar.

Houston had earlier ordered the Alamo abandoned. However, Houston's order was countermanded by provisional governor Henry Smith, who dispatched Colonel William Travis to reinforce the mission. On March 6, Santa Anna attacked the Alamo, killing all 188 of its defenders. Three weeks later, while Houston was en route with his meager army to the Brazos River, Santa Anna defeated James Fannin's force at Goliad, executing Fannin and 350 men.

THE FALL OF THE ALAMO

On March 2, 1836, while the Texas Declaration of Independence was being signed, nearly 4,000 Mexican soldiers had surrounded the tiny mission called the Alamo in San Antonio and were continuing to bombard it with cannon fire. The siege, which had begun on February 24, was directed by Antonio López de Santa Anna, the on-again, off-again president of Mexico and commander of its army. The Alamo served as the southernmost fortification in Texas.

Inside the Alamo, 188 defenders attempted to thwart the relentless assault on the mission. The commander of the Alamo's little army was William Barret Travis, a South Carolina-born lawyer who had arrived in January to reinforce the mission's 120 men under the leadership of James Bowie. Bowie was seriously ill and had turned over the command to Travis. Also present was the former Tennessee congressman, Davy Crockett. A dozen sharpshooters he called his Tennessee Mounted Volunteers followed him to the Alamo.

Originally a mission, the Alamo was named after a nearby grove of alamo (cottonwood) trees.

On March 6, Santa Anna ordered his army to attack and to give "no quarter." After the Mexicans scaled the walls and entered the mission, gunfire gave way to fierce hand-to-hand combat. During 90 minutes of intensive fighting, all of the defenders were killed, but not before they slew eight Mexicans for every one of them. A handful of women and children, a slave, and a San Antonian who was not one of the defenders were spared. Recently found documents suggest that Crockett was not slain while defending the Alamo's southeast wall, but rather, he may have been captured and executed by the Mexican forces. Bowie was killed while fighting from his sickbed, and according to his sister-in-law, the Mexicans tossed his body "on their bayonets until his blood covered their bodies and dyed them red."

The arrogant Santa Anna, while strolling through the carnage after the battle, murmered, "It was but a small affair." The days that followed proved him wrong.

Before confronting Santa Anna's huge and well-provisioned force, Houston wanted to buy time to strengthen his puny army with volunteers. He conducted a zigzagging march through east and south Texas not only to fragment and confuse the Mexican army but also to enlist more troops. Everywhere he marched, he inspired enlistments to the cause by speaking of the Alamo and Goliad.

Houston shrewdly bided his time until April 21, 1836, six weeks after the Alamo's fall. He brought his army of 783 men to the juncture of Buffalo Bayou and the San Jacinto River to do battle with Santa Anna and his force of 1,400. At mid-morning, while the exhausted Mexican troops slept, Houston led his ragtag band through the prairie grass with shouts of "Remember the Alamo!" and "Remember Goliad!"

The 20-minute battle was little more than a slaughter. When the smoke cleared, 630 of the Mexican army lay dead, another 208 were wounded, and 730 were taken prisoner. Included among the prisoners was the self-styled Napoleon of the West, Santa Anna, who was dressed in a private's uniform. Houston, who took a painful ankle wound during the fighting, suffered the loss of nine men and 34 wounded. After signing a document declaring the independence of the province of Texas y Coahuila, Santa Anna was permitted to take the remnant of his army across the Rio Grande.

Houston was elected the first president of the new Republic of Texas. His platform included provisions of frugality in the administration of the new government and the immediate seeking of recognition of the Republic by the United States and then annexation into the Union. Recognition was granted in March 1837, but the annexation question languished for the next eight years. Whig opposition in Congress to Texas statehood was based on the belief that Jackson had promoted the revolution to add a new Democratic state to the Union. Opposition also centered around the provision in the Texas constitution that permitted slavery. As Houston's political career flourished amid the controversy, his personal life improved as well. In 1840, he married Margaret Moffette Lea of Alabama.

On December 29, 1845, President James K. Polk signed the act that admitted Texas into the Union. Houston served in Washington as the state's first senator, a post he held for 14 years. Among the issues that were dear to his heart were Indian affairs, antislavery, and the preservation of the Union. When he was elected governor of Texas in 1859, he continued to oppose the secession of southern states from the Union, making impassioned speeches that warned of the war it would create. When Texas voted to secede despite his warnings, he resisted joining the Confederacy and refused to swear an oath of loyalty to it. As a result, the Texas legislature declared the office of governor vacant, and Houston retired to his farm in Huntsville.

He died of pneumonia on July 26, 1863. Houston's final words were "Texas—Texas—Margaret!"

Commanding 783 men, Sam Houston routed Mexican troops at San Jacinto to secure Texas's independence.

PHILIP H.
SHERIDAN

1831–1888

"The only good Indians I ever saw were dead." These infamous words were spoken candidly by General Phil Sheridan and frequently misquoted in the 20th century as "the only good Indian is a dead Indian."

Sheridan's hard-bitten philosophy was forged in the unforgiving arena of frontier warfare, and it reflected the pragmatic if ethnocentric viewpoint of 19th-century pioneers who felt it was their right to take possession of the last West.

The son of Irish immigrants, the combative Philip Henry Sheridan was born on March 6, 1831, in Ireland, onboard a ship bound for America, or in New England. The following year, the Sheridans moved to Somerset, a village in Ohio where Phil was reared.

From age 14 to 17, Phil worked as a store clerk, but the direction of his life changed in 1848 when he received an appointment to West Point. While at the Academy, his inclination to brawl brought him within five demerits of expulsion. A bout in front of the barracks even cost him a year's suspension. Finally, he graduated in 1853, 34th in a class

Philip Sheridan knew the army couldn't counter mobile bands of guerrillas; his winter strategy engaged Indians in their large, semi-permanent winter camps.

of 52. The new second lieutenant was assigned to the 1st Infantry and posted to isolated Fort Duncan on the Rio Grande in Texas.

Not long after, he was transferred to the Pacific Coast, and by 1856, he was campaigning in Oregon and Washington against the Yakima nation. Stationed at Fort Vancouver, Lieutenant Sheridan was detailed to lead 40 dragoons to relieve a blockhouse besieged by Yakima warriors. Sheridan's men disembarked from the steamer *Belle* on the north bank of the Lower Cascades of the Columbia River in Washington. The soldiers immediately fell under fire, and skirmishing continued for hours until the Yakima withdrew at sundown. The next morning, Sheridan led his force against the blockhouse, and, supported by another relief column, they successfully lifted the siege.

When the Civil War began, Sheridan was sent east as a captain. His initial assignment was in Missouri as chief commissary and quartermaster for the Army of the Southwest, but in May 1862, he was promoted to colonel of the 2nd Michigan Cavalry. "He fights! He fights!" exclaimed General William Rosecrans of the cool but aggressive Sheridan. Sheridan proved to be a brilliant cavalry commander, and within a few months his rank had soared to major general of volunteers.

After the war, Sheridan was sent to command a large force along the Rio Grande in support of rebelling Mexican Nationalists, which contributed directly to Austrian archduke Maximillian's defeat as emperor of Mexico. Later, Sheridan was appointed military governor of the Fifth District, comprising Texas and Louisiana, but his harsh implementation of Reconstruction policies resulted in his removal by President Andrew Johnson within six months.

At this point, Sheridan was placed in command of the Department of the Missouri (Illinois, Missouri, Oklahoma, Colorado, and New Mexico), where the objective was to subdue Indians and confine them to reservations. Charged with the immediate problem of subduing the Southern Cheyenne who had raided in Kansas during the summer of 1868, Major General Sheridan determined upon a winter campaign. Plains Indians generally rode the war trail during the summer when grass was tall, then retired for the winter into the vast plains. More recently, however, the Cheyenne, Kiowa, and Comanche had taken to raiding in the spring and summer, then spending the winter on their reservations in Oklahoma.

Sheridan was advised that winter campaigning was impossible, but he reasoned that grain-fed cavalry mounts would fare better than grass-fed Indian ponies during the winter when there was little natural forage. He also counted on the value of surprise, because Plains Indians felt secure in their homeland during the winter months. Sheridan studied meteorological records of the frontier outposts; consulted with officers, settlers, scouts, and teamsters about winter conditions; and planned his logistics carefully.

Numerous scouts were employed, supplies were gathered, and troops were assembled at

SHERIDAN'S "HEROES"

In 1875, when Texas legislators were considering a bill to protect the last of the state's rapidly dwindling buffalo herds, General Philip Sheridan appeared before the legislators and urged them to kill it. According to Sheridan, the men who destroyed the buffalo were heroes. Rather than stopping them from hunting the shaggy beasts, they should instead be given "a hearty, unanimous vote of thanks" and a bronze medal "with a dead buffalo on one side and a discouraged Indian on the other." Sheridan continued:

"These men have done in the last two years, and will do in the next year, more to settle the vexed Indian question than the entire regular army has done in the last 30 years. They are destroying the Indians' commissary; and it is a well-known fact that an army losing its base of supplies is placed at a great disadvantage. Send them the powder and lead, if you will; but for the sake of a lasting peace, let them kill, skin, and sell until the buffaloes are exterminated. Then your prairies can be covered with speckled cattle and the festive cowboy, who follows the hunter as a second forerunner of an advanced civilization."

In the end, Sheridan's words proved to be all too true. Military campaigns against the Plains Indians often proved effective, but almost never in a decisive way. Virtually every nation that offered resistance held out to some degree until starvation—due to the depletion of the buffalo—drove them to finally accept reservation life.

various points. In November, three main columns began to converge toward northwestern Oklahoma. Camp Supply was established as a base for the primary striking force, which was Lieutenant Colonel George Armstong Custer's 7th Cavalry. A protégé of Sheridan after spectacular service in the Civil War, Custer led his men through a snowstorm to seek the Cheyenne, and the climax of his efforts was the vicious Battle of the Washita.

One of Philip Sheridan's first victories against Native Americans came in 1856 when he lifted the Yakima siege at Fort Vancouver.

This type of forceful campaign during the winter influenced the Cheyenne to reside permanently on their reservation. Henceforth, the winter campaign was utilized regularly by the army, and it became a major factor in the rapid decline of the so-called "wild tribes."

Another key factor in the decline of the Plains Indians was Sheridan's encouragement of buffalo hunters to violate the Medicine Lodge Treaty of 1867. The treaty had pledged that the army would protect western buffalo herds from hunters. Sheridan reasoned that if the army ignored the treaty, hunters would decimate the vast herds, which were fundamental to the Plains Indians' way of life. Within a few years, the buffalo herds would all but disappear.

In 1869, Sheridan was promoted to lieutenant general and given command of the entire troubled region between the Mississippi River and the Rocky Mountains. As Native Americans waged war on encroaching whites, Sheridan continued his forceful policies. For several years, some Native Americans living in Mexico regularly crossed the Rio Grande and raided deep into Texas, driving thousands of stolen horses and cattle below the border. In 1873, Sheridan and Secretary of War W. W. Belknap traveled to Fort Clark, Texas, for two days of secret conferences with Colonel Ranald Mackenzie of the crack 4th Cavalry. Mackenzie was directed to pursue the hostiles into Mexico regardless of international repercussions. A few days later, the young colonel executed a slashing raid into Mexico, destroying three villages of those Native Americans deemed to be hostile. He then scrambled back across the border ahead of Mexican troops. Mexican officials protested vehemently but to little effect. A precedent had thus been set for future actions into Mexico whenever border control was considered inadequate.

When William T. Sherman vacated his position as commanding general in 1883, Sheridan took his place. By the late 1880s, he had become corpulent and was suffering from heart disease. In June 1888, a bedridden Sheridan was promoted to full general, but he died the following August at the age of 57. Although best remembered as a magnificent Civil War general, Sheridan played a preeminent role in subduing Native Americans.

WILLIAM TECUMSEH
SHERMAN

After the Civil War, William Tecumseh Sherman was assigned command of the U.S. Army's Division of the Missouri with the rank of lieutenant general. During the years of his command, 1866–1869, he never saw action, but he did participate in treaty signings with several Native American nations. He unwillingly served on the Peace Commission of 1867, whose job it was to solve the "Indian problem" in the West.

In 1867, Ulysses S. Grant was commanding general of the army. The United States signed a treaty with the Comanche and Kiowa bands of Texas, which relocated them from their traditional homeland in the Staked Plains to neighboring Indian Territory. The treaty promised that the two nations could maintain hunting rights in the Staked Plains. This was an example of Grant's so-called Peace Policy toward Native Americans.

Sherman succeeded Grant as commanding general of the army two years later. Sherman's primary consideration became the maintenance of peace among white settlers and western Native American nations. His idea of maintaining that peace can be understood from his attitude toward the Comanche and Kiowa.

In 1871, some Kiowa led by Satanta crossed into Texas and made an attack on a freight caravan. Sherman was inspecting army posts in the area in which the raid took place and actually passed by the spot only hours later. Sherman used this incident to "prove" that Grant's Peace Policy did not work, and he resolved to take more militant action.

Tensions mounted as the Comanche and Kiowa continued to raid, and white buffalo hunters devastated the buffalo herds in vast numbers, thereby threatening the Native American way of life. In the Red River War of 1874–1875, which pitted Comanche and Kiowa against buffalo hunters in the Staked Plains, Sherman gave General Phil Sheridan free rein to launch a massive campaign to force all Native Americans onto reservations. In September 1874, the army annihilated a large joint Comanche-Kiowa camp in the Palo Duro Canyon, located in the Staked Plains. The strength of the two nations was broken forever.

When Sherman retired in 1883, Sheridan took his place, ensuring little change in policy toward Native Americans.

Sherman helped develop the modern tactic of total war.

GEORGE CROOK

1829–1890

"Indian warfare is, of all warfare, the most trying and the most thankless . . . " reflected General George Crook. "In it you are required to serve without the incentive of promotion or recognition, in truth, without favor or hope of reward."

George Crook engaged in Indian warfare during four different decades, and while most officers of the era found it almost impossible to move up in grade, Crook's abilities were so exceptional that he won promotion to major general. His final experience in the Indian Wars readily explains the bitterness of his tone, but the enormity of his overall success made his recognition a certainty. Crook achieved this success by understanding the Native Americans and by treating his longtime opponents with sympathy, respect, and dignity. "He never lied to us," summed up Chief Red Cloud. "His words gave the people hope."

George Crook learned guerrilla tactics in the 1850s while fighting the Yakima and others in the Northwest, and he employed those tactics in the Civil War.

Born on September 23, 1829, Crook was reared on an Ohio farm near Dayton. At age 18, he was admitted to West Point, where Phil Sheridan was his roommate. Graduating near the bottom of his class in 1852, he was commissioned a lieutenant of the 4th Infantry.

Crook served for eight years on the Pacific Coast, where he helped build military posts, escorted explorers' parties, and campaigned against Native Americans in the Rogue River War and the Yakima War. On June 10, 1857, First Lieutenant Crook led Company D of the 4th Infantry into an inconclusive clash against hostiles on the Pit River in California. The only casualty was Crook, who caught an arrow in the side. Surgeons extracted the shaft but were unable to remove the arrowhead, which remained with Crook throughout his life.

During these campaigns and skirmishes, Crook learned to fight frontier-style, emulating the guerrilla tactics of the Native Americans and subsisting off the land while in the field. He respected his opponents and regarded them as human, which was more than many military officers and soldiers did. With determination, he drilled his troops and instructed them in marksmanship.

Early in the Civil War, Crook obtained the colonelcy of the 36th Ohio Volunteer Infantry. After taking the novel step of intensively training his regiment of volunteers, Crook led them into combat in what is now West Virginia and employed his troops in a guerrilla campaign. In May 1862, he was granted a special commission as a major of regulars after a victory at Lewisburg, during which he was badly wounded. Three months later, Crook was promoted to brigadier general of volunteers. He then led his brigade at Antietam. In 1863, he was given command of the 2nd Cavalry Division. After heavy campaigning, he was promoted to command one of Sheridan's corps and placed in charge of West Virginia. During the final months of the war, Sheridan placed him at the head of one of his cavalry divisions, and Crook saw combat in the actions leading to Appomattox. By war's end, he had advanced to major general of volunteers. As his military career progressed, his personal life was enriched by his marriage to Mary Dailey on August 22, 1865.

Crook returned to the frontier late in 1866 as a lieutenant colonel of the 23rd Infantry in command of troops in the Northwest. Upon reaching Idaho Territory, he rode at the head of Company F of the 1st Cavalry in pursuit of Paiute raiders. Crook's actions against the Paiute indicated his skill in skirmishing with the Native Americans. Time after time, he managed to kill or capture sufficient numbers of the enemy to secure a victory while losing only a man or two.

On December 26, 1866, Crook encountered a war party at Owyhee Creek and soundly defeated them, slaying 30 Paiute and capturing seven. Only one trooper was killed and one wounded. Within two weeks, Crook and Company F cornered hostile Paiute at the Malheur River in Oregon. Crook directed the action so skillfully that there were no casualties on either side, but 30 Native Americans were forced to surrender. Three weeks later, at Stein's Mountain in Oregon, Crook led Company M of the 1st Cavalry against a large band of Paiute. One civilian employee was slain and three troopers were wounded, while Crook and his men killed 60 hostiles and rounded up 27 captives.

Crook continued to hound the Paiute throughout the spring and summer of 1867. His final clash with them occurred on March 14, 1868, at the picturesquely named Donner and Blitzen Creek. Although three of his men were wounded, 12 Paiute were killed and two were captured. Crook's innovative methods and unremitting pressure against the Paiute pacified the Northwest region within a year and a half. The Oregon Legislature expressed its gratitude, and Crook's superiors, recognizing a virtuoso performance, issued commendations.

By this time, Crook was known as an inveterate outdoorsman who tended to travel ahead of his column for solitary hunting and scouting forays. During his years in the West, he hunted animals of virtually every known species and caught almost every type of fish. He eventually became a taxidermist to preserve his trophies. Crook often made significant contributions to the mess supplies of his men with his hunting and fishing. When his men were on the march and saw smoke ahead, pack animals were sent forward to carry whatever game Crook had killed.

A fine hunter, George Crook learned how to supplement his troops' food supply with available resources from the surrounding countryside.

His personal probes also taught him a great deal about the plant life and terrain of the area in which he was stationed, information that he used in planning his campaigns. Crook almost always refused an escort, not wanting to overwork his men. He shunned uniforms, preferring to wear canvas clothes and a straw hat. Crook liked to ride a mule, with a rifle or shotgun balanced across his pommel for quick use. He never used liquor, tobacco, tea, coffee, or profanity. He was tall, lean, erect, and sported a forked beard.

Crook exacted loyalty, affection, and supreme effort from his men. He incessantly pumped his subordinates for information but never revealed his plans to them. He did not bother his officers with detailed instructions, expecting them to exercise initiative. Two keys to Crook's success against Native Americans were his use of mule pack trains, which provided far greater mobility than wagon trains, and the liberal employment of Native American scouts. Crook worked his native allies hard in the field, thus keeping his troopers fresh for combat. He also found it much easier to locate renegades with the use of Native American scouts. Native American allies could settle old scores with a vengeance, so the employment of native scouts reduced the potential number of hostiles.

In 1871, President Ulysses S. Grant ordered that Crook be placed in charge of the Department of Arizona, where the ferocious

The keys to General Crook's Arizona campaign were the Apache scouts he used. They alone had the skill to locate Apache renegades.

and resourceful Apache raided at will. The Southwest proved a more difficult region to secure against Native American hostilities. The warm weather foiled surprise winter campaigns, while the terrain was too treacherous for major assaults. Part of Crook's strategy involved moving rapidly with his patrols into the heart of Apache lands. To penetrate areas previously unknown to the army, he employed Apache scouts—a tactic that proved vital to his success. An old Southwestern proverb maintains that "It takes an Apache to catch an Apache." Crook took advantage of the group's warring factions to hire Apache scouts from one band to track those from another band. "An Indian in his mode of warfare is more than the equal of the white man," Crook wrote. "The only hope of success lies in using their own methods, and their own people." Crook was nicknamed Gray Wolf by the Apache, because he tracked them with the skill and tenacity of a cunning timber beast.

The following year, Crook learned of a plot by Native Americans to kill him the next time he visited Camp Date Creek. While conversing with Crook, the chief conspirator was supposed to roll and light a cigarette. The first puff was to be the signal to murder Crook and any other whites present. Crook's next visit to Camp Date Creek occurred when the camp's commandant died. Arriving on September 8, 1872, Crook strolled into the midst of the reservation Indians, accompanied by his aide, Lieutenant William J. Ross, and several packers, who were veteran frontiersmen bristling with revolvers and knives. As planned, the chief conspirator rolled a cigarette and puffed it, whereupon a brave beside him aimed a carbine at Crook and fired. Ross struck the warrior's arm, and the bullet went astray. A hand-to-hand melee ensued, and those Apache who did not flee were overwhelmed.

Crook's military tactics and sympathetic diplomacy placed most Apache on reservations by 1873. The Arizona Territorial Legislature commended Crook, and he was promoted to brigadier general to fill the vacancy of the recently slain E.R.S. Canby. Crook was advanced over numerous officers, and his

$13 A MONTH

Whether scouting the movements of Native Americans, escorting emigrants across the prairie, or participating in battle, thousands of U.S. military patrols crisscrossed the American West during the army's 100 years of service there. Permanent posts typically served as the headquarters for most army units, but smart commanders quickly learned the usefulness of patrols. The use of far-traveling squads of men—usually cavalry—proved to be the best means for policing the thousands of square miles of Indian territories that separated the forts.

A typical patrol of the late 1870s consisted of detachments of one to several companies of cavalry. Each company featured 50 to 100 mounted men. On patrol, each soldier was supplied for a journey of several days. His equipment consisted of a rifle, pistol, extra ammunition, canteen, tin cup, knife, shelter half, haversack, saddle bags, poncho, and a feed bag for his horse. His food while on the trail consisted of bacon, hardtack, and coffee.

For all his efforts, the enlisted man was paid $13 a month!

The members of Troop E of the 6th Cavalry, shown here in 1881, rode out of Fort Union, New Mexico Territory.

controversial promotion was resented by many men with greater seniority (and less ability). Aware of his own talents and industriousness, Crook scorned his critics and remained as outspokenly contemptuous of them as he had been of ineffective officers during the Civil War.

After gold was discovered in the Black Hills, General Crook was given command of the Department of the Platte in anticipation of trouble with Sioux and Cheyenne warriors. When hostilities erupted, he was not reluctant to be active in the field. On March 18, 1876, Crook and an escort rode to the mouth of Little Powder Creek to visit the position of Colonel J. J. Reynolds, who had attacked a Cheyenne camp the previous day. While en route, Crook caught sight of the rear guard of a Cheyenne and Sioux war party. The general threw up his rifle and shot one of the braves off his horse. Crook's men captured nearly 100 horses from the fleeing warriors, but that night the Indians returned to snipe at the soldiers' campfires, apparently intending to recapture their ponies. Hoping to remove their excuse for lurking about, Crook ordered the ponies killed. The dying animals trumpeted pathetically, and the warriors yelled in anger, fired a few parting shots, then disappeared. The soldiers and scouts broiled steaks from the carcasses.

In May of that year, Crook marched out of Fort Fetterman with 1,300 men. His force represented one of three columns that were to converge on the rebellious Sioux and Cheyenne. At dawn on June 17, Crook broke camp on the Rosebud River in Montana and began to move up the canyon with his command of cavalrymen, infantrymen mounted on mules, Native American scouts, and civilians. This force was attacked by warriors under the leadership of Crazy Horse, who headed a force of considerable size. The ensuing six-hour Battle of the Rosebud was the largest in scale during the long history of warfare between whites and Native Americans.

Crook's Native American scouts held Crazy Horse's forces at bay for 20 minutes while the soldiers arrayed in line of battle. When Crook realized the unprecedented numbers of warriors opposing him, he intended to fight Civil War-style, in orderly lines. However, the terrain—a broken battle front that was three miles long, heavily timbered, and dotted with ravines—did not permit such an engagement. Neither would Crazy Horse, who attacked one flank and then another, hoping to draw the soldiers out group by group. The battle took the form of small, hard-fought clashes.

There were several hand-to-hand encounters, charges and countercharges, and considerable long-range sniping. Though Crook's men fired 25,000 cartridges during the battle, all of the fighting produced few casualties. Crazy Horse later admitted that three dozen of his braves were killed and 63 were wounded, while Crook suffered nine losses and 21 wounded. In midafternoon, Crazy Horse pulled his warriors away to the north, perhaps hoping to ambush the soldiers in the rugged Montana countryside. Crook claimed victory because he maintained possession of the battlefield. But the Native Americans were emboldened not only by their good showing but also by the lack of further pressure from Crook, who remained in camp for the next eight weeks. Eight days after the Battle of the Rosebud, the same Sioux-Cheyenne force met Custer at the Little Bighorn and devastated the 7th Cavalry.

Gray Wolf returned to Arizona in 1882 when restless Apache began raiding off the reservations. Combining his usual relentless campaigning with compassionate diplomacy, Crook attempted to subdue the raiders. The highlight of his efforts was one of the most dangerous expeditions of the Indian Wars, a daring probe into forbidding country never before visited by white men. During May and June of 1883, Crook led 50 soldiers and nearly 200 Native American scouts into Mexico, intending to crush Apache resistance by penetrating their Sierra Madre stronghold. Advance detachments skirmished with surprised Apache, and Apache leaders Geronimo, Nana, and Loco all had tense conferences with Crook. More than 300 Apache, including Nana and Loco, marched back to the United States with Crook. In ensuing months, other bands drifted back to their reservations from Mexico. Finally, in February 1884, Geronimo and his people crossed the border.

Two years later, Geronimo led another breakout, and Crook returned to Mexico for further conferences with renegade leaders. Although some of the bands came back, Geronimo was adamant and remained in Mexico. When civilians, newspapers, and even General Sheridan criticized his methods, Crook resigned his command. He was replaced by his rival, Nelson A. Miles, who ultimately accepted Geronimo's surrender. Crook was returned to the Department of the Platte.

Crook had not approved of some of the military's policies against the Native Americans. He was not enthusiastic, for example, about rounding up old men, women, children, and the infirmed so they could be transported to an unfamiliar and unsuitable destination selected for them by the government. Yet, he carried out his duty.

When the War Department stripped his old Apache scouts of their honors and then sent them to Florida with the renegades and raiders, Crook was incensed. He strongly protested this action and launched a vigorous correspon-

George Crook (second from right) at a council in March 1886 discusses surrender with Geronimo (second from left).

dence to see justice done. His efforts were fruitless.

In 1888, Crook was promoted to major general and assigned to the Division of the Missouri. Crook and his wife moved to the headquarters in Chicago, where he died two years later of a heart attack. He was buried at Oakland, Maryland, then transferred to Arlington National Cemetery. When the Apache at the San Carlos Reservation learned of his death, they wept for Gray Wolf.

AL
SIEBER

1844–1907

Though a friend to the Apache who served under him as scouts, Al Sieber was a relentless and resourceful foe to warriors he was paid to pursue. Sieber became a legendary scout in Arizona during the 1870s and 1880s and watched as his fame spread nationwide following campaigns against Victorio and Geronimo.

Albert Sieber was born on February 29, 1844, in Mingolsheim, Germany. His father died when Al was only one year old, but his indomitable mother managed to immigrate with her large brood to the United States in 1849. The Siebers settled in Lancaster, Pennsylvania, and lived there for seven years. When he was 12, Al moved with his mother and married sister to the logging settlement of Minneapolis, in Minnesota Territory. As a teenager, he apparently worked as a teamster and as a volunteer policeman.

At age 18, Sieber joined Company B of the 1st Minnesota Volunteers. His first Civil War campaign was at the siege of Yorktown, Virginia, where his skill with a rifle earned

While running the San Carlos Reservation, Al Sieber was shot in the foot during a melee.

him duty as a sharpshooter. He fought at Chancellorsville and at Gettysburg. During a charge at Gettysburg, Sieber was wounded in the head and leg, and he spent five months in the hospital. Although promoted to corporal in 1864, Sieber saw no further combat.

Sieber headed west of the Mississippi early the following year. He drifted around, working at a variety of occupations. He lived in San Francisco for a few months, then became a tie cutter for the Central Pacific Railroad. He ventured to the mining district of Nevada, where he worked as a road grader near the mining town of Virginia City. He prospected at White Pine in Utah, and he helped drive a horse herd from southern California to Prescott, Arizona, in 1868.

In Prescott, he made the acquaintance of such noted scouts and guides as Dan O'Leary, Ed Peck, and John Benjamin Townsend. From these veteran scouts, Sieber received invaluable instruction about the countryside and about Native Americans. This information proved helpful when he became the foreman of a ranch in Williamson Valley, which was frequently raided by Indians. Sieber saw his first action against Apache while riding in pursuit parties.

By 1871, Sieber was scouting for the cavalry. He also tried his hand at prospecting once again, but he was unsuccessful. For the rest of his life, he periodically worked various claims.

MILITARY SCOUTS

The conquest by rank-and-file officers and men of the U.S. Army over the Native American nations in the West would not have been possible without military scouts. The army scout had no rank within the military, but he was as respected as any officer.

A breed apart, scouts were loners who were accustomed to spending long periods of time by themselves. They understood nature like no others, save for Native Americans. When hunting and tracking, they navigated by the map of the terrain they carried in their heads. Most importantly, they were walking encyclopedias of facts about the Native Americans whom they were hired to trail.

A scout's job included more than just leading an expedition to its destination or trailing Native Americans. Often, scouts were in charge of finding game to eat and a sufficient water supply. When trailing, a scout gathered information by studying the land for clues. Broken twigs, displaced rocks, hoofprints, even manure provided valuable data to help him locate his quarry, be it man or beast. For this specialized and sometimes dangerous work, they were paid about the same as a captain.

Some army scouts—such as Kit Carson, Thomas Fitzpatrick, and Jim Bridger—had been fur trappers. Their knowledge of the terrain, game, and Native Americans resulted from their experiences as mountain men. Other army scouts, including Wild Bill Hickok and Buffalo Bill Cody, were men who had lived and worked on the frontier long enough to have a keen knowledge of

For General Crook, Fel-ay-tay (a member of the Yuma nation) scouted the Apache.

the Native Americans who lived there.

Scouts were also selected from a group of men who had more knowledge of the wilderness than any fur trapper or frontiersman: Native Americans. Frequently employed by the army, they often proved to be the most efficient scouts. Several eastern nations furnished scouts for the army, including the Delaware and Iroquois. Among the western peoples, the Pawnee, Apache, Cheyenne, Crow, and Sioux scouts proved to be essential to the success of the army's campaigns.

One group excelled in this line of work—the Seminole-Negro scouts. In the early 1800s, they had fled their homeland in Florida and migrated to Texas where they performed outstanding service for the army.

That year, General George Crook was assigned the command of the Department of Arizona, and the gifted Indian fighter needed men like Al Sieber. Crook developed a strategy of systematically crisscrossing Apache territory with small units that regularly fought or harassed any Indians encountered, thus making life on the reservation seem more desirable. A key to Crook's success was his widespread use of reservation braves as scouts. Sieber and other experienced Arizona frontiersmen found steady employment leading these Native American allies.

Sieber was hired during the flurry of activity following the Loring Massacre on November 5, 1871, in which six men on a stagecoach were killed by Apache near Wickenburg. His pay was $125 a month compared to the $13 per month received by army privates. At the conclusion of the winter campaign of 1872–1873, Sieber was one of the few scouts retained on a steady basis.

During the late winter and spring of 1874, Lieutenant Walter Schuyler led a sweeping expedition consisting of Company K of the 5th Cavalry, a pack train of 80 mules, and 122 scouts commanded by Sieber. The expedition ranged 1,500 miles in three months, regularly routing bands of Apache after Sieber's scouts had located their *rancherias*.

Sieber tended to discipline his scouts strictly, and on this particular expedition, at least one was executed by hanging. On other occasions, Sieber was known to shoot disobedient scouts. One or two of his men once decided to kill him in camp. Forewarned by a loyal scout, Sieber shot one of the would-be murderers in the head as he crept toward his bedroll. The other culprit tried to run, but Sieber shot him dead as well.

In a great act of bravery, Al Sieber halted an intertribal melee by standing in-between the skirmishing parties.

When the column returned to Camp Verde late in May, the women who had been captured during the operation were asked where they wanted to go. About 50 of them walked over to stand beside some of the Apache scouts. The scouts in turn agreed to marry them. Schuyler felt that a ceremony was in order, and he turned to Sieber. The chief of scouts explained the white man's concept of marriage, told them to join hands, and pronounced them man and wife.

From 1873 through 1879, Sieber was regularly in the field as the chief of scouts and the only permanent guide at Camp Verde. In 1875, the Verde Reservation was closed, although the military post remained in operation. Nearly 1,500 Native Americans were transferred to the San Carlos Reservation. While en route, an intertribal battle erupted, causing at least 15 casualties. The toll might have been higher if it hadn't been for Sieber, who stepped between the lines, braved the rain of crossfire, and quelled the shooting by his raw courage.

Throughout the 1880s, Sieber remained employed as chief of scouts in Arizona. When Crook was reassigned to Arizona in 1883, Sieber accompanied him on a dangerous mission into Mexico's Sierra Madre Apache stronghold. Afterward, Sieber and Lieutenant Britton Davis were given a relatively free hand to run San Carlos Reservation. Unfortunately, Sieber's negligence in forwarding a warning from Davis to Crook in 1885 led to a breakout by 134 Chiricahuas. Davis and Sieber led a pursuit column into Mexico, but after several fruitless weeks, Crook ordered Sieber to return to San Carlos to pacify the Apache there. Consequently, Sieber missed the climactic campaign that resulted in Geronimo's final surrender in 1886.

On January 1 of the following year, Sieber was wounded in a melee at San Carlos involving the Apache Kid, who had served as a scout under Sieber. The Apache Kid had killed a man over the death of his father. Deciding to give himself up, the Kid rode into San Carlos with several followers. Sieber persuaded the Kid and his friends to hand over their guns. As Sieber placed the weapons near his tent, shooting began. He darted into a tent for a gun, but when he emerged an Apache named Curley shattered his left foot with a rifle slug. The Apache Kid fled. He was later arrested, but he escaped again and was never recaptured.

Bedridden at San Carlos for several months, Sieber never regained full use of his left leg. He traveled by train to Minneapolis for a visit with his family in 1889, and not long after his return to San Carlos, he was fired by the commandant, Captain John L. Bullis. Sieber disapproved of the way Bullis treated the Apache. When his criticism became too vociferous, the captain found a pretext for dismissal.

After his days as a scout were over, Sieber drifted around Arizona, finding permanence in neither job nor home. Around the turn of the century, he moved to Roosevelt, where he managed a gang of Apache who were grading a road to the site of the future Roosevelt Dam.

On February 19, 1907, on the Tonto Road near Globe, Arizona, Sieber was crushed to death by falling rock while on the job. Though rumors circulated that Apache workmen had toppled the rock deliberately, most considered Sieber's death accidental. The noted old chief of scouts was buried in Globe.

Al Sieber respected the Native American scouts that he led and was fired when he protested their treatment.

RANALD MACKENZIE

1840—1889

Ranald Slidell Mackenzie, the army's best Indian fighter, was born in New York City on July 27, 1840. His father, a naval commander who also authored several popular books, died when Ranald was eight, and his mother moved the family to Morristown, New Jersey. Ranald entered Williams College at age 15 to begin an unenthusiastic study of the law. In 1858, he secured an appointment to West Point, primarily to relieve his mother of the financial burden of his education.

To the surprise of his family, the frail young man demonstrated a keen aptitude for the military, graduating in 1862, the first in a class of 28. During the Civil War, Mackenzie distinguished himself at Second Bull Run, Chancellorsville, Gettysburg, Petersburg, and other battles. Wounded six times, he held the rank of major general of volunteers by the age of 24. Electing to remain in the regular army after the war, Mackenzie became a captain of engineers. Predictably, he found construction work tedious, and in 1867, he accepted the

After a raid in the Palo Duro Canyon in 1874, Ranald Mackenzie killed more than 1,000 horses belonging to the Comanche and Kiowa.

colonelcy of the 41st Infantry, an African-American regiment assigned to the Texas frontier. A strict disciplinarian whose men had threatened to shoot him during the Civil War, Colonel Mackenzie whipped his inexperienced soldiers into a top unit. Unfortunately for Mackenzie, his regiment did not see combat, and in December 1870, he accepted a transfer to the 4th Cavalry.

Mackenzie transformed his new regiment into the army's finest Indian-fighting outfit. His men found him solemn, strong-willed, modest, and dignified. He displayed great stamina and often worked far into the night, but he was impatient and frequently irritable, perhaps as a result of his several wounds. When he became nervous, he habitually snapped the stumps of two fingers that had been shot off his right hand during the Civil War at Petersburg. Native Americans dubbed him Bad Hand and Threefingers.

After a training period, the 4th was stationed at Fort Richardson. From there, Mackenzie led campaigns in 1871 and 1872 into Comanche and Kiowa territory. During the 1871 expedition, a great deal of information about the hitherto unexplored Staked Plains was compiled, although there was no decisive combat.

During a skirmish on October 15, 1871, at Blanco Canyon, Mackenzie spurred forward to the point of action, and a barbed arrow thudded into his thigh. Chagrined at having been wounded again, Mackenzie did not mention the injury in his official report. The wound remained troublesome, and a fortnight later, a surgeon informed the restless Mackenzie that amputation might become necessary unless he submitted to bed rest. Mackenzie angrily hurled his crutch at the doctor and sent him scurrying from the tent.

In the fall of 1872, Mackenzie returned to Comanche territory with 284 soldiers. Early in the summer, Texas newspapers had reported erroneously that Mackenzie and a number of troops had been massacred by Indians, but it was an alive and purposeful Bad Hand who struck a village of 262 lodges on the North Fork of the Red River on September 29. The warriors fought bitterly and launched two counterattacks, but the village was vanquished within half an hour. Two nights later, a band of warriors raided Mackenzie's camp and retrieved a number of horses, including Bad Hand's own mount and many other cavalry animals. Mackenzie would not forget this raid.

In 1873, Mackenzie and the 4th were transferred to Fort Clark to focus their attention on the Kickapoos from northern Mexico, who were raiding deep into Texas and escaping back across the Rio Grande. General Philip Sheridan and Secretary of War W. W. Belknap met with Mackenzie for two days in April, confidentially instructing him to violate the Mexican border and punish the invading raiders. Mackenzie ordered his men to grind their sabers to a razor edge, and then he put them through grueling daily drills and carbine practice.

A few weeks later, Mackenzie learned of a raid against a nearby ranch. He mounted a column of more than 400 men and started out. He did not tell them of their mission until they reached the Rio Grande. There, Mackenzie directed his troopers to stuff their saddlebags with rations and to fill their pockets with cartridges, after which the pack mules were cut loose. With Mackenzie in the lead, the command pushed into Mexico under cover of darkness.

Mackenzie drove his men through the night. Just after dawn on May 18, they set up to strike three Native American villages near Remolino, Mexico. All three villages were destroyed and prisoners were taken. Heading back to the border immediately, the soldiers had no rest, ate only whatever hardtack they had shoved into their packs, and rode at a trot or gallop through a second night. When the prisoners began to fall off their horses, Mackenzie ordered them tied to their mounts. With Mexican cavalry in pursuit, the exhausted soldiers reached the safety of the Rio Grande before dawn on May 19, having ridden 140 miles in 38 hours.

Following the Battle of Adobe Walls and other attacks by the Comanche and Kiowa on buffalo hunters in the Texas Panhandle, General Sheridan organized a campaign according to a plan Mackenzie had designed in 1872. Five columns totaling 46 companies and 3,000 men converged on the Panhandle in the fall of 1874. Mackenzie led a column that

THE DECLINE OF THE BUFFALO

When Lewis and Clark made their way to the Pacific Ocean and back again in 1804 through 1806, as many as 60 million buffalo roamed the Great Plains. By 1886, when scientists from the National Museum in Washington, D.C., went to the great West searching for buffalo to use in a new exhibit at the Smithsonian Institution, they hunted the Montana plains for eight weeks before they found the 25 specimens they needed.

The rapid demise of the buffalo was caused by the wholesale slaughter of them by both pleasure and market hunters as well as by the destruction of their native habitat. Shooting buffalo became the sport of the West, with railroad passengers often taking aim into large herds as they whisked by on trains. If these practices were not officially sanctioned by U.S. officials, particularly during the years following the Civil War, they were at least consciously overlooked.

Several nations of buffalo-hunting Plains Indians fought the white hunters and the military for their very survival. For example, the Kiowa and Comanche waged war against the hunters in Texas after witnessing the extensive slaughter of the buffalo in the early 1870s. The white hunters had previously killed the buffalo during the winters when their coats were long and shaggy. However, by 1870, a new tanning process had been developed that made short-hair hides usable as well. Between the new tanning process and the use of high-powered, telescopic Sharps rifles that could kill the animals from long distances, the rate of slaughter accelerated.

After destroying the herds in Kansas, the hunters moved to the Staked Plains of Texas, setting up a base with their skinners at Adobe Walls. Quanah Parker and his Comanche braves, along with their Kiowa allies, attacked the hunters at Adobe Walls on June 26, 1874, but the hunters held their own. The incident launched a series of skirmishes between the Comanche-Kiowa and the white settlers known as the Red River War, which quickly led to a massive offensive against the Comanche-Kiowa by the U.S. Army.

Probably the most important factor in the surrender of the Native American Plains nations was the wholesale slaughter of their most vital resource, the buffalo.

totalled over 600 men, including numerous scouts, eight companies of the 4th, and five infantry companies.

When scouts reported Indian signs nearby, Mackenzie recalled the night raid by Comanche and Kiowa in 1872, and he took every precaution. Guards were stationed every 15 feet around the camp, skirmishers were strategically placed, and every animal was hobbled, cross-sidelined, and tethered by a thick rope to its individual iron stake. When 250 warriors struck that night, they were repulsed by Mackenzie's men. They reappeared the next morning but withdrew, heading for their long-time refuge, Palo Duro Canyon.

Mackenzie knew about Palo Duro Canyon, perhaps as a result of torturing the location out of a *Comanchero* trader. As daylight broke on September 28, Mackenzie's men scrambled down the precipitous trail into the Palo Duro, where native camps stretched for three miles along the canyon floor. One troop raced for a huge horse herd, capturing over 1,400 ponies, while Mackenzie led two companies in a charge through the villages. Only three Native Americans were killed, but in their scramble for safety, everything was abandoned. Mackenzie ordered all lodges, equipment, and immense stores of food burned. After cutting out 350 of the best Indian ponies, the balance of the herd was shot. With Palo Duro Canyon now closed to them and their winter food supply destroyed, the Comanche and Kiowa were eventually forced onto reservations. The Battle of Palo Duro Canyon proved to be a major turning point in the Red River War. The 4th was transferred to Fort Sill to supervise the Comanche and Kiowa as they adapted to reservation life.

During the late 1870s, Mackenzie and the 4th were transferred around the Southwest to quell trouble at various reservations and hotpoints. Once, General Sherman ordered Mackenzie to Arizona, where Apache were conducting raids and Navajo were bellicose. Mackenzie skillfully placed six companies of the 4th in position to block any possible Apache and Navajo union. Sherman was so pleased that he appointed Colonel Mackenzie in command of all troops in the Department of Arizona, a move that understandably infuriated the two generals who were thereby technically subordinate to the colonel. Within five weeks, Colonel Mackenzie reported that the Apache had either surrendered or fled to Mexico.

On October 26, 1882, Mackenzie was promoted to brigadier general. His success was spoiled by the collapse of his health. By his early 40s, the once-slender officer had become overweight, and an earlier abstinence from alcohol had been replaced by habitual drinking. Overwork and the long-range effects of his multiple wounds led to a deterioration of his mental abilities. Following a lengthy medical leave, the 43-year-old bachelor announced his engagement to a San Antonio widow, but it became painfully obvious that he was unbalanced. In 1884, he was placed on the retired list. His sister cared for him until he died at the age of 48, on January 19, 1889, in New Brighton, New York.

Mackenzie was interred at West Point alongside other military greats. A brilliant and heroic general during the Civil War, he continued his selfless service during the Indian Wars and proved himself to be the army's most effective troubleshooter. His determined efforts were key to the army's success in subjugating the Indians of the southern plains

NELSON A.
MILES

1839–1925

Nelson Appleton Miles was born on August 8, 1839, and raised on a Massachusetts farm. As a teenager, Miles worked as a clerk in Boston while spending his leisure hours in regular attendance at lectures, in night school, and in pursuit of a broad reading program. By 1860, he concluded that civil war was inevitable and that success in combat could provide the opportunity for the fame and position he craved. Miles began to study military volumes, and he joined a small group that employed a French veteran to provide them with drill instruction.

When hostilities erupted, Miles raised $3,500 to organize a volunteer company of infantry, but he was denied the captaincy by an ungrateful governor and resentfully accepted a lesser commission. The experience taught him a bitter lesson about the value of friends in high places. Throughout his career, Miles would shamelessly exploit every conceivable contact to promote his advancement.

During the Civil War, courage and a gift for utilizing terrain vaulted Miles to high rank. He experienced heavy combat duty and was wounded four times, while his exploits at Chancellorsville earned him a Medal of Honor. By the end of the war, he held the rank of major general of volunteers. In order to continue his military career, Miles had to accept a colonelcy in the regular army.

Marriage to Mary Sherman, niece of General William T. Sherman and of Ohio senator John Sherman, gave Miles invaluable contacts in his drive to the top of the frontier army. In 1869, Miles assumed command of the 5th Infantry at Fort Hays, Kansas. Combat against many of the Native Americans of the West was spearheaded by cavalry, however.

Nelson Miles's rise through the ranks of the military came as much through his skillful politicking as it did through his abilities as a combat leader.

As the years passed, the ambitious Miles chafed at the exclusion of his regiment from campaigns that promised glory and promotion. At last, in 1874, he was assigned to lead a column in the Red River War in the Texas Panhandle. Miles finally received his initiation into Indian fighting, and he carried along a newspaper correspondent to insure personal publicity.

A tall, handsome officer, Miles repeatedly exhibited courage, boldness, and organizational skills while campaigning in the West. Unfortunately, he was also vain, pompous, and ruthless in his personal ambitions. He was loathe to give credit to other officers and was deeply jealous of West Point graduates. Yet for a decade and a half, he was an efficient and relentless Indian fighter who successfully employed infantry in wars otherwise dominated by cavalry.

In 1876, Miles was assigned to lead five companies of the 5th as part of the general pursuit of the Sioux after Custer's demise at the Little Bighorn. Overcoming temperatures of 60 degrees below zero, the 5th marched hundreds of miles and forced the surrender of nearly 2,000 Native Americans. The following year, when Chief Joseph was outmaneuvering the army, General O. O. Howard sent a dispatch asking Miles to intercept the Nez Percé in their flight toward Canada. After 12 hours of hurried preparations in the darkness, Miles eagerly readied his entire available force—five cavalry companies and five infantry troops, four of which were mounted on captured Indian ponies. Miles was a prominent figure in the remainder of the Nez Percé campaign, emerging as the only successful officer of the entire operation.

Displaying incessant and tactless self-promotion, Miles clashed increasingly with his superiors, even with his uncle by marriage, General William T. Sherman. His qualifications were undeniable, however, and when a vacancy occurred in 1880, he finally received his long-sought star. From 1881 to 1885, General Miles commanded the Department of the Columbia.

In 1886, Geronimo and a few renegade Apache escaped custody after having been corralled by General George Crook. Pressured into resigning, Crook was replaced by Miles, who placed guard details at water holes and mountain passes, organized a system of pursuit parties, and established a network of 30 heliograph stations. The elusive Apache were hounded relentlessly, and Geronimo and a handful of followers finally surrendered. Miles eagerly accepted total credit for the victory, ignoring years of effort by Crook and numerous junior officers. A public subscription for an engraved sword for Miles for his efforts at capturing Geronimo fell far short of the needed amount. Miles quietly paid the difference, then basked in the presentation ceremonies at Tucson.

When two vacancies occurred at the rank of major general, Miles launched a vigorous campaign to be awarded the rank. Though he exploited every possible connection, he was not given a second star. After his keenest rival, Major General George Crook, died in 1890, he made another determined effort at

Shown en route to Indian Territory after their capture by Miles, the Nez Percé had been promised that they could stay in the Northwest. Miles later helped them win the right to return to their homeland.

WOUNDED KNEE

While Christmas Day, 1890, was being celebrated by the American soldiers at the Pine Ridge Reservation, Minniconjou chief Big Foot lay seriously ill several miles away. Days before, his friend Sitting Bull had been killed by Sioux policemen on the Standing Rock Reservation. Big Foot and several of Sitting Bull's Hunkpapa followers, who had fled Standing Rock after their leader's murder, were on their way to Pine Ridge to seek the counsel of Chief Red Cloud.

On December 28, Big Foot's party sighted four companies from the 7th U.S. Cavalry, commanded by Major Samuel Whitside. Big Foot ordered that a white flag be raised. When Whitside entered the Sioux camp, the pneumonia-stricken Big Foot personally greeted the major. Although Whitside had orders to disarm Big Foot's band, scout John Shangreau persuaded him to wait until the Sioux regrouped next to the army's encampment on nearby Wounded Knee Creek.

Once at Wounded Knee, Whitside again delayed disarming the Sioux due to the late hour. He ordered his men to assist the Indians in making camp and had rations issued to them. Then, he gave Big Foot a portable camp stove to put in his tent and sent the regimental surgeon to look after the sick chief.

During the night, Colonel James W. Forsyth arrived in the army camp, relieved Major Whitside, and told him to prepare the Sioux for movement to a prison in Omaha. The next morning, the 7th Cavalry surrounded the tent village, awoke the Indians, and demanded that they disarm. A young Minniconjou named Black Coyote balked at turning over his newly purchased rifle. When several soldiers forcibly took the weapon, someone fired a shot. The soldiers surrounding the Native American camp opened fire into the crowd. Within minutes, 146 Sioux men, women, and children lay dead in the fresh snow. Among the dead was Big Foot. Over two dozen soldiers were killed, and 39 were wounded.

Bad weather was imminent, so the soldiers left the dead Sioux where they lay. Later, when a burial detail returned, the corpses were frozen to the ground.

The survivors of Wounded Knee were taken to Pine Ridge, and after being exposed to the elements without shelter, they were finally taken in by members of the Episcopal mission. "We tried to run," exclaimed a survivor, "but they shot us like we were a buffalo. . . . soldiers must be mean to shoot women and children. Indian soldiers would not do that to white children."

In a grisly scene, a burial detail prepares a mass grave for the dead of Wounded Knee.

the promotion. He even secured an interview with President Benjamin Harrison. Finally, Miles obtained the promotion he so coveted.

Assuming command of the Division of the Missouri, Miles was confronted by a problem with the Sioux, who were living a discontented existence on reservations. By the end of 1890, the religious frenzy of the Ghost Dance had spread with such fervor that the military feared an uprising. Tensions mounted after respected Sioux leader Sitting Bull was slain in an incident on December 15.

Miles established a command post at Rapid City, South Dakota, and tried to smother further resistance to authority. When 350 Sioux escaped the reservation, their movement was blocked by the 7th Cavalry at Wounded Knee Creek. The ensuing "battle" of Wounded Knee resulted in at least 200 Native American casualties, including numerous women and children among the 146 dead. Incensed at what he regarded as a blunder, Miles increased military pressure gradually while working through personal diplomacy to divide Sioux leadership. Further bloodshed was averted, and on January 15, 1891, the Sioux submitted to Miles's authority.

In 1895, Miles was appointed commanding general and moved his family to Washington, D.C. Two years later, he went to Europe as a military representative to Queen Victoria's Jubilee and as an observer of the Greco-Turkish War. During his European tour, he visited the German, French, Italian, Russian, and Austrian standing armies. After returning to the United States, he campaigned for a stronger American military force. Miles also published his *Personal Recollections* in 1897.

Upon the outbreak of the Spanish-American War in 1898, Miles vigorously pushed for

naval action while the army prepared for combat in the tropics. He urged an assault on Puerto Rico, which lay along the sea route from Spain to Cuba. Miles opposed the hurried invasion of Cuba, and when he asked the

In the field, Miles proved himself to be a shrewd military strategist time and again.

president for permission to command the assault force, he was ignored. Shortly after Cuba surrendered, Miles landed in Puerto Rico with 3,500 men, conquering the defending troops in a skillfully executed 19-day campaign.

After the war, Miles continued to clash with the War Department and with Presidents McKinley and Roosevelt. In 1902, Roosevelt censured him after a public feud with Secretary of War Russell A. Alger. Miles was awarded the rank of lieutenant general, but he was denied a combat role in the Philippines.

When the United States entered World War I, the 77-year-old retiree eagerly volunteered for duty, but Miles's services were declined. Miles died on May 15, 1925, and was buried in Arlington National Cemetery.

GEORGE ARMSTRONG
CUSTER

1839—1876

Born on December 5, 1839, in New Rumley, Ohio, George Armstrong Custer was the son of the village blacksmith and the great-grandson of a Revolutionary War veteran. Impressed by his father's participation in a local militia unit, young Autie—as he was called—drilled near the men in a little uniform and with a toy musket. As a teenager, Autie attended an academy in Monroe, Michigan, where he lived with his married half-sister. There he met the lovely girl who later would become his devoted wife, Elizabeth "Libbie" Clift Bacon.

Custer became a rural schoolteacher at the ripe old age of 16, but the next year, he received an appointment to West Point, where he excelled at horsemanship. With each term, however, Cadet Custer piled up great numbers of demerits for slovenliness and tardiness. He was an inept pupil, graduating in 1861 as the last in a class of 34.

When the Civil War commenced, Custer proved audacious and fearless in combat. He saw action from First Bull Run to Gettysburg to Appomattox, with countless skirmishes between major engagements. By 1863, he was a captain in the 5th U.S. Cavalry, but because of his spectacular exploits, he was vaulted to brigadier general of the Michigan Volunteer Cavalry. The Boy General was the youngest United States officer ever to wear a star.

Above: Custer wears the uniform he designed for himself as a general in the volunteer army. **Right:** Clad in these showy buckskins, Custer set off for his fateful encounter with the Sioux nation.

General Custer designed for himself a uniform of blue velvet that was festooned with swirls of gold braid on the sleeves, silver stars on the collar, and a scarlet neckerchief. His thin, blond hair grew to shoulder length, inspiring his men to call him Old Curly. Despite his foppishness, he fought with distinction, leading victorious charges that earned him a second star, considerable publicity, and the admiration of such influential men as Generals Sheridan and Grant.

When the war ended, Phil Sheridan summoned Custer's unit to Texas for Reconstruction duty. His men grew disenchanted with Custer, considering him a martinet who cared nothing for the rank and file. Early in 1866, Major General of Volunteers Custer reverted to his regular army rank of captain, which entailed a salary reduction from $8,000 to $2,000 per year. He considered an offer of $16,000 to serve with the Mexican Army, but he turned it down when he could not obtain a year's leave of absence. Private business opportunities were also declined, and twice he refused an appointment as lieutenant colonel of the black 9th Cavalry because he wished "to be attached to an organization of *white* troops."

Custer's professional status was settled in late 1866 when General Sheridan secured for him the lieutenant colonelcy of the newly formed 7th Cavalry. In October 1866, Custer and his wife joined the regiment at Fort Riley, Kansas. Since the colonel was almost never present, Custer commanded the 7th in practice, if not in name.

The 7th's first campaign occurred in the spring and summer of 1867, when General Winfield Scott Hancock directed large-scale but ineffective efforts against the Cheyenne in Kansas. Custer was court-martialed for leaving his command without permission, using ambulances on personal business, ordering his officers to shoot deserters without trial, and abusing men and animals. One glaring example of foolishness occurred while Custer's column was on the march in Kansas. Custer was an avid hunter and had keenly anticipated pursuing his first buffalo. Early one morning, he spurred his big thoroughbred toward distant antelope, accompanied only by his bugler and a few greyhound hunting dogs. When he spotted a lone buffalo, he raced

Custer confers with his scouts on an 1870s mission to protect railroad workers as they pushed onto Indian lands in the northern plains.

after the beast for so great a distance that he was completely alone. When the buffalo finally turned to charge, Custer fired his pistol—into the brain of his horse! Afoot in Indian territory, with no idea of how far or in what direction his troops were, Custer trusted the instincts of two of his dogs. He trudged after them for miles, finally encountering the regiment and sending a detail after his gear.

Equally irresponsible was a forced march that Custer ordered, ostensibly to procure

Custer's expedition snakes out of the Black Hills toward Fort Abraham Lincoln after the initial survey of the region in 1874.

supplies from Fort Harker, but actually to provide him an opportunity to visit Libbie at Fort Riley. Custer drove his escort of 75 men night and day, covering 150 miles in 55 hours. When Indians jumped his rear guard and killed two men, Custer did not pause even to recover the bodies. When at last he allowed a rest halt at Fort Hays, he pushed on to Fort Harker with four men, taking just 12 hours to travel 60 more miles. He then took a train to Fort Riley, where he was soon in Libbie's arms—while most of his regiment remained in the field.

Custer was convicted at a court-martial and suspended from duty for one year. General Sheridan persuaded the Custers to accept his quarters at Fort Leavenworth. In September 1868, Sheridan directed his protégé to resume duties with the 7th and join a fall campaign that resulted in Custer's brutal conquest of the Cheyenne chief Black Kettle at the Battle of the Washita.

Custer executed a forced march south from Camp Supply in Indian Territory, pushing through a snowstorm in order to be in position for a dawn attack on November 27. Deciding to launch the type of headlong charge that had won him victories and fame during the Civil War, Custer deployed his troopers into four squadrons to surround the quiet lodges. The regimental band was with Custer's detail and under orders to blast out the stirring tune "Garry Owen" when the assault commenced. Buglers with each column began to blow the charge, but all instruments froze up after just a few notes.

Black Kettle was killed as the troopers attacked the camp. Custer surged into hand-to-hand fighting astride a black stallion: He fired a revolver slug into the head of a warrior; he ruthlessly rode down another brave; then he positioned himself in the middle of the village and directed his command. Warriors fought desperately to defend their fleeing families. Over 100 Indians were slain, 53 women and children were captured, and 875 ponies were seized. Also seized were 1,100 buffalo robes, 4,000 arrows, 1,000 pounds of lead, and 500 pounds of gunpowder. Soldiers pulled down the lodges, piled up the confiscated food and domestic gear, burned these piles, and methodically shot the ponies. There were 19 dead and 14 wounded soldiers, but when the 7th marched away from the devastated village at midafternoon, Custer again had them strike up "Garry Owen."

By this time, Custer had molded the 7th into a crack regiment. Each troop rode the same color horse, and a training program—an unusual practice among frontier units—was instituted. The program featured daily target practice, and the best 40 marksmen were formed into an elite unit of sharpshooters exempt from menial duties.

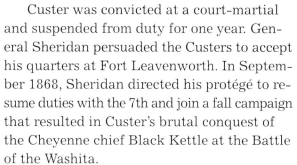

Nevertheless, many of his officers and men continued to resent Custer's disregard for the safety and comfort of those under his command, particularly since he indulged himself luxuriously even while campaigning. Custer always maintained a large, well-appointed tent and was attended in the field by a female cook, while Libbie often accompanied her husband on campaigns. In the field and on the post, Custer was boisterous and highly energetic. When he received good news at home, he was given to hurling furniture across the room in exuberance.

In 1873, Custer led the 7th during the Yellowstone Expedition, which comprised 1,500 officers and men, over 2,300 horses and mules, and 275 wagons and ambulances. The force was out for three months and traveled over 900 miles. The 7th was assigned to protect Northern Pacific survey parties, but Custer frequently journeyed ahead of the expedition with two companies to break a trail through the rugged country.

While reconnoitering with his two troops on August 4, 1873, Custer and 90 cavalrymen of the 7th were jumped by 300 Sioux warriors near the mouth of Montana's Tongue River. Custer coolly dismounted his men and conducted a determined defense for three hours. Choosing his moment shrewdly, Custer finally ordered his troopers into the saddle and led a smashing charge that routed the superior force.

A week later, Custer took eight companies and set out in pursuit of a large band of warriors along the north bank of the Yellowstone River. When several hundred braves suddenly approached his column, Custer ordered the band to blare out "Garry Owen,"

THIS PHOTOGRAPH WAS MADE AT
FORT LINCOLN, DAKOTA TERRITORY, 1874

then led a charge. The braves scattered in flight, and the cavalry pressed a close pursuit for nine miles before finally breaking off the chase. Custer's first mount was shot dead under him during the skirmish, but he soon set himself astride another horse and directed his troops to victory.

Custer sits with officers of the 7th and their wives at Fort Abraham Lincoln. Most of these men would die at the hands of Sioux warriors.

THE BATTLE OF THE
LITTLE BIGHORN

The annihilation of a large part of Lieutenant Colonel George Armstrong Custer's 7th U.S. Cavalry at the Little Bighorn River on June 25, 1876, climaxed the army's summer campaign against the Sioux and Cheyenne on the northern plains. The plan called for

Montana and to engage the large Sioux-Cheyenne encampment there. When Crook's command was defeated in mid-June at the nearby Rosebud River, the task was left to Gibbon and Terry.

Lieutenant Colonel Custer marched upstream

This painting shows the traditional version of the Little Bighorn incident, with Custer falling with the last of his men.

the forces of General George Crook from Fort Fetterman, General Alfred H. Terry from Fort Abraham Lincoln, and Colonel John Gibbon from Fort Ellis to rendezvous in southeastern

from the mouth of the Rosebud Creek with 600 men of the 7th Cavalry. Custer's scouts located the enemy camp on the morning of June 25. Despite warnings from his scouts that the enemy numbered as many as the "blades of grass" on

the ground, Custer prepared to engage them. He split his regiment into three battalions. Custer kept Companies C, E, F, I, and L with him while he assigned Major Marcus Reno and Captain Frederick Benteen three companies each. The remaining company of the regiment was ordered to stay with the supply wagons.

Custer and Reno approached the encampment while Benteen was sent to reconnoiter the bluffs along the river. Reno crossed the stream and was immediately engaged by a large party of Sioux.

Reno was forced to retreat, and when he finally hooked up with Benteen, the two battalions marched north to relieve Custer. Custer, in the meantime, had taken a position on a knoll about a half-mile above the Little Bighorn River. Benteen and Reno heard vigorous firing. As they began their march

north toward the battle scene, their commands were attacked and they were forced to retreat to Benteen's orginal position. They fought off several waves of Sioux and Cheyenne until the following day when the commands of Terry and Gibbon rescued them.

The men later learned that Custer had been attacked by large forces of Sioux warriors under the leadership of Gall and Crazy Horse. All the men in Custer's command were killed, including his two brothers, Boston and Tom, and his nephew, Henry "Autie" Reed. Benteen and Reno lost 47 men while 52 were wounded. Accurate numbers for the Native American losses are difficult to uncover, but it is generally thought that no more than 100 Native Americans were killed.

In 1874, Custer commanded the Black Hills Expedition, reconnoitering the sacred Sioux land in violation of recent treaties. With 1,000 men and 110 vehicles, Custer explored the region, verifying reports of gold deposits and earning the name "Chief of Thieves" from the Sioux. The subsequent gold rush to the Black Hills triggered unrest with the Sioux, and a massive campaign was planned for 1876 in which Custer was to play a prominent part.

Frank statements Custer made while testifying against graft in the War Department resulted in orders to remain in Chicago while the 7th marched against the Sioux. Only a flurry of pleas by the 36-year-old officer allowed him to march at the head of his regiment, perhaps in hopes of scoring a spectacular success that would confound his opponents and generate political opportunities.

On June 25, 1876, Custer pushed the 7th to find a large Sioux-Cheyenne encampment reported by scouts to be on the Little Bighorn River. Leaving one company to guard the supply train, Custer sent two battalions of three companies each in search of the encampment. Clad in a blue flannel shirt and buckskin breeches and armed with a brace of English double-action revolvers and a Remington sporting rifle, Custer rode at the head of the remaining five companies. In the command of 215 men were his brothers, officers Boston and Tom (who had won two Medals of Honor during the Civil War); his brother-in-law Lieutenant James Calhoun; and his favorite nephew, 18-year-old Henry Reed.

First contact was made by the battalion of Major Marcus Reno. Hearing the gunfire, Custer hurried to attack the enormous village, which contained more than 10,000 Indians, including perhaps 3,000 warriors.

Custer's force was overwhelmed, with every man killed. Custer was found among the last group of soldiers to fall. According to ten Cheyenne and Sioux warriors who were the first to meet Custer's column, he rode in the lead and took a bullet in the chest, possibly the first soldier to get hit. As his stunned troops began to pull back, the stricken Custer was lifted into the saddle and carried along until the remnants of his command made the famous "last stand." Although it is impossible to refute Native American claims that he was knocked out of action early in the battle, it is equally impossible to refute the popular image of Custer going down fighting with the last of his troopers.

Only a courageous defense saved the rest of the regiment from destruction, and Medals of Honor were awarded to 24 soldiers who battled valiantly on July 25 and 26. Custer and his men were buried on the battlefield, but in 1877 the remains of Custer and nine other officers were removed for reinterment at West Point. Coyotes had burrowed into the shallow grave and torn apart Custer's body, and only a double handful of bones could be found to place inside his coffin.

Employing the aggressive tactics that had produced victory throughout his military career, Custer led the 7th Cavalry against an insurmountable force. Custer and his men fell courageously, against an equally fearless foe, and the tragedy at the Little Bighorn became the most famous battle of the Indian Wars. And thus, the flawed but fierce Custer became a legendary leader in the Indian-fighting army.

The Crow scout Curley warned Custer against riding on the hostile encampment and left the soldiers when Custer refused to heed his advice.

BUFFALO
SOLDIERS

When the Civil War ended in 1865, the U.S. Army found itself with a large surplus of soldiers it no longer needed. Added to the thousands of white troops were nearly 200,000 African-American soldiers who had served as part of the U.S. Colored Troops during the War. The army was reduced to ten cavalry and 25 infantry regiments. Several regiments remained in the South to enforce Reconstruction, but many more were sent west of the Mississippi River to patrol the vast mountains and plains.

To employ the large number of black soldiers, Congress authorized the formation of the 9th and 10th Cavalry and the 24th and 25th Infantry regiments in 1866. These four units consisted entirely of black troops, but they were commanded by white officers.

Native Americans are credited with the term buffalo soldiers. The soldiers were supposedly called this because their hair was reminiscent of the bison's woolly mane. The troopers accepted their moniker proudly, with the 10th incorporating a buffalo into

Members of the 10th Cavalry form ranks at Fort Apache. These soldiers participated in the campaigns against the Southwest Indians in the 1870s.

Though the buffalo soldiers had a remarkably good record, serving in the military was not easy for them. They suffered discrimination and hostility from the settlers and townspeople they protected. Several officers, including George Armstrong Custer and Eugene A. Carr, refused to lead them.

After the Indian Wars of the West, the buffalo soldiers maintained their hard-earned reputation when they participated in the Spanish-American War and served in the Philippines. In 1916, they served with General John "Black Jack" Pershing—so named because he had commanded the 10th Cavalry—in his expedition against Pancho Villa.

its regimental crest. Men of the four regiments continued to be known as buffalo soldiers until the 1950s, when the U.S. Army was totally integrated.

When the men of the 9th, 10th, 24th, and 25th regiments reached their posts in the trans-Mississippi West, they became involved in some of the most vicious fighting in the history of the army. The two cavalry regiments saw extensive action in New Mexico and Arizona among the Apache, with the 9th earning a reputation for always arriving in the nick of time to save settlers or other soldiers. The 24th and 25th combated elements of the northern plains nations, including the Sioux and Cheyenne. For their outstanding bravery and valor, 18 buffalo soldiers were awarded Medals of Honor during the Indian Wars. The African-American troops generally had high enlistment rates, good morale, and very low desertion rates. The black regiments also had fewer court-martials for drunkenness.

Top: This Frederic Remington painting "Captain Dodge's Colored Troopers to the Rescue" depicts the 9th Cavalry in action. Remington spent time with these troops in Arizona. **Above:** This soldier and other members of the 9th were dispatched to Pine Ridge after the Wounded Knee massacre to help restore order.

OUTLAWS

Gunslinger, shootist, pistoleer, hired gun. Such terms conjure up an image of a western hero protecting lawful citizens on America's uncivilized frontier. Yet the romanticizing of the Old West has clouded the precise meanings of these words over time. None of these terms are synonyms for lawman or outlaw, because in the Wild West, gunfighters frequently worked both sides of the law.

Outlaws and lawmen represented two sides of the same coin. Sometimes only the hand of fate tossing the coin determined which side a gunslinger was on. The vast expanses of land and sparse population in the West meant that there were not enough citizens—let alone authorities—to enforce the law as it was known in the East. Guns were a basic tool for survival in the West, and those who possessed the skill and nerve to make their living as gunfighters hired out to those who did not. In areas where the law was ineffectual or nonexistent, gunslingers were sometimes employed to protect the interests of powerful cattle barons and mine owners from rustlers and highwaymen. Hiring a gunslinger in such an

The raucous atmosphere of the western saloon incited brawls and gunplay, which could turn a gunslinger into a bona fide outlaw.

instance was considered reasonable and lawful. Other gunslingers, such as Killin' Jim Miller, were hired as thugs to eliminate or bully political or economic rivals. A thin line separated the hired *gun* from the hired *assassin*, and only a change in political power or a public outcry was necessary to recast a champion of justice into an outlaw.

The rip-roaring, wide-open atmosphere of the cow towns and boomtowns bred lawlessness and instability. Towns such as Dodge City and Abilene attracted a criminal element that included gamblers, thieves, raucous cowboys, and con artists. The saloons and gambling dens spawned such brawls and free-for-alls that the folks of Tombstone claimed their town had "a dead man for break-

The corners of this illustration depict Arizona's Canon Diablo Gang, while their captors peer out from the center.

fast every morning." The lawmen hired by townspeople to keep the bad element in check were often gunslingers who had made their notorious reputations settling disputes and conflicts in the saloons of other cow towns or boomtowns. They were more at home gambling in such famous saloons as the Alamo, Alhambra, Crystal, Oriental, No. 10, and Long Branch than presiding over law and order from a sheriff's office. In fact, they sometimes consorted with the very people they were hired to eradicate. Gambler and gunman Luke Short, for example, befriended Bat Masterson and Wyatt Earp, with only a badge separating Short from his two confederates.

Aside from the mayhem and murder associated with gunslingers, the West fostered other types of crime. Western gangs—often bound by family ties—

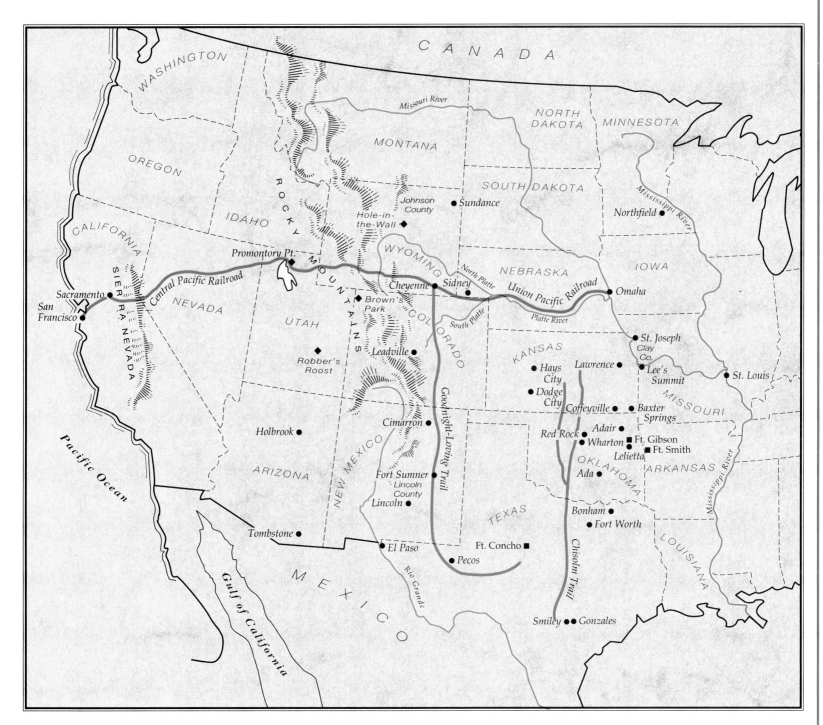

As law and order arrived in the West, outlaws and gunslingers were pushed out of the cow towns and boomtowns and into more remote regions.

pulled daring raids against trains, stages, and banks. Some bands of outlaws evolved from the hatred and bitterness of the Civil War era. Hostilities between Southern sympathizers and antislavery factions peaked along the Kansas-Missouri border, where bands of guerrilla raiders, night riders, looters, and even murderers operated from the 1850s through the Civil War. These violent times proved to be training grounds for some of the West's most notorious outlaws. Frank and Jesse James as well as Cole and Jim Younger rode with the guerrilla bands of William Clarke Quantrill and Bloody Bill Anderson.

The James-Younger Gang is often credited with the first daylight bank robbery in U.S. history in 1866. Over the next decade, the violent but lucrative exploits of this gang launched the careers of many imitators, who were lured by the prospect of easy money and adventure. As pioneered by the James-Younger Gang, bank robberies were pulled by splitting a gang into

Right: If train guards were reluctant to open the express car doors, then the Hole-in-the-Wall Gang dynamited the cars to oblivion.
Above: Several posses pursued the Hole-in-the-Wall Gang, but few proved successful.

two groups. One group of three or four held up the bank, while another group of one or two watched the horses and kept any bystanders at bay. After the robbery, the gang whooped, hollered, and blasted their guns in the air, creating confusion as they galloped away.

When stage lines were established to carry people and cargo across the vast expanse of the West, they also provided a means for companies to ship gold, silver, and other valuables. In the time it took for far-thinking outlaws to learn stage schedules and routes, highway robbery became an industry in the West. By 1877, Wells, Fargo & Company reported 200 highwaymen regularly robbing its stages.

So many trains were robbed between 1865 and 1900 that the railroads could not hire enough private detectives (many of them gunslingers) to guard them. Methods used by gangs to pull train holdups varied. To stop a

These two hired guns served as express guards for the robbery-plagued Wells, Fargo & Company.

train, gang members sometimes forced a railroad worker to throw a switch to send an oncoming locomotive onto a siding, where the outlaws would descend upon it. Or an obstruction was placed on the tracks in the hope that the engineer might see it in time to stop. If the gang was after the express car, a bundle of well-placed dynamite blew off the locked door, sometimes obliterating the car in the explosion—a technique favored by the Hole-in-the-Wall Gang.

Cattle and horse rustling were capital offenses in the West. Rustlers risked being shot or hung. Horse stealing was so intolerable that thieves were often

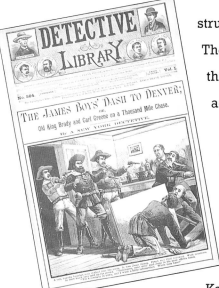

strung up from the nearest tree as soon as they were caught. The significance of cattle to the economy of the West and the importance of horses to survival in the vast landscape account for the harsh response to these crimes.

Hatred and intolerance of stock rustling contributed to the eruption of the range wars. Cattle barons hired gunslingers to protect their herds from rustlers and small ranchers, but often the gunfighters went after alleged "rustlers" without benefit of proof. In 1889, Cattle Kate Watson was lynched by the associates of rich cattlemen for an alleged involvement in cattle rustling. Most of the charges against her were trumped up after she was hung.

Dime novels about the James brothers (above) and Dalton Gang (right) recast the outlaws as victims of bad breaks.

Generally regarded as the lowest of criminals, the stock rustlers were rarely glorified—unlike gunslingers, gamblers, and outlaw gangs. Just as they had done for lawmen, dime novels and popular publications such as the *Police Gazette* romanticized the outlaws' stories. In the blurring of fact and fiction, gunslingers became defenders of justice and outlaws were turned into western Robin Hoods. A key to this transformation involved presenting the gunslingers, outlaws, and desperadoes as victims of injustice, defenders of the people, or both. In the dime novels, a fictionalized Jesse James was driven to a life of crime because he was refused a pardon after the Civil War. Like the Jameses, whom they admired, the Dalton brothers claimed to be victims of government authority. They supposedly turned to crime because a corrupt administration had fleeced them out of their salaries after they risked their lives as federal law officers.

In truth, Jesse James was a greedy thief with a deep resentment for the Union, which he used to rationalize his life of crime. He killed innocent by-standers during robberies and coldly gunned down bank clerks who refused to cooperate. The Daltons were fired from their posts as deputy U.S. marshals because they were suspected of being stock rustlers, among other things.

For all the glamorization of life outside the law, reality dictated that few outlaws or gunslingers reached middle age. The lifestyle was seedy and dangerous, with little economic compensation in the long run. In explaining his decision to voluntarily turn himself in to authorities, Frank James described the life of an outlaw: "I have been hunted for 21 years. I have literally lived in the saddle. I have never known a day of perfect peace. . . . When I slept, it was literally in the midst of an arsenal. If I heard dogs bark more fiercely than usual, or the feet of horses in a greater volume than usual, I stood to my arms. Have you any idea what a man must endure who leads such a life? No, you cannot."

At the end of the outlaw trail, imprisonment or death al-most always awaited. Sometimes, outlaws, gunslingers, and rustlers were captured and brought to justice by lawmen; sometimes death came at the hands of vigilantes. When disor-der, banditry, and violence plagued those frontier areas where the law was nonexistent or too slow, vigilance commit-tees brought justice swiftly and severely. Even in relatively large towns with sheriffs and marshals, lynch law often ruled. Rancher N. K. Boswell's vigilante group in Laramie City, Wyoming, stormed into the Bucket of Blood saloon, dragged out thief and murderer Big Steve Long, and lynched him in his stock-ing feet. His accomplices, Ace and Con Moyer, were hung with him. Captain

In this period illustra-tion, Frank James waves to well-wishers. Tired of the outlaw trail, Frank surrendered in September 1882.

Big Steve Long—a thief, gunslinger, and co-owner of the Bucket of Blood—was hung by vigilantes in 1868.

Jack Slade, a former superintendent for the Overland stage company, was lynched by offended spectators in Virginia City, Nevada, because he roared out to an actress to strip onstage. It was not uncommon for citizens to take the law into their own hands: By 1900, vigilance committees throughout the West had killed over 700 alleged criminals.

Detailed accounts of the deaths of outlaws and gunslingers circulated widely in the West, which revealed a strange fascination with that subject. Outlaws met their ends in any number of ways, and the exact circumstances quickly became shrouded in legend and lore. Countless photographs show lifeless bodies twisting from lynch mobs' ropes or bullet-riddled corpses propped up against the flimsy buildings of a western town. These photos served many purposes. They offered proof that a notorious outlaw or gunslinger was indeed dead, because unsubstantiated rumors of their deaths were always circulating. They served as a warning to other lawbreakers and miscreants. Sometimes, photos were taken as mementoes for the arresting lawman, particularly if the outlaw had been widely known. Often, the photos were turned into souvenir postcards that would be sold for years at a price as high as one dollar.

The desire for souvenirs of dead gunslingers and outlaws reached grisly proportions. As Bob Dalton lay dead in the street after a failed bank robbery in Coffeyville, Kansas, townspeople clipped locks of his hair for keepsakes. Even family members were not immune to the potential profit to be made from death souvenirs. William Clarke Quantrill's mother requested her son's bones be disinterred so she could bury him in the family plot. Later, she was caught selling his bones to souvenir hunters.

Photos, pebbles from graves, chips from tombstones, locks of hair, and even bones were not only souvenirs of the famous but also relics of a wild, adventurous era that was fading right before everyone's eyes. Perhaps the townspeople, farmers, and other ordinary folks who dipped their handkerchiefs in the blood of the notorious or spent their hard-earned dollars on postcards of corpses wanted to salvage the spirit of the Wild West and so turned to the wildest among them—the outlaws and gunfighters. The spirit they sought found a voice not in Frank James's sorrowful lament at the time of his surrender but in Bob Dalton's dying words. As his brother Emmett reached to him amid a haze of gun smoke, Bob shuddered one last time and gasped, "Good-bye Emmett. Don't surrender; die game."

Souvenir photos of outlaws, particularly in their coffins, made an interesting keepsake and served as a warning not to follow their crooked path.

265

JESSE AND FRANK JAMES

In 1842, Robert and Zerelda James moved from Kentucky to a farm in Clay County, Missouri, where Reverend James assumed the pastorate of a nearby Baptist church. On January 10, 1843, their first child, Alexander Franklin, was born, followed by another son, Jesse Woodson, on September 5, 1847. Frank and Jesse lost their father, who succumbed to gold fever and journeyed to California, where he fell ill and died. Strong-willed Zerelda quickly remarried, but this marriage failed, reportedly because their new stepfather was mean to Frank and Jesse.

Legend elevated Jesse (top) and Frank (bottom) James to folk heroes, but sometimes they killed bystanders without regard.

Zerelda entered her third marriage in 1855, with docile, prosperous Dr. Reuben Samuel. The growing family remained on the old James farm, even acquiring a few slaves. They were sympathetic to the Confederacy when the Civil War erupted, resulting in their mistreatment by Unionists. Frank joined William Quantrill's infamous band of Missouri guerrillas, participating in the vicious raid on Lawrence, Kansas, on August 21, 1863. Jesse began to ride with the raiders the next year: He was one of 30 men led by Bloody Bill Anderson into Centralia, Missouri, on September 27, 1864. There, the guerrillas executed 25 unarmed Union soldiers in cold blood.

Jesse suffered severe wounds twice while riding with Quantrill, but he recovered to loot and raid until the end of the war. Jesse and Frank returned to the family farm after the war, but their wartime experiences had stimulated their natural inclination to grip revolvers instead of plows. On the morning of February 13, 1866, a dozen riders pulled off the first daylight bank robbery in United States history, looting the Clay County Savings Bank in Liberty, Missouri, of $57,000. As the gang galloped out of town whooping the rebel yell, they gunned down local college student George Wymore. It has long been assumed that the Jameses and Cole Younger, who was a former lieutenant of Quantrill's, were the ringleaders behind the Liberty job.

For the next decade, the James-Younger Gang robbed banks, stores, and stagecoaches. After 1873, they struck trains in Missouri and in surrounding states. Cole Younger and his brothers, Jim, Bob, and John, were stalwarts of the band, and Frank James was a frequent participant. Jesse, despite being younger than Frank and Cole Younger, became the leader of the gang. Ruthless, assertive, smart, and quick on the trigger, Jesse was a natural outlaw leader. Cole, who disliked Jesse, sometimes led his own holdups, but they were in addition to those he committed with the James-Younger Gang.

Because of their notoriety, the James-Younger Gang tended to get the blame for every robbery in the multistate region. Jesse sometimes published letters proclaiming his innocence, insisting he had alibis for the times when certain holdups had occurred.

Folklore tends to portray Frank and Jesse James as the Robin Hoods of the Wild West, preying on banks and railroads. They are painted as romantic figures who attacked institutions that heralded the modern, industrialist age at the expense of America's agrarian heritage. In other words, they supposedly struck back at the banks and railroads who had taken the land out from under small farmers and poor country folk. But the members of the James-Younger Gang were not folk heroes; they were violent men who robbed and occasionally killed.

One of their more violent robberies occurred on December 7, 1869, in Gallatin, Missouri. The James brothers nursed a grudge against the bank's proprietor, John W. Sheets, who was a former Civil War officer. Posing as customers, Jesse and Frank entered the bank and engaged in a minor transaction with Sheets. When Sheets began writing, one of the brothers shot him in the head and heart. As clerk William McDowell bolted for the door, he was wounded in the arm, but he shouted that Sheets had been killed. The robbers dashed outside with several hundred dollars. During the commotion, the brothers lost one of their mounts and rode out of Gallatin on one horse. They stole another from a farmer, then fled southwest toward Clay County.

Jesse (center) and Frank James (right) started killing as rebel irregulars in William Quantrill's gang during the Civil War.

A reward of $3,000 was offered for Frank and Jesse after the Gallatin murder and robbery. A week later, four bounty hunters surrounded the James family farm. As Deputy Sheriff John Thomason approached the farmhouse, Jesse and Frank surged out of the barn astride swift mounts. A wild exchange of gunfire ensued, followed by a running chase with Thomason leading the pursuit. At one point, Thomason reined in his horse, dismounted, and rested his gun across his saddle to fire at the fleeing brothers. The deputy's horse bolted unexpectedly and, riderless, pulled up beside the outlaws. One of the brothers shot the horse dead, and the Jameses outdistanced their pursuers.

Legends about Frank and Jesse James also stress their regard for the common folk, but on more than one occasion, innocent bystanders were harmed or killed during their robberies. In the fall of 1872, the gang attempted what they thought would be an easy heist. Three mounted gang members robbed the ticket seller at the Kansas City Fair. One of the thieves, perhaps Jesse, seized the tin cashbox and cleaned it out. As he was fighting off ticket seller Ben Wallace, the thief pulled a pistol and fired a wild shot, hitting a little girl in the leg. At that point, the robbers galloped away.

The James-Younger Gang branched out into train robbery on July 21, 1873, at Adair, Iowa. To stop their target, the outlaws pulled up a rail from the tracks, which sent the Chicago, Rock Island & Pacific train into a ditch, killing the engineer. The bandits looted the express

Jesse James (far left) was a natural leader and took the reins of the James-Younger Gang. Jesse had a deep hatred of the government and the Pinkertons that was intensified by the bombing of his mother's house.

car, then collected valuables in the passenger coaches before escaping.

Ruthlessness aside, the James brothers were not without a sense of humor. On January 31, 1874, five masked members of the James-Younger Gang barged into the depot at Gad's Hill, Missouri, and held everyone at gunpoint until a train pulled into the station. After robbing the passengers and express car of the train, the outlaws left a note detailing exactly what they had done, but they deliberately left the amount of stolen money blank. They explained, "We prefer this to be published in the newspapers rather than the grossly exaggerated accounts that usually appear after one of our jobs."

The governor of Missouri offered a $2,000 reward for each member of the gang, while the U.S. postal authorities kicked in another $5,000, and the governor of Arkansas added $2,000. The Pinkerton Detective Agency put one of its finest operatives, John W. Witcher, on the case, but within a month he was found dead. He had been shot in the stomach, head, and shoulder, and most of his face had been eaten away by wild hogs. Certain that Jesse and gang member Clell Miller had killed Witcher, the Pinkerton Agency launched a determined effort to crush the outlaws.

Gang members went underground, but on April 23, Jesse married his lifelong sweetheart, Zee Mimms. Such family functions as Jesse's marriage led the Pinkertons to discover that Jesse and Frank periodically slipped back to the old farm to visit their kin.

A posse of unidentified men, who were probably Pinkertons, surrounded the James farm one night in January 1875, erroneously thinking that the James brothers were inside. Hoping to flush the outlaws, the posse tossed

THE
NORTHFIELD RAID

The James-Younger Gang arrived in Northfield, Minnesota, on September 7, 1876, to do some banking. Frank James, Jim Younger, and Bill Chadwell (alias Stiles) lingered at the edge of town to serve as rear guard. Cole Younger and Clell Miller stayed outside the First National Bank while Jesse James, Bob Younger, and Charlie Pitts entered. When a local citizen approached the bank, he was grabbed by Miller. Pulling away, the man ran down the street screaming, "Robbery! Robbery!" Frank, Jim, Chadwell, Cole, and Miller rode up and down the street shooting into the air to scare citizens and create confusion during the robbery.

Inside the bank, Jesse and the others had their hands full. When the cashier, Joseph L. Heywood, told the gang that a time lock controlled the opening of the safe, he was hit over the head by Pitts and then slashed in the throat. Employees Alonzo E. Bunker and Frank J. Wilcox were roughed up by Jesse and Bob. Ironically, the time lock was not in operation. The safe door was closed with the bolts in place, but the dial on the safe was not turned.

In the confusion, Bunker escaped out the back to warn others of the robbery in progress. Realizing that their plans had failed, the three bandits exited the bank. One of them turned and shot Heywood. A vicious street fight ensued. Townsman Nicholas Gustavson was slain, but so were outlaws Miller and Chadwell. Bob Younger was severely wounded and his horse was killed. One of his brothers picked him up under heavy fire and galloped out of town along with the other survivors.

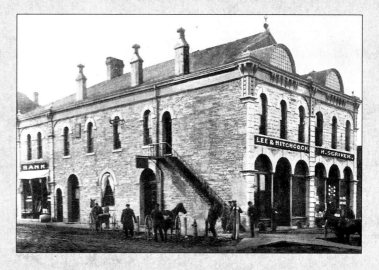

The string of conquests experienced by the James-Younger Gang stopped after failing to rob this bank in Northfield, Minnesota. With the Youngers captured, the Jameses were on their own.

As posses combed the Minnesota countryside, Jesse reportedly tried to persuade Cole to abandon or finish off Bob. When Cole stiffly refused, Jesse and Frank split with the gang. A couple of weeks later, Pitts was killed in a shoot-out with lawmen. Cole, Bob, and Jim Younger—who were all suffering from multiple wounds—surrendered. The James brothers made it back to Missouri, where they tried to disappear.

incendiary devices through the windows. An unexpected explosion killed the nine-year-old half-brother of Frank and Jesse and wounded their mother, resulting in the amputation of her hand. The incident aroused public anger against the Pinkertons, and there were efforts to secure amnesty for the James boys.

Jesse and Frank utilized this type of popular sympathy and support to avoid arrest. That sympathy and support began to wane during the mid-1870s because by that time they had become hardened criminals with no intention of giving up their outlaw way of life.

In 1876, the gang left their familiar Kansas-Missouri countryside to rob a bank at Mankato, Minnesota. The venture proved to be the downfall of the James-Younger Gang. In Mankato, they were frightened away by a group of rugged citizens, so the outlaws decided to shift their raid to nearby Northfield. On September 7, 1876, the gang failed in their attempt to rob the First National Bank there. Three gang members were killed while all three Younger brothers were captured, effectively destroying the James-Younger Gang.

The James brothers made it back to Missouri and then disappeared for a time. Using various aliases, Jesse and Zee lived in Texas, Kansas City, and Tennessee, where their son and daughter were born. On numerous occasions, Jesse was reported killed, but on July 15, 1881, he led his new gang onto a Chicago, Rock Island & Pacific train at Winston, Missouri, and cleaned it out.

Under the name of Thomas Howard, Jesse moved his family to St. Joseph to plan more robberies. However, with more than $50,000 in rewards posted for Jesse, living in anonymity grew more and more difficult.

Bob and Charles Ford joined his new gang with the intention of earning this fortune. On Monday morning, April 3, 1882, Jesse finished breakfast and entered his living room with the Ford brothers, perhaps to finalize plans for a bank holdup the next day. When Jesse stepped up on a chair to straighten a picture, Bob Ford recognized his chance. Bob drew a revolver and triggered a bullet into the back of Jesse's head. As Jesse fell dead, Zee rushed to his side. The Ford brothers headed for a

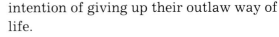

Above: The myth of the Jameses as Robin Hoods was advanced by dime novels. **Right:** In later years, Frank appeared in a Wild West show with Cole Younger.

telegraph office to claim their rewards, while townspeople swarmed to the house to view the infamous outlaw's remains.

Jesse was buried in the front yard of his mother's farm. For years afterward, his mother permitted tourists to visit the old James farm and her son's grave for 25 cents. Also included in the price was Mrs. Samuel's "performance." She cursed detectives, wept melodramatically over the persecution of her sons, and wished damnation upon the Ford brothers. Mrs. Samuel also sold pebbles from Jesse's grave for 25 cents each and regularly replenished her supply from a nearby creek. The Ford brothers were treated with contempt, and Charles committed suicide in 1884. Bob was shot and killed in 1892.

A few months after Jesse's death, on October 4, 1882, Frank surrendered himself to Missouri Governor Thomas T. Crittenden. Following a series of trials and legal moves, he was acquitted and released from custody. Frank lived a quiet, honest existence for 30 years. He worked as a race starter at county fairs, as a theater doorman, and as an attraction in traveling companies. In 1903, he became partners with Cole Younger in the James-Younger Wild West Show. Eventually, Frank returned to the old Missouri farm, where he died at the age of 72 on February 18, 1915.

There were rumors that Jesse was not the man murdered in 1882, and for decades impostors claimed to be the outlaw. Jesse did live on, however, as a romanticized legend in novels, in movies, and in the public imagination. Though he was a thief and murderer, even as esteemed a figure as Theodore Roosevelt wrote, "Jesse W. James is America's Robin Hood."

"I HAVE KILLED JESSE JAMES"

Bob Ford did not attain the success and fame he wanted after his murder of Jesse James in St. Joseph, Missouri, on April 3, 1882. Ford and his brother, Charles, had been members of Jesse's last outlaw gang.

Ford shot the notorious outlaw in the back while Jesse was straightening a picture on his living room wall. Immediately afterward, Ford telegraphed Missouri Governor Thomas T. Crittenden, stating "I have killed Jesse James." The local sheriff arrested Ford, and he was convicted of murder by a jury. After Governor Crittenden pardoned Ford, "the dirty little coward who shot Mr. Howard," as the folk song went, was forced by public opinion to leave Missouri. Charles Ford committed suicide in 1884.

After traveling with P. T. Barnum's sideshow, where he proudly narrated his epic version of the killing of Jesse James, Bob Ford moved to Colorado and opened a saloon in the mining town of Creed. He married one of the dancers and tried to start a new life. In June 1892, a former lawman named Edward (Red) O. Kelly strolled into Ford's saloon and accused Bob of telling lies about him. The two men scuffled, and Ford had Kelly thrown out of the bar. Kelly went across the street, picked up a shotgun, and went back to the saloon, where he shot Ford dead.

Bob Ford died the way he lived, amidst the violence and treachery of his times.

THE YOUNGER
BROTHERS

From left: Cole, Jim, and Bob Younger embraced lives as desperadoes when they rounded out the James-Younger gang.

"We are rough men and used to rough ways." A bedridden Bob Younger spoke for his wounded brothers, Cole and Jim, after they were shot and captured following a bank robbery attempt in 1876 in Northfield, Minnesota. For more than a decade, the Youngers had lived extremely rough and dangerous lives while establishing themselves as western outlaws of the front rank.

There were 14 Youngers, the sons and daughters of a Missouri politician and slaveholder who farmed near Lee's Summit, Missouri. The seventh child was Cole, born in 1844; Jim was born four years to the day after Cole; John came along in 1851; and the rugged baby brother of the outlaw gang, Bob, was born two years later. Their father, although a slave owner, was a Union sympathizer. His farm was raided prior to the Civil War by Kansas Jayhawkers, and he was killed in 1862.

Cole joined William Clarke Quantrill's Missouri Bushwhackers, a band of Southern guerrilla raiders. During the Civil War, he alternated between fighting with regular Confederate troops and raiding with Quantrill's guerrillas. Cole Younger was a hard-bitten man but highly skilled with a gun. During a skirmish between Quantrill's force and Federal troops on November 10, 1861, Cole killed his first man with a remarkable pistol shot that was measured at 71 yards. The following year, in a Kansas City saloon on Christmas Day, Cole encountered one of the men responsible for his father's murder and shot him to death.

Stationed in Texas in 1863, Cole met a tempestuous 16-year-old, Myra Belle Shirley. The relationship between Cole and Myra Belle, who later became notorious as Belle Starr, is one that has been exaggerated and fictionalized in western lore and literature. Starr herself did much to embellish the facts of their relationship, claiming that her daughter Pearl had been sired by Cole.

Hoping to avenge his father's murder, Jim followed Cole into the ranks of Quantrill's raiders. Jim remained with the guerrilla leader throughout the remainder of the war, raiding and looting and acquiring the outlook and attitude of an outlaw.

Young John became increasingly bitter and moody after his father's murder, and at the age of 15, he killed his first man. It occurred while John was arguing with a man named Gillereas, who slapped him with a dead fish and then threatened him with a slingshot. John responded by producing a revolver and shooting him. A coroner's jury acquitted him on grounds of self-defense. After his mother died in 1870, John grew more temperamental and surly—and murderous.

After the war, Cole returned to Lee's Summit, where he encountered a neighbor, Frank James. Frank, a former Quantrill rider, introduced him to his brother Jesse James, another Quantrill veteran. A few weeks later, Frank and Cole are thought to have teamed up to lead the first daylight bank robbery in the United States, on the morning of February 13, 1866, in Liberty, Missouri. A dozen desperadoes rode to the Clay County Savings Bank. Two of them dismounted, entered the bank, and then emerged with grain sacks bulging with more than $57,000. As the bandits thundered out of town, whooping the rebel yell, they gunned down a passerby, a college student named George Wymore.

Cole and several family members spent the next few months enjoying the holdup profits in Texas and Louisiana. When Cole returned to Missouri, the Younger brothers and the James brothers organized a bandit gang that ran rampant for years. The aggressive, ruthless Jesse became the acknowledged leader of the gang, but Cole never got along with Jesse and led several robberies himself. The James-Younger Gang committed holdups throughout Missouri and the surrounding states, and in time, almost every bank, train, or stagecoach robbery was attributed to the bold outlaw band. The Youngers maintained their home base in Missouri, but when pressured by the law, they left the state, usually for Texas.

Jim, who had finished the Civil War in a military prison at Alton, Illinois, returned to Lee's Summit and quietly worked the family farm—until he began helping Cole and the James brothers rob banks. When Bob joined the gang as a teenager, he pursued the outlaw's life with no regrets. The malignant John, who went for his guns at the slightest provocation, also eagerly embraced outlawry.

Following a train robbery at Gad's Hill, Missouri, on January 31, 1874, John and Jim took refuge at the home of a friend at Monegaw Springs. Several weeks afterward, they were located by Pinkerton agents Louis J. Lull and John Boyle and Deputy Sheriff Ed Daniels, who began snooping around the neighborhood in an attempt to capture the fugitives. On March 16, the two Youngers rode after the lawmen, and the hunted found the hunters that afternoon on the Chalk Level Road.

Jim whipped out a brace of revolvers and John leveled a shotgun and ordered the stunned officers to disarm themselves. When Jim dismounted to collect the weapons, Lull suddenly pulled a pistol from his hip pocket and shot John in the throat. John emptied both barrels of his shotgun into Lull, who pitched from the saddle and died the next day in a nearby house. Daniels managed to shoot Jim in the leg, but the Youngers turned their fire on the deputy and gunned him down. Boyle abandoned his dying comrades and spurred to safety, while John collapsed and died. Jim arranged for friends to take care of John's body, then fled. Cole and Bob

QUANTRILL'S RAIDERS

Just prior to the Civil War, the Kansas Territory was torn with violence over the issue of entering the Union as a proslavery or antislavery state. One of the most vicious of the pro-Southern factions proved to be Quantrill's raiders. The raiders were organized during the early days of the war by William Clarke Quantrill. They skirmished with U.S. troops, Kansas Jayhawkers, and anyone else who espoused the Union cause.

On August 21, 1863, Quantrill and 450 followers raided the town of Lawrence, Kansas, a stronghold for abolitionists and pro-Union sympathizers. Within a few violent minutes, Quantrill's guerrillas had killed at least 150 of the town's residents and burned much of Lawrence to the ground. Two months later, the raiders killed 17 non-combatants near Baxter Springs, Kansas. Following these two atrocities, Quantrill's band split up, with smaller elements drifting to Texas. At the end of the war, Quantrill was killed by Union troops.

Quantrill's raiders were considered criminals, not soldiers, by the Union.

were in Mississippi when they read about the shoot-out in the newspaper.

In an unusual move, the James-Younger Gang ventured north to Minnesota in 1876, intending to take a bank there. Although it's unclear what prompted them to make a strike so far from their home territory, the plan was likely the suggestion of gang member Bill Chadwell, a native of Minnesota who was intimately familiar with the terrain of the area. The gang selected a bank in the town of Mankato, but they were frightened away by a crowd of tough-looking citizens. At the suggestion of Chadwell, they shifted their target to the First National Bank of Northfield. On September 7, 1876, the eight bandits donned linen dusters to hide their weapons and rode into Northfield. Jim and two others took a position at the bridge leading into the main part of town, while Cole and Clell Miller kept people away from the bank. Bob entered the bank with Jesse and Charlie Pitts.

The robbery was a failure, resulting in the deaths of gang members Chadwell and Miller. Bob's horse was shot in the head, and when Bob sprinted for cover, a rifle bullet tore along his right arm to the elbow. Jim spurred onto the scene, with his reins in his teeth and a revolver in each hand, while Cole galloped by and picked up Bob. The Youngers, the Jameses, and Charlie Pitts fought their way out of Northfield, but the area was soon swarming with posses. With the wounded Bob barely able to stay in the saddle and Jim and Cole having to ride double, the gang couldn't move quickly. Worse yet, the only one familiar with the region, Bill Chadwell, lay dead in the streets of Northfield.

After a few days, the James brothers split from the rest of the gang and escaped after

Jesse unsucessfully tried to convince the others to abandon Bob Younger. Cole, Jim, Bob, and Pitts struggled through unfamiliar country-side, a fortnight of starvation, clashes with posses, and the agony of wounds. On September 21, a final shoot-out erupted with a seven-man posse in the small town of Medalia. Pitts was killed, Cole was shot 11 times, and Jim and Bob were hit five times each.

When a wagon brought the brothers to the nearest town, the severely wounded Cole managed to stand up and make a sweeping bow to the ladies who were watching. The Youngers pled guilty in order to escape hanging and were sentenced to life imprisonment.

Bob became a model prisoner, spending several years in the study of medicine, but he contracted tuberculosis and died in 1889. Jim Younger had been hit in the jaw during the shoot-out and suffered immensely from this injury. The slug had shattered his jaw and lodged just below his brain. The pain remained so intense that three years after his capture, he prevailed upon a prison hospital

From left: Bob, Jim, and Cole Younger—shown with sister Rhetta—had been able to shoot their way out of scrapes several times before the Northfield raid, but an obdurate citizenry finally put an end to the Youngers' villainy.

intern to operate. After working at intervals over two days, the doctor finally removed the bullet.

Cole and Jim were paroled in 1901. Jim fell in love with newspaperwoman Alice J. Miller, but he was legally forbidden to marry. His efforts to find work were unsuccessful. Despondent and emaciated from illness, Jim shot himself to death on October 19, 1902. His shattered jawbone was obtained by the Minnesota Historical Society and placed on display.

Cole adapted to law-abiding life successfully. For a brief time, he peddled tombstones, then he became an insurance salesman. Cole tried a Wild West Show venture with Frank James before hitting the lecture circuit, relating his adventures and expounding on the evils of crime. Finally retiring to Lee's Summit, he passed away at the age of 71 on February 21, 1916.

John had been buried in a Missouri cemetery near the site of his last gunfight. Cole, Jim, and Bob were laid to rest in the family plot at Lee's Summit.

KILLIN' JIM
MILLER

1866–1909

The West's premier assassin was called Killin' Jim or Killer Miller—but never to his face. James B. Miller was born in Arkansas in 1866, but the family moved to Texas the following year. Within a few years, young Jim's parents died, and he was taken to Evant, Texas, to live with his grandparents. The boy's at-

Killin' Jim Miller (wearing white hat at table) enjoys a game of faro in Pecos, Texas.

traction to violence began early. His grandparents were murdered in their home when he was just eight years old, and Jim was arrested for the chilling crime but never prosecuted. Jim was sent to live with his sister and her husband, J. E. Coop, on their nearby farm. Jim clashed with Coop, and when he was 17, he shot his brother-in-law in the head while he slept on a porch. Convicted of murder and

sentenced to life in prison, Miller won release on a legal technicality.

Miller went to work as a cowboy on the ranch of Mannen Clements. When the hard-bitten gunman Clements was shot to death by Ballinger City Marshal Jim Townsend in 1887, Killin' Jim shotgunned Townsend out of the saddle from ambush. Four years later, Miller married Sallie Clements, Mannen's daughter, who brought him into the Methodist church with such outward enthusiasm that he became known as Deacon Jim.

Deacon Jim pinned on a badge as a deputy sheriff in Reeves County, then became town marshal of the county seat, Pecos. For a time he also served as a Texas Ranger. Prudently, Killin' Jim began wearing a steel breastplate under his clothing, a precaution that saved his life twice during a feud with Bud Frazer. While Frazer was sheriff of Reeves County, he arrested Marshal Miller for stealing a pair of mules. When Killin' Jim was free to walk the streets of Pecos once again, Frazer realized that he could be a target. On April 12, 1894, Sheriff Frazer shot Marshal Miller without warning. Hit in the right arm, Miller opened fire with his left hand but succeeded only in wounding an innocent bystander. Frazer then emptied his gun into Miller's chest, knocking him off his feet. However, Miller was saved because the bullets hit the breastplate.

The following December, Frazer, now an ex-sheriff, opened fire on Miller once again, striking him in the left leg and right arm. Miller again fought back with his left hand, and when two more bullets bounced off the breastplate, a demoralized Frazer turned and fled. Frazer left Texas for New Mexico. Two years later, he returned to the Pecos area to visit his mother and sister. Learning of Frazer's presence, Killer Miller found Frazer in a saloon and blew away most of his head with a shotgun. When cursed by the dead man's sister, he threatened to shoot her, too.

Miller won acquittal on grounds that "he had done no worse than Frazer." Three weeks after the trial, he ambushed and killed Joe Earp, who had testified against him, then galloped 100 miles to establish an alibi. When the district attorney who had prosecuted Miller died of food poisoning soon thereafter, it was widely speculated that Killin' Jim had slipped arsenic to him.

The Millers moved to Fort Worth, where Sallie opened a rooming house and Deacon Jim spoke regularly at prayer meetings. Between prayer meetings, however, Killin' Jim was increasingly busy as word spread that his services were available for $150 per victim. Miller was paid $500 to dispatch Lubbock lawyer James Jarrott. In 1904, he carried out a contract on Frank Fore in a Fort Worth hotel, and two years later he shotgunned Deputy U.S. Marshal Ben Collins in Emet, Oklahoma. Killin' Jim was also widely suspected in the 1908 murder of famed lawman Pat Garrett.

The following year, Miller was paid $2,000 to kill rancher A. A. Bobbitt in Ada, Oklahoma. After ambushing Bobbitt at his ranch, Miller hastened back to Fort Worth. Texas officials happily extradited him to Ada, where he was lynched, along with his three employers, on April 19, 1909.

The day of the gunslinger had ended. Delivered to a lynch mob by 20th-century authorities, the last—and perhaps the worst—of the notorious hired gunmen vanished from the West.

With chilling effectiveness, frontier justice finally catches up to Killin' Jim Miller and his coconspirators.

CHEROKEE BILL

1876–1896

The notorious outlaw known as Cherokee Bill was only 19 when he was sentenced to hang, but Judge Isaac Parker accurately described the vicious young killer as "a most ferocious monster."

The monster was born Crawford Goldsby at Fort Concho, Texas, in February of 1876. His multiracial father, a soldier, had met his part Cherokee, part white, part black mother while stationed at Fort Gibson in Indian Territory. In 1878, Sergeant Goldsby abandoned his family after being implicated in a shoot-out between soldiers and civilians. Crawford and his baby brother, Clarence, were brought to the Cherokee Nation by their mother. When Crawford was seven, he left home to attend the Indian school at Cherokee, Kansas. After three years, he was sent away to the famous Indian school in Carlisle, Pennsylvania.

He came home to Fort Gibson at the age of 12, but his mother had remarried, and Crawford disliked his new stepfather. He began carousing and drinking with rough companions. When he was 15, he moved to Nowata to live with his sister. He found that he disliked her husband, Mose Brown, and decided to leave Nowata. Returning to

Cherokee Bill became feared for his viciousness during his short life.

Graciously posing with the posse that will bring him in for murder, Cherokee Bill (center) shows the confidence he held that no hangman would ever put a rope around him.

Fort Gibson, he worked at a few odd jobs and continued to carouse.

Early in 1894, while at a dance near Fort Gibson, 18-year-old Crawford, who was now called Cherokee Bill, tangled with Jake Lewis, an African American in his 30s. A fistfight ensued, and Lewis pounded his younger opponent. Two days later, Cherokee Bill sought out Lewis, shot him twice, and galloped away. Lewis survived his wounds.

Cherokee Bill took up with a pair of criminal brothers named Bill and Jim Cook. On July 18, 1894, Bill and the Cooks stopped for supper at the Halfway House, an eating establishment operated by relatives of the Cook brothers. When an eight-man posse appeared, led by Sheriff Ellis Rattling Gourd, the three fugitives seized their Winchesters, and a furious fight erupted. Jim Cook was wounded seven times, and officer Sequoyah Houston was slain, apparently by Cherokee Bill. The posse retreated, allowing Cherokee Bill and Bill Cook a chance to escape.

Soon after this incident, Bill Cook organized the Cook Gang, and Cherokee Bill readily assisted in a succession of robberies and murders that terrorized the Cherokee and Creek Nations. Less than two weeks after the gunbattle with Sheriff Gourd, Cherokee Bill shot and killed J. M. Mitchell while looting the Lincoln County Bank of Chandler. In September 1894, following another disagreement with Mose Brown, he gunned down his brother-in-law. On November 8, while robbing a store in Lenapah, Cherokee Bill put a Winchester bullet in the brain of Ernest Melton. This was the murder for which he would hang.

Cherokee Bill was known to meet his sweetheart, Maggie Glass, at the cabin of Ike Rogers and his wife, who was Maggie's aunt. A mixture of Cherokee and African American, Rogers held a commission as a deputy U.S. marshal, but he was an ineffectual lawman. Cherokee Bill felt reasonably safe at his cabin, located five miles east of Nowata. Unbeknownst to Cherokee Bill, Rogers agreed to a plan to capture the outlaw for a one-third share of the reward money. On January 30, after a night-long sojourn with Maggie, Cherokee Bill was jumped by Rogers and Clint Scales. After a vicious struggle, Cherokee Bill was overpowered, then whisked by wagon to confinement at Fort Smith, Arkansas.

Convicted and sentenced to hang, Cherokee Bill engineered an escape attempt from Murderer's Row on July 26, 1895. With a revolver and ammunition that had been smuggled into his cell, he killed guard Lawrence

Keating, then traded shots with other officers for 15 minutes. Another notorious inmate, Henry Starr, persuaded Cherokee Bill to give up his gun, and Judge Parker promptly issued a second murder charge.

On the day of his execution, March 17, 1896, Cherokee Bill was visited by his mother, brother, and sister, as thousands of sightseers crowded into Fort Smith. He gave away his personal possessions, then calmly faced the gallows and reportedly said, "Good-bye, all you chums down that way."

Before he was hung on St. Patrick's day, 1896, Cherokee Bill calmly accepted his fate, saying, "This is about as good a day to die as any.

A year after his brother was hanged, Clarence Goldsby shot Ike Rogers in the neck. When Rogers fell on his back, Clarence pumped two more slugs into his face. Clarence took his brother's gun from Rogers's corpse, eluded a posse, and disappeared. From somewhere "down that way" Cherokee Bill must have smiled.

JOHN WESLEY
HARDIN

1853–1895

The son of a Methodist preacher, John Wesley Hardin was named after the founder of his father's denomination. Hardin taught school in a one-room classroom, and he later became a lawyer. He conducted school, however, while hiding out from lawmen, and he studied for the bar while serving a prison term for murder. The preacher's kid was actually one of the most prolific killers of the last days of the Old West.

Hardin was born on May 26, 1853, in Bonham, Texas. His Methodist father selected the boy's name in the hope that he might become a minister. In order to supplement his income, Reverend Hardin taught school and practiced law, and when Wes was two, the family moved to southeastern Texas. While he was still a boy, Wes learned to handle guns in order to hunt game, then he refined his skill by using an effigy of Abraham Lincoln for target practice. Wes revealed his killer instinct at the tender age of 14 when he stabbed a boy in the chest and back during a knife fight. The boy recovered, but Wes moved on to more violent behavior the next year.

In November 1868, Wes visited an uncle's farm near Moscow in East Texas. During a

John Wesley Hardin claimed to have stared down Wild Bill Hickok in Abilene in 1871, though some historians dispute the story.

wrestling match between Wes, his cousin, and a former slave named Mage, Mage became angry, probably for good reason. The next day as Wes was riding home, Mage stepped into the road with a stick in his hand. Young Hardin, filled with the racist resentments prevalent in Texas during Reconstruction, hauled out his .44 and pumped three slugs into Mage.

Hardin hid out at the farm of a friend near Sumpter. Learning that three occupation soldiers were coming to arrest him for the murder of Mage, he armed himself with a shotgun and revolver, and he set an ambush at a nearby creek. When the troopers rode near, Hardin let loose with both barrels of the shotgun, killing two of his prey. The third soldier managed to shoot Wes in the left arm, but Hardin dropped the man with his .44. Hardin fled the area, and several ex-Confederate soldiers concealed the Union corpses.

Reverend Hardin took his deadly son to Navarro County, where there were numerous sympathetic relatives. A cave provided a secluded hideout. The nearby community of Pisgah Ridge offered employment as a teacher in a one-room school where bullies had run off a succession of schoolmarms. Hardin was only 16 and fuzzy-cheeked, but he commanded rapt attention from his pupils by wearing a pair of cap-and-ball revolvers at his waist. Professor Hardin gave up the classroom to work as a cowboy near Corsicana, Texas.

The number of gunfights in which two opponents face off in the street has been greatly exaggerated by western lore and literature, but John Wesley Hardin did engage in such a shoot-out in tiny Towash, Texas, on Christmas Day of 1869. He had been arguing over a card game with a gambler named Bradly, and late in the day, the two antagonists met on the street. Bradly missed Hardin with a pistol shot, but Wes gunned down his opponent with bullets to the head and chest.

On the run again, Hardin proved to be hot-tempered and quick on the trigger. Like a good street fighter who always threw the first punch, he did not hesitate to go for the opening shot as soon as he saw trouble brewing. There were other altercations, followed by fatal shootings.

While in Smiley in South Texas during September 1871, Hardin learned he was being hunted by two African-American state policemen, Green Parramore and John Lackey. The young gunfighter boldly approached the unsuspecting officers, who were eating crackers and cheese at the general store, and asked them if they knew Hardin. They replied that they had never seen Hardin, but that they intended to find and arrest him. "Well," snapped Wes, drawing a revolver, "you see him now!" Wes shot Parramore dead and wounded Lackey in the mouth. Lackey bolted out of the store, thus surviving his encounter with Hardin.

The young killer took time away from gambling and fighting to marry Jane Bowen in 1872, and they eventually became the parents of two daughters and a son. Marriage did little to settle him down.

Hardin was eventually arrested, but he was rescued from jail by Mannen Clements. He then joined his Clements cousins in the violent Sutton-Taylor feud, a personal conflict that had been going on between the Suttons and the Taylors since they had lived in South Carolina in the 1840s. The Clements sided with the Taylors. Each family recruited gangs of about 200 "regulators" to protect their interests. In a Cuero saloon in April 1873, Hardin killed J. B. Morgan, who worked as a deputy for DeWitt County Sheriff Jack Helm. Helm was a leader of the Sutton Regulators. In July 1873, Hardin and Jim Taylor encountered Helm in Albuquerque, Texas. Wes blasted Helm in the chest with a load of buckshot, and Taylor emptied his revolver into the fallen man's head.

The next year, Wes celebrated his 21st birthday by winning heavily at horse racing in Comanche, Texas. Afterward, he quarreled in a saloon with Deputy Sheriff Charles Webb, and the two men pulled their pistols and fired. Hardin was struck in the side, but Webb took a bullet in the head. Webb jerked his trigger as he was hit, and two of Hardin's companions pumped slugs into the officer as he went down. An enraged mob chased Hardin and his party out of town. Hardin escaped, but his brother, Joe, and two others were lynched in Comanche. Eventually, five more cousins and friends of Hardin died as retribution for Webb's death.

Posing as J. H. Swain, Jr., Hardin traveled with his family by steamboat to Florida. For three years he tried to remain anonymous by working for a living. He traded in cattle and horses, operated a saloon, and ran a logging business. It worked until 1877 when he was spotted by Texas Ranger John Armstrong on a train at a depot in Pensacola. Unable to get to his gun, which got caught in his suspenders, Hardin was jumped by several lawmen. Armstrong clubbed him senseless with his long-barreled .45, and the fugitive was whisked back to Texas.

Tried for the murder of Deputy Webb, Hardin was sentenced to 25 years in the penitentiary at Huntsville. While in prison, he joined

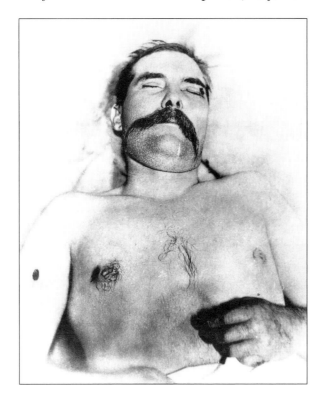

John Wesley Hardin was shot through the back of the head. Note the bullet hole through his left eye.

a debating society, became superintendent of the Sunday school, and studied for the bar. He maintained an extensive correspondence with his wife, and his letters were sometimes surprisingly poignant for having come from the pen of a seemingly cold-hearted killer. Jane Hardin worked ceaselessly for his release, but she died a year before Hardin was granted a full pardon in 1894.

For a time, he lived with his children in Gonzales, Texas, where he opened a law office. He moved his legal practice to Junction and married teenager Callie Lewis. Callie left him on their honeymoon. He gravitated to El Paso, a notorious border town that was one of the last gunfighter haunts. Drinking and carousing with a hard crowd, he kept company with a married woman, a former prostitute known as Beulah McRose. Beulah left Hardin, but that did not stop him from trying to protect her. After she was arrested by John Selman, Jr., Hardin ran into John Selman, Sr., and threatened to kill him and his son.

A 53-year-old gunfighter who understood the menace in Hardin's threats, Selman was determined to face the trouble. The elder Selman charged into the Acme Saloon on the evening of August 19, 1895, and opened fire on Hardin's back. A slug crashed into the outlaw's head and emerged from his left eye. Selman fired again but missed Hardin as he fell. He then walked over to Hardin's prostrate form and deliberately pumped two more slugs into his victim. John Selman, Jr., ran into the saloon, clutched his father's arm, and shouted, "Don't shoot him anymore, he's dead."

He was indeed dead, at the age of 42. Not long after Hardin's death, a manuscript was discovered titled *The Life of John Wesley Hardin, As Written by Himself.* The autobiography, which ends abruptly in the 1880s, describes more than two dozen killings, though other sources attribute over 40 shooting deaths to Hardin. While these numbers are unreliable, there is no question that from 1868 through 1874, young Wes Hardin was one of the most lethal shootists in frontier history.

HARDIN GOES TO JAIL

John Wesley Hardin spent 15 years in the Huntsville prison in Texas on a second-degree murder charge stemming from the killing of Deputy Sheriff Charles Webb. While serving his time, Hardin proved to be surprisingly industrious and hard working. Much has been made of the fact that he spent the latter years of his term engaged in a variety of intellectual pursuits; he studied, among other things, theology, algebra, and law from his prison cell.

When he first arrived at Huntsville, however, Hardin devoted his energies to some less-admirable activities. He aggressively worked at stirring up other inmates and inciting unrest in the prison, and he also made repeated attempts at escape during the first ten years of his sentence. In one incident, Hardin led a group of prisoners in a revolt and nearly captured the prison armory. After an overnight standoff, the inmates were subdued when additional forces arrived to back up the prison guards.

For his rebellious actions, Hardin repeatedly received severe beatings and was kept in solitary confinement for long periods and restricted to subsistence rations. Through it all, his spirit proved to be remarkably resilient. Many prisoners and guards alike came to respect and admire his tenacity and provided him with food, blankets, and other items against prison orders during his punishments.

The following excerpt from his autobiography *The Life of John Wesley Hardin* details his ongoing efforts to escape from a jail in Austin, Texas, where he was held during his unsuccessful appeal of the trial.

"The rangers took me back to Austin to await the result of my appeal. Judge White affirmed the decision of the lower court and they took me back to Comanche in the latter part of September, 1878, where I received my sentence of twenty-five years with hard labor.

"While I was in that Austin jail I had done everything in my power to escape. The cells were made of good material and in fact the jail was a good one, with one set of cages on top of the other, separated by sheet iron. I soon got so I could make a key that would unlock my cell door and put me in the runaround. I made a key to unlock that and now all I had to do was to climb to the window and saw one of the bars. I could then easily escape.

"But some 'trusties' found out the scheme and gave it away to the jailor, who placed a guard inside the jail day and night. Thus it became impossible for me to do the work in the window though I had the key to the cell and the runaround.

"There were from 60 to 90 prisoners in that jail all the time and at least 50 of these stood ready to inform on me at any time. [That] was the trouble [in] getting out. . . ."

LUKE
SHORT
1854—1893

Luke Short was a dapper gambler whose name aptly described his frame; he was five feet six inches tall, and weighed 125 pounds. That name was also recognizable across the

Luke Short possessed an elegant taste in clothing and a crass appetite for violence.

West because its owner was a fierce and deadly gunfighter. Always a fastidious dresser, Short sported tailored clothes with his right pants pocket cut extra long and lined with leather

to hold his Colt revolver—a revolver that appeared in his hand at the slightest provocation.

Born in 1854 in Mississippi, Luke moved with his family to Texas when he was two. Like so many adolescent boys of his era, Luke became a cowboy, trailing herds to the Kansas railheads. In those freewheeling cow towns, Short ran across the coolheaded, fast-living gamblers who plied their trades in the raucous saloons. Fascinated with the lifestyle, he set about changing his occupation from cowboy to gambler.

Drifting to Sidney, Nebraska, in 1876, he became acquainted with a gang of whiskey peddlers. He joined their enterprise, which consisted of selling firewater to the Sioux—a federal offense. The hazards and dangers of such a venture were many, and Short later claimed that he killed six braves on various occasions while peddling his whiskey. The army put Short out of business, and shortly thereafter, he began working for the military, carrying dispatches.

Short was enjoying the life of a gambler by 1879, when he was living in Leadville, Colorado. It was there that Short's reputation as a fierce gunman began to circulate. At first, saloon patrons hounded Short about his natty attire, but those comments stopped when the diminutive gambler clubbed a barfly with his Colt after the man made a remark about

Short's suit. Soon after that, Short became involved in a shoot-out one evening with a man named Brown. Brown had apparently been meddling in Short's bets at the faro table, perhaps trying to instigate gunplay. Short's verbal warning to stop made Brown go for his gun. Short snaked out his revolver and shot Brown. The bullet tore through his face, ripping through both cheeks. Brown was not fatally wounded, and Short was not charged. Lawmen maintained that Short had a right to protect his bets.

Luke moved to Dodge City and spent two quiet years as a house dealer in the famous Long Branch Saloon. Attracted to booming Tombstone in 1881, Short relocated there to work as a house dealer in the Oriental Saloon. One of the most famous saloons in the West, the Oriental was reportedly the site of some 200 deaths by gunplay. Short worked alongside Wyatt Earp, who owned a quarter interest in the saloon, and Bat Masterson, who ran one of the tables. Doc Holliday idled away most of his hours gambling in the Oriental.

Short added to the notorious reputation of the saloon during the brief time he was there. On February 25, 1881, Short quarreled with Charles Storms after Storms accused him of cheating. Masterson restrained Short and Charles Storms from coming to blows, but a short time later, Storms returned to resume the dispute. This time the quarrel escalated to gunplay. With the gun barrel of his

This is a portrait of Hattie Buck, a Dodge City woman purported to be the wife of Luke Short.

.45, Storms traced around Short's mustache, which set off the fiery gunfighter. The two gamblers reached for their guns, and Short quickly pumped out three fatal rounds. One slug broke Storms's neck while a second tore into his heart. After being cleared of any charges on the grounds of self-defense, Short returned to Dodge City.

Short purchased an interest in the Long Branch in 1883, but almost immediately, he became embroiled in the so-called Dodge City War, which was a dispute between reformers and saloon owners. Short had returned to Dodge during an era when reform had thoroughly gripped the city. The reform movement in Dodge had begun about 1878, when a law was passed that allowed only legitimate gambling. The goal was to get rid of the card sharps who were provoking incidents of violence. As the years passed, the reformers became more rigid and puritanical in their goals, at one point campaigning for the banishment of alcohol. By the time Short returned, they had begun cracking down on prostitution, gambling, and other pastimes associated with saloons.

One of the reformers' tactics was to ban women employees in saloons, resulting in the arrest of three of Short's female "singers." Short fumed and growled threats. One Saturday night in the spring of 1883, he encountered Special Policeman and City Clerk L. C. Hartman on Front Street. "There is one of the sons of bitches," muttered Short to his companion, referring to Hartman's status as part of the reform administration. "Let's throw it to him."

Short shot two rounds at Hartman, who dove for cover. Thinking he had killed his man, Short walked away. An uninjured Hartman pulled his gun and fired a shot, sending

Luke Short was called the "Undertaker's Friend" because he "shot 'em where it didn't show."

Short scurrying into the darkness. Luke was arrested and kicked out of town.

Angered, Short made for Topeka, where he spoke to the press. He also sent telegrams to the illustrious circle of gunfighters he called his friends, asking them to help him out. Soon, such notables as Wyatt Earp, Bat Masterson, and Doc Holliday began to drift into Dodge. In addition, several colorful but

less memorable gunmen rode ominously into town, including Black Jack Bill, Cold Chuck Johnny, Dynamite Sam, Dark Alley Jim, Three-Fingered Dave, Six-Toed Pete, and Rowdy Joe Lowe. The sheriff panicked and telegraphed the governor, who interceded by dispatching his adjutant general to try to prevent an altercation. The state militia was put on alert.

The press had a field day speculating on what might happen once all of these gunmen sided with Short against the reformers. Short and his pals marched into Dodge, but violence was avoided when the reformers caved in immediately. Before leaving town, the most famous of the gunfighters, who called themselves the Dodge City Peace Commission, posed for a photograph with Short.

The following year, Short tried to sue Dodge City for throwing him out of town. He settled out of court and then left Dodge for good.

Establishing himself in Fort Worth, Short purchased a one-third interest in Jake Johnson's White Elephant Saloon. Johnson had been paying protection money to Longhair Jim Courtright, a notorious gunfighter who had formerly served as city marshal of Fort Worth. Short balked at paying extortion money to Courtright, triggering a bitter conflict. Although Short sold his interest in the saloon on February 7, 1887, Courtright angrily confronted him the next day, in the company of Bat Masterson.

"No time was wasted in the exchange of words once the men faced each other," recalled Masterson. Courtright drew first, but the hammer of his six-gun caught in Short's watch chain, giving Luke time to pull his revolver. He fired a bullet, which shattered the

The Dodge City Peace Commission helped Short (back row, center) bully the town's reform-minded government and included famous lawmen Bat Masterson (back row, right) and Wyatt Earp (front row, second from left).

cylinder of Courtright's weapon. Short then fired methodically, triggering slugs into Courtright's right shoulder, right thumb, and heart. Longhair Jim collapsed and died within minutes. Short was later cleared on grounds of justifiable homicide.

Short's final gunfight erupted in Fort Worth on December 23, 1890. Angry over a gambling dispute, saloon owner Charles Wright ambushed Short with a shotgun blast from behind. Hit in the left leg, Short gamely palmed his revolver and opened fire on his assailant. Wright managed to escape, but one of Short's bullets broke his wrist before he reached safety.

Short developed a condition known as dropsy not long after. He went to the mineral spa at Gueda Springs, Kansas, but his condition worsened, and he died on September 8, 1893. His body was taken to Fort Worth's Oakwood Cemetery, where he was interred only a few steps from Jim Courtright. Though Short was known as a ruthless and deceitful gunfighter, Bat Masterson painted a different portrait. Pointing out that "he was one of the best-hearted men who ever lived," Masterson stated that Short "owed less and had more money due him when he died than any gambler who ever lived."

BILLY THE KID

1859–1881

"*Quien es? Quien es?*"
Translated from Spanish as "Who is it? Who is it?" these were the last words uttered by the notorious outlaw Billy the Kid. Also known as William Bonney, Kid Antrim, and William Antrim, he was actually born Henry McCarty in New York City in 1859. Legend has it that he killed 21 men, one for every year of his life; it has also been claimed that he escaped death in New Mexico at the hands of Pat Garrett to live a venerable existence as Brushy Bill Roberts of Hico, Texas. The question might well be asked of the Kid, *"Quien es? Quien es?"*

Henry McCarty's father died when Henry was a boy, and by 1865 Catherine McCarty had moved with Henry and his older brother to Indiana. There she met Bill Antrim, who moved with the McCartys to Wichita, Kansas, a few years later. In 1871, this familial group relocated to Santa Fe, New Mexico, where

One of the few known likeness of Henry Mc-Carty, a.k.a. Billy the Kid, shows a confident, cool-headed killer.

Antrim and Catherine wed in 1873. The family moved to Silver City, New Mexico, where Catherine died of tuberculosis in 1874.

While in his mid-teens, Kid Antrim, as he was known during this period, drifted into trouble. He was arrested in Silver City for theft but escaped jail and left town. Heading for Arizona, he worked briefly at the big ranch of Henry C. Hooker. He began to rustle horses near Camp Grant, where he became embroiled in his first killing. On August 17, 1877, the Kid tangled with F. P. Cahill in George Adkins's saloon. The burly blacksmith wrestled the Kid to the floor, but the slender teenager pulled a revolver and shot him. Cahill died the next day, and the Kid was indicted by a coroner's jury for criminal and unjustifiable murder.

By this time, the Kid had already fled, gravitating to lawless Lincoln County, New Mexico. Settled primarily by ranchers, including cattle king John Chisum, the vast county covered the southeastern quarter of New Mexico. Outlawry and bloodshed were commonplace in sparsely settled Lincoln County, and the Kid became one of the Boys, a band of horse rustlers led by Jesse Evans. By this time, he was known as Billy Bonney, a likable but volatile drifter who spoke fluent Spanish and was especially popular with Mexican women.

After Jesse Evans was arrested, the Kid spent a few months hunting with George Coe on his ranch south of Lincoln. The Kid then found employment on the nearby ranch of John

Tunstall, a young Englishman involved in the factional difficulties that exploded into the bloody Lincoln County War. Indeed, Tunstall's murder before the Kid's eyes on February 18, 1878, triggered the brewing hostilities.

Attracted to trouble and chagrined at failing to protect his employer from assassins, the Kid swore vengeance—and fully partook of it during the full-scale war that ensued. The Kid eagerly joined a group called the Regulators, which was led by Tunstall's foreman, Dick Brewer. The Regulators chased down two of the chief suspects in Tunstall's murder, Frank Baker and William Morton, and shot them dead on March 9.

The leader of the Tunstall murderers was Lincoln County Sheriff William Brady, and the Kid boldly hatched a scheme to kill the lawman in Lincoln. Accompanied by five Regulators, the Kid set up an ambush behind a low adobe wall overlooking Lincoln's dusty main street. About mid-morning on April 1, Brady walked by, along with Deputy George Hindman, Billy Matthews, Jack Long, and George Peppin. Suddenly, the Regulators stood up and opened fire, killing Brady and Hindman. Matthews was also hit, but he managed to scramble for cover with Long and Peppin. The Kid was nicked in the side when he tried to pick up the dead lawmen's Winchesters. The young bushwhackers then mounted up and galloped away.

Three days later, the Kid rode with a dozen other Regulators scouring the countryside for members of the opposition. At Blazer's Mill, they stopped for a meal. Shortly after their arrival, Andrew L. "Buckshot" Roberts rode into their midst unsuspectingly. Armed with a brace of six-guns and a carbine, Roberts was hunting Regulators for the $200 reward that had been posted for the killers of Sheriff Brady. Undaunted by the odds, Buckshot Roberts took on the Regulators, wounding two of his opponents and killing Dick Brewer before succumbing to a bullet from Charlie Bowdre.

The Lincoln County War came to a bloody climax during the five-day Battle of Lincoln in mid-July of 1878. The Kid and ten gunmen were besieged in the 12-room house of Tun-

A drawing from the *Illustrated Police News* depicts Billy the Kid gunning down one of his many victims.

stall's friend Alexander McSween, while other Regulators fought from nearby positions. Opposing gunmen were reinforced by troopers from Fort Stanton. The house was burned to the ground, and McSween was shot by opponents. Five Regulators were hit, but the Kid sprinted away unscathed.

Now a hunted outlaw, the Kid surrendered to the authorities in exchange for amnesty from Territorial Governor Lew Wallace. Apprehensive over the formalities of his approaching trial, the Kid left Lincoln, thus violating the terms of his amnesty agreement. The Kid formed a gang of rustlers, which included Dave Rudabaugh, Charlie Bowdre, and Tom O'Folliard.

Boldly refusing to leave Lincoln County, the Kid rustled livestock and accepted shelter from numerous friends and sweethearts. In November 1880, the Kid was nearly caught by a posse when he was trapped in a ranch house near White Oaks with two other outlaws. After darkness fell, he shot his way free.

By this time, Sheriff Pat Garrett was leading a relentless manhunt. On the night of December 19, 1880, the Kid led five other fugitives into Fort Sumner for food and recreation, but Garrett and his posse opened fire. Tom O'Folliard was mortally wounded, but the others escaped. The Kid and his men were trailed through the snow to a hideout at Stinking Springs. After Charlie Bowdre was killed, the Kid, who was surrounded and outgunned, finally surrendered to Garrett.

Tried, convicted, and sentenced in Mesilla, the Kid was incarcerated in Lincoln to await hanging. On April 28, 1881, he procured a revolver, which may have been planted in an outhouse, and killed guard J. W. Bell. Bob Olinger, a guard who had bullied the Kid and threatened him with his shotgun, came running to see what the problem was. He was met

REWARD
($5,000.00)

Reward for the capture, dead or alive, of one **Wm. Wright**, better known as

"BILLY THE KID"

Age, 18. Height, 5 feet, 3 inches. Weight, 125 lbs. Light hair, blue eyes and even features. He is the leader of the worst band of desperadoes the Territory has ever had to deal with. The above reward will be paid for his capture or positive proof of his death.

JIM DALTON, Sheriff.

DEAD OR ALIVE!
"BILLY THE KID"

This reward poster attests to the Kid's diminutive stature as well as his ominous reputation.

by the Kid, who was brandishing Olinger's shotgun. "Hello, Bob," the Kid sneered. The ominous greeting was punctuated with the roar of both barrels blasting into Olinger. The Kid tossed the shotgun into the dust beside his tormentor's body, reportedly shouting, "You won't follow me any more with that gun." Once again he escaped, and once again he brazenly hid out in the nearby countryside.

On the night of July 14, 1881, Garrett led two deputies into Fort Sumner, then ventured alone into the darkened bedroom of Pete Maxwell to ask the whereabouts of the Kid. That evening, the Kid had come in to visit a sweetheart. About midnight, he slipped his double-action .41 into the waistband of his pants, picked up a butcher knife, and walked in his stocking feet to Maxwell's quarters. Intending to ask for the key to the meat house so he could cut a steak, he passed the two deputies and peered at the dim form sitting on Maxwell's bed. He asked, *"Quien es? "Quien es?"* As a reply, Garrett triggered a bullet into the Kid's heart. He was buried the next day in the Fort Sumner cemetery between confederates Tom O'Folliard and Charlie Bowdre.

In a four-year span, he fought in at least 16 shoot-outs, he killed four men himself, and he helped to kill five others. Who was Billy the Kid? He was a bold and deadly gunfighter who earned his ostentatious reputation.

THE
LINCOLN COUNTY WAR

Although the name Billy the Kid is closely associated with the Lincoln County War, the troubles in that remote New Mexico county during the late 1870s and early 1880s went far deeper than the youthful Kid. Like most range wars in the West, this one had its origins in pure greed. On one side of the war was a powerful Lincoln merchant named Lawrence G. Murphy and on the other were several cattlemen, including John Chisum.

Murphy, an Irishman who had migrated to the United States as a teenager, owned L. G. Murphy & Company, a general store that he opened in the county seat of Lincoln in 1874. Early on, Murphy became an ally of the Republican leadership of the territory, which helped him corner lucrative government contracts to provide beef and other supplies to army posts and Indian reservations. Murphy's associates included James Riley and James Dolan, a hothead who did not hesitate to use a gun.

Murphy was resisted by Chisum, a cattle baron who wanted to monopolize the government-owned public range for his own purposes. The situation was further complicated in 1875 when John Tunstall, a well-to-do Englishman, went into the cattle business with Alexander McSween, a lawyer. Tunstall and McSween, who also wanted to secure government contracts for beef, became allies of Chisum. They opened a store in direct competition with Murphy and his associates, and they also started a bank.

After Murphy sold his interest of L. G. Murphy & Company to his partners, sales lagged, and Riley and Dolan found many of their customers switching their allegiances to Tunstall and McSween. Accusations and threats were hurled from both sides, and each mounted a force of men and associates for protection.

When some of Dolan's men murdered Tunstall, the war was triggered. Billy the Kid, who was employed by the Englishman, swore revenge. Tunstall's foreman headed a force called the Regulators, who were loyal to McSween. Over the next several months, members of both sides were killed in cold blood. The violence between the two factions climaxed in mid-July of 1878 when McSween's house was burned down and he was shot dead. By that time, Murphy had drunk himself to death. With Murphy, Tunstall, and McSween all dead, the Lincoln County War soon ended.

James Riley and James Dolan bought out Lawrence Murphy's interest in this store and other Lincoln, New Mexico, enterprises just before the start of the Lincoln County War.

BLACK BART

1830?—1917?

When Wells, Fargo & Company became the preferred carrier of bullion from the California goldfields during the 1850s, it also became the preferred target of a great many bandits. A gang of outlaws led by Rattlesnake Dick waylaid a Wells Fargo mule train in 1855 and relieved it of some $80,000 dollars in gold dust. This first Wells Fargo robbery was the costliest, but over the next 15 years, more than 300 holdups occurred, with losses totaling $415,000.

The most infamous of the California highwaymen was a solitary bandit known as Black Bart. He was born Charles E. Boles, probably in 1830 in Jefferson County, New York. Boles apparently abandoned a wife and four children to seek his fortune in California during the gold rush.

Black Bart was said to have impressed the stage drivers he robbed with his bold but respectful demeanor.

Later he claimed to have served as a Union officer during the Civil War, but his commission cannot be documented.

Certainly he was back in California after the war, because on July 26, 1875, he robbed a Wells Fargo stagecoach of $300. Wearing a linen duster and a derby hat perched atop a flour sack with eye holes, he intercepted the stage on a steep grade near Copperopolis and indicated a band of concealed confederates, whose gun barrels were pointing through nearby bushes. After the strongbox was dropped to the ground, he produced a small ax, extracted the gold coins, then disappeared on foot. The driver soon returned to retrieve the strongbox, only to discover that the gang's guns were merely sticks tied to the bushes.

Encouraged by his success, the stagecoach robber executed at least 28 holdups during the next seven years. He always hit Wells Fargo vehicles; he always wore the duster, flour sack mask, and derby; and he always worked on foot. His schedule was unpredictable: Sometimes he waited months between holdups, but he once robbed stages on successive days 30 miles apart. Occasionally he left behind short, light-hearted verses, which he signed "Black Bart, the Po-8." Black Bart left his first doggerel on a scrap of paper following his third robbery:

> I've labored long and hard for bread
> for honor and for riches
> But on my *corns too* long youve tred
> *You fine haired Sons of Bitches.*

To plan his strikes, the highwayman roamed through the countryside observing Wells Fargo routes. Posing as an itinerant laborer, he dressed in rough clothes, and his boots were slit to relieve the corns referred to in his poem. When not working, he led a more urbane life, residing at a San Francisco hotel, nattily attired in a derby hat and business suit and sporting a diamond ring and stickpin, a gold watch and chain, and a walking cane.

Black Bart's persistent thievery was an embarrassment to Wells Fargo, and they launched a rigorous investigation with their own highly trained company police. They made little progress until 1882, when the bandit staged a holdup at the site of his initial robbery, near Copperopolis. At the bottom of the grade, driver Reason McConnell dropped off Jimmy Rolleri, who prowled for game with a hunting rifle. Near the top of the hill, Black Bart stepped into the road brandishing a shotgun. Taking McConnell's rifle, he discovered that the strongbox was bolted to the floor of the coach. Black Bart ordered McConnell to unhitch the team and lead the animals away, so that he could chop open the box in the coach.

By the time Black Bart loped off with his loot, McConnell had reunited with Rolleri. McConnell seized the rifle, but twice missed the retreating outlaw. Rolleri took his rifle back and drew a bead. "I'll get him and I won't kill him, either." The words and his shot were true. Wounded, Black Bart held onto the gold but dropped several items before escaping into the wilderness. Wells Fargo detectives later found a laundry mark on a handkerchief he had left at the site, and a painstaking search revealed a San Francisco laundry whose records identified the handkerchief owner as Charles "Bolton."

Bolton, who turned out to be Boles, matched the physical description of Black Bart—five feet eight inches, broad shoulders, blue eyes, a large gray mustache—and soon he was arrested. After pleading guilty in a San Andreas court in November 1883, he was sentenced to six years in San Quentin. Pardoned after four years and two months, he was rumored to have moved to Harrisburg, Pennsylvania, to marry a childhood sweetheart. Other rumors held that Wells Fargo paid him not to return to robbery. During his career, Black Bart never shot anyone and never robbed a passenger, and his Wells Fargo loot totaled only $18,000. But his one-man campaign of banditry against the West's most prestigious express company assured him of a special place in the history of American outlawry.

THE DALTON
BROTHERS

On October 5, 1892, Bob, Emmett, and Grat Dalton achieved a lifelong ambition. They staged the most spectacular bank holdup in western history. The Dalton gang simultaneously hit two banks in Coffeyville, Kansas, and in the bloodbath that followed, a dozen men were shot, including all three Dalton brothers and their two confederates.

The outlaw trio was born in Cass County, Missouri: Grattan was born in 1865, Bob in 1868, and Emmett in 1871. All the Dalton children—ten sons and five daughters—were reared by Lewis and Adeleine Dalton on a succession of farms, including an Oklahoma homestead near the Kansas bordertown of Coffeyville. Post-Civil War Kansas and the Indian Territories were awash in the violence that was a legacy of the border

Bob Dalton and sweetheart Eugenia Moore had this photo taken at a studio in Indian Territory in 1889.

conflicts and the influence of the James-Younger Gang. The Daltons were distant relatives of the Youngers, and they claimed an even more distant kinship to the Jameses. Most of the children grew up to be law-abiding, but four of them claimed that outlawry was in their blood.

An older brother, Frank Dalton, was killed by whiskey runners while serving as a deputy

Emmett Dalton, in 1910, had long since abandoned his violent outlaw life.

U.S. marshal under Judge Isaac Parker. Seeking revenge, Grat, Bob, and Emmett promptly sought lawmen badges themselves. Grat was appointed to take Frank's place as a deputy U.S. marshal. Bob joined Grat as a member of his regular posse and then later became a deputy marshal. Emmett, who worked on a ranch for a while, served as a posse member for his two brothers. The Dalton brothers proved to be able lawmen because they had nerves of steel and they could shoot fast and straight. Unfortunately, they tended to break the law as much as they protected it. They rustled herds of horses and cattle and sold them in Kansas. When Judge Parker found out about the Daltons' sideline, he revoked their appointments and issued warrants for their arrest.

By this time, the brothers had fled to Oklahoma, where they visited their mother and siblings. Lewis Dalton had died in 1889. Bob and Grat wanted to move their brothers to California to join a couple of other brothers, Littleton and Bill. They had plans to become train and bank robbers, but Charles and Henry Dalton refused, declaring they wanted no part of being outlaws. In the end, Charles, Henry, and Emmett stayed in Oklahoma to take care of their mother, while Bob and Grat left for California. Emmett wanted desperately to go to California, but Grat thought him too young for the life of a train and bank robber.

Grat rode west to join Littleton and Bill, and Bob followed. Grat, Bill, and Bob attempted to rob a Southern Pacific train in February 1891 near Alila, California. While Bill kept the passengers subdued by firing over their heads, Bob and Grat forced the engineer to take them to the express car. The engineer tried to slip away but was killed by a shot to the stomach. When Grat and Bob reached the express car, the guard refused to open the door. When he fired down on the Daltons through a small hole in the door, the brothers gave up and rode away.

Bill and Grat were apprehended, but Bob eluded capture and returned to Oklahoma. Grat was quickly tried and sentenced to 20 years in prison. On April 1, he made a spectacular escape and returned to Oklahoma, where Bob had already organized a band of outlaws.

Members of the gang included Bob, Emmett, and Grat, Bill Doolin, Bitter Creek Newcomb, Dick Broadwell, Charley Pierce, Bill Powers, and "Black Faced" Charley Bryant. Bob's sweetheart, Eugenia Moore, who was also known as Flo Quick, was the gang's advance agent until she died of cancer. Emmett also had a sweetheart, whose name was Julia Johnson. He realized that his outlaw life would make it difficult for a wife and family, so he bid Julia farewell, telling her he

was sure he was headed for Boot Hill. Emmett later reflected, "What had I to offer Julia, a man with a price on his head and no clear way to extricate myself from the compounding results of crime? I rode away. An outlaw has no business having a girl, no business thinking of marriage."

For a year and a half, the Daltons terrorized the region, pulling train holdups in such Oklahoma whistle stops as Wharton, Lelietta, Red Rock, and Adair. The gang was blamed for a number of other area robberies as well. After they had a number of robberies under their belts, they planned their most daring job—the looting of two banks in Coffeyville.

On the way into Coffeyville, Bill Doolin's horse pulled up lame, leaving the three Daltons, Dick Broadwell, and Bill Powers to ride into town. They had planned to hitch their horses in front of the banks, but a repair party had removed the hitch rails, and the gang tied their animals to a fence in a nearby alley. Bob and Emmett proceeded to the First National Bank, while Grat led Powers and Broadwell across the street to the Condon Bank.

The Daltons were recognized by a citizen who quietly spread the word that bank robbers were among them. As Bob and Emmett dumped $21,000 into a grain sack, townspeople began shouting orders and arming themselves in nearby hardware stores. The brothers emerged from the bank with hostages in front of them, but gunfire forced them back inside, and they fled through a rear door toward their horses.

Their way was blocked by a pistol-wielding man named Lucius Baldwin. Bob dropped him with a fatal Winchester slug to the chest. As the brothers sprinted down the street, Bob spotted George Cubine and Charles Brown, bootmakers who were old acquaintances since boyhood. But old acquaintances were forgotten that day because Cubine held a Winchester. Bob dropped him with one shot, then he shot Brown dead when the old man angrily picked up the rifle. Filled with the lust of battle, Bob then shot bank cashier Thomas G. Ayers through the left cheek.

Inside the Condon Bank, cashier Charley Ball bluffed Grat, Powers, and Broadwell with a story about a time lock on the vault. When a bullet crashed through a window and hit Broadwell in the arm, Grat quickly scooped $1,500 into his bag, then led his men around the corner toward the alley. City Marshal Charles T. Connelly was on their heels, firing rapidly, but Grat killed him with one shot.

Suddenly, livery stable owner John J. Kloehr stepped into "Death Alley" and triggered a rifle bullet into Bob's chest. Grat whirled toward Kloehr, but the livery man coolly shot him in the neck. When Grat collapsed, Powers jumped onto his horse, only to be shot out of the saddle. When Broadwell also clambered aboard a mount, he, too, met a deadly fusillade. Emmett tried to pick up Bob, but Kloehr shot him in the hip, and barber Carey Seaman blasted a load of buckshot into Emmett's back and shoulders.

Seven townspeople were wounded, including three fatally, but among the wounded outlaws, only buckshot-riddled Emmett stayed alive. While Emmett was carried to a hotel bed, souvenir hunters snipped locks of hair

The Condon Bank in Coffeyville shows obvious signs of the Daltons' infamous failed raid.

Dead or dying, Bob (left) and Grat (right) Dalton are propped up for display on the streets of Coffeyville.

from Bob's head. The outlaws were propped up to be photographed alongside the victorious townspeople, and Grat's arms were pumped up and down to make blood spurt from his neck.

Having escaped the massacre, Bill Doolin formed a gang of "Oklahombres," but he was killed by a posse in 1896. Embittered by the treatment of his brothers' corpses, Bill Dalton turned outlaw. He served as Doolin's lieutenant, then organized his own gang. Following an 1894 bank robbery, he was slain by lawmen. Nursed back to health by his mother and sweetheart, Emmett was sentenced to life in prison, but he was pardoned in 1907. He finally married the long-suffering Julia. He began a successful career as a building contractor, real estate agent, and, after moving to Los Angeles, a movie consultant. Until his death in 1937, the last of the outlaw Daltons worked as a vigorous anti-crime crusader.

EMMETT DALTON ON OUTLAWRY

Once pardoned from prison in 1907, Emmett Dalton "went straight." He turned to honest labor to make a living, including working as a building contractor and a real estate agent. After he moved to Hollywood, he parlayed his colorful background as an authentic Wild West outlaw into a brief career as a technical adviser for Hollywood westerns. He even appeared in a couple of silent films himself. In 1909, he returned to Coffeyville to act as the adviser on a short film about the Daltons' famous raid.

Emmett also used his former career to try to keep others on the straight and narrow. He spent much of his time crusading against crime by describing the tragic and violent deaths of his brothers, Bob, Grat, and Bill. He declared that anyone who thought he could beat the law was "the biggest fool on earth," and he pointed to his brothers as examples.

He detailed his exploits as an outlaw in numerous lectures and writings, including *When the Daltons Rode,* published in 1931.

"One thing I must say to the credit of the old-fashioned badman. He seldom shot his victim in the back. He had a certain pride at arms, a code of craft, a certain *punctilio* in his deadly dealings. His reputation didn't hang on potting someone in the rear or on the run—which requires no guts at all. When he came a-smokin' it was in the face of his challenger. . . . In this respect the Western gunplay was more like the older duello. It was entirely unlike the savage behavior of the modern city gangster or mountain feudist who places his victim 'on a spot' without a chance, to be mowed down in the dark with machine guns or rifles spitting from ambush."

CLAY
ALLISON

At the height of the Civil War, Confederate doctors deemed that the services of one Robert A. Clay Allison were no longer required by the Tennessee Light Artillery. For the good of the South, they issued a rare medical discharge to the private, citing a condition "of a mixed character, partly epileptic and partly maniacal." Clay Allison lived up to the latter part of the diagnosis, going on to become a vicious murderer who unpredictably exploded into fits of raging violence.

Allison was born with a club foot around 1840 in Waynesboro, Tennessee, and he spent the first two decades of his life on the family farm. After his brief stint in the Confederate Army, he moved to Texas with several other family members. Clay signed on as a cowboy with Charles Goodnight and Oliver Loving and probably was one of the 18 drovers who followed the two cattlemen on the historic 1866 drive through West Texas, New Mexico, and

At age 26, Clay Allison was living the life of a law-abiding cattleman in the Southwest. In time, he would earn a reputation as a volatile, emotionally disturbed killer.

Colorado that blazed the famous Goodnight-Loving Trail. Soon Clay became a trail boss for a partnership between his brother-in-law, Lewis Coleman, and Isaac W. Lacy. In 1870, Coleman and Lacy relocated their operation to New Mexico on a spread in Colfax County. Clay agreed to lead their herd to the new ranch in exchange for 300 head of good livestock. Starting with this small herd, Allison established his own ranch and built it into a lucrative operation near Cimarron, New Mexico.

Clay seemed to fit in with the good folks of Cimarron well enough until an act of vigilantism revealed his disturbed other side. On October 7, 1870, he led a mob that broke into the jail in nearby Elizabethtown and lynched an accused murderer named Charles Kennedy in a slaughterhouse. This act alone was not that unusual, but a wild-eyed Allison also decapitated Kennedy and then placed the head on a pole in Henri Lambert's saloon in Cimarron.

Allison squared off against known gunfighter Chunk Colbert over an 1874 horse race between them that had ended in a tie. While the men dined together at the Clifton House inn after the race, Colbert reached for another cup of coffee with one hand and slowly raised a revolver above the table with the other. Allison snatched out his own weapon, and Chunk hurried his shot, blasting a slug into the tabletop. Allison's answering round drilled Colbert just above the right eye. Colbert died instantly and was buried behind the Clifton House. Charles Cooper—the judge of the race who was also present at the fatal dinner—mysteriously disappeared two weeks later. Eventually, Clay was charged with Cooper's murder, but he was released for lack of evidence.

Clay became involved in another lynching on October 30, 1875, heading a mob that seized suspected murderer Cruz Vega. Vega was hanged from a telegraph pole, then shot in the back for good measure. Once again, a bloodthirsty Allison abused the victim, tying the lynch rope to his saddle horn and dragging the corpse over rocks and brush. Two nights later, Clay put three slugs in Cruz's employer, Pancho Griego, as the men talked over drinks in the St. James Hotel.

While drunkenly disturbing the patrons of the Olympic Dance Hall in Las Animas, Colorado, Clay and his brother John were confronted by lawman Charles Faber and two deputies on December 21, 1876. As Faber sprayed buckshot across John's chest and shoulder, Clay pulled his revolver and squeezed off four rounds, slamming the first bullet into the constable's chest. Faber dropped in his tracks and died within moments. The two deputies fled and were pursued by Clay, who emptied his gun at them from the front of the steps of the Olympic. Clay then dragged the mortally wounded Faber over to his fallen brother, repeatedly assuring John that the lawman was dead and vengeance was achieved. John was carried away, while Clay surrendered to the county sheriff. Eventually John recovered from his wounds, and Clay was released from custody.

After moving his ranch to Hemphill County in the Texas Panhandle, Clay took a wife in 1881 who later bore him two daughters. Family life reduced Clay's carousing, although he remained prone to violent outbursts. While in Cheyenne on a cattle drive, he saw a dentist about a bad tooth. When the dentist began working on the wrong tooth, Clay sought out another practitioner for proper repairs. The enraged Allison then returned to the first dentist, held him down in his own chair, and yanked out one of his teeth with a pair of pliers. Allison was working on another tooth when the poor man's shrieks brought a crowd to his rescue.

On July 3, 1887, Allison fell out of a supply wagon he was driving to his newest ranch, north of Pecos, Texas. A wheel rolled over him and broke his neck, and he died within an hour. His widow, Dora, remarried three years later, moved to Fort Worth, and lived until 1939.

In 1975, as a part of local efforts to emphasize the Old West past of Pecos, Allison's remains were exhumed and reinterred downtown at the Pecos Park. A wooden marker somewhat inaccurately proclaims him "Clay Allison Gentleman Gunfighter," while a granite headstone announces: "He never killed a man that did not need killing."

BUTCH CASSIDY
AND THE
SUNDANCE KID

Butch and Sundance started out with more pedestrian names—Robert LeRoy Parker and Harry Alonzo Longabaugh. While still in

This famous photo taken in Fort Worth, Texas, shows the Wild Bunch: Left to right, Harry Longabaugh, William Carver, Ben Kilpatrick, Harvey Logan, and Butch Cassidy.

adolescence, each young man acquired his colorful sobriquet as he launched a criminal career.

Robert LeRoy Parker was born on April 13, 1866, in Beaver, Utah, where his father ran a store. His father and mother and their families had migrated from England during the 1850s in response to Brigham Young's requests for workmen to come to Utah and help build Mormon communities. Bob was the first of 13 children born to Max and Annie Parker, and he took after his father, who was far less devout a Mormon than Annie Parker. When Bob was 13, his father moved the family to a small ranch three miles south of Circleville, Utah. As an adolescent, Bob showed an affinity for animals and became a horsebreaker.

The Circleville area was a hangout for outlaws. In his mid-teens, Bob developed a hero worship for a ruffian named Mike Cassidy. Cassidy taught Bob how to shoot, and he gave his young friend a gun and saddle. Bob began to run with Cassidy, perhaps even engaging in a little rustling. Bob left home under a cloud, and in 1886, he was accused of horse theft near Telluride, Colorado. Using the name Roy Parker, he continued to drift and associate with such criminal types as Matt Warner and Tom McCarty.

On June 24, 1889, Warner, McCarty, and Parker robbed a bank in Telluride of more than $20,000. Now a fugitive, Parker took refuge in Brown's Park, an isolated region where small ranchers took a liking to the affable young man. There he met Elzy Lay and several other young felons. Having discovered one of the classic outlaw haunts in the West, he worked as a bronc buster, cowboyed on Herb Bassett's ranch, and rustled a few horses. He left Brown's Park for a few months and, using the alias George Cassidy, found employment with a butcher in Rock Springs, Wyoming. Because he worked in a butcher shop, people began to call him Butch, the name he would be known by for the rest of his life.

Cassidy and a confederate named Al Hanier were arrested for horse theft after lawmen Bob Calverly and John Chapman tracked them to Auburn, Wyoming. Hanier was captured at a sawmill, but Cassidy was taken at his hideout, a cabin near town. Hainer was eventully acquitted and released, but Butch wasn't so lucky. In July 1894, George "Butch" Cassidy was ordered to serve a two-year sentence in the Wyoming Territorial Prison at Laramie. Pardoned in January 1896, Cassidy promptly returned to Brown's Park and resumed a criminal's career, becoming the leader of a band of carousing outlaws, "That wild bunch from Brown's Park."

On August 13, 1896, Butch Cassidy, Elzy Lay, and Bob Meeks looted the bank at Montpelier, Idaho, of $7,000. This same trio stole $8,000 in the robbery of a coal mine payroll in Castle Gate, Utah, on April 21, 1897. Hiding out in another notorious outlaw haunt, Robber's Roost, Butch and his henchmen pitched a tent in a barren canyon. When they were joined by Elzy Lay and his wife, another tent went up. Then a third tent was erected to accommodate the Sundance Kid and his sweetheart, Etta Place.

The Sundance Kid—Harry Alonzo Longabaugh—was born near Phoenixville, Pennsylvania, probably in 1867. Harry was the youngest of five children, and his father, Josiah, was a common laborer who frequently uprooted his family for new jobs. By the time Harry reached his teens, he had left home to find menial work of his own. He read dime novels and learned to shoot with an old pistol. Hoping to secure employment in an urban

In Utah, a youthful Robert Parker tends to his horse sometime before he took the name Butch Cassidy.

area, he traveled to Philadelphia, New York, and Boston, but he had no luck. He joined some cousins in Illinois for a wagon trek to Colorado. Harry worked as a horse wrangler on the LC Ranch, then hired on with a cattle drive on its way to Montana, where he was hired by the N Bar N near Miles City. It was in Colorado that Harry may have met Butch Cassidy, Matt Warner, and other future criminal associates, while he was probably introduced to the murderous Harvey Logan in Montana.

Laid off along with a host of other cowboys during the severe winter of 1886–1887, Harry stole a horse, saddle, and six-gun from the VVV Ranch near Sundance, Wyoming, on February 27, 1887. Returning to Miles City, young Longabaugh was arrested on April 8 by Sheriff James Ryan. Sheriff Ryan made a lengthy detour by train because of business in St. Paul, Minnesota. When Ryan went to the lavatory, Longabaugh picked the locks on his handcuffs and leg irons, then jumped off the speeding train.

Incredibly, the youthful fugitive went back to Miles City, where he was arrested two months later. This time, handcuffed and shackled, he was driven in a buckboard directly to Sundance, where he pled guilty to horse theft. Sentenced to 18 months of hard labor, he was permitted to serve his term in the county jail at Sundance rather than at the Wyoming Territorial Prison because he was still a minor. Now called the Sundance Kid, he was released in February 1889, trying his luck first in Deadwood, South Dakota, then at the Colorado home of his cousins.

After heading north, the Sundance Kid tried crime again on September 29, 1892, helping to rob a Great Northern train near Malta, Montana. The take was minuscule, and Sundance's two henchmen were taken into custody two days after the holdup. Sundance was arrested, too, at the depot in Malta, but he escaped and headed for the outlaw hideout at Hole-in-the-Wall near Kaycee, Wyoming. During the next few years, he appeared occasionally in Montana and Canada, and he briefly worked with a band of horse rustlers who operated in northeastern Montana. Sundance also acquired a lover, Etta Place, a comely brunette of obscure background who

was reputed to have worked as a schoolmarm. By 1897, Sundance and Etta had found refuge under a tent in Robber's Roost.

For the next few years, members of the Wild Bunch committed numerous holdups, concentrating so frequently on railroad express cars that they sometimes were called the Train Robbers' Syndicate. Key members of the gang included Butch and Sundance, Harvey Logan and his brother Lonnie, Ben "The Tall Texan" Kilpatrick, Elzy Lay, "Deaf" Charley Hanks, Will Carver, and "Flatnose" George Currie. Between robberies, Butch rendezvoused with Mary Boyd and other sweethearts. He also liked to lead fellow gang members on roisterous vacations to such retreats as Denver, San Antonio, and Fort Worth.

Usually operating in small groups, members of the Wild Bunch avoided arrest by moving along the Outlaw Trail, which ran from Hole-in-the-Wall to Brown's Park to Robber's Roost. A few weeks after Butch engineered the Castle Gate payroll robbery in April 1897, Sundance led "Flatnose" George Currie, Lonnie Logan, 15-year-old George Putney, and a drunken Tom O'Day against the Butte County Bank in Belle Fourche, South Dakota. The holdup was abbreviated when O'Day, who had neglected to tie up his mount, spooked his horse and fellow thieves by foolishly triggering a shot into the air. Bolting out of the bank with only $97, the four men with horses galloped out of town with a huge posse in pursuit, while O'Day ducked into an outhouse. O'Day was captured in this dubious hideout and incarcerated in Deadwood.

The other outlaws split up, but after a couple of months in Hole-in-the-Wall, Sundance, young Putney, and Harvey Logan rode north to Montana. In camp near Lavina on September 24, 1897, the fugitive trio was jumped by a posse. The three outlaws were jailed with O'Day in Deadwood, but on October 31, the four desperadoes overpowered a deputy and rode to freedom on horses that had been staked out by an accomplice. The following summer, Sundance, Harvey Logan, and Currie pulled a couple of jobs, then scurried back to Brown's Park.

In 1899, Cassidy planned the most ambitious Wild Bunch robbery to date, involving Sundance, Harvey and Lonnie Logan, "Flatnose" George Currie, Ben Kilpatrick, and Will Carver. Two hours past midnight on June 2, two gang members boarded a Union Pacific train between Wilcox and Medicine Bow, Wyoming. At gunpoint, the engineer was forced to advance his train across a bridge, which was then blown up while the passenger cars were uncoupled. The train and express car steamed forward two miles to a rendezvous with the rest of the gang, who blew open the express car door. The safes were blown open with charges that demolished the car, and the bandits gathered $30,000 in loot.

After rewards totaling $18,000 put such accomplished detectives as Charles Siringo and Joe LeFors on his trail, Cassidy discreetly inquired about the possibilities of amnesty. The Union Pacific agreed not to prosecute him if he never robbed a U.P. train again. U.P. officials even offered him a job as an express guard. Amnesty didn't work out, however.

The Wild Bunch dynamited this Union Pacific express car outside Wilcox, Wyoming, and made off with $30,000.

THE
HOLE-IN-THE-WALL GANG

The hideout for outlaws called Hole-in-the-Wall existed among the jagged outcroppings along the eastern face of the Rocky Mountains in central Wyoming. Attractive primarily because of its isolation, the surrounding area contained only a few scattered homesteads whose inhabitants seemed willing to tolerate the presence of outlaws as long as it caused them no loss or inconvenience.

The gang that frequented the place was a loose-knit group of robbers and bandits who hid there when their trails were hot.

Although the chain of command among the members of the Hole-in-the-Wall gang was somewhat relaxed, it was Butch Cassidy who was the real leader, assisted by Harvey Logan, known throughout the country as Kid Curry.

Among the other notorious members of the Wild Bunch were Tom O'Day, O. C. Hanks, Elzy Lay, Will Roberts, Harry Longabaugh (known as the Sundance Kid), Bob Lee, Dave Atkins, and Peg Leg Elliott. The Bunch's files took up considerable space in the Pinkerton Agency's cabinets.

Historian James D. Horan has called Harvey Logan, alias Kid Curry, the "tiger" of the Wild Bunch. Logan, who was born in Kentucky but raised in Missouri, was part Cherokee. When he was 19, Logan killed his first man, thus commencing his career as an outlaw. Over the next few years, he became proficient at bank robberies and killing. In the late 1890s, Logan hooked up with Butch Cassidy at Hole-in-the-Wall, and for the next few years, traveled all over the country plying his trade as a bank and train robber.

In December 1901, in far-away Knoxville, Tennessee, Logan was captured by city police after he wounded two officers. William Pinkerton warned Knoxville officials to watch out for Logan. "He has not one single redeeming feature," the head of the Pinkertons wrote. After spending nearly one and a half years in jail, Logan outwitted a guard and escaped on June 27, 1903. He had become such a noted inmate in the Knoxville prison that when he died in Colorado in 1904, the Pinkertons sent a man from Knoxville to identify the body.

Harvey Logan killed himself on June 8, 1904, to avoid capture after a train robbery.

When U.P. officials were late—delayed by a storm—for a meeting at a remote rendezvous point, Cassidy became skittish and disappeared. The outlaw leader left an angry note for his attorney, Douglas Preston, who was accompanying the U.P. men: "Damn you Preston you have double crossed me. I waited all day but you did not show up. Tell the U.P. to go to hell and you can go with them." Cassidy and three accomplices robbed another U.P. train in Wyoming after midnight on August 29, 1900, riding away with more than $55,000. In December 1900, while carousing in Hell's Half Acre in Fort Worth, Butch, Sundance, Kilpatrick, Carver, and Harvey Logan donned three-piece suits and derbies and posed for a studio photograph. Perhaps the most famous outlaw photo ever shot, the likeness aided detectives in their pursuit of Wild Bunch fugitives.

Butch and Sundance continued their vacation in San Antonio, visiting Fanny Porter's sporting house and other favorite haunts. Sundance journeyed to New Orleans, accompanied by Etta Place. The couple visited Sundance's relatives in Pennsylvania, toured Niagara Falls, then met Cassidy in New York City and spent three weeks vacationing in America's largest city. On February 20, 1901, under the aliases James Ryan and Mr. and Mrs. Harry Place, Butch, Sundance, and Etta boarded a steamer for Argentina.

The trio homesteaded a ranch at Cholila, near the border of Chile. After a couple of years, Sundance returned with Etta to the United States. She may have had an appendectomy at a Denver hospital, or an abortion, or she might even have borne a child. Etta went back to South America for a time, then returned north for an obscure end in the United States.

By 1904, Butch and Sundance knew that Pinkerton detectives had investigated their activities in South America. Fearing that American detectives or Argentine officials might ferret them out for the reward money, Butch and Sundance abandoned the Cholila ranch and pulled at least four robberies. They went on the run throughout Argentina, Chile, and Bolivia.

The Union Pacific employed posses such as this one to ride down the Hole-in-the-Wall Gang and other train bandits.

After what turned out to be their final holdup, Butch and Sundance rode mules into the remote Bolivian village of San Vicente on November 6, 1908. Arriving early in the evening, they were confronted by an armed posse consisting of two soldiers and a police inspector, who were led by a captain. A shoot-out erupted between the officers and the bandits. Cassidy fatally wounded soldier Victor Torres, but he was shot in the arm. Sundance took several bullets in the same limb. Everyone ducked for cover, whereupon Cassidy apparently shot Sundance in the head, then committed suicide.

Rumors persisted that Cassidy escaped the Bolivian gun battle and returned to the West, where he occasionally saw relatives, searched for caches of stolen loot, and lived under an assumed identity until 1937. Less persistent rumors suggested that Sundance, too, slipped back to the United States to live a quiet life. Perhaps no one wanted to believe that the last of the great Wild West outlaws were truly gone.

RAILROADS

On May 10, 1869, at Promontory Point, Utah, officials of the Union Pacific and Central Pacific Railroads drove the last spike into the tracks that connected the two companies' rail lines. For the first time, the East was linked to the West via the railways. It was the culmination of a dream that had its beginnings 20 years earlier.

When national attention focused on the vast West in the late 1840s, one of the most pressing issues became the establishment of a route for the transcontinental railroad. In the halls of Congress, politicians from the North and the South tried to outmaneuver each other to establish the railroad where it would most benefit them. By 1853, Congress had passed legislation that ordered the U.S. Army Corps of Topographical Engineers to survey several routes to the

The Central Pacific train *Jupiter* chugs toward the ceremony at Promontory Point on May 10, 1869.

Pacific. The central route won the competition. When the golden spike was driven at Promontory Point on that May day in 1869, the rail line that was completed connected Omaha with Sacramento.

The railroad in America proved its value long before a completed line reached all the way from the Mississippi River to California. For example, when laborers drove the last spikes into the line at Abilene, the town was converted almost overnight into a shipping depot for transporting Texas cattle to

the East. After the transcontinental railroad was completed, the possibility of traversing the entire 3,000 miles between New York and California within a matter of days made traveling and shipping goods much simpler and cheaper. The golden age of the railroad had begun.

Ultimately, the railroad was more than just a convenient way to travel or to ship goods. It brought thousands of emigrants from the East to the inexpensive lands of the West. The railroads themselves got into the emigration business by advertising the sale of vast amounts of real estate for only pennies an acre. Soon, there was not just one transcontinental railroad, but several. The Northern Pacific, the Southern Pacific, and the Atchison, Topeka & Santa Fe were just a few of the main lines that completed an east-west connection.

The advent of the transcontinental railroad and the encroachment of more and more white settlements added to the swift destruction of the Plains Indians' way of life. New railroad towns sprang up on the Great Plains where nothing but prairie grass had grown the year before. The buffalo, which were so significant to the Native American livelihood, were destroyed at a rapid rate, and Native Americans were pressured to submit to reservation life.

The railroad served as one of the final instruments of conquest of the American West—a distinction that has both positive and negative connotations.

Chinese laborers became the backbone of the workforce for the Central Pacific.

In over 7,000 popular prints, Currier and Ives chronicled life in 19th-century America. Here, the significance of the railroad is captured in "Across the Continent."

Index